Elements of Artificial Neural Networks

Complex Adaptive Systems

John H. Holland, Christopher G. Langton, and Stewart W. Wilson, advisors

Adaptation in Natural and Artificial Systems: An Introductory Analysis with Applications to Biology, Control, and Artificial Intelligence, John H. Holland

Toward a Practice of Autonomous Systems: Proceedings of the First European Conference on Artificial Life, edited by Francisco J. Varela and Paul Bourgine

Genetic Programming: On the Programming of Computers by Means of Natural Selection, John R. Koza

Genetic Programming: The Movie, John R. Koza and James P. Rice

From Animals to Animats 2: Proceedings of the Second International Conference on Simulation of Adaptive Behavior, edited by Jean-Arcady Meyer, Herbert L. Roitblat, and Stewart W. Wilson

Intelligent Behavior in Animals and Robots, David McFarland and Thomas Bösser

Advances in Genetic Programming, edited by Kenneth E. Kinnear, Jr.

Genetic Programming II: Automatic Discovery of Reusable Programs, John R. Koza

Genetic Programming II Video: The Next Generation, John R. Koza

Turtles, Termites, and Traffic Jams: Explorations in Massively Parallel Microworlds, Mitchel Resnick

From Animals to Animats 3: Proceedings of the Third International Conference on Simulation of Adaptive Behavior, edited by Dave Cliff, Philip Husbands, Jean-Arcady Meyer, and Stewart W. Wilson

Artificial Life IV: Proceedings of the Fourth International Workshop on the Synthesis and Simulation of Living Systems, edited by Rodney A. Brooks and Pattie Maes

Comparative Approaches to Cognitive Science, edited by Herbert L. Roitblat and Jean-Arcady Meyer

Artificial Life: An Overview, edited by Christopher G. Langton

Evolutionary Programming IV: Proceedings of the Fourth Annual Conference on Evolutionary Programming, edited by John R. McDonnell, Robert G. Reynolds, and David B. Fogel

An Introduction to Genetic Algorithms, Melanie Mitchell

Catching Ourselves in the Act: Situated Activity, Interactive Emergence, and Human Thought, Horst Hendriks-Jansen

Toward a Science of Consciousness: The First Tucson Discussions and Debates, edited by Stuart R. Hameroff, Alfred W. Kaszniak, and Alwyn C. Scott

Genetic Programming: Proceedings of the First Annual Conference, edited by John R. Koza, David E. Goldberg, David B. Fogel, and Rick L. Riolo

Evolutionary Programming V: Proceedings of the Fifth Annual Conference on Evolutionary Programming, edited by Lawrence J. Fogel, Peter J. Angeline, and Thomas Bäck

Advances in Genetic Programming, Volume 2, edited by Peter J. Angeline and Kenneth E. Kinnear, Jr.

Elements of Artificial Neural Networks, Kishan Mehrotra, Chilukuri K. Mohan, and Sanjay Ranka

Elements of Artificial Neural Networks

Kishan Mehrotra

Chilukuri K. Mohan

Sanjay Ranka

A Bradford Book
The MIT Press
Cambridge, Massachusetts
London, England

Second printing, 2000

This book was set in Times Roman by Windfall Software using ZzTEX and was printed and bound in the United States of America.

Library of Congress Cataloging-in-Publication Data

Mehrotra, Kishan.
    Elements of artificial neural networks / Kishan Mehrotra.
    Chilukuri K. Mohan, Sanjay Ranka.
        p.   cm. — (Complex adaptive systems / A Bradford Book)
        Includes bibliographical references and index.
        ISBN 0-262-13328-8
        1. Neural networks (Computer science)   I. Mohan, Chilukuri K.
    II. Ranka, Sanjay.   III. Title.   IV. Series.
    QA76.87.M45   1996
    006.3—dc20   96-20178
                                                            CIP

For

Rama,
Sudha,
and
Deepa

Contents

Preface

This book is intended as an introduction to the subject of artificial neural networks for readers at the senior undergraduate or beginning graduate levels, as well as professional engineers and scientists. The background presumed is roughly a year of college-level mathematics, and some amount of exposure to the task of developing algorithms and computer programs. For completeness, some of the chapters contain theoretical sections that discuss issues such as the capabilities of algorithms presented. These sections, identified by an asterisk in the section name, require greater mathematical sophistication and may be skipped by readers who are willing to assume the existence of theoretical results about neural network algorithms.

Many off-the-shelf neural network toolkits are available, including some on the Internet, and some that make source code available for experimentation. Toolkits with user-friendly interfaces are useful in attacking large applications; for a deeper understanding, we recommend that the reader be willing to modify computer programs, rather than remain a user of code written elsewhere.

The authors of this book have used the material in teaching courses at Syracuse University, covering various chapters in the same sequence as in the book. The book is organized so that the most frequently used neural network algorithms (such as error backpropagation) are introduced very early, so that these can form the basis for initiating course projects. Chapters 2, 3, and 4 have a linear dependency and, thus, should be covered in the same sequence. However, chapters 5 and 6 are essentially independent of each other and earlier chapters, so these may be covered in any relative order. If the emphasis in a course is to be on associative networks, for instance, then chapter 6 may be covered before chapters 2, 3, and 4. Chapter 6 should be discussed before chapter 7. If the "non-neural" parts of chapter 7 (sections 7.2 to 7.5) are not covered in a short course, then discussion of section 7.1 may immediately follow chapter 6. The inter-chapter dependency rules are roughly as follows.

$1 \rightarrow 2 \rightarrow 3 \rightarrow 4$

$1 \rightarrow 5$

$1 \rightarrow 6$

$3 \rightarrow 5.3$

$6.2 \rightarrow 7.1$

Within each chapter, it is best to cover most sections in the same sequence as the text; this is not logically necessary for parts of chapters 4, 5, and 7, but minimizes student confusion.

Material for transparencies may be obtained from the authors. We welcome suggestions for improvements and corrections. Instructors who plan to use the book in a course should send electronic mail to one of the authors, so that we can indicate any last-minute corrections needed (if errors are found after book production). New theoretical and practical developments continue to be reported in the neural network literature, and some of these are relevant even for newcomers to the field; we hope to communicate some such results to instructors who contact us.

The authors of this book have arrived at neural networks through different paths (statistics, artificial intelligence, and parallel computing) and have developed the material through teaching courses in Computer and Information Science. Some of our biases may show through the text, while perspectives found in other books may be missing; for instance, we do not discount the importance of neurobiological issues, although these consume little ink in the book. It is hoped that this book will help newcomers understand the rationale, advantages, and limitations of various neural network models. For details regarding some of the more mathematical and technical material, the reader is referred to more advanced texts such as those by Hertz, Krogh, and Palmer (1990) and Haykin (1994).

We express our gratitiude to all the researchers who have worked on and written about neural networks, and whose work has made this book possible. We thank Syracuse University and the University of Florida, Gainesville, for supporting us during the process of writing this book. We thank Li-Min Fu, Joydeep Ghosh, and Lockwood Morris for many useful suggestions that have helped improve the presentation. We thank all the students who have suffered through earlier drafts of this book, and whose comments have improved this book, especially S. K. Bolazar, M. Gunwani, A. R. Menon, and Z. Zeng. We thank Elaine Weinman, who has contributed much to the development of the text. Harry Stanton of the MIT Press has been an excellent editor to work with. Suggestions on an early draft of the book, by various reviewers, have helped correct many errors. Finally, our families have been the source of much needed support during the many months of work this book has entailed.

We expect that some errors remain in the text, and welcome comments and corrections from readers. The authors may be reached by electronic mail at *mehrotra@syr.edu, ckmohan@syr.edu,* and *ranka@cis.ufl.edu.* In particular, there has been so much recent research in neural networks that we may have mistakenly failed to mention the names of researchers who have developed some of the ideas discussed in this book. Errata, computer programs, and data files will be made accessible by Internet.

Elements of Artificial Neural Networks

1 Introduction

If we could first know where we are, and whither we are tending,
we could better judge what to do, and how to do it.
—Abraham Lincoln

Many tasks involving intelligence or pattern recognition are extremely difficult to automate, but appear to be performed very easily by animals. For instance, animals recognize various objects and make sense out of the large amount of visual information in their surroundings, apparently requiring very little effort. It stands to reason that computing systems that attempt similar tasks will profit enormously from understanding how animals perform these tasks, and simulating these processes to the extent allowed by physical limitations. This necessitates the study and simulation of *Neural Networks*.

The neural network of an animal is part of its nervous system, containing a large number of interconnected *neurons* (nerve cells). "Neural" is an adjective for neuron, and "network" denotes a graph-like structure. *Artificial neural networks* refer to computing systems whose central theme is borrowed from the analogy of biological neural networks. Bowing to common practice, we omit the prefix "artificial." There is potential for confusing the (artificial) poor imitation for the (biological) real thing; in this text, non-biological words and names are used as far as possible.

Artificial neural networks are also referred to as "neural nets," "artificial neural systems," "parallel distributed processing systems," and "connectionist systems." For a computing system to be called by these pretty names, it is necessary for the system to have a labeled directed graph structure where nodes perform some simple computations. From elementary graph theory we recall that a "directed graph" consists of a set of "nodes" (vertices) and a set of "connections" (edges/links/arcs) connecting pairs of nodes. A graph is a "labeled graph" if each connection is associated with a label to identify some property of the connection. In a neural network, each node performs some simple computations, and each connection conveys a signal from one node to another, labeled by a number called the "connection strength" or "weight" indicating the extent to which a signal is amplified or diminished by a connection. Not every such graph can be called a neural network, as illustrated in example 1.1 using a simple labeled directed graph that conducts an elementary computation.

EXAMPLE 1.1   The "AND" of two binary inputs is an elementary logical operation, implemented in hardware using an "AND gate." If the inputs to the AND gate are $x_1 \in \{0, 1\}$ and $x_2 \in \{0, 1\}$, the desired output is 1 if $x_1 = x_2 = 1$, and 0 otherwise. A graph representing this computation is shown in figure 1.1, with one node at which computation (multiplication) is carried out, two nodes that hold the inputs (x_1, x_2), and one node that holds one output. However, this graph cannot be considered a neural network since the connections

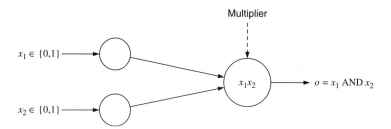

Figure 1.1
AND gate graph.

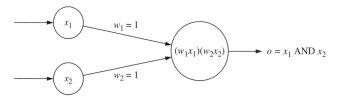

Figure 1.2
AND gate network.

between the nodes are fixed and appear to play no other role than carrying the inputs to the
node that computes their conjunction.

We may modify the graph in figure 1.1 to obtain a network containing weights (connection strengths), as shown in figure 1.2. Different choices for the weights result in different
functions being evaluated by the network. Given a network whose weights are initially
random, and given that we know the task to be accomplished by the network, a "learning algorithm" must be used to determine the values of the weights that will achieve the
desired task. The graph structure, with connection weights modifiable using a learning algorithm, qualifies the computing system to be called an artificial neural network.

EXAMPLE 1.2   For the network shown in figure 1.2, the following is an example of a
learning algorithm that will allow learning the AND function, starting from arbitrary values of w_1 and w_2. The trainer uses the following four examples to modify the weights:
$\{(x_1 = 1, x_2 = 1, d = 1), (x_1 = 0, x_2 = 0, d = 0), (x_1 = 1, x_2 = 0, d = 0), (x_1 = 0, x_2 = 1, d = 0)\}$. An (x_1, x_2) pair is presented to the network, and the result o computed by the
network is observed. If the value of o coincides with the desired result, d, the weights are
not changed. If the value of o is smaller than the desired result, w_1 is increased by 0.1;
and if the value of o is larger than the desired result, w_1 is decreased by 0.1. For instance,

if $w_1 = 0.7$ and $w_2 = 0.2$, then the presentation of $(x_1 = 1, x_2 = 1)$ results in an output of $o = 0.14$ which is smaller than the desired value of 1, hence the learning algorithm increases w_1 to 0.8, so that the new output for $(x_1 = 1, x_2 = 1)$ would be $o = 0.16$, which is closer to the desired value than the previous value ($o = 0.14$), although still unsatisfactory. This process of modifying w_1 or w_2 may be repeated until the final result is satisfactory, with weights $w_1 = 5.0$, $w_2 = 0.2$.

Can the weights of such a net be modified so that the system performs a different task? For instance, is there a set of values for w_1 and w_2 such that a net otherwise identical to that shown in figure 1.2 can compute the OR of its inputs? Unfortunately, there is no possible choice of weights w_1 and w_2 such that $(w_1 \cdot x_1) \cdot (w_2 \cdot x_2)$ will compute the OR of x_1 and x_2. For instance, whenever $x_1 = 0$, the output value $(w_1 \cdot x_1) \cdot (w_2 \cdot x_2) = 0$, irrespective of whether $x_2 = 1$. The node function was predetermined to multiply weighted inputs, imposing a fundamental limitation on the capabilities of the network shown in figure 1.2, although it was adequate for the task of computing the AND function and for functions described by the mathematical expression $o = w_1 w_2 x_1 x_2$.

A different node function is needed if there is to be some chance of learning the OR function. An example of such a node function is $(x_1 + x_2 - x_1 \cdot x_2)$, which evaluates to 1 if $x_1 = 1$ or $x_2 = 1$, and to 0 if $x_1 = 0$ and $x_2 = 0$ (assuming that each input can take only a 0 or 1 value). But this network cannot be used to compute the AND function.

Sometimes, a network may be capable of computing a function, but the learning algorithm may not be powerful enough to find a satisfactory set of weight values, and the final result may be constrained due to the initial (random) choice of weights. For instance, the AND function cannot be learnt accurately using the learning algorithm described above if we started from initial weight values $w_1 = w_2 = 0.3$, since the solution $w_1 = 1/0.3$ cannot be reached by repeatedly incrementing (or decrementing) the initial choice of w_1 by 0.1.

We seem to be stuck with a one node function for AND and another for OR. What if we did not know beforehand whether the desired function was AND or OR? Is there some node function such that we can simulate AND as well as OR by using different weight values? Is there a different network that is powerful enough to learn every conceivable function of its inputs? Fortunately, the answer is *yes*; networks can be built with sufficiently general node functions so that a large number of different problems can be solved, using a different set of weight values for each task.

The AND gate example has served as a takeoff point for several important questions: what are neural networks, what can they accomplish, how can they be modified, and what are their limitations? In the rest of this chapter, we review the history of research in neural networks, and address four important questions regarding neural network systems.

1. How does a single neuron work?

2. How is a neural network structured, i.e., how are different neurons combined or connected to obtain the desired behavior?

3. How can neurons and neural networks be made to learn?

4. What can neural networks be used for?

We also discuss some general issues important for the evaluation and implementation of neural networks.

1.1   History of Neural Networks

Those who cannot remember the past are condemned to repeat it.
—Santayana, "The Life of Reason" (1905–06)

The roots of all work on neural networks are in neurobiological studies that date back to about a century ago. For many decades, biologists have speculated on exactly how the nervous system works. The following century-old statement by William James (1890) is particularly insightful, and is reflected in the subsequent work of many researchers.

The amount of activity at any given point in the brain cortex is the sum of the tendencies of all other points to discharge into it, such tendencies being proportionate

1. to the number of times the excitement of other points may have accompanied that of the point in question;

2. to the intensities of such excitements; and

3. to the absence of any rival point functionally disconnected with the first point, into which the discharges may be diverted.

How do nerves behave when stimulated by different magnitudes of electric current? Is there a minimal threshold (quantity of current) needed for nerves to be activated? Given that no single nerve cell is long enough, how do different nerve cells communicate electrical currents among one another? How do various nerve cells differ in behavior? Although hypotheses could be formulated, reasonable answers to these questions could not be given and verified until the mid-twentieth century, with the advance of neurology as a science.

Another front of attack came from psychologists striving to understand exactly how learning, forgetting, recognition, and other such tasks are accomplished by animals. Psycho-physical experiments have helped greatly to enhance our meager understanding of how individual neurons and groups of neurons work.

McCulloch and Pitts (1943) are credited with developing the first mathematical model of a single neuron. This model has been modified and widely applied in subsequent work.

System-builders are mainly concerned with questions as to whether a neuron model is sufficiently general to enable learning all kinds of functions, while being easy to implement, without requiring excessive computation within each neuron. Biological modelers, on the other hand, must also justify a neuron model by its biological plausibility.

Most neural network learning rules have their roots in statistical correlation analysis and in gradient descent search procedures. Hebb's (1949) learning rule incrementally modifies connection weights by examining whether two connected nodes are simultaneously ON or OFF. Such a rule is still widely used, with some modifications. Rosenblatt's (1958) "perceptron" neural model and the associated learning rule are based on gradient descent, "rewarding" or "punishing" a weight depending on the satisfactoriness of a neuron's behavior. The simplicity of this scheme was also its nemesis; there are certain simple pattern recognition tasks that individual perceptrons cannot accomplish, as shown by Minsky and Papert (1969). A similar problem was faced by the Widrow-Hoff (1960, 1962) learning rule, also based on gradient descent. Despite obvious limitations, accomplishments of these systems were exaggerated and incredible claims were asserted, saying that intelligent machines have come to exist. This discredited and discouraged neural network research among computer scientists and engineers.

A brief history of early neural network activities is listed below, in chronological order.

1938 Rashevsky initiated studies of neurodynamics, also known as neural field theory, representing activation and propagation in neural networks in terms of differential equations.

1943 McCulloch and Pitts invented the first artificial model for biological neurons using simple binary threshold functions (described in section 1.2.2).

1943 Landahl, McCulloch, and Pitts noted that many arithmetic and logical operations could be implemented using methods containing McCulloch and Pitts neuron models.

1948 Wiener presented an elaborate mathematical approach to neurodynamics, extending the work initiated by Rashevsky.

1949 In *The Organization of Behavior,* an influential book, Hebb followed up on early suggestions of Lashley and Cajal, and introduced his famous learning rule: repeated activation of one neuron by another, across a particular synapse, increases its conductance.

1954 Gabor invented the "learning filter" that uses gradient descent to obtain "optimal" weights that minimize the mean squared error between the observed output signal and a signal generated based upon the past information.

1954 Cragg and Temperly reformulated the McCulloch and Pitts network in terms of the "spinglass" model well-known to physicists.

1956 Taylor introduced an associative memory network using Hebb's rule.

1956 Beurle analyzed the triggering and propagation of large-scale brain activity.

1956 Von Neumann showed how to introduce redundancy and fault tolerance into neural networks and showed how the synchronous activation of many neurons can be used to represent each bit of information.

1956 Uttley demonstrated that neural networks with modifiable connections could learn to classify patterns with synaptic weights representing conditional probabilities. He developed a linear separator in which weights were adjusted using Shannon's entropy measure.

1958 Rosenblatt invented the "perceptron," introducing a learning method for the McCulloch and Pitts neuron model.

1960 Widrow and Hoff introduced the "Adaline," a simple network trained by a gradient descent rule to minimize mean squared error.

1961 Rosenblatt proposed the "backpropagation" scheme for training multilayer networks; this attempt was unsuccessful because he used non-differentiable node functions.

1962 Hubel and Wiesel conducted important biological studies of properties of the neurons in the visual cortex of cats, spurring the development of self-organizing artificial neural models that simulated these properties.

1963 Novikoff provided a short proof for the Perceptron Convergence Theorem conjectured by Rosenblatt.

1964 Taylor constructed a winner-take-all circuit with inhibitions among output units.

1966 Uttley developed neural networks in which synaptic strengths represent the mutual information between fixing patterns of neurons.

1967 Cowan introduced the sigmoid fixing characteristic.

1967 Amari obtained a mathematical solution of the credit assignment problem to determine a learning rule for weights in multilayer networks. Unfortunately, its importance was not noticed for a long time.

1968 Cowan introduced a network of neurons with skew-symmetric coupling constants that generates neutrally stable oscillations in neuron outputs.

1969 Minsky and Papert demonstrated the limits of simple perceptrons. This important work is famous for demonstrating that perceptrons are not computationally universal, and infamous as it resulted in a drastic reduction in funding support for research in neural networks.

In the next two decades, the limitations of neural networks were overcome to some extent by researchers who explored several different lines of work.

1. Combinations of many neurons (i.e., neural networks) can be more powerful than single neurons. Learning rules applicable to large NN's were formulated by researchers such as Dreyfus (1962), Bryson and Ho (1969), and Werbos (1974); and popularized by McClelland and Rumelhart (1986). Most of these are still based on gradient descent.

2. Often gradient descent is not successful in obtaining a desired solution to a problem. Random, probabilistic, or stochastic methods (e.g., Boltzmann machines) have been developed to combat this problem by Ackley, Hinton, and Sejnowski (1985); Kirkpatrick, Gelatt, and Vecchi (1983); and others.

3. Theoretical results have been established to understand the capabilities of non-trivial neural networks, by Cybenko (1988) and others. Theoretical analyses have been carried out to establish whether networks can give an approximately correct solution with a high probability, even though the correct solution is not guaranteed [see Valiant (1985), Baum and Haussler (1988)].

4. For effective use of available problem-specific information, "hybrid systems" (combining neural networks and non-connectionist components) were developed, bridging the gulf between symbolic and connectionist systems [see Gallant (1986)].

In recent years, several other researchers (such as Amari, Grossberg, Hopfield, Kohonen, von der Malsburg, and Willshaw) have made major contributions to the field of neural networks; such as in self-organizing maps discussed in chapter 5 and in associative memories discussed in chapter 6.

1.2   Structure and Function of a Single Neuron

In this section, we begin by discussing biological neurons, then discuss the functions computed by nodes in artificial neural networks.

1.2.1   Biological neurons

A typical biological neuron is composed of a cell *body*, a tubular *axon*, and a multitude of hair-like *dendrites*, shown in figure 1.3. The dendrites form a very fine filamentary brush surrounding the body of the neuron. The axon is essentially a long, thin tube that splits into branches terminating in little end bulbs that almost touch the dendrites of other cells. The small gap between an end bulb and a dendrite is called a *synapse*, across which information is propagated. The axon of a single neuron forms synaptic connections with many other

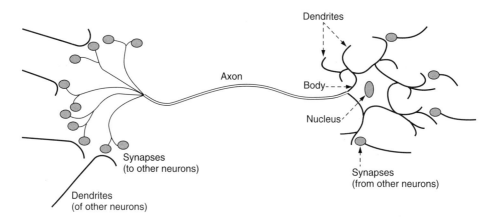

Figure 1.3
A biological neuron.

neurons; the *presynaptic* side of the synapse refers to the neuron that sends a signal, while the *postsynaptic* side refers to the neuron that receives the signal. However, the real picture of neurons is a little more complicated.

1. A neuron may have no obvious axon, but only "processes" that receive and transmit information.

2. Axons may form synapses on other axons.

3. Dendrites may form synapses onto other dendrites.

The number of synapses received by each neuron range from 100 to 100,000. Morphologically, most synaptic contacts are of two types.

Type I: Excitatory synapses with asymmetrical membrane specializations; membrane thickening is greater on the postsynaptic side. The presynaptic side contains round bags (synaptic vesicles) believed to contain packets of a neurotransmitter (a chemical such as glutamate or aspartate).

Type II: Inhibitory synapses with symmetrical membrane specializations; with smaller ellipsoidal or flattened vesicles. Gamma-amino butyric acid is an example of an inhibitory neurotransmitter.

An electrostatic potential difference is maintained across the cell membrane, with the inside of the membrane being negatively charged. Ions diffuse through the membrane to maintain this potential difference. Inhibitory or excitatory signals from other neurons are transmitted to a neuron at its dendrites' synapses. The magnitude of the signal received by a neuron (from another) depends on the *efficiency* of the synaptic transmission, and can be thought of as the strength of the connection between the neurons. The cell membrane becomes electrically active when sufficiently excited by the neurons making synapses onto this neuron. A neuron will *fire*, i.e., send an output impulse of about 100mV down its axon, if sufficient signals from other neurons fall upon its dendrites in a short period of time, called the *period of latent summation*. The neuron fires if its net excitation exceeds its inhibition by a critical amount, the *threshold* of the neuron; this process is modeled by equations proposed by Hodgkin and Huxley (1952). Firing is followed by a brief *refractory period* during which the neuron is inactive. If the input to the neuron remains strong, the neuron continues to deliver impulses at frequencies up to a few hundred impulses per second. It is this frequency which is often referred to as the output of the neuron. Impulses propagate down the axon of a neuron and reach up to the synapses, sending signals of various strengths down the dendrites of other neurons.

1.2.2   Artificial neuron models

We begin our discussion of artificial neuron models by introducing oft-used terminology that establishes the correspondence between biological and artificial neurons, shown in table 1.1. Node output represents firing frequency when allowed to take arbitrary non-binary values; however, the analogy with biological neurons is more direct in some artificial neural networks with binary node outputs, and a node is said to be fired when its net input exceeds a certain threshold.

Figure 1.4 describes a general model encompassing almost every artificial neuron model proposed so far. Even this noncommittal model makes the following assumptions that may lead one to question its biological plausibility.

1. The position on the neuron (node) of the incoming synapse (connection) is irrelevant.

2. Each node has a single output value, distributed to other nodes via outgoing links, irrespective of their positions.

Table 1.1
Terminology

Biological Terminology	Artificial Neural Network Terminology
Neuron	Node/Unit/Cell/Neurode
Synapse	Connection/Edge/Link
Synaptic Efficiency	Connection Strength/Weight
Firing Frequency	Node Output

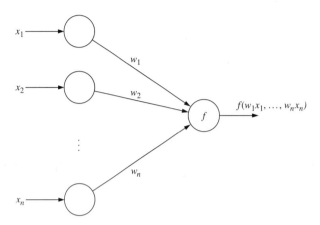

Figure 1.4
General neuron model.

3. All inputs come in at the same time or remain activated at the same level long enough for computation (of f) to occur. An alternative is to postulate the existence of buffers to store weighted inputs inside nodes.

The next level of specialization is to assume that different weighted inputs are summed, as shown in figure 1.5. The neuron output may be written as $f(w_1x_1 + \cdots + w_nx_n)$ or $f(\sum_{i=1}^{n} w_i x_i)$ or $f(net)$, where $net = \sum_{i=1}^{n} w_i x_i$. The simplification involved here is the assumption that all weighted inputs are treated similarly, and merely summed. When examining biological plausibility of such models, we may pose questions such as the following: If different inputs to a biological neuron come in at different locations, exactly how can these be added up before any other function (f) is applied to them?

Some artificial neuron models do *not* sum their weighted inputs, but take their product, as in "sigma-pi" networks [see Feldman and Ballard (1982), Rumelhart and McClelland (1986)]. Nevertheless, the model shown in figure 1.5 is most commonly used, and we elaborate on it in the rest of this section, addressing the exact form of the function f. The simplest possible functions are: the identity function $f(net) = net$; the non-negative identity function $f(net) = \max(0, net)$; and the constant functions $f(net) = c$ for some constant value c. Some other functions, commonly used in neural networks, are described below. Node functions whose outputs saturate (e.g., $\lim_{x \to \infty} f(x) = 1$ and $\lim_{x \to -\infty} f(x) = 0$) are of great interest in all neural network models. Only such functions will be considered in this chapter. Inputs to a neuron that differ very little are expected to produce approximately the same outputs, which justifies using continuous node functions. The motivation for us-

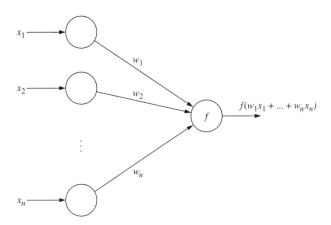

Figure 1.5
Weighted input summation.

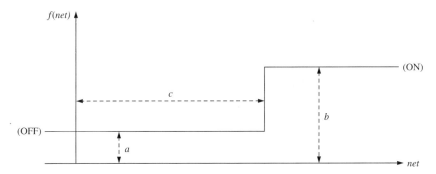

Figure 1.6
Step function.

ing differentiable node functions will become clear when we present learning algorithms
that conduct gradient descent.

Step functions   A commonly used single neuron model is given by a simple step function, shown in figure 1.6. This function is defined in general as follows.

$$f(net) = \begin{cases} a & \text{if} \quad net < c \\ b & \text{if} \quad net > c \end{cases} \tag{1.1}$$

and at c, $f(c)$ is sometimes defined to equal a, sometimes b, sometimes $(a+b)/2$ and
sometimes 0. Common choices are $c = 0, a = 0, b = 1$; and $c = 0, a = -1, b = 1$. The

latter case is also called the signum function, whose output is $+1$ if $net > 0$, -1 if $net < 0$, and 0 if $net = 0$.

The step function is very easy to implement. It also captures the idea of having a minimum threshold ($= c$ in figure 1.6) for the net weighted input that must be exceeded if a neuron's output is to equal b. The state of the neuron in which $net > c$, so that $f(net) = b$, is often identified as the active or ON state for the neuron, while the state with $f(net) = a$ is considered to be the passive or OFF state, assuming $b > a$. Note that b is not necessarily greater than a; it is possible that a node is activated when its net input is less than a threshold.

Though the notion of a threshold appears very natural, this model has the biologically implausible feature that the magnitude of the net input is largely irrelevant (given that we know whether net input exceeds the threshold). It is logical to expect that variations in the magnitudes of inputs should cause corresponding variations in the output. This is not the case with discontinuous functions such as the step function. Recall that a function is continuous if small changes in its inputs produce corresponding small changes in its output. With the step function shown in figure 1.4, however, a change in net from $c - \epsilon/2$ to $c + \epsilon/2$ produces a change in $f(net)$ from a to b that is large when compared to ϵ, which can be made infinitesimally small. Biological systems are subject to noise, and a neuron with a discontinuous node function may potentially be activated by a small amount of noise, implying that this node is biologically implausible.

Another feature of the step function is that its output "saturates," i.e., does not increase or decrease to values whose magnitude is excessively high. This is desirable because we cannot expect biological or electronic hardware to produce excessively high voltages.

The outputs of the step function may be interpreted as class identifiers: we may conclude that an input sample belongs to one class if and only if the net input exceeds a certain value. This interpretation of the step-functional neuron appears simplistic when a network contains more than one neuron. It is sometimes possible to interpret nodes in the interior of the network as identifying features of the input, while the output neurons compute the application-specific output based on the inputs received from these feature-identifying intermediate nodes.

Ramp functions   The ramp function is shown in figure 1.7. This function is defined in general as follows.

$$f(net) = \begin{cases} a & \text{if } net < c \\ b & \text{if } net > d \\ a + ((net - c)(b - a))/(d - c) & \text{otherwise} \end{cases} \quad (1.2)$$

Common choices are $c = 0, d = 1, a = 0, b = 1$; and $c = -1, d = 1, a = -b$.

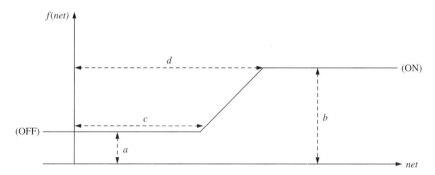

Figure 1.7
Ramp function.

As in the case of the step function, $f(net) = \max(a, b)$ is identified as the ON state, and $f(net) = \min(a, b)$ is the OFF state. This node function also implies the existence of a threshold c which must be exceeded by the net weighted input in order to activate the node. The node output also saturates, i.e., is limited in magnitude. But unlike the step function, the ramp is continuous; small variations in net weighted input cause correspondingly small variations (or none at all) in the output. This desirable property is gained at the loss of the simple ON/OFF description of the output: for $c < net < d$, in figure 1.7, $f(net) \neq a$ and $f(net) \neq b$, so the node output cannot be identified clearly as ON or OFF. Also, though continuous, the node function f is not differentiable at $net = c$ and at $net = d$.

Sigmoid functions   The most popular node functions used in neural nets are "sigmoid" (S-shaped) functions, whose output is illustrated in figure 1.8. These functions are continuous and differentiable everywhere, are rotationally symmetric about some point ($net = c$), and asymptotically approach their saturation values (a, b)

$$\lim_{net \to \infty} f(net) = b$$

and

$$\lim_{net \to -\infty} f(net) = a.$$

Common choices are $a = 0$ or $a = -1$, $b = 1$, and $c = 0$. Some possible choices of f are

$$f(net) = z + \frac{1}{1 + \exp(-x \cdot net + y)} \tag{1.3}$$

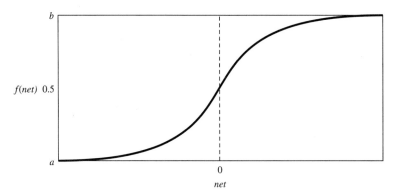

Figure 1.8
A sigmoid function; the graph of $f(net) = 1/(1 + \exp(-2(net)))$.

and

$$f(net) = \tanh(x \cdot net - y) + z, \tag{1.4}$$

where x, y, and z are parameters that determine a, b, and c for figure 1.8. The advantage
of these functions is that their smoothness makes it easy to devise learning algorithms
and understand the behavior of large networks whose nodes compute such functions. Ex-
perimental observations of biological neurons demonstrate that the neuronal firing rate
is roughly sigmoidal, when plotted against the net input to a neuron. But the Brooklyn
Bridge can be sold easily to anyone who believes that biological neurons perform any precise mathematical operation such as exponentiation. From the viewpoint of hardware or
software implementation, exponentiation is an expensive computational task, and one may
question whether such extensive calculations make a real difference for practical neural
networks.

Piecewise linear functions   Piecewise linear functions are combinations of various linear functions, where the choice of the linear function depends on the relevant region of
the input space. Step and ramp functions are special cases of piecewise linear functions
that consist of some finite number of linear segments, and are thus differentiable almost
everywhere, with the second derivative = 0 wherever it exists. Piecewise linear functions
are easier to compute than general nonlinear functions such as sigmoid functions, and have
been used as approximations of the same, as shown in figure 1.9.

Gaussian functions   Bell-shaped curves such as the one shown in figure 1.10 have come
to be known as Gaussian or radial basis functions. These are also continuous; $f(net)$

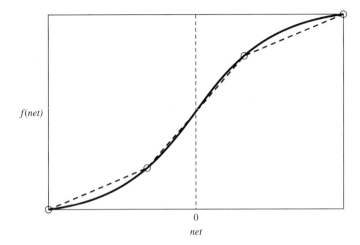

Figure 1.9
A piecewise linear approximation of a sigmoid function.

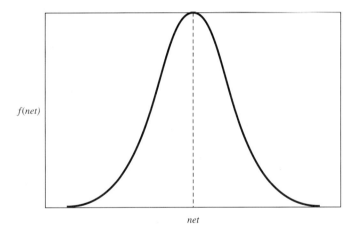

Figure 1.10
Gaussian node function: the graph of $(2\pi\sigma^2)^{-1/2}\exp(-(net-\mu)^2/2\sigma^2)$.

asymptotically approaches 0 (or some constant) for large magnitudes of *net*, and $f(net)$ has a single maximum for $net = \mu$. Algebraically, a Gaussian function of the net weighted input to a node may be described as follows.

$$f(net) = \frac{1}{\sqrt{2\pi}\sigma} \exp\left(-\frac{1}{2}(\frac{net - \mu}{\sigma})^2\right). \tag{1.5}$$

For analyzing various input dimensions separately, we may use a more general formula with a different μ_i and σ_i, for each input dimension x_i.

$$f(w_1 x_1, w_2 x_2, \ldots, w_n x_n) = c \exp\left(-\frac{1}{2}\left(\left(\frac{w_1 x_1 - \mu_1}{\sigma_1}\right)^2 + \ldots + \left(\frac{w_n x_n - \mu_n}{\sigma_n}\right)^2\right)\right).$$

All the other node functions examined are monotonically non-decreasing or non-increasing functions of net input; Gaussian functions differ in this regard. It is still possible to interpret the node output (high/low) in terms of class membership (class 1/0), depending on how close the net input is to a chosen value of μ. Gaussian node functions are used in Radial Basis Function networks, discussed in chapter 4.

1.3   Neural Net Architectures

A single node is insufficient for many practical problems, and networks with a large number of nodes are frequently used. The way nodes are connected determines how computations proceed and constitutes an important early design decision by a neural network developer. A brief discussion of biological neural networks is relevant, prior to examining artificial neural network architectures.

Different parts of the central nervous system are structured differently; hence it is incorrect to claim that a single architecture models all neural processing. The cerebral cortex, where most processing is believed to occur, consists of five to seven layers of neurons with each layer supplying inputs into the next. However, layer boundaries are not strict and connections that cross layers are known to exist. Feedback pathways are also known to exist, e.g., between (to and from) the visual cortex and the lateral geniculate nucleus. Each neuron is connected with many, but not all, of the neighboring neurons within the same layer. Most of these connections are excitatory, but some are inhibitory. There are some "veto" neurons that have the overwhelming power of neutralizing the effects of a large number of excitatory inputs to a neuron. Some amount of indirect self-excitation also occurs—one node's activation excites its neighbor, which excites the first node again.

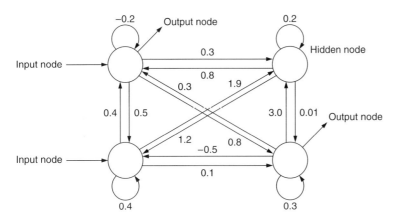

Figure 1.11
A fully connected asymmetric network.

In the following subsections, we discuss artificial neural network architectures, some of which derive inspiration from biological neural networks.

1.3.1   Fully connected networks

We begin by considering an artificial neural network architecture in which every node is connected to every node, and these connections may be either excitatory (positive weights), inhibitory (negative weights), or irrelevant (almost zero weights), as shown in figure 1.11.

This is the most general neural net architecture imaginable, and every other architecture can be seen to be its special case, obtained by setting some weights to zeroes. In a fully connected asymmetric network, the connection from one node to another may carry a different weight than the connection from the second node to the first, as shown in figure 1.11.

This architecture is seldom used despite its generality and conceptual simplicity, due to the large number of parameters. In a network with n nodes, there are n^2 weights. It is difficult to devise fast learning schemes that can produce fully connected networks that generalize well. It is practically never the case that every node has direct influence on every other node. Fully connected networks are also biologically implausible—neurons rarely establish synapses with geographically distant neurons.

A special case of fully connected architecture is one in which the weight that connects one node to another is equal to its symmetric reverse, as shown in figure 1.12. Therefore,

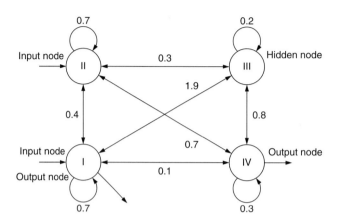

Figure 1.12
A symmetric fully connected network. Note that node I is an input node as well as an output node.

these networks are called fully connected symmetric networks. In chapter 6, we consider these networks for associative memory tasks. In the figure, some nodes are shown as "Input" nodes, some as "Output" nodes, and all others are considered "Hidden" nodes whose interaction with the external environment is indirect. A "hidden node" is any node that is neither an input node nor an output node. Some nodes may not receive external inputs, as in some recurrent networks considered in chapter 4. Some nodes may receive an input as well as generate an output, as seen in node I of figure 1.12.

1.3.2 Layered networks

These are networks in which nodes are partitioned into subsets called layers, with no connections that lead from layer j to layer k if $j > k$, as shown in figure 1.13.

We adopt the convention that a single input arrives at and is distributed to other nodes by each node of the "input layer" or "layer 0"; no other computation occurs at nodes in layer 0, and there are no intra-layer connections among nodes in this layer. Connections, with arbitrary weights, may exist from any node in layer i to any node in layer j for $j \geq i$; intra-layer connections may exist.

1.3.3 Acyclic networks

There is a subclass of layered networks in which there are no intra-layer connections, as shown in figure 1.14. In other words, a connection may exist between any node in layer i and any node in layer j for $i < j$, but a connection is not allowed for $i = j$.

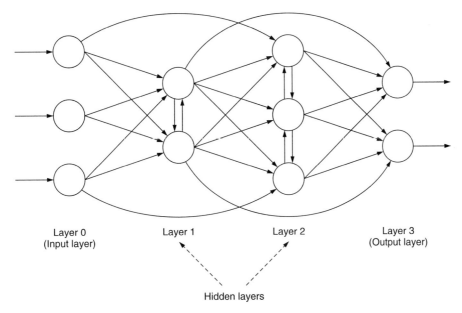

Figure 1.13
A layered network.

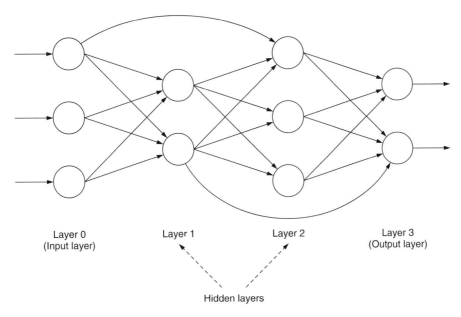

Figure 1.14
An acyclic network.

The computational processes in acyclic networks are much simpler than those in networks with exhaustive, cyclic, or inter-layer connections. Networks that are not acyclic are referred to as *recurrent* networks.

1.3.4 Feedforward networks

This is a subclass of acyclic networks in which a connection is allowed from a node in layer i only to nodes in layer $i + 1$, as shown in figure 1.15.

These networks are succinctly described by a sequence of numbers indicating the number of nodes in each layer. For instance, the network shown in figure 1.15 is a 3-2-3-2 feedforward network; it contains three nodes in the input layer (layer 0), two nodes in the first hidden layer (layer 1), three nodes in the second hidden layer (layer 2), and two nodes in the output layer (layer 3).

These networks, generally with no more than four such layers, are among the most common neural nets in use, so much so that some users identify the phrase "neural networks" to mean only feedforward networks. Conceptually, nodes in successively higher layers abstract successively higher level features from preceding layers. In the literature on neural networks, the term "feedforward" has been used sometimes to refer to layered or acyclic networks.

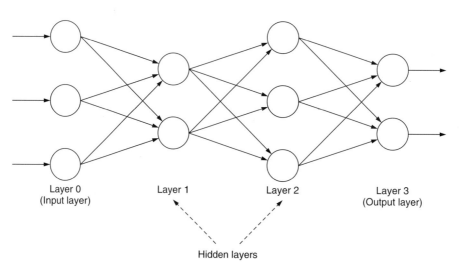

Figure 1.15
A feedforward 3-2-3-2 network.

1.3.5   Modular neural networks

Many problems are best solved using neural networks whose architecture consists of several modules, with sparse interconnections between modules. Modularity allows the neural network developer to solve smaller tasks separately using small (neural network) modules and then combine these modules in a logical manner. Modules can be organized in several different ways, some of which are illustrated in figure 1.16.

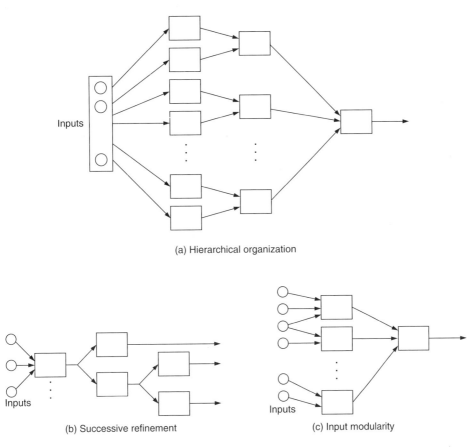

(a) Hierarchical organization

(b) Successive refinement   (c) Input modularity

Figure 1.16
Examples of modular neural networks (each box represents a network of neurons). (a) Hierarchical organization: each higher level module processes the outputs of the previous level module. (b) Successive refinement: each module performs some operations and distributes tasks to next higher level modules. (c) Input modularity: each first level module processes a different subset of inputs (subsets need not be disjoint).

1.4   Neural Learning

It is reasonable to conjecture that neurons in an animal's brain are "hard wired." It is equally obvious that animals, especially the higher order animals, learn as they grow. How does this learning occur? What are possible mathematical models of learning? In this section, we summarize some of the basic theories of biological learning and their adaptations for artificial neural networks. In artificial neural networks, learning refers to the method of modifying the weights of connections between the nodes of a specified network.

1.4.1   Correlation learning

One of the oldest and most widely known principles of biological learning mechanisms was described by Hebb (1949), and is sometimes called "Hebbian learning." Hebb's principle is as follows.

When an axon of cell A is near enough to excite a cell B and repeatedly or persistently takes place in firing it, some growth process or metabolic change takes place in one or both cells such that A's efficiency, as one of the cells firing B, is increased.

For artificial neural networks, this implies a gradual increase in strength of connections among nodes having similar outputs when presented with the same input. The strength of connections between neurons eventually comes to represent the correlation between their outputs. The simplest form of this weight modification rule for artificial neural networks can be stated as

$$\Delta w_{i,j} = c \, x_i \, x_j \tag{1.6}$$

where c is some small constant, denotes the strength of the connection from the jth node to the ith node, and x_i and x_j are the activation levels of these nodes. Many modifications of this rule have been developed and are widely used in artificial neural network models. Networks that use this type of learning are described in chapter 6.

1.4.2   Competitive learning

Another principle for neural computation is that when an input pattern is presented to a network, different nodes compete to be "winners" with high levels of activity. The competitive process involves self-excitation and mutual inhibition among nodes, until a single winner emerges. The connections between input nodes and the winner node are then modified, increasing the likelihood that the same winner continues to win in future competitions (for input patterns similar to the one that caused the adaptation). This leads to the development of networks in which each node specializes to be the winner for a set of similar patterns. This process has been observed in biological systems, and artificial neural networks that conduct this process are discussed in chapter 5.

Competition may be viewed as the consequence of resources being limited, drawing from the analogy of ecological systems. In the brain, maintaining synapses and high connection strengths requires resources, which are limited. These resources would be wasted if a large number of neurons were to respond in identical ways to input patterns. A competitive mechanism can be viewed as a way of ensuring selective neural responses to various input stimuli. Resource conservation is also achieved by allowing connection strengths to decay with time.

The converse of competition is cooperation, found in some neural network models. Cooperative activity can occur in several different ways. Different nodes may specialize in different subtasks, so that together they accomplish a much bigger task. Alternatively, several nodes may learn the same (or a similar) subtask, providing for fault tolerance: errors made by a single node may then be compensated for by other nodes. Connections may exist from each member of such a set of nodes to another higher level node so that the higher level node comes to represent an abstract concept or generalization that combines the concepts represented by the members of the lower level nodes.

1.4.3   Feedback-based weight adaptation

Animals learn as time passes, based on feedback obtained from the environment. Each interaction with the environment can be viewed as measuring the performance of the system, and results in a small change in the system's behavior such that performance improves in the future. If moving limbs in one direction leads towards food (positive feedback), this reinforces the animal's behavior in response to a presented input. The same principle forms the basis of much of machine learning. In the context of neural networks, for instance, if increasing a particular weight leads to diminished performance or larger error, then that weight is decreased as the network is trained to perform better.

The amount of change made at every step is very small in most networks to ensure that a network does not stray too far from its partially evolved state, and so that the network withstands some mistakes made by the teacher, feedback, or performance evaluation mechanism. If the incremental change is infinitesimal, however, the neural network will require excessively large training times. Some training methods cleverly vary the rate at which a network is modified.

1.5   What Can Neural Networks Be Used for?

Practically every non-mechanical task performed by animals requires the interaction of neural networks. Perception, recognition, memory, conscious thought, dreams, sensorimotor control—the list goes on. The desire to simulate some of these tasks has motivated the development of artificial neural networks. In this section, we present the reasons for studying neural networks from the viewpoint of the computational tasks for which they can be used. For each task, we identify performance measures that can be used to judge the degree of success of a neural network in performing the task.

At a high level, the tasks performed using neural networks can be classified as those requiring *supervised* or *unsupervised* learning. In supervised learning, a teacher is available to indicate whether a system is performing correctly, or to indicate a desired response, or to validate the acceptability of a system's responses, or to indicate the amount of error in system performance. This is in contrast with unsupervised learning, where no teacher is available and learning must rely on guidance obtained heuristically by the system examining different sample data or the environment. A concrete example of supervised learing is provided by "classification" problems, whereas "clustering" provides an example of unsupervised learning. The distinction between supervised and unsupervised learning is illustrated in the following examples.

EXAMPLE 1.3   (a) An archaeologist discovers a human skeleton and has to determine whether it belonged to a man or woman. In doing this, the archaeologist is guided by many past examples of male and female skeletons. Examination of these past examples (called the training set) allows the archaeologist to learn about the distinctions between male and female skeletons. This learning process is an example of supervised learning, and the result of the learning process can be applied to determine whether the newly discovered skeleton belongs to a man.

(b) In a different situation, the archaeologist has to determine whether a set of skeleton fragments belong to the same dinosaur species or need to be differentiated into different species. For this task, no previous data may be available to clearly identify the species for each skeleton fragment. The archaeologist has to determine whether the skeletons (that can be reconstructed from the fragments) are sufficiently similar to belong to the same species, or if the differences between these skeletons are large enough to warrant grouping them into different species. This is an unsupervised learning process, which involves estimating the magnitudes of differences between the skeletons. One archaeologist may believe the skeletons belong to different species, while another may disagree, and there is no absolute criterion to determine who is correct.

EXAMPLE 1.4   Consider the table in appendix B.1 containing Fisher's iris data. This data consists of four measurements: the lengths and widths of sepals and petals of iris flowers. Class membership of each data vector is indicated in the fifth column of this table. This information is used in supervised learning. But if we remove the fifth column of the data, all we have is a set of 150 vectors (of widths and lengths of petals and sepals of iris flowers). To separate all 150 vectors into different groups of iris flowers, we would use procedures that depend only on the four values in each vector, and the relative proximity of different vectors. Such training is unsupervised because no *a priori* information is used regarding class membership, i.e., there is no teacher.

1.5.1   Classification

Classification, the assignment of each object to a specific "class" (one of many predetermined groups), is of fundamental importance in a number of areas ranging from image and speech recognition to the social sciences. We are provided with a "training set" consisting of sample patterns that are representative of all classes, along with class membership information for each pattern. Using the training set, we deduce rules for membership in each class and create a classifier, which can then be used to assign other patterns to their respective classes according to these rules.

Neural networks have been used to classify samples, i.e., map input patterns to different classes. For instance, each output node can stand for one class. An input pattern is determined to belong to class i if the ith output node computes a higher value than all other output nodes when that input pattern is fed into the network. In some networks, an additional constraint is that the magnitude of that output node must exceed a minimal threshold, say 0.5.

For two-class problems, feedforward networks with a single output node are adequate. If the node output has permissible values ranging from 0 to 1, for instance, a value close to 1 (say > 0.9) is considered to indicate one class, while a value close to 0 (say < 0.1) indicates the other class.

Neural networks have been used successfully in a large number of practical classification tasks, such as the following.

1. Recognizing printed or handwritten characters

2. Classifying loan applications into credit-worthy and non-credit-worthy groups

3. Analyzing sonar and radar data to determine the nature of the source of a signal

1.5.2   Clustering

Clustering requires grouping together objects that are similar to each other. In classification problems, the identification of classes is known beforehand, as is the membership of

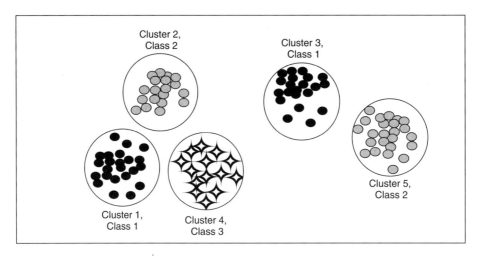

Figure 1.17
Five clusters, three classes in two-dimensional input space.

some samples in these classes. In clustering problems, on the other hand, all that is available is a set of samples and distance relationships that can be derived from the sample descriptions. For example, flowers may be clustered using features such as color and number of petals.

Most clustering mechanisms are based on some distance measure. Each object is represented by an ordered set (vector) of features. "Similar" objects are those that have nearly the same values for different features. Thus, one would like to group samples so as to minimize intra-cluster distances while maximizing inter-cluster distances, subject to constraints on the number of clusters that can be formed. One way to measure intra-cluster distance would be to find the average distance of different samples in a cluster from the cluster center. Similarly, inter-cluster distance could be measured using the distance between the centers of different clusters. Figure 1.17 depicts a problem in which prior clustering (into five clusters) is helpful in a classification pattern.

The number of clusters depends on the problem, but should be as small as possible. Figure 1.18 shows three ways of clustering the same data, of which the first is preferable since it has neither too many nor too few clusters.

Some neural networks accomplish clustering by the following method. Initially, each node reacts randomly to the presentation of input samples. Nodes with higher outputs to an input sample learn to react even more strongly to that sample and to other input samples geographically near that sample. In this way, different nodes *specialize*, responding

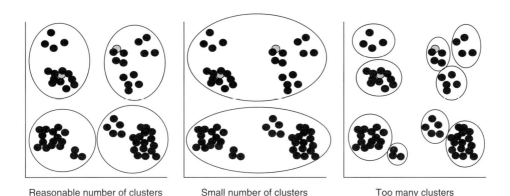

Reasonable number of clusters   Small number of clusters   Too many clusters

Figure 1.18
Three different ways of clustering the same set of sample points.

strongly to different clusters of input samples. This method is analogous to the statistical approach of *k-nearest neighbor* clustering, in which each sample is placed in the same cluster as the majority of its immediate neighbors.

1.5.3   Vector quantization

Neural networks have been used for compressing voluminous input data into a small number of weight vectors associated with nodes in the networks. Each input sample is associated with the nearest weight vector (with the smallest Euclidean distance). *Vector quantization* is the process of dividing up space into several connected regions (called "Voronoi regions"), a task similar to clustering. Each region is represented using a single vector (called a "codebook vector"). Every point in the input space belongs to one of these regions, and is mapped to the corresponding (nearest) codebook vector. The set of codebook vectors is a compressed form of the set of input data vectors, since many different input data vectors may be mapped to the same codebook vector. Figure 1.19 gives an example of such a division of two-dimensional space into Voronoi regions, called a Voronoi diagram (or "tessellation"). For two-dimensional input spaces, the boundaries of Voronoi regions are obtained by sketching the perpendicular bisectors of the lines joining neighboring codebook vectors.

1.5.4   Pattern association

In pattern association, another important task that can be performed by neural networks, the presentation of an input sample should trigger the generation of a specific output pattern. In *auto-association* or *associative memory tasks* (see figure 1.20), the input sample

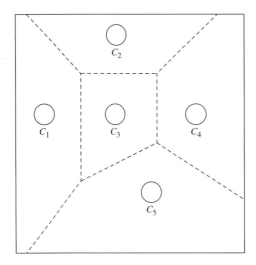

Figure 1.19
Voronoi diagram in two-dimensional space, with five Voronoi regions, and codebook vectors $C_1, \dots, C_5$.

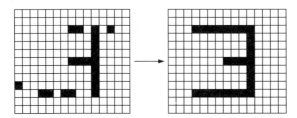

Figure 1.20
Auto-association.

is presumed to be a corrupted, noisy, or partial version of the desired output pattern. In *hetero-association* (see figure 1.21), the output pattern may be any arbitrary pattern that is to be associated with a set of input patterns. An example of an auto-associative task is the generation of a complete (uncorrupted) image, such as a face, from a corrupted version. An example of hetero-association is the generation of a name when the image of a face is presented as input.

In the context of neural networks, "auto/hetero-association" refers to the task of setting up weights that represent the mappings between input and output patterns, whereas "recall" refers to the retrieval of the output pattern corresponding to a specific input pattern. A typical auto-associative neural network consists of a single layer of nodes, each

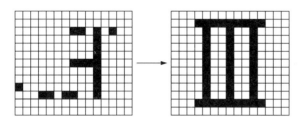

Figure 1.21
Hetero-association.

node corresponds to each input pattern dimension, and the recall process involves repeatedly modifying node outputs until the resulting output pattern ceases to change. For
hetero-associative recall, a second layer of nodes is needed to generate the output pattern
corresponding to an input pattern. These concepts are discussed in greater detail in chapter 6.

1.5.5   Function approximation

Many computational models can be described as functions mapping some numerical input
vectors to numerical outputs. The outputs corresponding to some input vectors may be
known from training data, but we may not know the mathematical function describing the
actual process that generates the outputs from the input vectors. *Function approximation*
is the task of learning or constructing a function that generates approximately the same
outputs from input vectors as the process being modeled, based on available training data.

Figure 1.22 illustrates that the same finite set of samples can be used to obtain many
different functions, all of which perform reasonably well on the given set of points. Since

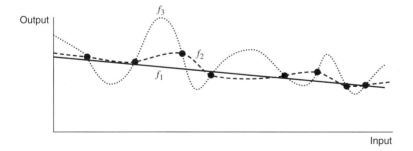

Figure 1.22
Function approximation: different networks implement functions that have the same behavior on training
samples.

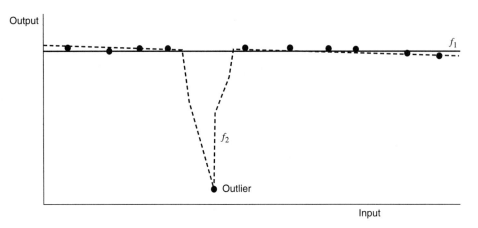

Figure 1.23
Presence of an outlier and function approximation.

infinitely many functions exist that coincide for a finite set of points, additional criteria are necessary to decide which of these functions are *desirable*. Continuity and smoothness of the function are almost always required. Following established scientific practice, an important criterion is that of simplicity of the model, i.e., the neural network should have as few parameters as possible.

These criteria sometimes oppose the *performance* criterion of minimizing error, as shown in figure 1.23. This set of samples contains one *outlier* whose behavior deviates significantly from other samples. Function f_2 passes through all the points in the graph and thus performs best; but f_1, which misses the outlier, is a much simpler function and is preferable. The same is true in the example in figure 1.22, where the straight line (f_1) performs reasonably well, although f_2 and f_3 perform best in that they have zero error. Among the latter, f_2 is certainly desirable because it is smoother and can be represented by a network with fewer parameters. Implicit in such comparisons is the assumption that the given samples themselves might contain some errors due to the method used in obtaining them, or due to environmental factors.

Function approximation can be performed using the networks described in chapters 3 and 4. Many industrial or manufacturing problems involve stabilizing the behavior of an object, or tracking the behavior of a moving object. These can also be viewed as function approximation problems in which the desired function is the time-varying behavior of the object in question.

1.5.6   Forecasting

There are many real-life problems in which future events must be predicted on the basis of past history. An example task is that of predicting the behavior of stock market indices. Weigend and Huberman (1990) observe that prediction hinges on two types of knowledge: knowledge of underlying laws, a very powerful and accurate means of prediction, and the discovery of strong empirical regularities in observations of a given system. However, laws underlying the behavior of a system are not easily discovered, and empirical regularities or periodicities are not always evident, and can often be masked by noise.

Though perfect prediction is hardly ever possible, neural networks can be used to obtain reasonably good predictions in a number of cases. For instance, neural nets have succeeded in learning the 11-year cycle in sunspot data (cf. figure 1.24) without being told *a priori* about the existence of such a cycle [see Li et al. (1990); Weigend, Huberman, and Rumelhart (1990)].

At a high level, the prediction problem is a special case of function approximation problems, in which the function values are represented using *time series*. A time series is a sequence of values measured over time, in discrete or continuous time units, e.g., $S = \{v(t) : 1 \leq t \leq N\}$ represents a collection of N observations collected at times $t = 1, 2, \ldots, N$. For a network that is to make predictions based upon d most recent values of

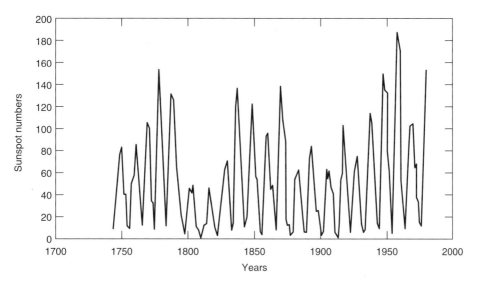

Figure 1.24
Yearly sunspot numbers, showing cyclic fluctuations.

the variable, we extract from S a training set of $(d+1)$-tuples. Each such tuple contains $d+1$ consecutive elements from S, of which the first d components represent network inputs and the last component represents the desired output for those inputs. At each step in the training phase, a d-tuple of input data (recent history) is presented to the network. The network attempts to predict the next value in the time sequence. In this way, the forecasting problem reduces to a function approximation problem.

In forecasting problems, it is important to consider both short-term ("one-lag") and long-term ("multilag") predictions. In one-lag prediction, we forecast the next value based only on actual past values. In multilag prediction, on the other hand, some predicted values are also used to predict future values. For instance, a five-input network is first used to predict a value n_6 from observed input data $i_1, \ldots i_5$, then the next network prediction n_7 is made using inputs $i_2, \ldots, i_5, n_6$, followed by the network prediction n_8 using inputs i_3, i_4, i_5, n_6, n_7. But one-lag prediction at the eighth instant is made using only the actual input data values i_3, i_4, i_5, i_6, i_7. Multilag prediction is required, for example, if we want to predict the value of a variable six months from today, not knowing the values for the next five months.

A better understanding of difficult problems is often obtained by studying many related variables together rather than by studying just one variable. A multivariate time series consists of sequences of values of several variables concurrently changing with time. The variables being measured may be significantly correlated, e.g., when similar attributes are being measured at different geographic locations. Values for each variable may then be predicted with greater accuracy if variations in the other variables are also taken into account. To be successful, forecasting must be based on all available correlations and empirical interdependencies among different temporal sequences.

Feedforward as well as recurrent networks have been used for forecasting and are discussed in chapters 3 and 4.

1.5.7 Control applications

Many manufacturing and industrial applications have complex implicit relationships among inputs and outputs. *Control* addresses the task of determining the values for input variables in order to achieve desired values for output variables. This is also a function approximation problem, for which feedforward, recurrent, and some specialized neural networks have been used successfully. Adaptive control techniques have been developed for systems subject to large variations in parameter values, environmental conditions, and signal inputs. Neural networks can be employed in adaptive control systems to provide fast response, without requiring human intervention.

Systems modeled in control problems may be *static* or *dynamic*; in the latter, the system may map inputs to outputs in a time-dependent manner, and the system's input-output

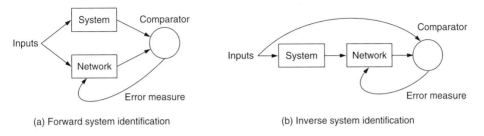

(a) Forward system identification   (b) Inverse system identification

Figure 1.25
Forward and inverse control problems.

mapping may change with time. A simple example of a static control system is one that maps input voltages into mechanical displacements of a robotic arm. Irrespective of the history of the system, an input voltage will always generate the same output displacement. By contrast, the inverted pendulum control task, where the behavior of a pendulum depends on time-dependent input variables such as velocity, is a dynamic control task.

Neural networks have been used for two tasks associated with control; in both tasks, learning is supervised because the system's behavior dictates what the neural network is to accomplish. These tasks, illustrated in figure 1.25, are as follows.

1. *System (forward) identification* is the task of approximating the behavior of a system using a neural network or other learning method. If the system maps a set of input variables I to output variables O, then forward identification is conducted by a feedforward neural network whose inputs correspond to I and outputs correspond to O, trained to minimize an error measure that captures the difference between the network outputs and actual control system outputs.

2. *Inverse identification* is the task of learning the inverse of the behavior of a system, possibly using neural networks. For instance, given the amount of force applied to a robotic arm system, the system's behavior results in displacement by a certain amount. The inverse problem in this case consists of determining the force required to produce a desired amount of displacement. This can be conducted using a feedforward network that uses components of O as its inputs and components of I as its outputs, using an error measure that captures the difference in actual system inputs (i) from the result ($N(S(i))$) of applying the actual system on those inputs, followed by the neural network.

If the neural network has been successfully trained to perform inverse system identification, it can generate values for system inputs needed to obtain desired system outputs. If the system behavior changes with time, the same network that is used to generate inputs for the system may also be continually trained on-line, i.e., its weights are adjusted depending on the error measure

$$N(i) - N(S(N(i))),$$

the deviation between the network outputs $N(i)$ and the result of applying the network to the system's output when applied to the network's outputs.

If the system's input-output mapping is not completely known, or varies with time, a neural network may have to be continually trained to track changes in system behavior. A *feedback* control system is then appropriate, in which the error between actual and desired system output is used to modify the input signal, in order to produce the desired behavior.

Feedforward neural networks (discussed in chapter 3) have been applied to many control problems, such as pole-balancing [Tolat and Widrow (1988)], robot arm control [Guez, Eilbert, and Kam (1988)], truck backing-up [Nguyen and Widrow (1990)], and inverse robot kinematics [Josin, Charney, and White (1988)]. These systems have been successful due to the following features.

1. Realization of fast decision making and control by parallel computation

2. Ability to adapt to a large number of parameters

3. Natural fault tolerance due to the distributed representation of information

4. Robustness to variations in parameters not modeled, due to the generalization properties of networks

1.5.8 Optimization

Many problems in business and scientific modeling can be represented as optimization problems in which the goal is to optimize (maximize or minimize) some functions, subject to some constraints. An example is the task of arranging components on a circuit board such that the total length of wires is minimized, with additional constraints that require certain components to be connected to certain others, as shown in figure 1.26. Some such problems can also be solved using neural networks.

The best solutions for complex optimization problems are often obtained using networks with stochastic behavior in which network behavior has a significant random or probabilistic component. Chapter 7 discusses neural networks and stochastic algorithms for optimization.

1.5.9 Search

Search problems and their solutions occupy a central place in Artificial Intelligence. Search problems are characterized by a set of states, a description of how transitions (or

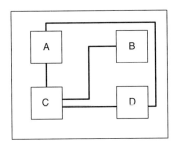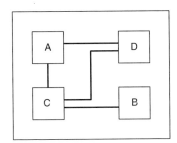

Figure 1.26
Two layouts of components on a circuit board with different wire lengths, but with the same inter-component connections.

moves) may be made among different states, and methods of making moves that make it possible to reach a goal, possibly minimizing the number of moves or computational expense. Many problems discussed in preceding subsections (and solved using neural networks) can be viewed as search problems: for instance, each "state" in a neural network is a possible weight matrix, each "move" is the possible change in the weight matrix that may be made by the learning algorithm, and the "goal" state is one for which the mean squared error is at a local minimum.

Neural networks can also be applied to certain other search problems often solved using symbolic reasoning systems. In attempting to solve a search problem using neural networks, the first (and possibly the hardest) task is to obtain a suitable representation for the search space in terms of nodes and weights in a network. For instance, in a neural network to be used for game playing, the inputs to the network describe the current state of the board game, and the desired output pattern identifies the best possible move to be made. The weights in the network can be trained based on an evaluation of the quality of previous moves made by the network in response to various input patterns.

1.6   Evaluation of Networks

A human learner's capabilities can be evaluated in the following ways.

1. How well does the learner perform on the data on which the learner has been trained, i.e., what is the difference between the expected and actual results generated by the learner?

2. How well does the learner perform on new data not used for training the learner?

3. What are the computational resources (time, space, effort) required by the learner?

The performance of neural networks can also be evaluated using the same criteria, discussed in the following subsections.

1.6.1   Quality of results

The performance of a neural network is frequently gauged in terms of an error measure. The error measure most often used is the Euclidean distance $(\sum_i (d_i - o_i)^2)^{1/2}$ where d_i is the ith element of the desired output vector and o_i is the ith element of the actual network output vector. In some neural networks, discussed in chapter 5, when an input vector i is used, the closest weight vector $w_j \in \{w_1, \ldots, w_k\}$ needs to be determined; when vectors are normalized to have unit length, this can be accomplished by maximizing the vector dot product which is exactly the same as the net input received by a node.

$$w_j \cdot i = w_{j,0} i_0 + \ldots + w_{j,n} i_n$$

Thus, in some instances, the vector dot product can also be used as a negative distance measure.

Among other measures, $\sum_i |d_i - o_i|$, the Manhattan distance or Hamming distance, is often used, especially in pattern association tasks. These measures are generalized to the Minkowski norms $(\sum_i |d_i - o_i|^k)^{1/k}$, for various values of $k > 0$.

These distance measures give equal emphasis to all dimensions of input data. Sometimes, it is more meaningful to use weighted distance measures that attach different degrees of importance to different dimensions. For instance, if in a two-dimensional input vector the first dimension is height, measured in meters, and the second dimension is weight, measured in kilograms, the Euclidean distance between (1.5, 60) and (1.5, 58) is more than the distance between (1.5, 60) and (1.0, 60), which is counter-intuitive in the context of human measurements: the first two individuals differ in weight only by a small amount (two kilograms), whereas the difference in height is significantly larger in the second pair. A more appropriate distance measure, in such cases, is of the form

$$\|x_1 - x_2\| = \sqrt{a^2(x_{1,1} - x_{1,2})^2 + b^2(x_{2,1} - x_{2,2})^2}$$

where the choice of a and b reflects the amount of variation in two components, respectively, which depends on the problem. For the (*height, weight*) problem, $a = 1$ and $b = 0.03$ correspond to reasonable choices for the distance measure.

In general, such a measure could be written as

$$\|x - y\| = ((x - y)^T A^T A (x - y))^{\frac{1}{2}}$$

where A is an $n \times n$ matrix and n is the number of input dimensions. When A is a diagonal matrix, $||\mathbf{x} - \mathbf{y}|| = \sqrt{a_{11}^2(x_1 - y_1)^2 + \ldots + a_{nn}^2(x_n - y_n)^2}$ which reduces to the Euclidean distance when A is the identity matrix. When A has non-zero, non-diagonal entries, $||\mathbf{x} - \mathbf{y}||^2$ is an arbitrary quadratic function.

The nature of the problem sometimes dictates the choice of the error measure. In classification problems, in addition to the Euclidean distance, another possible error measure is the fraction of misclassified samples.

$$E = \frac{\text{Number of misclassified samples}}{\text{Total number of samples}}$$

If the network outputs are be interpreted as probabilities, the error measure chosen may be the probability of misclassification.

For clustering problems, it is desirable that the number of clusters should be small, intra-cluster distances should be small and inter-cluster distances should be large, leading to a generic error measure such as

$$E = \alpha(\text{No. of clusters}) + \beta \sum_{\substack{\text{all} \\ \text{clusters}}} (\text{Intra-cluster Distance})$$

$$- \gamma \sum_{\substack{\text{pairs of} \\ \text{clusters}}} (\text{Inter-cluster Distance})$$

where α, β, γ are non-negative; a frequent choice for fixed number of clusters (k) is

$$\gamma = 0, \quad \beta = 1, \quad \text{and } \alpha = \begin{cases} 0, & \text{if the number of clusters} \leq k \\ \infty, & \text{if the number of clusters} > k. \end{cases}$$

Intra-cluster distance may be expressed as the sum or maximum of distances between all possible pairs of objects in each cluster, or between the centroid and other objects in each cluster. Similarly, inter-cluster distances may be computed by adding the distances between centroids or pairs of objects in different clusters.

1.6.2 Generalizability

It is not surprising for a system to perform well on the data on which it has been trained. But good generalizability is also necessary, i.e., the system must perform well on new test data distinct from training data. Consider a child learning addition of one digit numbers. Suppose the child is taught the result of the additions $3 + 4$ and $33 + 44$. Given these numbers, the child will find the right answer. However, would the child be able to add 333 and 444 (for which the answer was not provided earlier)? This can occur if the child has *learned* how to extrapolate addition to larger numbers, rather than merely *memorized* the answers provided for training examples. The same distinction between learning and memorization is also relevant for neural networks.

In network development, therefore, available data is separated into two parts, of which one part is the training data and other part is the test data. It has been observed that excessive training on the training data sometimes decreases performance on the test data. One way to avoid this danger of "overtraining" is by constant evaluation of the system using test data as learning proceeds. After each small step of learning (in which performance of the network on training data improves), one must examine whether performance on test data also improves. If there is a succession of training steps in which performance improves only for the training data and not for the test data, overtraining is considered to have occurred, and the training process should be terminated.

1.6.3   Computational resources

Once training is complete, many neural networks generally take up very little time in their execution or application to a specific problem. However, training the networks or applying a learning algorithm can take a very long time, sometimes requiring many hours or days. Training time increases rapidly with the size of the networks and complexity of the problem. For fast training, it helps significantly to break down the problem into smaller subproblems and solve each one separately; modular networks that use such problem decomposition techniques were described in section 1.3.5.

The capabilities of a network are limited by its size. Despite this, the use of large networks increases training time and reduces generalizability. Size of a network can be measured in terms of the number of nodes, connections, and layers in a network. Complexity of node functions, possibly estimated as the number of bits needed to represent the functions, also contributes to network complexity measures.

1.7   Implementation

Although most networks are currently implemented in software, hardware implementations offer significant improvement in speed. Most learning algorithms, however, have been devised without clear hardware implementation considerations. For instance, neural hardware can generally allow only weights whose magnitudes are severely limited. Most chips also have limited fanout (pin-count), so networks with very high connectivity are difficult to implement.

Computations proceed in lockstep or in a strict pre-ordered sequence in some networks, which are said to be synchronous. More biologically plausible are asynchronous networks in which any node or group of nodes may perform its computations at any instant. The time sequence of computations becomes especially relevant in recurrent or cyclic networks. In layered networks it is generally assumed that all computations of layer i nodes occur (in parallel) strictly before computations of layer $(i + 1)$ nodes. When there are intra-layer connections, it is assumed that the previous output of one node is fed into the other node at the same layer, and vice versa. If f_i is the node function of the ith node and $x_i[t]$ is that node's output at time t, then

$$x_i[t + 1] = f_i(\sum_{j \in \mathcal{P}} w_{ij} x_j[t + 1] + \sum_{j \in \mathcal{S}} w_{ij} x_j[t]), \qquad (1.7)$$

where $\mathcal{P}$ is the set of nodes in preceding layers and $\mathcal{S}$ denotes the set of nodes in the same or higher level layers, according to this computational rule. Asynchrony is essential for proving the correctness properties of some networks.

Parallelizability is another important consideration for neural networks. Depending on the hardware, synchronous or asynchronous computation models may be appropriate. Most existing learning methods have been devised for serial hardware, although some parallel implementations have also been developed.

1.8   Conclusion

The computing paradigm of artificial neural networks has become increasingly important, based on successes in many practical applications. In this chapter, we have examined some of the main principles underlying such systems.

Most neural network models combine a highly interconnected network architecture with a simple neuron model. The use of a learning algorithm is assumed, which stores the knowledge specific to a problem in the weights of connections between neurons.

Neural networks have been used for several different kinds of tasks, such as classification, clustering, function approximation, and optimization. Each task requires a different kind of network and learning algorithm, whose details are discussed in the chapters that follow. So far, we have only examined the commonalities between these networks and attempted to present a general framework within which various neural network models can be understood. Where possible, we will point out the relations to other well-known statistical and mathematical procedures, often cloaked under the cover of neural network terminology.

For many of the tasks discussed earlier in this chapter, neural networks have been found to be at least as successful as previously used statistical methods. This is partly because neural networks are non-parametric estimators, making no assumptions about input distributions, and use non-linear node functions. By contrast, non-parametric and non-linear statistical procedures are relatively complex and harder to implement than neural networks. However, statistical procedures are useful in suggesting the limitations of different neural network models, and also point to the directions for future research in neural networks. For instance, results of statistical analysis can be carefully interpreted, and measures of confidence can be formulated for results generated by statistical procedures; these are unavailable for neural network procedures.

There are some problems for which the alternative to a neural net is a rule-based expert system. The latter is suitable if knowledge is readily available. Neural networks can be applied more easily if raw data is available and if it is difficult to find an expert whose knowledge can be codified into rules.

"Case-based reasoning," in which new cases are directly compared with stored cases, is another alternative that competes with neural nets that perform clustering tasks. Again, the amount of external or expert assistance available may dictate the preferential use of the non-neural alternatives, although hardware or parallel implementations weigh in favor of neural nets.

Many books and thousands of papers have been written on the subject of neural networks since the decade of the 1980s, which has been called the "renaissance" period for the subject, probably beginning with the publication of the book *Parallel Distributed Processing* (D. Rumelhart and J. McClelland, 1986). Anderson and Rosenfeld (1988) and Cowan (1990) are good sources that discuss the history of neural networks. A series of important network models are cataloged in *Artificial Neural Systems* (Simpson, 1988). For the interested and mathematically inclined reader, *Neural Networks: A Comprehensive Foundation* by Haykin (1994), and *Introduction to the Theory of Neural Computation* by Hertz, Krogh, and Palmer (1991) should serve as useful followups to this text. Books have also appeared on specific applications of neural networks, in areas such as chemistry and geography. Research papers appear in journals such as *Neural Networks*, *IEEE Transactions on Neural Networks*, *Neurocomputing*, *Journal of Artificial Neural Networks*, and *Biological Cybernetics*; important papers also appear in many other journals in the areas of artificial intelligence, statistics, pattern recognition, physics, biology, parallel computing, and cognitive science. Many neural network tools are also freely available on the Internet.

It is easy to be lost in this immense literature on neural networks. Not all networks are described here, nor anywhere else, for that matter: new networks, algorithms, and heuristics appear in the literature every month. We hope that this book will help in the newcomer's first forays into this field and whet the reader's appetite for more details.

1.9   Exercises

1. For each of the following problems, indicate whether it can be considered a problem of classification, clustering, pattern association, optimization, forecasting, function approximation, or other appropriate category. For which of these problems would it be appropriate to use neural networks, as opposed to rule-based expert systems, statistical procedures, or other traditional techniques, and why? In each case, certain "inputs" specific to a particular situation may be available, as well as some knowledge stored in a neural network or some other system.

  a. Decide whether a person is smiling, based on an analysis of the visual input you receive.

  b. Remember the name of a person.

  c. Determine whether a person is suffering from malaria.

  d. Determine what actions will make a person leave you alone.

2. How useful is it to have a clustering system where the number of clusters equals the number of input patterns?

3. Give an example of a classification task where clustering is not helpful.

4.   a. Can any network developed for function approximation be used for classification purposes?

  b. Can any network developed for function approximation be used for clustering purposes?

  c. Can any network developed for optimization be used for classification purposes?

  d. Can any network developed for optimization be used for clustering purposes?

5. Estimate the effort and expense involved in building an artificial neural network that contains as many neurons and connections as the human brain, assuming that the brain's functioning becomes fully understood at some future time.

6. Compare the relative difficulty of the following tasks, for problems for which these tasks can be performed successfully.

  a. Finding a straight line that separates data belonging to two different classes

  b. Finding the equation of an elliptic curve that separates data belonging to two different classes

  c. Finding a straight line that separates data into two equal sets such that the first set contains as many samples of one class as possible and the other set contains as many samples of the second class as possible

d. Finding a straight line that minimizes the sum of the distances of all data points from the line

7.   a. Present a two-class classification example to illustrate that minimizing mean squared error can produce a different result than minimizing the number of misclassifications.

b. Given two-dimensional data points, let E be the total Euclidean distance of all data points from a line, and let M be the total Manhattan distance of all data points from a line. Present an example to show that a straight line that minimizes E need not minimize M.

8. The grading problem consists of assigning letter grades (A, B, C, D, F) to students whose aggregate scores in a course are known; three instances of this problem are given below, where the maximum possible score is assumed to be 100.

a. 95, 75, 65, 55, 54, 52, 51, 35, 30, 20, 5, 0

b. 90, 85, 80, 75, 70, 65, 60, 55, 50, 45, 40, 35, 30, 25, 20

c. 90, 89, 85, 84, 60, 59, 40, 39, 20, 19, 0

How would you categorize this problem (classification, clustering, etc.)? Discuss the issues and difficulties involved in constructing a neural network for this task.

2 Supervised Learning: Single-Layer Networks

Seek simplicity, and distrust it.
—Alfred North Whitehead

In this chapter, and in chapters 3 and 4, we discuss neural networks trained using well-known supervised learning algorithms, which are applicable when the desired result is known for samples in the training data. The networks discussed in this chapter are the simplest, consisting of only one layer of nodes at which computation is performed, frequently with only one node in this layer. The learning algorithms are hence simpler and do not have to address the more difficult question of how to modify weights among computing nodes. The main focus of this chapter is on the description, use, capabilities, and limitations of simple *perceptrons*, among the oldest and simplest artificial neural networks known; many variations of this model were developed and studied by Rosenblatt (1958). We also examine the related Least Mean Squares (LMS) and pocket algorithms. The basic ideas of the algorithms studied in this chapter are also applicable to more complex neural networks, and will prepare us for the study of multilayer supervised learning algorithms.

2.1 Perceptrons

Rosenblatt (1958) defines a *perceptron* to be a machine that learns, using examples, to assign input vectors (samples) to different classes, using a linear function of the inputs. Minsky and Papert (1969) instead describe the perceptron as a stochastic gradient-descent algorithm that attempts to linearly separate a set of n-dimensional training data. In this text, we use the word *perceptron* in the former sense as a machine, following Rosenblatt, and refer explicitly to the "perceptron learning algorithm" whenever necessary.

In its simplest form, a perceptron has a single output whose values determine to which of two classes each input pattern belongs. Such a perceptron can be represented by a single node that applies a step function to the net weighted sum of its inputs. The input pattern is considered to belong to one class or the other depending on whether the node output is 0 or 1.

EXAMPLE 2.1   Consider two-dimensional samples $(0, 0)$, $(0, 1)$, $(1, 0)$, $(-1, -1)$ that belong to one class, and samples $(2.1, 0)$, $(0, -2.5)$, $(1.6, -1.6)$ that belong to another class. These classes are linearly separable. The *dichotomy* or two-class partition of the input space is also shown in figure 2.1. A perceptron that separates samples of opposite classes is shown in figure 2.1(b). The node function is a step function, whose output is 1 if the net weighted input exceeds 2, and 0 otherwise. If x_1 and x_2 are the two input dimensions,

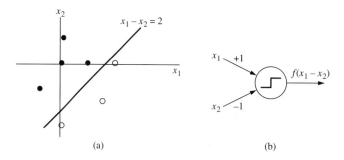

Figure 2.1
Samples from two linearly separable classes, and the associated perceptron whose output $= 1$ if $(x_1 - x_2) > 2$ and 0 otherwise.

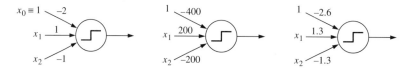

Figure 2.2
Equivalent perceptrons that use a constant input $= 1$ instead of a threshold.

the node function chosen is such that the output is 1 if and only if $x_1 - x_2 > 2$. Samples in one part of the input space are those with $x_1 - x_2 > 2$, and the perceptron considers them all to be in a class other than those samples for which $x_1 - x_2 \leq 2$. An artificial input whose value is always equal to 1 is used in alternate representations of the same perceptron, shown in figure 2.2. This commonly used artifice allows us to replace the threshold by a weight from an input to the node, and makes it easier to write learning algorithms.

If one set of weights exists that solves a two-class classification problem, then there are infinitely many sets of weights that describe the same dichotomizer. For instance, each of the perceptrons in figure 2.2 performs the same task. Since the equation of a line can be expressed in infinitely many ways (for example, $x_1 - x_2 = 2$, $2x_1 - 2x_2 = 4$, $100x_1 - 100x_2 = 200$), infinitely many sets of weights represent functionally equivalent perceptrons.

For practical hardware implementations, one of the important concerns is that the weight values are neither too large nor too small, so that the weights can be represented with sufficient accuracy by hardware devices whose outputs have limited range. For these reasons, weight magnitudes not exceeding 1 are often preferred.

2.2   Linear Separability

For two-dimensional inputs, if there exists a line (whose equation is $w_0 + w_1x_1 + w_2x_2 = 0$) that separates all samples of one class from the other class, then an appropriate perceptron (with weights w_0, w_1, w_2 for the connections from inputs $1, x_1, x_2$, respectively) can be derived from the equation of the separating line. Such classification problems are said to be "linearly separable," i.e., separable by a linear combination of inputs.

The close correspondence between perceptron weights and the coefficients of terms in the equations of lines can be used to arrive at the converse result as well: if there is a simple perceptron (with weights w_0, w_1, w_2 for the connections from inputs $1, x_1, x_2$, respectively) that can separate samples of two classes, then we can obtain the equation $(w_0 + w_1x_1 + w_2x_2 = 0)$ of a line that separates samples of the two classes.

Therefore, if the samples are NOT linearly separable, i.e., no straight line can possibly separate samples belonging to two classes, then there CANNOT be any simple perceptron that achieves the classification task. This is the fundamental limitation of simple perceptrons, considered here for two-dimensional input samples. Examples of linearly nonseparable classes are illustrated in figure 2.3. Most real–life classification problems are linearly nonseparable, and hence cannot be solved using perceptrons.

So far, we have examined problems with two input dimensions (say x_1, x_2). If there is only one input dimension (say x), then the two–class problem can be solved using a perceptron if and only if there is some value x_0 of x such that all samples of one class occur for $x > x_0$, and all samples of the other class occur for $x < x_0$ (see figure 2.4).

If there are three input dimensions, a two-class problem can be solved using a perceptron if and only if there is a plane that separates samples of different classes. As in the two-dimensional case, coefficients of terms in the equation of the plane correspond to the weights of the perceptron.

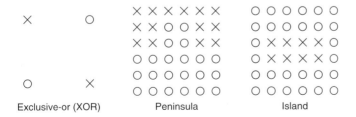

Figure 2.3
Examples of linearly *nonseparable* classes: crosses indicate samples of one class, and circles indicate samples of another class.

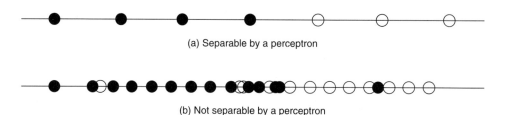

(a) Separable by a perceptron

(b) Not separable by a perceptron

Figure 2.4
Classification problems in one-dimensional input space.

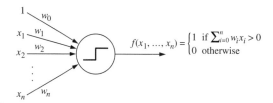

$$f(x_1, \ldots, x_n) = \begin{cases} 1 & \text{if } \sum_{i=0}^{n} w_i x_i > 0 \\ 0 & \text{otherwise} \end{cases}$$

Figure 2.5
Generic perceptron for n-dimensional input space, implementing the hyperplane $\sum_{i=0}^{n} w_i x_i = 0$.

For spaces of higher number of input dimensions, our geometric intuitions need to be suitably extended, imagining "hyperplanes" that can separate samples of different classes. Each hyperplane in n dimensions is defined by the equation

$$w_0 + w_1 x_1 + w_2 x_2 + \ldots + w_n x_n = 0,$$

dividing the n-dimensional space into two regions, in which $w_0 + w_1 x_1 + w_2 x_2 + \ldots + w_n x_n > 0$ and $w_0 + w_1 x_1 + w_2 x_2 + \ldots + w_n x_n < 0$, respectively. This again corresponds exactly with the decision made by the perceptron whose weights are $w_1, w_2, \ldots, w_n$ and threshold is w_0, as shown in figure 2.5.

For simple examples, and for two-dimensional input spaces, it is relatively easy to determine by geometric construction whether two classes are linearly separable. But this becomes very difficult for higher-dimensional spaces. Is there a mechanical procedure that will help us obtain the weights of a suitable perceptron for any linearly separable problem? This question is answered in the following section.

2.3 Perceptron Training Algorithm

A learning procedure called the "perceptron training algorithm" can be used to obtain mechanically the weights of a perceptron that separates two classes, whenever possible. From

Algorithm Perceptron;
   Start with a randomly chosen weight vector w_0;
   Let $k = 1$;
   while there exist input vectors that are misclassified by w_{k-1}, **do**
      Let i_j be a misclassified input vector;
      Let $x_k = class(i_j).i_j$, implying that $w_{k-1} \cdot x_k < 0$;
      Update the weight vector to $w_k = w_{k-1} + \eta x_k$;
      Increment k;
   end-while;

Figure 2.6
Perceptron Training Algorithm.

the weights, the equation of the separating hyperplane can be derived. The perceptron developed in this manner can be used to classify new samples, based on whether the node output is 0 or 1 for the new input vector.

In what follows, we denote vectors by rows of numbers (rather than columns), for ease of presentation. If $w = (w_1, w_2, \ldots, w_n)$ and $x = (x_1, x_2, \ldots, x_n)$ represent two vectors, then their "dot product" or "scalar product" $w \cdot x$ is defined as $(w_1 x_1 + w_2 x_2 + \ldots + w_n x_n)$. The Euclidean length $\|v\|$ of a vector v is $(v \cdot v)^{1/2}$. The presentation of the learning is simplified by using perceptron output values $\in \{-1, 1\}$ instead of $\{0, 1\}$; we hence assume that the perceptron with weight vector w has output 1 if $w \cdot x > 0$, and output -1 otherwise, corresponding to the other class.

The perceptron training algorithm (figure 2.6) does not assume any *a priori* knowledge about the specific classification problem being solved: initial weights are random. Input samples are repeatedly presented and the performance of the perceptron observed. If the performance on a given input sample is satisfactory, i.e., the current network output is the same as the desired output for a given sample, the weights are not changed in this step. But if the network output differs from the desired output, the weights must be changed in such a way as to reduce system error. Let w be the weight vector (including the threshold) and i be the input vector (including the dummy input constant $i_0 = 1$) for a given iteration of the while loop. If i belongs to class 0 (for which the desired node output is -1) but $w \cdot i > 0$, then the weight vector needs to be modified to $w + \Delta w$ so that $(w + \Delta w) \cdot i < w \cdot i$. The consequence of this modification is that i would have a better chance of being classified correctly in the following iteration. This can be done by choosing Δw to be $-\eta i$ where η is some positive constant, since

$$(w + \Delta w) \cdot i = (w - \eta i) \cdot i = w \cdot i - \eta i \cdot i < w \cdot i,$$

because $i \cdot i$ is the square of the length of the non-zero vector i and is hence always positive.

Similarly, if $w \cdot i < 0$ when the desired output value is 1, the weight vector needs to be modified so that $(w + \Delta w) \cdot i > w \cdot i$, which can be done by choosing Δw to be ηi for $\eta > 0$, since $(w + \eta i) \cdot i = w \cdot i + \eta i \cdot i > w \cdot i$. This is the essential rationale for the perceptron training algorithm.

Let $i_1, i_2, \ldots, i_p$ denote the training set, containing p input vectors. Each input vector $i_j = (i_{j,0}, i_{j,1}, \ldots, i_{j,n})$ includes the constant component $(i_{j,0} \equiv 1)$ associated with the threshold weight. For the training set, we define a function *class* that maps each sample to either $+1$ or -1; *class* $(i_j) = 1$ if the sample belongs to class C_1, and *class* $(i_j) = -1$ if the sample belongs to class C_0. Samples are presented repeatedly to train the weights. Samples that do not change the weights can be ignored when we consider the sequence of steps at which weights change.

EXAMPLE 2.2   This example illustrates the execution of the perceptron training algorithm on 7 one-dimensional input patterns [shown in figure 2.4(a)] that are linearly separable. Samples $\{0.0, 0.17, 0.33, 0.50\}$ belong to one class (with desired output 0), whereas samples $\{0.67, 0.83, 1.0\}$ belong to the other class (with desired output 1). The perceptron attempts to find the values of w_1, w_0 such that the input patterns are separated by the point $(-w_0/w_1)$ defined by $w_1 x_1 + w_0 = 0$.

For this example, we assume that we present all samples in some fixed cyclic sequence, although this assumption is not necessary for the algorithm to terminate. For the initial randomly chosen value of $w_1 = -0.36$, and for $w_0 = -1.0$, the samples $\{0.83, 0.67, 1.0\}$ are misclassified. For the presentation of sample 0.83, the net input to the step function is $(0.83)(-0.36) - 1.0 = -1.2$ implying that the sample is placed by the perceptron in the class labeled -1, which is an error. For $\eta = 0.1$, since the desired output is 1 in each of these cases, the result of presenting sample 0.83 results in the new weight

$$w_1 = -0.36 + (0.1)(0.83) = -0.28, \quad w_0 = -1 + (0.1)(1) = -0.9,$$

for which these same samples are still misclassified. Subsequent changes result in the weight modifications and number of misclassifications shown in figure 2.1; these are results obtained after each sample presentation, in a fixed sequence. The final result is $w_1 = 0.3$, $w_0 = -0.2$ which corresponds to a separation between the classes at $x_1 \approx 0.667$.

EXAMPLE 2.3   This example illustrates the execution of the perceptron training algorithm on 27 one-dimensional input patterns [shown in figure 2.4(b)] that are not linearly separable. Samples $\{0.05, 0.1, 0.15, 0.2, 0.25, 0.3, 0.35, 0.4, 0.45, 0.49, 0.52, 0.56, 0.57, 0.82\}$ belong to one class (with desired output 0), whereas samples $\{0.12, 0.47, 0.48, 0.5, 0.55, 0.6, 0.65, 0.7, 0.75, 0.8, 0.85, 0.9, 0.95\}$ belong to the other class (with desired output 1).

Table 2.1
Results of perceptron training on linearly separable data.

Presentation No.	2	3	4	5	6	7	8	9
Sample	0.33	0.67	0.17	1.00	0.50	0.00	0.83	0.33
Desired output	−1	1	−1	1	−1	−1	1	−1
Net input	−0.99	−1.10	−0.80	−1.00	−0.80	−0.70	−0.80	−0.60
w_1	−0.28	−0.21	−0.21	−0.11	−0.11	−0.11	−0.03	−0.03
w_0	−0.90	−0.80	−0.80	−0.70	−0.70	−0.70	−0.60	−0.60
Number misclassified	3	3	3	3	3	3	3	3

Presentation No.	10	...	17	...	24	25	26	27
Sample	0.67	...	0.67	...	0.67	0.17	1.00	0.50
Desired output	1	...	1	...	1	−1	1	−1
Net input	−0.62	...	−0.15	...	−0.01	−0.04	0.25	0.01
w_1	0.04	...	0.29	...	0.35	0.35	0.30	0.30
w_0	−0.50	...	−0.20	...	−0.10	−0.10	−0.10	−0.20
Number misclassified	3	...	1	...	2	2	2	0

For this data, several samples are misclassified by even the best performing perceptron, for which the separating point is roughly near 0.5. (See table 2.1.)

The specific sequence in which inputs were supplied to the perceptron was (0.05, 0.5, 0.82, 0.15, 0.75, 0.3, 0.65, 0.35, 0.95, 0.45, 0.12, 0.57, 0.55, 0.2, 0.6, 0.4, 0.7, 0.1, 0.8, 0.85, 0.9, 0.25, 0.47, 0.48, 0.49, 0.52, 0.56). We assume a learning rate of $\eta = 0.1$. The bias weight was initialized at -1.0, as in the previous example. For the initial value of $w_1 = -0.36$, chosen randomly, the separation imposed by the perceptron is at $x_1 \approx 2.7$, and all the samples with desired output 1 are misclassified. The presentation of input 0.5 results in the weights being modified to $w_1 = -0.36 + (0.1)(0.5) = -0.31$, and $w_0 = -1.0 + (0.1)(1) = -0.9$, implying that the network places almost all samples in class 1. It takes 19 such sample presentations for the number of mistakes to be reduced: for $w_1 = 0.2$, $w_0 = -0.1$, corresponding to separating the classes at $x_1 = 0.5$, only seven samples are misclassified. However, the weights of the perceptron continue to change with subsequent sample presentations, and the quality of the final result depends on the point at which computation is stopped.

The following important questions remain to be answered. Note that these questions are relevant for other learning algorithms as well.

1. How long should we execute this procedure, i.e., what is the termination criterion if the given samples are not linearly separable?

2. What is the appropriate choice for the learning rate η?

3. How can the perceptron training algorithm be applied to problems in which the inputs are non-numeric values (e.g., values of the attribute "color" instead of numbers)?

4. Is there a guarantee that the training algorithm will always succeed whenever the samples are linearly separable?

5. Are there useful modifications of the perceptron training algorithm that work reasonably well when samples are not linearly separable?

The rest of this section addresses the first three questions, and the latter questions are answered in sections 2.4 and 2.5.

2.3.1 Termination criterion

For many neural network learning algorithms, one simple termination criterion is: "halt when the goal is achieved." For perceptrons and other classifiers, the goal is the correct classification of all samples, assuming these are linearly separable. So the perceptron training algorithm can be allowed to run until all samples are correctly classified. Termination is assured if η is sufficiently small, and samples are linearly separable.

The above termination criterion allows the procedure to run indefinitely if the given samples are not linearly separable or if the choice of η is inappropriate. How can we detect that this may be the case? One method is to compare the amount of progress achieved in the recent past. If the number of misclassifications has not changed in a large number of steps, the samples may not be linearly separable. However, the problem may be with the choice of η, and experimenting with a different choice of η may yield improvement. If we know that the two classes overlap (i.e., are not linearly separable) to some known degree, or if the performance requirements allow some (known) amount of misclassification, then this information can be used to modify the termination criterion of the perceptron training procedure. For instance, it may be known that at least 6% of the samples will be misclassified, no matter which hyperplane is chosen to separate the two classes. Alternatively, the user may be satisfied with a misclassification rate of 6% even though it is not known *a priori* whether better classification is possible. We can then terminate the perceptron training procedure as soon as 94% of the samples are correctly classified.

2.3.2 Choice of learning rate

The examination of extreme cases can help derive a good choice for η. If η is too large (e.g., $\eta = 1,000,000$), then the components of $\Delta w = \pm \eta x$ can have very large magnitudes, assuming components of x are not infinitesimally small. Consequently, each weight update swings perceptron outputs completely in one direction, so that the perceptron now considers all samples to be in the same class as the most recent one. This effect is reversed when a new sample of the other class is presented: now the system considers all samples to be in that class. The system thus oscillates between extremes.

We now consider the other alternative, choosing a very small value for η. Clearly, if $\eta = 0$, the weights are never going to be modified. If η equals some infinitesimally small value, the change in weights in each step (with $\Delta w = \pm \eta x$) is going to be infinitesimally small, assuming components of x are not very large in magnitude. So if the initial (random) choice of weights was not exactly the desired choice of weights for the perceptron, an extremely large number of such (infinitesimally small) changes to weights are needed. This makes the algorithm exceedingly slow, and such a choice of η is hence undesirable.

What is an appropriate choice for η, which is neither too small nor too large? A common choice is $\eta = 1$, leading to the simple weight change computational rule of $\Delta w = \pm x$, so that $(w + \Delta w) \cdot x = w \cdot x \pm x \cdot x$. Note that there is no assurance that the sample x is as yet correctly classified by the perceptron, since it is possible that $|w \cdot x| > |x \cdot x|$.

In order to ensure that the sample x is correctly classified following the weight change, we need a choice of $\Delta w = \pm \eta x$ such that $(w + \Delta w) \cdot x$ and $x \cdot x$ have opposite signs, i.e.,

$$|\Delta w \cdot x| > |w \cdot x|,$$

that is,

$$\eta |x \cdot x| > |w \cdot x|,$$

that is,

$$\eta > \frac{|w \cdot x|}{|x \cdot x|}.$$

2.3.3   Non-numeric inputs

In some problems, the input dimensions are non-numeric, and their values do not have any inherent order. For instance, the input dimension may be "color," and its values may range over the set {red, blue, green, yellow}. If these values are depicted as points on an axis, e.g., red–blue–green–yellow, the resulting figure depicts erroneous implicit inter-relationships, e.g., that "red" is closer to "blue" than to "green" or "yellow." How may the perceptron method be used to solve problems with such inputs? Note that this is not a problem if the attribute "color" was allowed to take on only two values.

The simplest alternative is to generate four new dimensions ("red," "blue," "green," and "yellow") instead of the single "color" dimension, and replace each original attribute-value pair by a binary vector with one component corresponding to each color. For instance, color = "green" is represented by the input vector (0, 0, 1, 0) standing for red=0, blue=0, green=1, yellow=0. In the general case, if an attribute can take one of n different values, then n new dimensions are obtained, and each sample has a 1 or 0 value for each of these dimensions. The disadvantage of this approach is a drastic increase in the number of dimensions, as well as the loss of the information that the attribute has a unique value, e.g., that an object cannot be both blue and red.

EXAMPLE 2.4   The day of the week (Sunday/Monday/ . . .) is an important variable in predicting the amount of electric power consumed in a geographical region. However, there is no obvious way of sequencing weekdays, so it is inappropriate to use a single variable whose values range from 1 to 7. Instead, seven different variables should be chosen (eight, if a separate category of "holiday" is needed), and each input sample has a value of 1 for one of these coordinates, and a value of 0 for others. It may also be reasonable to combine some of these variables into a single one, e.g., to combine Tuesday, Wednesday, and Thursday, for which the input-output mapping is similar.

Another possible approach departs from the notion that each weight must be a single real number. Using this approach, each weight is essentially a function that maps its input to a real number. For instance, for an input node intended to denote color={red, blue, green, yellow}, the weight function on the connection from the color node to the jth node at the next level may be of the form

$$w_{j,color}(x) = \begin{cases} c_1 & \text{if } x = red \\ c_2 & \text{if } x = blue \\ c_3 & \text{if } x = green \\ c_4 & \text{if } x = yellow. \end{cases}$$

In applying a gradient descent rule to modify such a weight, when a blue input pattern is presented to the network, a modification made will be to c_2 but not to c_1, c_3, or c_4. This rule is analogous to having four separate inputs (one for each color) carrying 0 or 1 values.

2.4   Guarantee of Success

In this section, we prove that the perceptron training algorithm terminates with a set of weights that correctly classifies samples belonging to two linearly separable classes: C_0 and C_1. This property of the perceptron was demonstrated by Novikoff (1963).

Let w_k be the "current" weight vector after the kth weight change. We need to prove that there is an upper bound on k; the termination criterion ensures that the resulting weight vector correctly classifies all samples.

Suppose it takes m sample presentations to train the perceptron; in general $m > p$. Since the given classes are linearly separable, there must exist a vector of weights w^* that correctly separates them, This implies that $\boldsymbol{w}^* \cdot \boldsymbol{i}_k > 0$ whenever $\boldsymbol{i}_k$ belongs to the class with desired output 1 and $\boldsymbol{w}^* \cdot \boldsymbol{i}_k < 0$ when $\boldsymbol{i}_k$ belongs to the class with desired output -1. Define

$$\boldsymbol{x}_k = \begin{cases} \boldsymbol{i}_k & \text{if desired output is 1} \\ -\boldsymbol{i}_k & \text{if desired output is } -1, \end{cases}$$

so that $\boldsymbol{w}^* \cdot \boldsymbol{x}_k > 0$ whenever $\boldsymbol{x}_k$ is correctly classified by the perceptron with weight vector $\boldsymbol{w}^*$.

THEOREM 2.1   Given training samples from two linearly separable classes, the perceptron training algorithm terminates after a finite number of steps, and correctly classifies all elements of the training set, irrespective of the initial random non-zero weight vector $\boldsymbol{w}_0$.

Proof   We assume $\eta = 1$, without loss of generality. After executing the perceptron training algorithm for k steps, the resulting weight vector is

$$\boldsymbol{w}_k = \boldsymbol{w}_0 + \boldsymbol{x}_1 + \boldsymbol{x}_2 + \ldots + \boldsymbol{x}_k. \tag{2.1}$$

Since the given classes are linearly separable, there must exist a vector of weights $\boldsymbol{w}^*$ that correctly classifies them, with $sgn(\boldsymbol{w}^* \cdot \boldsymbol{i}_k) = class(\boldsymbol{i}_k)$, where "sgn" is the step function whose outputs are 1 and -1, with the discontinuity located at 0. Taking the scalar product of each side of equation 2.1 with $\boldsymbol{w}^*$, we have

$$\boldsymbol{w}^* \cdot \boldsymbol{w}_k = \boldsymbol{w}^* \cdot \boldsymbol{w}_0 + \boldsymbol{w}^* \cdot \boldsymbol{x}_1 + \ldots + \boldsymbol{w}^* \cdot \boldsymbol{x}_k.$$

For each input vector $\boldsymbol{i}_j$, the dot product $\boldsymbol{w}^* \cdot \boldsymbol{i}_j$ has the same sign as $class(\boldsymbol{i}_j)$. Since the corresponding element of the training sequence $\boldsymbol{x} = class(\boldsymbol{i}_j)\boldsymbol{i}_j$, we can be assured that

$$\boldsymbol{w}^* \cdot \boldsymbol{x} = \boldsymbol{w}^* \cdot (class(\boldsymbol{i}_j)\boldsymbol{i}_j) > 0.$$

Therefore, there exists an $\varepsilon > 0$ such that $\boldsymbol{w}^* \cdot \boldsymbol{x}_i > \varepsilon$ for every member $\boldsymbol{x}_i$ of the training sequence. Hence

$$\boldsymbol{w}^* \cdot \boldsymbol{w}_k > \boldsymbol{w}^* \cdot \boldsymbol{w}_0 + k\varepsilon. \tag{2.2}$$

By the Cauchy–Schwarz inequality,

$$\|\boldsymbol{w}^* \cdot \boldsymbol{w}_k\|^2 \le \|\boldsymbol{w}^*\|^2 \|\boldsymbol{w}_k\|^2. \tag{2.3}$$

Without loss of generality we may assume that $\boldsymbol{w}^*$ is of unit length, i.e., $\|\boldsymbol{w}^*\| = 1$, since the unit length vector $\boldsymbol{w}^*/\|\boldsymbol{w}^*\|$ also correctly classifies the same samples. Using this unit-length assumption and equations 2.2, 2.3, we obtain the following lower bound for the square of the length of the weight vector.

$$\|\boldsymbol{w}_k\|^2 > (\boldsymbol{w}_0 \cdot \boldsymbol{w}^* + k\varepsilon)^2 \tag{2.4}$$

On the other hand, since $\boldsymbol{w}_j = \boldsymbol{w}_{j-1} + \boldsymbol{x}_j$, the following upper bound can be obtained for this vector's squared length.

$$\begin{aligned}
\|\boldsymbol{w}_j\|^2 &= \boldsymbol{w}_j \cdot \boldsymbol{w}_j \\
&= \boldsymbol{w}_{j-1} \cdot \boldsymbol{w}_{j-1} + 2\boldsymbol{w}_{j-1} \cdot \boldsymbol{x}_j + \boldsymbol{x}_j \cdot \boldsymbol{x}_j \\
&= \|\boldsymbol{w}_{j-1}\|^2 + 2\boldsymbol{w}_{j-1} \cdot \boldsymbol{x}_j + \|\boldsymbol{x}_j\|^2
\end{aligned}$$

Since $\boldsymbol{w}_{j-1} \cdot \boldsymbol{x}_j < 0$ whenever a weight change is required by the algorithm, we have

$$\|\boldsymbol{w}_j\|^2 - \|\boldsymbol{w}_{j-1}\|^2 < \|\boldsymbol{x}_j\|^2. \tag{2.5}$$

Summation of the above inequalities over $j = 1, \ldots, k$ gives an upper bound

$$\|\boldsymbol{w}_k\|^2 - \|\boldsymbol{w}_0\|^2 < k \max \|\boldsymbol{x}_j\|^2. \tag{2.6}$$

Combining this with the inequality 2.4, we have

$$(\boldsymbol{w}_0 \cdot \boldsymbol{w}^* + k\varepsilon)^2 < \|\boldsymbol{w}_k\|^2 < \|\boldsymbol{w}_0\|^2 + k \max \|\boldsymbol{x}_j\|^2. \tag{2.7}$$

These inequalities establish two conflicting requirements on the size of $\|\boldsymbol{w}_k\|^2$: the lower bound increases at the rate of k^2 whereas the upper bound increases at linear rate k. But any quadratic function with positive coefficient for k^2 will eventually be larger than a linear function. In other words, there will be some finite value of k for which

$$(\boldsymbol{w}_0 \cdot \boldsymbol{w}^* + k\varepsilon)^2 > \|\boldsymbol{w}_0\|^2 + k \max \|\boldsymbol{x}_j\|^2. \tag{2.8}$$

This implies that k cannot increase without bound, so that the algorithm must eventually terminate. This completes the proof of the theorem.

2.5   Modifications

Nothing useful can be assumed about the behavior of the perceptron training algorithm when applied to classification problems in which the classes are not linearly separable. In some cases, non-separability of samples may be a result of noise, so that even complex multilayer neural network training algorithms, discussed in the following chapters, cannot succeed in learning how to separate the samples of different classes. For example, let the samples of one class be $\{(0, 0), (0, 0.2), (0.2, 0)\}$, and let the samples of the other class be $\{(1,1), (1,0.8), (0.8,1), (0.01,0.01)\}$. These samples cannot be linearly separated: the first sample of the first class is almost coincident with the last sample of the second class, possibly a result of noise or erroneous judgment by the person supplying the training examples. If the last sample is omitted, linear separation of the two classes is very easy to accomplish. A robust algorithm would give a reasonable separation between most of the samples of the two classes, minimizing the errors made.

In section 2.3.1 we considered some criteria to terminate a perceptron algorithm. Terminating the perceptron training algorithm as soon as the samples are correctly classified allows any of a large range of weight combinations to be evolved. The final results depend on the initial (randomly chosen) weights and the sequence in which samples are presented while training the perceptron. Furthermore, it is possible that the early presentation of a single "outlier" biases the weight so much that the training procedure does not converge to the desired solution.

In this section, we present two algorithms that attempt to achieve robust classification when the two classes are not linearly separable. These are the "pocket" algorithm of Gallant (1986) and the "Least Mean Squares" (LMS) algorithm of Widrow and Hoff (1960). The pocket algorithm stores information about the better weight vectors encountered in the process of modifying perceptron weights, while the LMS algorithm attempts to minimize mean squared error rather than the number of misclassified patterns.

2.5.1   Pocket algorithm

Any two weight vectors can be compared in terms of the number of samples presented that were correctly classified, i.e., the length of the *run* for which the weight vector was unchanged. Gallant (1986) has proposed a useful modification of the perceptron training algorithm in order to achieve this goal. Patterns are presented randomly to the neural network, whose weight change mechanism is exactly the same as that of the perceptron. In addition, the algorithm identifies the weight vector with the longest unchanged run as the best solution among those examined so far. Gallant's *pocket algorithm* uses this heuristic and separately stores (in a "pocket") the best solution explored so far, as well as the length of the run associated with it. The contents of the pocket are replaced whenever a new weight vector with a longer successful run is found.

The goal of this algorithm is to find the "optimal" set of weights, i.e., the linear classifier for which the number of misclassifications is the least. If the number of training samples is finite, and samples are presented randomly, then running the pocket algorithm long enough will ensure that the optimal set of weights is discovered with high probability.

A further variation of the pocket algorithm attempts to guard against the possibility that a lucky run of several successes allowed a poor solution to replace a better solution

Algorithm Pocket;
  Start with a randomly chosen weight vector w_0;
  Let $k = 0$, $best\_run\_length = 0$; $current\_run\_length = 0$;
  while $k <$ maximum allowed number of presentations **do**
    Increment k;
    Let i be a randomly selected input vector;
    Let $x_k = class(i).i$;
    if $w_{k-1} \cdot x_k > 0$,
    then increment $current\_run\_length$;
    else
        if ($best\_run\_length < current\_run\_length$) **and if** w_{k-1}
          misclassifies fewer samples than current
          pocket contents
        then replace pocket contents by w_{k-1} and
        $best\_run\_length$ by $current\_run\_length$;
        end-if
        Update the weight vector to $w_k = w_{k-1} + \eta x_k$;
    end-if
  end-while.

Figure 2.7
Pocket algorithm with ratchet check.

in the pocket. This approach, called the pocket algorithm with *ratchet*, ensures that the pocket weights always "ratchet up": a set of weights w_1 in the pocket is replaced by a set of weights w_2 with a longer successful run only after testing (on all training samples) whether w_2 does correctly classify a greater number of samples than w_1. While there is no guarantee of reaching the optimal weight vector, in a reasonable number of iterations, empirical evidence suggests that the pocket algorithm gives good results. (See figure 2.7.)

    The ratchet check is expensive if there are many samples, but needs to be invoked less frequently as the quality of the solution in the pocket improves. This suggests the alternative of using the ratchet only in later stages of computation, after several iterations with the training data have been conducted and a reasonably good solution has been moved into the pocket.

EXAMPLE 2.5   This example illustrates the execution of the pocket algorithm on the data of example 2.3, consisting of 27 one-dimensional input patterns that are not linearly separable. Samples $\{0.05, 0.1, 0.15, 0.2, 0.25, 0.3, 0.35, 0.4, 0.45, 0.49, 0.52, 0.56, 0.57, 0.82\}$ belong to one class (with desired output 0), whereas samples $\{0.12, 0.47, 0.48, 0.5, 0.55, 0.6, 0.65, 0.7, 0.75, 0.8, 0.85, 0.9, 0.95\}$ belong to the other class (with desired output 1).

As in the case of the perceptron, the bias weight was initialized at -1.0, the learning rate was chosen to be $\eta = 1.0$, and w_1 was initialized randomly.

The pocket algorithm was first run on this data for 100 sample presentations. Within about 50 presentations, the pocket contents were replaced by $w_1 = 0.18$, $w_0 = -0.1$ corresponding to separating samples at $x_1 \approx 0.56$, which results in seven misclassified samples. Since samples were chosen randomly, this weight vector had a successful run of a sequence of nine correctly classified samples. At the end of 100 sample presentations, this was the weight vector with the longest successful run.

When the algorithm was allowed to run for 10,000 sample presentations, the weight vector with the longest successful run (stored in the pocket) happened to be $w_1 = 0.26$, $w_0 = -0.1$, corresponding to a separation at about $x = 0.38$, again resulting in eight misclassified samples.

When the algorithm was allowed to run for 100,000 sample presentations, the best possible weight vector was discovered to have the longest successful run (and was stored in the pocket): $w_1 = 0.17$, $w_0 = -0.1$, corresponding to a separation at about $x = 0.59$, again resulting in six misclassified samples. This weight vector was stored in the pocket after roughly 50,000 sample presentations.

Although the best weight vector may have been encountered earlier by the algorithm, it was not then able to accumulate a successful run longer than its predecessors in the pocket. A ratchet check does not help this particular problem: the better weight choice never became a candidate for replacing the pocket contents, since its successful run length did not exceed that of the existing pocket contents. If the converse had been the case, i.e., if the better weight vector had first been in the pocket when another weight vector with a longer successful run was encountered, then the ratchet check would compare the number of samples misclassified by these weight choices, and therefore leave the pocket contents unchanged, so that the better weight choice survives in the pocket.

2.5.2 Adalines

The fundamental principle underlying the perceptron learning algorithm is to modify weights in such a manner as to reduce the number of misclassifications. Although perfect classification using a linear element may not be possible, it may nevertheless be desirable to obtain as robust a separation as possible (between samples of different classes). This may be achieved by minimizing the mean squared error (MSE) instead of the number of misclassified samples.

An adaptive linear element or *Adaline*, proposed by Widrow (1959, 1960), is a simple perceptron-like system that accomplishes classification by modifying weights in such a way as to diminish the MSE at every iteration. This can be accomplished using gradient

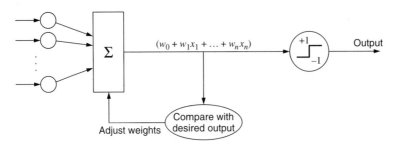

Figure 2.8
Adaptive linear element (Adaline).

descent, since MSE is a quadratic function whose derivative exists everywhere. Unlike the
perceptron, this algorithm implies that weight changes are made to reduce MSE even when
a sample is correctly classified by the network. The structure of an Adaline is indicated in
figure 2.8.

   In the training process, when a sample is presented, the linear weighted net input is
computed and compared with the desired output for that sample, generating an error signal
used to modify each weight in the Adaline. The weight change rule can be derived as
follows.

   Let $i_j = (i_0, i_1 \ldots, i_n)$ be an input vector for which d_j is the desired output value, with
$i_0 \equiv 1$. Let $\mathrm{net}_j = \sum_l w_l i_l$ be the net input to the node, where $w = (w_0, \ldots, w_n)$ is the
present value of the weight vector. On comparing desired output to net input, the squared
error is $E = (d_j - \mathrm{net}_j)^2$, so that

$$\frac{\partial E}{\partial w_k} = 2(d_j - \mathrm{net}_j)\frac{\partial}{\partial w_k}(\text{-}\mathrm{net}_j)$$

$$= (d_j - \mathrm{net}_j)\frac{\partial}{\partial w_k}\left(-\sum_{l=0}^{n} w_l i_{l,j}\right)$$

$$= -(d_j - \mathrm{net}_j)\, i_{k,j}.$$

A gradient descent rule would choose Δw_k to be a negative multiple of $\partial E/\partial w_k$, leading
to the weight update rule

$$\Delta w_k = \eta\left(d_j - \sum_l w_l i_{l,j}\right) i_{k,j} i = \eta(d_j - net_j)i_j. \tag{2.9}$$

Algorithm LMS-Adaline;
   Start with a randomly chosen weight vector w_0;
   Let $k = 1$;
   while mean squared error is unsatisfactory and computational
   bounds are not exceeded, **do**
      Let $i_j = (i_0, i_1 \ldots, i_n)$ be an input vector
      (chosen randomly or in some sequence)
      for which d_j is the desired output value, with $i_0 \equiv 1$;
      Update the weight vector to
$$w_k = w_{k-1} + \eta(d_j - \sum_l w_{k-1,l} i_l) i_j$$

      Increment k;
   end-while.

Figure 2.9
LMS (Adaline) training algorithm.

Thus, the weight vector w changes to $(w + \eta(d_j - \sum_{l=0}^n w_l i_{l,j}) i_j)$, when the input vector i_j is presented to the Adaline. The weight change procedure is repeatedly applied for various input vectors i_j. (See figure 2.9.)

A modification of this LMS rule was suggested by Widrow and Hoff (1960), making the weight change magnitude independent of the magnitude of the input vector. The resulting "α–LMS" or Widrow-Hoff delta rule is

$$\Delta w = \eta(d_j - \text{net}_j) \frac{i_j}{||i_j||}, \tag{2.10}$$

where, as before, $w = (w_0, w_1, \ldots, w_n)$ is the current weight vector, d_j is the desired output for the jth input i_j, $\text{net}_j = \sum_{l=0}^n w_i i_{l,j}$, and $||i||$ denotes the length of vector i.

So far, we have not discussed the threshold or step function at the output generation point of the Adaline. This step function plays no role in training the Adaline, but is called into action whenever the Adaline needs to generate an output for some input pattern. Once trained, the input-output mapping of the Adaline is identical to that of a perceptron, when used for classification purposes, i.e., the output of the Adaline is given by

$$o_j = \begin{cases} 1 & \text{if } \sum w_l i_{l,j} > 0 \\ -1 & \text{otherwise.} \end{cases}$$

The training part of the Adaline (preceding output generation via the step function) can be used for function approximation tasks as well, unlike the perceptron. In this respect, the behavior of the Adaline is seen to be identical to that of statistical "linear regression" [see Neter, Wasserman, and Kutner (1990)], where a set of $(n + 1)$ linear equations

$$\sum_{j=1}^{P}(d_j - (w_0 + w_1 i_{1,j} + \cdots + w_n, i_{n,j}))i_{i,j} = 0$$

must be solved for the unknown values $w_0, \ldots, w_n$; here P denotes the number of patterns.

EXAMPLE 2.6   This example illustrates the execution of the Adaline LMS training algorithm on the data of example 2.3, consisting of 27 one-dimensional input patterns which are not linearly separable. Samples {0.05, 0.1, 0.15, 0.2, 0.25, 0.3, 0.35, 0.4, 0.45, 0.49, 0.52, 0.56, 0.57, 0.82} belong to one class (with desired output −1), whereas samples {0.12, 0.47, 0.48, 0.5, 0.55, 0.6, 0.65, 0.7, 0.75, 0.8, 0.85, 0.9, 0.95} belong to the other class (with desired output 1). As in the case of the perceptron, a learning rate of 0.1 was chosen, the bias weight was initialized at −1.0, and w_1 was initialized randomly at $w_1 = -0.36$.

When the input sample 0.05 was presented, the net input to the Adaline was (0.05) $(-0.36) - 1 \approx -1.0$; since this was the desired output, there is no change in the weight vector. When the input sample 0.5 was presented, the net input to the Adaline was $(0.5)(-0.36) - 1 = -1.18$, leading to a change of $\delta w_1 = (0.1)(0.5)(1.0 - (-1.18)) = 0.109$, so that the new weight is $w_1 = -0.36 + 0.109 \approx -0.25$. Similarly, the bias weight changes to $w_0 = -1 + (0.1)(1.0 - (-1.18)) = -0.78$. The MSE is now 2.4, reducing to about 0.9 in the next 20 presentations, but the number of misclassified samples is still large (13). By the end of 1,000 presentations, the MSE reduces to 0.73, with the least possible number (6) of misclassified samples, for $w_1 = 2.06$, $w_0 = -1.2$, corresponding to a class separation at $x \approx 0.58$. In subsequent presentations, MSE remains roughly at this level, although the number of misclassifications occasionally increases during this process.

2.5.3   Multiclass discrimination

So far, we have considered dichotomies, or two-class problems. Many important real-life problems require partitioning data into three or more classes. For example, the character recognition problem (for the Roman alphabet) consists of distinguishing between samples of 26 different classes. A layer of perceptrons or Adalines may be used to solve some such multiclass problems. In figure 2.10 four perceptrons are put together to solve a four-class classification problem.

Each weight $w_{i,j}$ indicates the strength of the connection from the jth input to the ith node. A sample, supplied as input to a (trained) single-layer perceptron network, is con-

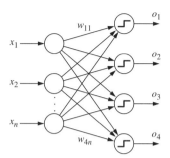

Figure 2.10
A four-node perceptron that solves a four-class problem in n-dimensional input space.

sidered to belong to the ith class if and only if the ith output $o_i = 1$, and every other output $o_k = 0$, for $k \neq i$. Such networks are trained in the same way as individual perceptrons; in fact, all the perceptrons can be trained separately, in parallel.

If all outputs are zeroes, or if more than one output value equals 1, the network may be considered to have failed in the classification task. In networks whose node outputs can have values in between 0 and 1, a "maximum-selector" can be used to select the highest-valued output, possibly subject to the requirement that the highest-valued output must at least exceed some small threshold level. In some m-class problems, one of the classes can be interpreted as an otherwise case, so that a network with only $m - 1$ nodes (in the perceptron layer) can be used; if all $m - 1$ outputs have low values, we assume that the network assigns that input sample to the mth class.

2.6   Conclusion

The perceptron and Adaline are the simplest neural network models; indeed, it may be argued that such single-node systems should not even be called networks. Their applicability is restricted to very simple problems. Their chief contribution is in indicating how a simple supervised learning rule similar to gradient descent can be used to make a network learn a task. The mathematical results discussed in this chapter are clean results that indicate the capabilities as well as limitations of these networks. Such easily interpretable results are difficult to obtain for the more complex networks discussed in later chapters.

Perceptrons have been used for pattern recognition tasks. There have been many applications of the Adaline in areas such as signal processing [see Widrow et al. (1975), Hassoun and Spitzer (1988)], and control [see Widrow and Smith (1964), Tolat and Widrow (1988)].

2.7   Exercises

1. Which of the following sets of points are linearly separable?

   a. Class 1: $(0, 0, 0)$, $(1, 1, 1)$, $(2, 2, 2)$
      Class 2: $(3, 3, 3)$, $(4, 4, 4)$, $(5, 5, 5)$

   b. Class 1: $(0, 0, 0)$, $(1, 1, 1)$, $(4, 4, 4)$
      Class 2: $(2, 2, 2)$, $(3, 3, 3)$

   c. Class 1: $(0, 0, 0, 0)$, $(1, 0, 1, 0)$, $(0, 1, 0, 1)$
      Class 2: $(1, 1, 1, 1)$, $(1, 1, 1, 2)$, $(1, 2, 1, 1)$

   d. Class 1: $(0, 0, 0, 0, 0)$, $(0, 1, 0, 1, 0)$, $(1, 0, 1, 0, 1)$
      Class 2: $(1, 1, 1, 1, 1)$, $(1, 1, 1, 1, 2)$, $(0, 1, 2, 1, 1)$

2. Generate 30 patterns in three-dimensional space such that 15 patterns belong to class 1 and the remaining 15 patterns belong to class 2, and they are linearly separable. Apply the perceptron algorithm on the data so generated and comment on the computational time and performance obtained using different learning rates, with $\eta \in \{10, 1, 0.1, 0.01\}$.

3. Train an Adaline for the data $\{(0, 0; 0)$, $(0, 1; 0)$, $(2, 0; 0)$, $(-1, -1; 0)$, $(-1, 0; 0)$, $(0, -1; 0)$, $(1, 1; 0)$, $(0, 3; 1)$, $(1, 3; 1)$, $(2, 3; 1)$, $(1, 2; 1)$, $(1, 0; 1)$, $(1, -1; 1)$, $(2, 0; 1)$, $(2, 1; 1)$, $(2, 2; 1)$, $(2, -1; 1)\}$, where the third element indicates class membership. Choose the initial weights randomly.

   Evaluate the performance using the following measures.

   a. Number of iterations in training

   b. Amount of computation time

   c. Number of misclassifications

   d. Mean squared error

4. For each of the following problems, determine the length of the perceptron training sequence, with $\eta = 1$, beginning from $w_0 = (1, 1, 1)$.

   a. Class 1: $(3, 1)$, $(4, 2)$, $(5, 3)$, $(6, 4)$
      Class 2: $(2, 2)$, $(1, 3)$, $(2, 6)$

   b. Class 1: $(0.03, 0.01)$, $(0.04, 0.02)$, $(0.05, 0.03)$, $(0.06, 0.04)$
      Class 2: $(0.02, 0.02)$, $(0.01, 0.03)$, $(0.02, 0.06)$

   c. Class 1: $(300, 100)$, $(400, 200)$, $(500, 300)$, $(600, 400)$
      Class 2: $(200, 200)$, $(100, 300)$, $(200, 600)$

5. Apply the pocket algorithm and the LMS algorithm to the following data sets.

   a. Class 1: (3, 1), (4, 2), (5, 3), (6, 4)
      Class 2: (2, 2), (1, 3), (2, 6), (6, 1)

   b. Class 1: (3, 1), (4, 2), (5, 3), (6, 4), (2.5, 2.5)
      Class 2: (2, 2), (1, 3), (2, 6), (2.6, 2.6)

6. For a specific problem, assume that we know that available data can be completely separated into two classes using a circle instead of a straight line. Suggest a modification of the perceptron algorithm that determines the equation of the appropriate circle.

7. Does the perceptron algorithm converge to a solution in a finite number of iterations (for linearly separable data) if the sequence of data points is not random, but chosen in a "malicious" manner by an adversary?

8. In the pocket algorithm, is there any advantage gained if we are allowed to store more than one tentative solution in the "pocket"?

9. Is there any advantage obtained by modifying the Adaline training algorithm to include the heuristic of the pocket algorithm (storing the best recent vector)?

10. Illustrate the development of the weights of an Adaline for the following data.

   a. Class 1: (0, 0, 0), (1, 1, 1), (2, 2, 2), (0, 0, 3), (4, 1, 4), (2, 5, 5)
      Class 2: (3, 3, 3), (4, 4, 4), (5, 5, 5), (3, 3, 0), (4, 4, 1), (5, 5, 2)

   b. Class 1: (0, 0, 0), (1, 1, 1), (4, 4, 4)
      Class 2: (2, 2, 2), (3, 3, 3)

11. Adalines without the step function can be used for function approximation. Illustrate the development of the weights of a two-input Adaline for the following data, where the third component of each data point is interpreted as the desired result of the network when the first two components are presented.

{(0, 0, 0), (1, 1, 1), (2, 2, 2), (0, 0, 3), (4, 1, 4), (2, 5, 5), (3, 3, 3), (4, 4, 4), (5, 5, 5), (3, 3, 0), (4, 4, 1), (5, 5, 2)}

What is the best possible mean squared error that can be obtained (using any other method) for the above data?

12. a. Assume that a two-class classification problem is such that samples belong to Class I if and only if

$$\sum_i c_i x_i + \sum_{i,j} c_{i,j} x_i x_j > 0,$$

   where $x_1, \ldots, x_n$ are input parameters, and the coefficients $(c_i, c_{i,j})$ are unknown. How would you modify the simple perceptron to solve such a classification problem?

   b. Assume that a function to be approximated is of the form

$$f(x_1, \ldots, x_n) = \sum_i c_i x_i + \sum_{i,j} c_{i,j} x_i x_j$$

   where $x_1, \ldots, x_n$ are input parameters, and the coefficients $(c_i, c_{i,j})$ are unknown. Suggest a simple modification of the Adaline that can learn to approximate such a function.

13. Would it be possible to train a perceptron in "batch mode," periodically invoking the following weight update rule after presenting all training samples to the perceptron?

$$\Delta w = \sum (\text{misclassified input vectors from class 1})$$

$$- \sum (\text{misclassified input vectors from class 2})$$

Support your answer by presenting a counterexample or by extending the perceptron convergence theorem.

14. Would it be possible to train a perceptron using a variant of the perceptron training algorithm in which the bias weight is left unchanged, and only the other weights are modified? Support your answer by presenting a counterexample or by extending the perceptron convergence theorem.

15. What is the performance obtainable on iris data, given in appendix B.1, using (a) a perceptron, (b) the LMS algorithm, and (c) the pocket algorithm (with ratchet)?

3 Supervised Learning: Multilayer Networks I

Each new machine or technique, in a sense, changes all existing machines and techniques, by permitting us to put them together into new combinations.
—Alvin Toffler (1970)

Perceptrons and other one-layer networks, discussed in the preceding chapter, are seriously limited in their capabilities. Feedforward multilayer networks with non-linear node functions can overcome these limitations, and can be used for many applications. However, the simple perceptron learning mechanism cannot be extended easily when we go from a single layer of perceptrons to multiple layers of perceptrons. More powerful supervised learning techniques for multilayer networks are presented in this chapter and the next.

The focus of this chapter is on a learning mechanism called error "backpropagation" (abbreviated "backprop") for feedforward networks. Such networks are sometimes referred to as "multilayer perceptrons" (MLPs), a usage we do not adopt, particularly since the learning algorithms used in such networks are considerably different from those of (simple) perceptrons. The phrase "backpropagation network" is sometimes used to describe feedforward neural networks trained using the backpropagation learning method.

Backpropagation came into prominence in the late 1980's. An early version of backpropagation was first proposed by Rosenblatt (1961), but his proposal was crippled by the use of perceptrons that compute step functions of their net weighted inputs. For successful application of this method, differentiable node functions are required. The new algorithm was proposed by Werbos (1974) and largely ignored by the scientific community until the 1980's. Parker (1985) and LeCun (1985) rediscovered it, but its modern specification was provided and popularized by Rumelhart, Hinton, and Williams (1986).

Backpropagation is similar to the LMS (least mean squared error) learning algorithm described earlier, and is based on gradient descent: weights are modified in a direction that corresponds to the negative gradient of an error measure. The choice of everywhere-differentiable node functions allows correct application of this method. For weights on connections that directly connect to network outputs, this is straightforward and very similar to the Adaline. The major advance of backpropagation over the LMS and perceptron algorithms is in expressing how an error at a higher (or outer) layer of a multilayer network can be propagated backwards to nodes at lower (or inner) layers of the network; the gradient of these backward-propagated error measures (for inner layer nodes) can then be used to determine the desired weight modifications for connections that lead into these hidden nodes. The backpropagation algorithm has had a major impact on the field of neural networks and has been widely applied to a large number of problems in many disciplines. Backpropagation has been used for several kinds of applications including classification, function approximation, and forecasting.

3.1 Multilevel Discrimination

In this section, we present a first attempt to construct a layered structure of nodes to solve linearly nonseparable classification problems, extending the perceptron approach of chapter 2. Such a network is illustrated in figure 3.1, and contains "hidden" (interior) nodes that isolate useful features of the input data. However, it is not easy to train such a network, since the ideal weight change rule is far from obvious. Given that the network makes an error on some input sample, exactly which weights in the network must be modified, and to what extent? This is an instance of a "credit assignment" problem, where credit or blame for a result must be assigned to many different entities that participated in generating that result.

If some detailed domain-specific information about the problem is available, methods such as the perceptron training procedure may be used in different successive steps to achieve successful classification. For instance, we may first allocate each sample to one subgroup or cluster by applying neural or non-neural clustering algorithms, and simple perceptrons may be successful in identifying each sample as belonging to one of these subgroups. Now, using the information about the subgroup to which an input sample belongs, one can make the final classification.

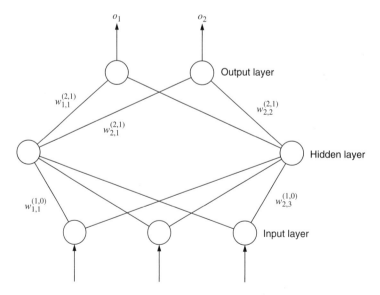

Figure 3.1
A feedforward network with one hidden layer.

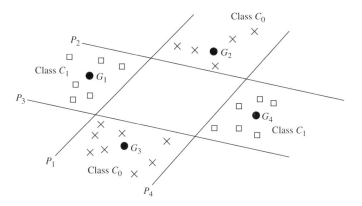

Figure 3.2
An instance of a two-class problem in which elements of each class are found in two clusters. Clusters can be separated by straight lines P_1, P_2, P_3, and P_4. G_1, G_2, G_3, and G_4 represent the cluster centers.

For instance, in the XOR-like problem of figure 3.2, a layer of four different perceptrons can be separately made to learn to which subgroup (G_1, G_2, G_3, G_4) an input sample belongs. Another (output) perceptron with four inputs can be trained to discriminate between classes C_1 and C_0 based on subgroup information alone. Crucial to this particular case is the availability of the information regarding subgroup membership of different samples. The remainder of this chapter does not assume any such information to be available, and the backpropagation learning algorithm includes mechanisms to train hidden nodes to solve appropriate subtasks.

3.2 Preliminaries

In this section, we discuss the architecture of neural networks for which the backpropagation algorithm has been used, and we also describe the precise task attempted by backpropagation. This is followed by the derivation of the backpropagation algorithm, in section 3.3.

3.2.1 Architecture

The backpropagation algorithm assumes a feedforward neural network architecture, outlined in chapter 1. In this architecture, nodes are partitioned into layers numbered 0 to L, where the layer number indicates the distance of a node from the input nodes. The lowermost layer is the input layer numbered as layer 0, and the topmost layer is the output layer numbered as layer L. Backpropagation addresses networks for which $L \geq 2$, containing "hidden layers" numbered 1 to $L - 1$. Hidden nodes do not directly receive inputs from nor send outputs to the external environment. For convenience of presentation, we will assume that $L = 2$ in describing the backpropagation algorithm, implying that there is only one hidden layer, as shown in figure 3.1. The algorithm can be extended easily to cases when $L \neq 2$. The presentation of the algorithm also assumes that the network is strictly feedforward, i.e., only nodes in adjacent layers are directly connected; this assumption can also be done away with.

Input layer nodes merely transmit input values to the hidden layer nodes, and do not perform any computation. The number of input nodes equals the dimensionality of input patterns, and the number of nodes in the output layer is dictated by the problem under consideration. For instance, if the task is to approximate a function mapping n-dimensional input vectors to m-dimensional output vectors, the network contains n input nodes and m output nodes. An additional "dummy" input node with constant input ($= 1$) is also often used so that the bias or threshold term can be treated just like other weights in the network. The number of nodes in the hidden layer is up to the discretion of the network designer and generally depends on problem complexity.

Each hidden node and output node applies a sigmoid function to its net input, shown in figure 3.3. As discussed briefly in chapter 1, the main reasons motivating the use of an S-shaped sigmoidal function are that it is continuous, monotonically increasing, invertible, everywhere differentiable, and asymptotically approaches its saturation values as $net \to \pm\infty$. These basic properties of the sigmoidal function are more important than the specific sigmoidal function chosen in our presentation below, namely,

$$S(net) = \frac{1}{1 + e^{(-net)}}.$$

3.2.2 Objectives

The algorithm discussed in this chapter is a supervised learning algorithm trained using P input patterns. For each input vector x_p, we have the corresponding desired K-dimensional output vector

$$d_p = (d_{p,1}, d_{p,2}, \ldots, d_{p,K})$$

for $1 \leq p \leq P$. This collection of input-output pairs constitutes the training set $\{(x_p, d_p) : p = 1, \ldots, P\}$. The length of the input vector x_p is equal to the number of inputs of the given application. The length of the output vector d_p is equal to the number of outputs of the given application.

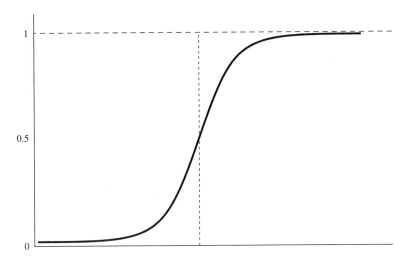

Figure 3.3
A sigmoid function.

The training algorithm should work irrespective of the weight values that preceded training, which may initially have been assigned randomly.

As with the other networks, one would expect that some training samples are such that any reasonably small network is forced to make some errors in the hope of better performance on the test data. Furthermore, many real-life problems are such that perfect classification or approximation using a small network is impossible, and not all training or test samples can be classified or approximated correctly. As in the case of perceptrons and Adalines, the goal of training is to modify the weights in the network so that the network's output vector

$$\boldsymbol{o}_p = (o_{p,1}, o_{p,2}, \ldots, o_{p,K})$$

is as close as possible to the desired output vector $\boldsymbol{d}_p$, when an input vector $\boldsymbol{x}_p$ is presented to the network. Towards this goal, we would like to minimize the cumulative error of the network:

$$\text{Error} = \sum_{p=1}^{P} Err(\boldsymbol{o}_p, \boldsymbol{d}_p). \tag{3.1}$$

As discussed in chapter 1, there are many possible choices for the error function Err above. The function Err should be non-negative, and should be small if o_p is close to d_p (and large otherwise).

One such function is the "cross-entropy" function, $\sum_p (d_p \log o_p + (1 - d_p) \log(1 - o_p))$, suggested by Hinton (1987). The more popular choices for Err are based on norms of the difference vector $d_p - o_p$.

An error measure may be obtained by examining the difference $\ell_{p,j} = |o_{p,j} - d_{p,j}|$ between the jth components of the actual and desired output vectors. For the entire output vector, a measure indicating its distance from the desired vector is $\ell_p = ((\ell_{p,1})^u + \cdots + (\ell_{p,K})^u)^{\frac{1}{u}}$, for some $u > 0$.

For the rest of the section, we will consider $u = 2$ and define the $Err(o_p, d_p)$ function to be $(\ell_p)^2$. This function is differentiable, unlike the absolute value function. It is also easy to apply gradient descent methods, since the derivative of the resulting quadratic function is linear and thus easier to compute.

Hence our goal will be to find a set of weights that minimize

$$\text{Sum Square Error} = \sum_{p=1}^{P} \sum_{j=1}^{K} (\ell_{p,j})^2 \qquad (3.2)$$

or mean squared error

$$MSE = \frac{1}{P} \sum_{p=1}^{P} \sum_{j=1}^{K} (\ell_{p,j})^2. \qquad (3.3)$$

3.3 Backpropagation Algorithm

The backpropagation algorithm is a generalization of the least mean squared algorithm that modifies network weights to minimize the mean squared error between the desired and actual outputs of the network. Backpropagation uses supervised learning in which the network is trained using data for which inputs as well as desired outputs are known. Once trained, the network weights are frozen and can be used to compute output values for new input samples.

The feedforward process involves presenting an input pattern to input layer neurons that pass the input values onto the first hidden layer. Each of the hidden layer nodes computes a weighted sum of its inputs, passes the sum through its activation function and presents the result to the output layer.

The following is the scenario for the pth pattern in a feedforward network with $L = 2$.

1. The ith node in the input layer holds a value of $x_{p,i}$ for the pth pattern.

2. The net input to the jth node in the hidden layer $= net_j^{(1)} = \sum_{i=0}^n w_{j,i}^{(1,0)} x_{p,i}$. This includes the threshold with $x_{p,0} = 1$; the connection from the ith input node to the jth hidden layer node is assigned a weight value $w_{j,i}^{(1,0)}$, as shown in figure 3.1.

3. The output of the jth node in the hidden layer $= x_{p,j}^{(1)} = \mathcal{S}\left(\sum_{i=0}^n w_{j,i}^{(1,0)} x_{p,i}\right)$ where $\mathcal{S}$ is a sigmoid function.

4. The net input to the kth node of the output layer $= net_k^{(2)} = \sum_j \left(w_{k,j}^{(2,1)} x_{p,j}^{(1)}\right)$, including the threshold; the connection from the jth hidden layer node to the kth output layer node is assigned a weight value $w_{k,j}^{(2,1)}$.

5. Output of the kth node of the output layer $o_{p,k} = \mathcal{S}\left(\sum_j w_{k,j}^{(2,1)} x_{p,j}^{(1)}\right)$ where $\mathcal{S}$ is a sigmoid function.

6. The desired output of the kth node of the output layer is $d_{p,k}$, and the corresponding squared error is $\ell_{p,k}^2 = |d_{p,k} - o_{p,k}|^2$.

In a more general setting, with $L > 2$, weight $w_{k,j}^{(i+1,i)}$ denotes the weight assigned to the link from node j in the ith layer to node k in the $(i+1)$th layer, and $x_{p,j}^{(i)}$ denotes output of the jth node in the ith layer for the pth pattern.

The error (for pattern p) is given by $E_p = \sum_k \left(\ell_{p,k}\right)^2$. We need to discover $\boldsymbol{w}$, the vector consisting of all weights in the network, such that the value of E_p is minimized.

Suppressing the suffix p for convenience, the expression to be minimized is $E = \sum_{k=1}^K (\ell_k)^2$. One way to minimize E is based on the gradient descent method. Since o_k depends on the network weights, E is also a function of the network weights. According to gradient descent, the direction of weight change of $\boldsymbol{w}$ should be in the same direction as $-\partial E / \partial \boldsymbol{w}$.

To simplify the calculation of $-\partial E / \partial \boldsymbol{w}$, we examine the weight change in a single weight. We calculate the value of $\partial E / \partial w_{k,j}^{(2,1)}$ for each connection from the hidden layer to the output layer. Similarly, we calculate the value of $\partial E / \partial w_{j,i}^{(1,0)}$ for each connection from the input layer to the hidden layer. The connection weights are then changed by using the values so obtained; this method is also known as the *generalized delta rule*. In brief, the following two equations describe the suggested weight changes.

$$\Delta w_{k,j}^{(2,1)} \propto \left(\frac{-\partial E}{\partial w_{k,j}^{(2,1)}}\right) \tag{3.4}$$

$$\Delta w_{j,i}^{(1,0)} \propto \left(\frac{-\partial E}{\partial w_{j,i}^{(1,0)}}\right) \tag{3.5}$$

The derivative of E with respect to a weight $w_{k,j}^{(2,1)}$ associated with the link from node j of the hidden layer to the kth node of the output layer is easier to calculate than for a weight $w_{j,i}^{(1,0)}$ connecting the ith node of the input layer to the jth node of the hidden layer. But both calculations use the same general idea—the chain rule of derivatives. We consider the chain rule in some detail in the following paragraphs as it applies to the backpropagation learning algorithm. We assume $\ell_k = |d_k - o_k|$ in the following derivation.

The error E depends on $w_{k,j}^{(2,1)}$ only through o_k, i.e., no other output term $o_{k'}$, $k' \neq k$ contains $w_{k,j}^{(2,1)}$. Hence, for the calculations that follow, it is sufficient to restrict attention to the partial derivative of E with respect to o_k and then differentiate o_k with respect to $w_{k,j}^{(2,1)}$. Since $E = \sum_{i \neq k} \ell_i^2 + (d_k - o_k)^2$, we obtain

$$\frac{\partial E}{\partial o_k} = -2(d_k - o_k). \tag{3.6}$$

Before differentiating o_k, we observe that the output o_k is obtained by applying a node function $\mathcal{S}$ to $net_k^{(2)}$, i.e., $o_k = \mathcal{S}(net_k^{(2)})$ and $net_k^{(2)}$ represents the total input to a node k in the output layer, i.e.,

$$net_k^{(2)} = \sum_j w_{k,j}^{(2,1)} \times x_j^{(1)}.$$

Hence $\partial o_k / \partial net_k^{(2)} = \mathcal{S}'(net_k^{(2)})$, where $S'(x) = dS(x)/dx$. Finally, $\partial net_k^{(2)} / \partial w_{k,j}^{(2,1)} = x_j^{(1)}$. Consequently, the chain rule

$$\frac{\partial E}{\partial w_{k,j}^{(2,1)}} = \frac{\partial E}{\partial o_k} \frac{\partial o_k}{\partial net_k^{(2)}} \frac{\partial net_k^{(2)}}{\partial w_{k,j}^{(2,1)}} \tag{3.7}$$

gives

$$\frac{\partial E}{\partial w_{k,j}^{(2,1)}} = -2(d_k - o_k)\mathcal{S}'(net_k^{(2)})x_j^{(1)}. \tag{3.8}$$

Next, consider the derivation of $(\partial E / \partial w_{j,i}^{(1,0)})$. The error E depends on $w_{j,i}^{(1,0)}$ through $net_j^{(1)}$, which, in turn, appears in each o_k for all $k = 1, \ldots, K$. Also, $o_k = \mathcal{S}(net_k^{(2)})$, $x_j^{(1)} = \mathcal{S}(net_j^{(1)})$, and $net_j^{(1)} = \sum_i w_{j,i}^{(1,0)} \times x_i$. Therefore, using the chain rule of derivatives, we obtain

$$\frac{\partial E}{\partial w_{j,i}^{(1,0)}} = \sum_{k=1}^{K} \frac{\partial E}{\partial o_k} \frac{\partial o_k}{\partial net_k^{(2)}} \frac{\partial net_k^{(2)}}{\partial x_j^{(1)}} \frac{\partial x_j^{(1)}}{\partial net_j^{(1)}} \frac{\partial net_j^{(1)}}{\partial w_{j,i}^{(1,0)}}$$

$$= \sum_{k=1}^{K} \left\{ -2(d_k - o_k) \mathcal{S}'\left(net_k^{(2)}\right) w_{k,j}^{(2,1)} \mathcal{S}'\left(net_j^{(1)}\right) x_i \right\}.$$

From equations 3.4 and 3.8, the weight changes at the outer layer of weights can be summarized as

$$\Delta w_{k,j}^{(2,1)} = \eta \times \delta_k \times x_j^{(1)} \tag{3.9}$$

and from equations 3.5 and 3.9, weight changes at the inner layer of weights are

$$\Delta w_{j,i}^{(1,0)} = \eta \times \mu_j \times x_i \tag{3.10}$$

where η is an independent parameter (a predetermined constant)[1] known as the "learning rate," and

$$\delta_k = (d_k - o_k) \mathcal{S}'\left(net_k^{(2)}\right) \tag{3.11}$$

and

$$\mu_j = \left(\sum_k \delta_k w_{k,j}^{(2,1)} \right) \mathcal{S}'\left(net_j^{(1)}\right). \tag{3.12}$$

Thus, similar equations determine the change in both layers of weights proportional to the product of the input to the weight in the forward direction ($x_j^{(1)}$ or x_i) and a generalized error term (δ_k or μ_j).

• The value of δ_k is proportional to the amount of error ($d_k - o_k$) multiplied by the derivative of the output node with respect to the net input to the output node.

• The value of μ_j is proportional to the amount of weighted error $\sum_k \delta_k w_{k,j}^{(2,1)}$ (using the previous layer's δ values) multiplied by the derivative of the output of the hidden node with respect to the net input of the hidden node.

Thus, the changes in weights for the two layers are similar. The only difference is that δ_k values are calculated using the actual error, ($d_k - o_k$), while μ_j values (at the hidden

---

1. Some variants of the algorithm use different learning rates (η) for different weights.

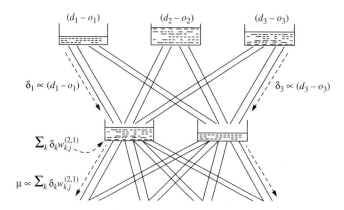

Figure 3.4
Flow of error in backprop.

nodes) are calculated using the weighted sums of errors coming to the hidden node from the higher level nodes (output nodes) to which this node is connected. Error terms are calculated in the direction opposite to most of the node output calculation, i.e., from output layer to the hidden layer. This idea, underlying the backpropagation algorithm, is pictorially explained in figure 3.4.

The above analysis does not make any assumption about the node function $\mathcal{S}$ except that $\mathcal{S}$ should be differentiable. For the sigmoid function $\mathcal{S}(x) = 1/(1 + \exp(-x))$, the derivative $\mathcal{S}'(x) = \partial \mathcal{S}(x)/\partial x$ satisfies the following property.

$$\mathcal{S}'(x) = \frac{\exp(-x)}{(1 + \exp(-x))^2}$$

$$= \frac{1}{(1 + \exp(-x))} - \frac{1}{(1 + \exp(-x))^2} \tag{3.13}$$

$$= \mathcal{S}(x)\,(1 - \mathcal{S}(x))\,.$$

Hence, if every node uses this node function, then

$$\delta_k = (d_k - o_k)o_k(1 - o_k) \tag{3.14}$$

and

$$\mu_j = \sum_k \delta_k w_{k,j}^{(2,1)} x_j^{(1)}(1 - x_j^{(1)}). \tag{3.15}$$

The above equations use terms that are available or calculated in the feedforward phase and thus δ_k and μ_j can be calculated very easily.

The above discussion is based on the error for one pattern: the subscript p was omitted in the preceding equations and expressions. Reintroducing the subscript, the amount of weight change caused by the error for the pth pattern is

$$\Delta w_{k,j}^{(2,1)} = \eta \delta_{p,k} x_{p,j}^{(1)}$$

and

$$\Delta w_{j,i}^{(1,0)} = \eta \mu_{p,j} x_{p,i},$$

where

$$\delta_{p,k} = (d_{p,k} - o_{p,k}) \times o_{p,k} \times (1 - o_{p,k})$$

and

$$\mu_{p,j} = \sum_k \delta_{p,k} w_{k,j}^{2,1} \times x_{p,j}^{(1)} \times (1 - x_{p,j}^{(1)}).$$

Note that the thresholds $w_{k,0}^{(j)}$ are learned in the same manner as the other weights; the coefficient of the threshold is thought of as a weight attached to a dummy unit whose value remains fixed at 1.

Figure 3.5 describes the main algorithm, which uses these weight update rules, assuming a one-hidden-layer network.

We begin by addressing the general multiclass classification problem, with K classes, denoting the kth class by $\mathcal{C}_k$. There are n_k exemplars or training samples of class $\mathcal{C}_k$, forming the set

$$T_k = \left\{ (x_p^k, d_p^k): \; p = 1, \dots, n_k, \text{ for } k = 1, \dots, K \right\}.$$

The complete training set is $T = T_1 \cup \dots \cup T_K$. The goal is to find a set of weights such that the output layer nodes respond with the desired output vector d_p^k whenever the corresponding input vector x_p^k is presented. In the simplest representation scheme, if the number of classes exceeds two, we use one node in the output layer for each class, i.e., there are K nodes in the output layer. The most natural choice for the desired output vector is

$$d^k = (0, 0, \dots 0, 1, 0, \dots, 0)$$

Algorithm Backpropagation;
   Start with randomly chosen weights;
   while MSE is unsatisfactory
         and computational bounds are not exceeded, **do**
         for each input pattern x_p, $1 \le p \le P$,
            Compute hidden node inputs $(net_{p,j}^{(1)})$;

            Compute hidden node outputs $(x_{p,j}^{(1)})$;

            Compute inputs to the output nodes $(net_{p,k}^{(2)})$;

            Compute the network outputs $(o_{p,k})$;

            Compute the error between $o_{p,k}$ and desired output $d_{p,k}$;

            Modify the weights between hidden and output nodes:

            $\Delta w_{k,j}^{(2,1)} = \eta (d_{p,k} - o_{p,k}) \mathcal{S}'(net_{p,k}^{(2)}) x_{p,j}^{(1)}$

            Modify the weights between input and hidden nodes:

            $\Delta w_{j,i}^{(1,0)} = \eta \sum_k \left((d_{p,k} - o_{p,k}) \mathcal{S}'(net_{p,k}^{(2)}) w_{k,j}^{(2,1)} \right) \mathcal{S}'(net_{p,j}^{(1)}) x_{p,i}$
      end-for
   end-while .

Figure 3.5
Backpropagation training algorithm, for a one-hidden-layer network; each node has the same activation function $\mathcal{S}$.

with a 1 at the kth position of the output vector if the given sample x_p^k belongs to the kth class. But if the node function is the sigmoid $1/(1 + \exp(-net))$, the output value will be 0 only when the net input is $-\infty$, and the output value will be 1 only when the net input is $+\infty$. Since $net_i = \sum_j w_{i,j} x_j$, and since x_j values (inputs and hidden node outputs) are finite, this requires weights of infinitely high magnitude. Moreover, since the magnitude of the first derivative of the sigmoid function is very small for large net inputs (cf. figure 3.6), the rate of change of output is very small for large net inputs.

For these reasons, it is preferable to use a smaller value $(1 - \epsilon)$ instead of 1, and larger value ϵ instead of 0, as the desired output values. In other words, for each class $\mathcal{C}_k$, the desired network output for a pattern x_p belonging to that class is a real vector d_p of length K, called the target vector for that class. When x_p belongs to class $\mathcal{C}_k$, the elements of d_p satisfy

$$d_{p,k} = 1 - \epsilon$$

$$d_{p,\ell} = \epsilon, \quad \text{for} \quad \ell \neq k,$$

where ϵ is a small positive real number. Typical choices of ϵ are between 0.01 and 0.1. For

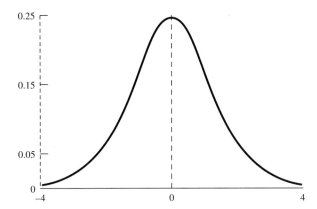

Figure 3.6
Graph of $\exp(-u)/(1 + \exp(-u))^2$, the derivative of a sigmoid function.

example, when $K = 3$ and $\epsilon = 0.05$, the target vectors for the three classes are as shown below.

$$d^1 = (0.95, 0.05, 0.05)$$

$$d^2 = (0.05, 0.95, 0.05)$$

$$d^3 = (0.05, 0.05, 0.95)$$

For classification problems, perfect classification may be possible even if $|o_{p,j} - d_{p,j}|$ is non-zero, and the network may be allowed to ignore any error that is inconsequential for the correct classification. This leads to the following definition of $\ell_{p,j}$.

1. If $d_{p,j} = (1 - \epsilon)$ and $o_{p,j} \geq d_{p,j}$, then $\ell_{p,j} = 0$.

2. If $d_{p,j} = \epsilon$ and $o_{p,j} \leq d_{p,j}$, then $\ell_{p,j} = 0$.

3. Otherwise, $\ell_{p,j} = |o_{p,j} - d_{p,j}|$, the absolute value of the difference between $o_{p,j}$ and $d_{p,j}$.

Figure 3.7 gives a pictorial description of these choices of $\ell_{p,j}$ for a two-class classification problem, using a single output node.

The backpropagation algorithm described in figure 3.5 can be adjusted to accommodate for this definition of $\ell_{p,j}$ to obtain faster convergence and improved results.

The above representation scheme implies that eight different output nodes are used for an eight-class problem. Is it not sufficient to use only three output nodes to generate eight possible output vectors $(0, 0, 0), (0, 0, 1), (0, 1, 0), (0, 1, 1), \ldots (1, 1, 1)$ where each

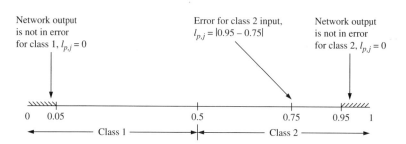

Figure 3.7
Two-class classification and the choice of $\ell_{p,j}$.

output vector represents a separate class? This requires training the network so that in
some cases the outputs of multiple outermost layer nodes are simultaneously high. Such a
binary encoding scheme is feasible, but training such a network is much more difficult than
training the network with as many output nodes as the number of classes. The inability to
obtain appropriate weights is partly due to a phenomenon called "cross-talk," defined as
follows: Learning is unsuccessful because different training samples require conflicting
changes to be made to the same weight. If there is a separate output node for each class,
each weight in the outer layer can focus on learning a specific task (for one class) rather
than on performing multiple duties.

After training is complete we can use the following procedures to determine the class
membership of a pattern, x_p.

1. Compute the output vector o_p and assign x_p to that class k for which

$$\|d^k - o_p\| \leq \|d^j - o_p\| \quad \text{for} \quad j \neq k, \text{where} \quad j = 1, \ldots, K,$$

where $\| \cdot \|$ denotes the Euclidean norm. If the output vector is equidistant from two desired
vectors, we arbitrarily assign the pattern to one of the two classes.

2. Assign x_p to class k if $o_{k,p} > o_{j,p}$ for all $j \neq k$, $1 \leq j \leq K$.

3. In the third procedure the original inputs are assumed to have a noise component of
small magnitude in each dimension. Given an input x_p, an odd number of random perturbations of it can be used separately to generate outputs, and the class to which a majority
of these outputs correspond is chosen as the class to which the given input x_p is assigned.

If the number of classes is only two, a pattern is assigned to class $\mathcal{C}_1$ if the only output o
exceeds 0.5 and to class $\mathcal{C}_2$ if $o \leq 0.5$. Each pattern is always assigned to exactly one class
by the network.

3.4 Setting the Parameter Values

So far, we have paid little attention to some important details.

1. How are weights initialized?

2. Do weights change after the presentation of each pattern or only after all patterns of the training set have been presented?

3. How is the value of η, the learning rate, chosen?

4. When should training stop?

5. How many hidden layers and how many nodes in each hidden layer should be chosen to build a feedforward network for a given problem?

6. How many patterns should there be in a training set?

7. How does one know that the network has learned something useful?

Many of the techniques described in this section address these concerns, but are relatively *ad hoc* and without substantial theoretical support. However, empirical evidence has shown them to be very useful for solving a variety of problems from many disciplines.

3.4.1 Initialization of weights

Training is generally commenced with randomly chosen initial weight values. Typically, the weights chosen are small (between -1.0 and 1.0 or -0.5 to $+0.5$), since larger weight magnitudes may drive the output of layer 1 nodes to saturation, requiring large amounts of training time to emerge from the saturated state; this phenomenon results from the behavior of the sigmoid functions.

    If the magnitudes of some of the inputs are much larger than others, random initialization may bias the network to give much greater importance to inputs whose magnitudes happen to be large. In such a situation, weights can be initialized as follows, so that the net input to each hidden node is roughly of the same magnitude.

$$w_{j,i}^{(1,0)} = \pm \frac{1}{2P} \sum_{p=1}^{P} \frac{1}{|x_i|} \tag{3.16}$$

and

$$w_{k,j}^{(2,1)} = \pm \frac{1}{2P} \sum_{p=1}^{P} \frac{1}{S(\sum w_{j,i}^{(1,0)} x_i)} \tag{3.17}$$

Another empirical heuristic for weight initialization has been suggested by Nguyen and Widrow (1990). They propose to modify the weights connecting input nodes to hidden nodes, after initial random allocation, by

$$w_{j,i}(\text{new}) \propto \frac{w_{j,i}(\text{old})}{||\bar{w}_j(\text{old})||}$$

where $\bar{w}_j$ denotes the average weight, computed over all values of i.

3.4.2 Frequency of weight updates

There are two approaches to learning.

1. In "per-pattern" learning, used in the algorithm as described in figure 3.5, weights are changed after every sample presentation.

2. In "per-epoch" (or "batch-mode") learning, weights are updated only after all samples are presented to the network. An *epoch* consists of such a presentation of the entire set of training samples. Weight changes suggested by different training samples are accumulated together into a single change to occur at the end of each epoch.

$$\Delta w = \sum_{p=1}^{P} \Delta w_p$$

Both methods are in wide use, and each has its advantages and disadvantages. In each case, training is continued until a reasonably low error is achieved, or until the maximum number of iterations allocated for training is exceeded. In the literature, "iteration" often refers to an epoch, although some authors use the term to indicate presentation of a single data item. For some applications, the input-output patterns are presented on-line, hence batch-mode learning is not possible. This is a feature of human learning; we are not provided with a lifetime of experience and suitable decisions all at once. But per-pattern training is more expensive then per-epoch training because the weights have to be changed after every sample presentation.

For large applications, the amount of training time is large, requiring several days even on the fastest processors, irrespective of whether the training method is per-epoch or per-pattern. The amount of training time can be reduced by exploiting parallelism in per-epoch training, where each of P different processors calculates weight changes for each pattern independently, followed by a phase in which all errors are summed up. Per-pattern training is not parallelizable in this manner.

One problem that may arise in per-pattern learning is that the network may just learn to generate an output close to the desired output for the current pattern, without actually

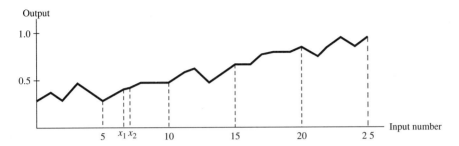

Figure 3.8
Input–output behavior of a training set.

learning anything about the entire training set. This phenomenon is observed in the following example, where a network is being trained using the per-pattern approach to learn the input-output relation shown in figure 3.8. Suppose that for the first pattern of the training set, the input is x_1, desired output is d_1, and the network output is o_1. If the value of o_1 happens to be close to d_1, only a small amount of weight changes are needed. When the network is presented with the next input x_2, the expected output would be close to o_1 (since $x_2 \approx x_1$). For the function given in figure 3.8, this would imply that the error for input x_2 would also be small (because $o_1 \approx o_2$). Again, the change of weights would be very small and would be such that the network produces o_2 for input x_2. This scenario may be repeated at every step. It would therefore seem that the network is making very little error at each step, when in fact the weights are being modified at every step to suit the current input and output (as x_k and o_k are close to x_{k+1} and o_{k+1}, respectively). At the end of the cycle, the network is observed to perform poorly on the samples presented earlier in the cycle, and, thus, the network performs poorly on the training set considered in its entirety. It may be possible to rectify this situation by presenting the input patterns in a randomized sequence, so that there is no correlation between inputs and outputs that are presented consecutively. However, this is only possible if all the patterns are available before training begins.

3.4.3   Choice of learning rate

Weight vector changes in backpropagation are proportional to the negative gradient of the error; this guideline determines the relative changes that must occur in different weights when a training sample (or a set of samples) is presented, but does not fix the exact magnitudes of the desired weight changes. The magnitude change depends on the appropriate choice of the learning rate η. A large value of η will lead to rapid learning but the weight may then oscillate, while low values imply slow learning. This is typical of all gradient descent methods. The right value of η will depend on the application. Values between 0.1 and 0.9 have been used in many applications.

There have been several studies in the literature on the choice of η. In some formulations, each weight in the network is associated with its own learning rate, adapted separately from the values for other weights and their associated learning rates. The following are some of the methods suggested for adapting the learning rate as computation proceeds.

1. A simple heuristic is to begin with a large value for η in the early iterations, and steadily decrease it; the rationale is that changes to the weight vector must be small to reduce the likelihood of divergence or weight oscillations, when the network has already converged to a (local) optimum. This is based on the expectation that larger changes in error would occur earlier in the training, while the error decreases more slowly in the later stages.

2. Another heuristic is to increase η at every iteration that improves performance by some significant amount, and to decrease η at every iteration that worsens performance by some significant amount.

3. One method to adjust the value of the learning rate is based on the philosophy of steadily doubling the learning rate until the error value worsens. Let w be the weight vector at some point during the training process, E the network error function, and $E'(w)$ the error gradient value at weight vector w. We assume that $\epsilon > 0$ is a constant small enough such that $E(w - E'(w)\epsilon) < E(w)$. The following procedure successively searches for a large enough learning rate $(2^i \epsilon)$ at which system error no longer decreases; we then choose $\eta = 2^{i-1}\epsilon$ as the largest learning rate (examined) for which error does decrease.

$i := 0; w_{new} := w - E'(w)\epsilon;$
while $E(w_{new}) < E(w)$ **do**
   $i := i + 1; w := w_{new};$
   $w_{new} := w - E'(w)2^i \epsilon$
end-while.

4. The second derivative of the error measure provides information regarding the rate with which the first derivative changes. If the second derivative is low in magnitude, it is safe to assume a steady slope, and large steps can be taken in the direction of the negative gradient, with confidence that error steadily decreases. But if the second derivative has high magnitude for a given choice of w, the first derivative may be changing significantly at w, and the error surface may be uneven in the neighborhood of w. Assumptions of steady slope are then incorrect, and a smaller choice of η may be appropriate. Although there is clear intuitive justification for this method, the main difficulty is that a large amount of computation is required to compute the second derivative with good precision. Furthermore, this method leads to choosing very small steps when the error surface is

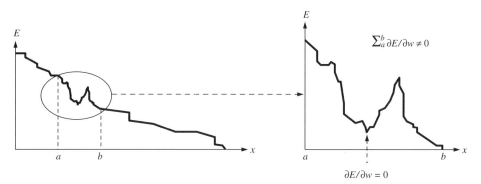

Figure 3.9
Graph of a jagged error surface, where the neighborhood averaging method may produce improved performance.

highly jagged (as in figure 3.9 where error is plotted against weight values), so that the system is certain to get stuck in the nearest local minimum of the error surface in the neighborhood of the current weight vector.

3.4.4 Momentum

Backpropagation leads the weights in a neural network to a local minimum of the MSE, possibly substantially different from the global minimum that corresponds to the best choice of weights. This problem can be particularly bothersome if the "error surface" (plotting MSE against network weights) is highly uneven or jagged, as shown in figure 3.9, with a large number of local minima. We may prevent the network from getting stuck in some local minimum by making the weight changes depend on the average gradient of MSE in a small region rather than the precise gradient at a point. Averaging $\partial E/\partial w$ in a small neighborhood can allow the network weights to be modified in the general direction of MSE decrease, without getting stuck in some local minima.

Calculating averages can be an expensive task. A shortcut, suggested by Rumelhart, Hinton, and Williams (1986), is to make weight changes in the ℓth iteration of the back-propagation algorithm depend on immediately preceding weight changes, made in the $(\ell - 1)$th iteration. This has an averaging effect, and diminishes the drastic fluctuations in weight changes over consecutive iterations. The implementation of this method is straight-forward, and is accomplished by adding a *momentum* term to the weight update rule,

$$\Delta w_{k,j}(t+1) = \eta \delta_k x_j + \alpha \Delta w_{k,j}(t), \tag{3.18}$$

where $\Delta w_{k,j}(t)$ is the weight change required at time t, and α is an additional parameter. The effective weight change is an average of the change suggested by the current gradient and the weight change used in the preceding step. However, direction for weight change chosen in early stages of training can strongly bias future weight changes, possibly restricting the training algorithm (with momentum) to explore only one region of the weight space.

Use of the momentum term in the weight update equation introduces yet another parameter, α, whose optimal value depends on the application and is not easy to determine *a priori*. Values for the momentum coefficient α can be obtained adaptively, as in the case of the learning rate parameter η. A well-chosen value of α can significantly reduce the number of iterations for convergence. A value close to 0 implies that the past history does not have much effect on the weight change, while a value closer to 1 suggests that the current error has little effect on the weight change.

3.4.5 Generalizability

Given a large network, it is possible that repeated training iterations successively improve performance of the network on training data, e.g., by "memorizing" training samples, but the resulting network may perform poorly on test data. This phenomenon is called over-training.

One solution is to constantly monitor the performance of the network on the test data. Hecht-Nielsen (1990) proposes that the weights should be adjusted only on the basis of the training set, but the error should be monitored on the test set. Training continues as long as the error on the test set continues to decrease, and is terminated if the error on the test set increases. Training may thus be halted even if the network performance on the training set continues to improve; this is illustrated in figure 3.10 for a typical problem.

To eliminate random fluctuations, performance over the test set is monitored over several iterations, not just one iteration. This method does *not* suggest using the test data for training: weight changes are computed solely on the basis of the network's performance on training data. With this stopping criterion, final weights do depend on the test data in an indirect manner. Since the weights are not obtained from the current test data, it is expected that the network will continue to perform well on future test data.

A network with a large number of nodes (and therefore edges) is capable of memorizing the training set but may not generalize well. For this reason, networks of smaller sizes are preferred over larger networks. Thus, overtraining can be avoided by using networks with a small number of parameters (hidden nodes and weights).

Injecting noise into the training set has been found to be a useful technique to improve the generalization capabilities of feedforward neural networks. This is especially the case when the size of the training set is small. Each training data point $(x_1, \ldots, x_n)$ is modified to a point $(x_1 \pm \alpha_1, x_2 \pm \alpha_2, \ldots, x_n \pm \alpha_n)$ where each α_i is a small randomly generated displacement.

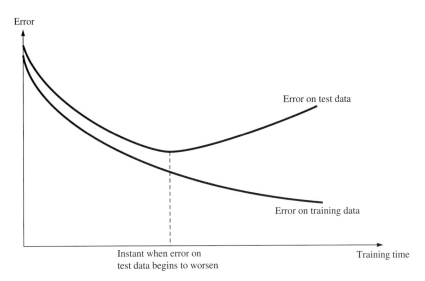

Figure 3.10
Change in error with training time, on training set and test set.

3.4.6   Number of hidden layers and nodes

Many important issues, such as determining how many training samples are required for successful learning, and how large a neural network is required for a specific task, are solved in practice by trial and error. These issues are complex because there is considerable dependence on the specific problem being attacked using a neural network.

With too few nodes, the network may not be powerful enough for a given learning task. With a large number of nodes (and connections), computation is too expensive. Also, a neural network may have the resources essentially to "memorize" the input training samples; such a network tends to perform poorly on new test samples, and is not considered to have accomplished learning successfully. Neural learning is considered successful only if the system can perform well on test data on which the system has not been trained. We emphasize capabilities of a network to *generalize* from input training samples, *not* to memorize them.

Adaptive algorithms have been devised that either begin from a large network and successively remove some nodes and links until network performance degrades to an unacceptable level, or begin from a very small network and introduce new nodes and weights until performance is satisfactory; the network is retrained at each intermediate state. Some such algorithms are discussed in the next chapter. Some researchers, e.g.,

Kung (1987) and Siet (1988), have proposed penalties for choosing the number of hidden nodes.

Lippmann (1988) has pointed out that for classification tasks solved using a feedforward neural network with d input nodes, first hidden layer nodes often function as hyperplanes that effectively partition d-dimensional space into various regions. Each node in the next layer represents a cluster of points that belong to the same class, as illustrated in figure 3.11. It is assumed that all members in a cluster belong to the same class, and samples of each class may be spread over different clusters.

For a one-hidden-layer network, Mehrotra, Mohan, and Ranka (1990) suggest the following approach to estimate the number of hidden nodes required to solve a classification problem in d-dimensional input space. If the problem is characterized by M clusters of points, where each cluster belongs to a separate region in d-dimensional space, then these regions need to be separated by segments of hyperplanes. Assuming each hyperplane corresponds to a hidden node, the number of hidden nodes needed (m) is a function of the number of clusters (M). In the worst case, as many as $M - 1$ hidden nodes (hyperplanes) may be needed to separate M clusters, e.g., to separate M collinear points in two-dimensional space, when adjacent points belong to different classes. In general, the number of hidden nodes needed will be sufficiently large so that $R(m, d) \geq M$, where $R(m, d)$ is the maximum number of regions into which m hyperplanes can divide d-dimensional space. Note that $R(m, 1) = m + 1$, and $R(1, d) = 2$, while $R(m, 0)$ is assumed to be 0.

For effective use of the above analysis in designing neural networks for a given classification task, certain clustering procedures may first be required as a preprocessing step. Using a first estimate of the number of clusters of samples, we can obtain an estimate of the number of regions to be separated by hyperplane segments.

3.4.7   Number of samples

How many samples are needed for good training? This is a difficult question whose answer depends on several factors. A rule of thumb, obtained from related statistical problems, is to have at least five to ten times as many training samples as the number of weights to be trained. Baum and Haussler (1989) suggest the following number, on the basis of the desired accuracy on the test set:

$$P > \frac{|W|}{(1 - a)} \tag{3.19}$$

where P denotes the (desired) number of patterns (i.e., the size of the training set), $|W|$ denotes the number of weights to be trained, and a denotes the expected accuracy on the test set. Thus, if a network contains 27 weights and the desired test set accuracy is

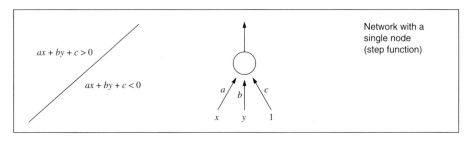

Network with a
single node
(step function)

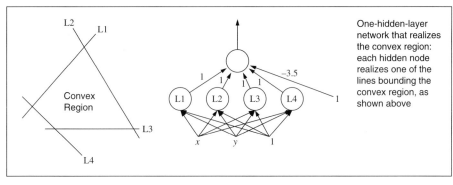

One-hidden-layer
network that realizes
the convex region:
each hidden node
realizes one of the
lines bounding the
convex region, as
shown above

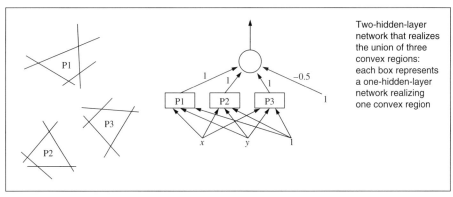

Two-hidden-layer
network that realizes
the union of three
convex regions:
each box represents
a one-hidden-layer
network realizing
one convex region

Figure 3.11
Types of decision regions that can be formed by two-input feedforward neural networks with one and two layers
of hidden units that implement step functions.

95% ($a = 0.95$), then their analysis suggests that the size of the training set should be at least $P > 27/0.05 = 540$. The above is a necessary condition. A sufficient condition that ensures the desired performance is

$$P \geq \frac{|W|}{(1-a)} \log \frac{n}{1-a} \tag{3.20}$$

where n is the number of nodes. The minimum number of hyperplane segments needed to separate samples can be used to provide a measure on the number of samples required for a given neural network for a classification task. We consider the case where the number of hidden nodes exceeds the minimum number required for successful classification of a given number of clusters. Let $A(m, d)$ denote the maximum number of hyperplane segments formed by mutual intersections among m hyperplanes in d-dimensional space. Note that $A(0, d) = 0$ and $A(m, 1) = m + 1$. Since each hyperplane contains at least one segment, $A(m, d) \geq m$. Since no hyperplane can be divided into more than 2^{m-1} segments by the $m - 1$ other hyperplanes, we must also have $A(m, d) \leq m \cdot 2^{m-1}$.

For $R(m, d) \geq M$, it can be shown that

$$\frac{\min(m, d)}{2} \leq \frac{A(m, d)}{R(m, d)} = \frac{m \, R(m - 1, d - 1)}{R(m, d)} \leq \frac{\min(m, 2d)}{2}. \tag{3.21}$$

The above result can be used to estimate the required number of "boundary samples," samples which are close to the region boundaries and hence provide the maximum information for classification. This number ought to be proportional to the number of hyperplane segments needed to separate various regions. When all hyperplanes intersect each other ($k = n$), equation 3.21 implies that this number is proportional to $\min(m, d).R(m, d)$. This gives the minimum number of boundary samples required for successful classification proportional to $\min(Mm, Md)$.

3.5 Theoretical Results*

This section discusses some theoretical properties of feedforward neural networks, illustrating their adequacy for solving large classes of problems. We first present a result of Cover (1965) that shows the usefulness of hidden nodes. We then discuss the ability of multilayer feedforward networks to represent and approximate arbitrary functions.

3.5.1 Cover's theorem

Cover (1965) showed that formulating a classification problem in a space of higher dimensionality (than the original problem) can help significantly, since the patterns of different classes may become linearly separable when transformed to the higher-dimensional space. This result indicates the usefulness of hidden nodes in various neural networks.

In the rest of this section, we assume that $\mathbf{f}$ is a function mapping $\mathfrak{R}^n$ to $\mathfrak{R}^h$, i.e., mapping n-dimensional input vectors to h-dimensional vectors. The role of $\mathbf{f}$ can be viewed as analogous to the activation of h hidden nodes when an input vector is presented to a neural network with n input nodes.

Consider the two-class classification problem based on the training samples $T = \{i_\ell : \ell = 1, \ldots, P\}$, where each i_ℓ is an n-dimensional input vector. This problem is said to be "$\mathbf{f}$-separable" if the result of applying $\mathbf{f}$ makes the data linearly separable, i.e., the set $\{\mathbf{f}(i) : i \in T\}$ is linearly separable. Thus $\mathbf{f}$-separability implies that there exists an h-dimensional weight vector w such that $w \cdot \mathbf{f}(i) \geq 1$ if i belongs to one class and $w \cdot \mathbf{f}(i) < 1$ if i belongs to the other class. (Using 1 in the inequalities, instead of the more commonly used 0, allows us to omit the threshold or bias terms.)

Cover's theorem derives the probability that sets of points in T are $\mathbf{f}$-separable, as a function of size of the training set P. It relies on Schlafli's formula for counting the number of sets of input vectors that are $\mathbf{f}$-separable. The result also depends on another important concept: the degrees of freedom of the function $\mathbf{f}$, denoted by $\#(\mathbf{f})$, which represents the dimensionality of the subspace defined by the elements in $\{\mathbf{f}(i_1), \ldots, \mathbf{f}(i_P)\}$. The relevance of the degrees of freedom of a function is easy to follow in terms of two simple examples. If we define $\mathbf{f}$ to map every input vector $i \in T$ to the h-dimensional zero vector, the data are hardly likely to be $\mathbf{f}$-separable, since all of the inputs are mapped to the same point. In this case we say that such a function has zero degrees of freedom. On the other hand, if $\mathbf{f}$ maps an input i to "general position" for all inputs, then there is zero probability that any non-trivial subset of $\{\mathbf{f}(i_1), \ldots, \mathbf{f}(i_P)\}$ with h elements is linearly dependent.

The statement of Cover's theorem is as follows. We will assume that degrees of freedom of $\mathbf{f}$ is h.

THEOREM 3.1   Let $\mathbf{f}$ be a function mapping $\mathfrak{R}^n$ to $\mathfrak{R}^h$, where h is a positive integer. Any set of P randomly chosen n-dimensional input vectors is $\mathbf{f}$-separable with probability

$$\sum_{j=0}^{h-1} \binom{P-1}{j} / 2^{P-1}.$$

For a fixed P, this probability increases as h increases. This implies that the use of many hidden nodes makes it very likely that a feedforward network with a step function at its output node will succeed in separating the input data into the appropriate classes. Samples are $\mathbf{f}$-separable with probability ≈ 1 when $P \approx h$, i.e., the number of hidden nodes is roughly equal to the number of input samples.

3.5.2 Representations of functions

A neural network with one hidden layer can represent any binary function. To understand the reason for this, suppose $f(x_1, \ldots, x_n)$ is a function in n variables such that $x_i \in \{0, 1\}$ for $i = 1, \ldots, n$, and the output $f(x_1, \ldots, x_n) \in \{0, 1\}$. Such a function has unique representation in disjunctive normal form.[2] If the desired output is a vector $\in \{0, 1\}^n$, then we can imagine a separate neural network module that predicts each component of this vector; hence it suffices to examine the single output case. The neural network interpretation of the disjunctive normal form representation is that f can be written as

$$\sigma \left(\sum_k w_k^{(2,1)} \sigma (\sum_j w_j^{(1,0)} x_j) \right)$$

where σ is a step function.

A similar result also holds in general for continuous functions and is known as Kolmogorov's theorem (1957). Let f be a continuous function such that

$$f(x_1, \ldots, x_n) \in R, x_i \in [0, 1] \text{ for } i = 1, 2, \ldots, n.$$

Kolmogorov's theorem tells us that f can be represented in terms of functions in one variable. There are two kinds of functions in terms of which the function f is expressed: fixed functions ($h_{i,j}$) and other functions (g_j) whose choice depends on f.

THEOREM 3.2 (Kolmogorov, 1957)   There exist fixed increasing continuous functions $\{\cdots, h_{i,j}, \cdots\}$ and properly chosen continuous functions $\{\cdots, g_j, \cdots\}$ so that every continuous function f can be written in the form

$$f(x_1, \ldots, x_n) = \sum_{j=1}^{2n+1} g_j \left(\sum_{i=1}^{n} h_{i,j}(x_i) \right)$$

where

$$h_{i,j} : [0, 1] \longrightarrow \Re \quad \text{for} \quad i = 1, \ldots, n; \ j = 1, \ldots, 2n + 1$$

---

2. As described in books such as Mattson (1993), an expression is in disjunctive normal form (DNF) if it is written as a disjunction (OR) of conjunctions (AND's) of variables (x_i) and complements of variables ($\overline{x_i}$). Any binary function of binary variables can be written in DNF, e.g., $(x_1 + x_2 x_3)(\overline{x_1} x_2 + \overline{x_3} x_4)$ can be written in DNF as $x_1 \overline{x_3} x_4 + \overline{x_1} x_2 x_3$, where addition represents OR, multiplication represents AND, and the horizontal bar above a variable indicates NOT.

and

$$g_j : \Re \longrightarrow \Re \quad \text{for} \quad j = 1, \ldots, 2n + 1.$$

Hecht-Nielsen (1987) suggested an obvious interpretation of this theorem in terms of neural networks: Every continuous function, whose argument is a vector of real components, can be computed by a two-hidden-layer neural network. Nodes in the first hidden layer of this network apply h transformations to each individual input (x_i), nodes at the second layer compute g transformations, and the output layer sums the outputs of the second-hidden-layer nodes.

There are some difficulties in obtaining practical applications for this very important mathematical result. This theorem is an existence theorem—it tells us that any multivalued continuous function can be expressed as described above. It is non-constructive since it does not tell us how to obtain h and g functions needed for a given problem. Results obtained by Vitushkin (1964, 1977) have shown that g and h functions may be highly non-smooth. On the other hand, as Girosi and Poggio (1989) have pointed out

In a network implementation that has to be used for learning and generalization, some degree of smoothness is required for the functions corresponding to the units in the network.

In addition, as described in earlier sections, the process of solving a problem using a feedforward network implies that smooth node functions are first chosen, architecture of the network is "guessed," and only the weights remain to be adjusted. Poggio and Girosi (1990) call such approximations "parameterized representations."

In view of the above observations, several researchers focus on a different issue: approximation of a continuous multivalued function within prespecified error limits. Pertinent results are discussed in the following subsection.

3.5.3   Approximations of functions

A well-known result in mathematics shows that functions can be approximated to any degree of accuracy using their Fourier approximations. This degree of approximation is measured in terms of mean squared error. Understanding the mathematical result requires defining a few technical terms. If $f(x_1, \ldots, x_n)$ is a function and

$$\int_{[0,1]^n} f^2(\boldsymbol{x}) d\boldsymbol{x} < \infty,$$

then the function is "square-integrable." Suppose $\hat{f}_N(\boldsymbol{x})$ is another function that approximates $f(\boldsymbol{x})$. We can measure the difference between $f(\boldsymbol{x})$ and $\hat{f}_N(\boldsymbol{x})$ in terms of

$$\int_{[0,1]^n} \left| f(x) - \hat{f}_N(x) \right|^2 dx,$$

which is called the mean squared error (MSE). Note that this definition of MSE is for continuous functions, whereas the definition presented in chapter 1 was for finite sets of training samples.

THEOREM 3.3 (Fourier series approximation) Let $f(x)$ be a square integrable function, being approximated by

$$\hat{f}_N(x) = \sum_{k_1=-N}^{N} \cdots \sum_{k_n=-N}^{N} c_k \, e^{2\pi \sqrt{-1}(k \cdot x)} \tag{3.22}$$

whose coefficients are defined in terms of $f(x)$ as

$$c_k = \int_{[0,1]^n} f(x) e^{-2\pi \sqrt{-1}(k \cdot x)},$$

where $k = (k_1, \ldots, k_n)$ is an n-dimensional vector.

Then the MSE of this approximation converges to 0 as $N \longrightarrow \infty$, i.e.,

$$\lim_{N \longrightarrow \infty} \int_{[0,1]^n} \left| f(x) - \hat{f}_N(x) \right|^2 dx = 0.$$

This Fourier series approximation can be obtained using a feedforward network with one hidden layer containing cosine node functions, as shown by Gallant and White (1988) and Hecht-Nielsen (1989). Therefore, given any $\epsilon > 0$ and a square integrable function $f(x)$, there exists a feedforward backpropagation neural network with one hidden layer that can approximate f to a desired level of accuracy with MSE $< \epsilon$. Since the quality of the approximation improves as N increases, this theorem appear to suggest that an arbitrarily large number of nodes in the hidden layer may be needed for desired accuracy.

There is one more difficulty with the above result: The coefficients c_k in equation 3.22 depend upon the functions f whose approximation is the goal of the learning procedure using the training set $\{(x, y_i) : i = 1, \ldots, P\}$. Theorem 3.3 does not guarantee that such weights can be learned by a feedforward backpropagation neural network.

In contrast to the previous result in which an attempt is made to implement Fourier series approximations, Cybenko (1988) and Hornik, Stinchcombe, and White (1989) have independently obtained results that describe the abilities of a traditional one-hidden-layer neural network. These researchers have shown that feedforward neural networks with one hidden layer and sigmoid node functions can approximate continuous functions with arbitrary precision. The approximation is measured in terms of absolute error, i.e.,

$|f(x) - \hat{f}_N(x)| < \epsilon$, for all $x \in [0, 1]^n$

where

$$\hat{f}_N(x) = \sum_{j=1}^{N} \alpha_j \sigma(w \cdot x) + w_{0j}.$$

The above universal approximation result assumes that no constraints are placed on the number of nodes or weight magnitudes. Subsequent research has established a connection between the quality of approximation and network size: Kurkova (1992) has derived upper bounds on the number of nodes needed for approximating an arbitrary continuous function to a desired degree of accuracy, using a two-hidden-layer feedforward network with sigmoidal non-linearities. Barron (1993) has shown that feedforward networks with one hidden layer of sigmoidal non-linearities can achieve integrated squared error of $O(1/(\text{number of nodes in the network}))$, in approximating a large class of functions. Therefore better approximations are obtained using neural networks than using series expansions, for a given number of parameters. This result assumes that the functions to be approximated have a bound on the first moment of the magnitude distribution of the Fourier transform.

3.6   Accelerating the Learning Process

The time required for training is proportional to the product of the number of iterations, the number of weights used in the network, and the number of samples. Thus, the computational requirements for training may be large even for networks of reasonable size. Several methods have been discussed in the literature to accelerate the learning process by reducing the number of iterations required for convergence. Two such approaches, the *Quickprop* and *conjugate gradient* methods, are discussed in this section.

3.6.1   Quickprop algorithm

This method relies on analytically determining the minimum of a paraboloid that passes through two known points. Fahlman's (1988) Quickprop algorithm is based on Newton's method. For a parabola $E = aw^2 + bw + c$, the first derivative $E' = \partial E / \partial w = 2aw + b$, is a linear function of w. If $w(t)$ and $w(t-1)$ are the values of the w at time t and $(t-1)$ respectively, and if $E'(t)$ and $E'(t-1)$ are the values of the error gradient at time t and $(t-1)$ respectively, then the assumption that E is a paraboloid function of w allows determination of the desired value $w(t+1)$ of the weight such that $E'(t+1) = 0$, as described below. The equations

$$\frac{\partial E(t)}{\partial w} = E'(t) = 2aw(t) + b$$

$$\frac{\partial E(t-1)}{\partial w} = E'(t-1) = 2aw(t-1) + b$$

imply that

$$2a = \frac{E'(t) - E'(t-1)}{w(t) - w(t-1)} = \frac{E'(t) - E'(t-1)}{\Delta w(t-1)}$$

and

$$b = E'(t) - \frac{(E'(t) - E'(t-1))w(t)}{\Delta w(t-1)}.$$

To find the minimum of E in the very next step, we set the gradient $\partial E(t+1)/\partial w = 0$, i.e., $2aw(t+1) + b = 0$, which implies that $w(t+1) = -b/2a$. Substituting for a and b from the above equations gives

$$w(t+1) = \left[\frac{\Delta w(t-1)}{E'(t) - E'(t-1)}\right] \frac{(E'(t) - E'(t-1))w(t) - E'(t)\Delta w(t-1)}{\Delta w(t-1)}$$

$$= w(t) + \left[\frac{E'(t)\Delta w(t-1)}{E'(t-1) - E'(t)}\right]. \tag{3.23}$$

Consequently,

$$w(t+1) - w(t) = E'(t)\Delta w(t-1)/(E'(t-1) - E'(t)).$$

This method often gives a good estimate for the minimum, especially if the error surface between the newly generated point and one of its generating points has a roughly paraboloidal shape. However, the method cannot be applied if the error gradient has not decreased in magnitude and has not changed sign at the preceding time step, i.e., if $|E'(t)| \geq |E'(t-1)|$ and $\mathrm{sgn}(E'(t)) = \mathrm{sgn}(E'(t-1))$, in which case this method would lead to taking a step "up" the current slope, or taking an infinitely large step.

Figure 3.12 shows the weight change suggested by the above formula, which results in faster progress towards error minimum than is the case with backpropagation.

3.6.2 Conjugate gradient

The *conjugate gradient* method [see Hestness and Stiefel (1952), Fletcher and Reeves (1964), and Shewchuk (1994)] is an iterative optimization procedure that conducts a spe-

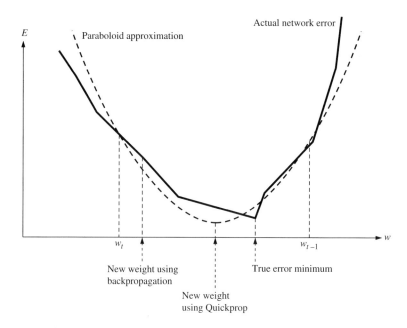

Figure 3.12
Quickprop and the paraboloidal approximation to minimize the error function.

cial kind of gradient descent in d-dimensional space. This is achieved by finding d directions along which the system state is successively transformed, where the largest possible step that decreases the cost (or error or energy) function is taken in each direction, and the $(i + 1)$th direction is chosen to be "conjugate" to the first i directions (two vectors $x_1 \neq \mathbf{0}$ and $x_2 \neq \mathbf{0}$ are said to be *conjugate* with respect to a matrix A, or A-orthogonal, if $x_1^T A x_2 = \mathbf{0}$).

For optimization problems, the relevant matrix A consists of the coefficients of the second order terms of the Taylor series expansion of the objective function being optimized. If the function is quadratic, or if the third order and higher order terms in the Taylor series expansion can be ignored, then the process of making the largest possible changes successively along various A-orthogonal directions is guaranteed to result in the optimum of the objective function. Even in non-quadratic functions, this method provides a useful approximation for the task of finding the best possible search direction.

In practice, the entire A matrix is not calculated exactly; just as we often approximate dy/dx at (x_i, y_i) by the difference ratio $(y_i - y_{i-1})/(x_i - x_{i-1})$, each new conjugate direction is obtained by an approximation that examines only the most recent among the previously obtained directions, and constructs a new vector that is approximately A-orthogonal to all the previously obtained directions.

In training a feedforward neural network, the conjugate gradient method can be applied to obtain the weights that minimize the error function E. The initial weights (w_0) are chosen randomly, as in the case of training algorithms such as backpropagation. Let w_i denote the weight vector in the ith iteration, and let $E'(w_i)$ denote the error gradient in that iteration, i.e., the derivative of E with respect to the weight matrix at $w = w_i$. In the application of the conjugate gradient method to feedforward neural network training, a series of direction vectors are computed along which modifications are successively made to the weight vector. In each step, the new weight is calculated as

$$w_{i+1} = w_i + \eta_i d_i,$$

where the vector d_i is approximately conjugate to the vectors $d_{i-1}, \ldots, d_1$ used in the immediately preceding iterations. The first direction for weight updates is

$$d_0 = -E'(w)$$

as in the case of backpropagation.

The coefficient η_i is obtained so as to minimize $E(w_i + \eta_i d_i)$ for the current choice of w_i and d_i, using a method analogous to "line search." The following subsections describe the methods of selecting w_i and η_i in greater detail.

Selection of magnitude of descent along current direction   There are several methods to obtain the optimum value of η. The basic idea is to differentiate $E(w + \eta d)$ with respect to η and solve the resulting equation obtained by equating the derivative equal to 0 (keeping other variables constant). Differentiation as well as solving of the resulting equation are easy if the function is approximated in the neighborhood of w by the first two terms of its Taylor series expansion. Equivalently, we may approximate the function by the equation of a paraboloid whose minimum is easy to obtain. This is essentially the traditional Newton-Raphson method. The Taylor series expansion of E gives

$$E(w + \eta d) \approx E(w) + \eta \left[E'(w)\right]^T d + \frac{\eta^2}{2} d^T E''(w) d.$$

Setting to zero the first derivative of E with respect to η, we obtain

$$\frac{d}{d\eta} E(w + \eta d) \approx \left[E'(w)\right]^T d + \eta d^T E''(w) d = 0$$

where $E''(w)$ denotes the Hessian matrix or the matrix of the second derivative of $E(w)$ with respect to w. The minimum of E is thus obtained at

$$\eta = -\frac{[E'(w)]^T d}{d^T E''(w)d}.$$

This method of obtaining η has one drawback: it requires evaluation of the matrix containing the second derivatives of the error function, which is difficult to obtain for feedforward networks, due to the size of the weight vector as well as the extensive computations required by the lengthy expressions describing the derivatives. The *secant method*, which approximates the second derivative by the difference of the first derivatives at two neighboring points, can be used to rectify this problem.

$$\frac{d^2}{d\eta^2} E(w + \eta d) \approx \frac{E'(w + \tau d) - E'(w)}{\tau}$$

The quality of this approximation depends on the size of the neighborhood parameter τ. By substitution, when the resulting derivative of $E(w + \eta d)$ with respect to η is zero,

$$\eta = \frac{-\tau [E'(w)]^T d}{d^T (E'(w + \tau d) - E'(w)d)}.$$

Selection of conjugate direction vectors   One can select each successive direction by the following rule,

$$d_{i+1} = r_{i+1} + \beta_{i+1} d_i,$$

where $r_{i+1} = -E'(w_{i+1})$. The coefficient β_{i+1} is calculated by using one of the following methods.

1. In the Fletcher-Reeves method,

$$\beta_{i+1} = \frac{r_{i+1}^T r_{i+1}}{r_i^T r_i}.$$

2. In the Polak-Ribière method,

$$\beta_{i+1} = \max \left\{ \frac{r_{i+1}^T (r_{i+1} - r_i)}{r_i^T r_i}, 0 \right\}.$$

Note that in the case of the Polak-Ribière method, $\beta_{i+1} = 0$ is equivalent to restarting the search.

3.7   Applications

In this section, we describe several small applications of feedforward networks trained using the backpropagation algorithm. The first application is a two-class medical classification problem for "weaning" patients from respiratory assistance. The second is a classification problem in which myoelectric signals are distinguished. The third is a financial forecasting problem, predicting values for flour prices in three cities. The fourth is a problem in automatic control, in which the behavior of a gantry crane is to be understood and manipulated.

3.7.1   Weaning from mechanically assisted ventilation

The first application is a medical decision-making problem. "Weaning" or discontinuing respiratory support to a patient receiving mechanical ventilation requires evaluating the patient's ability to sustain unassisted breathing without clinical or physiological deterioration. Premature weaning can harm a patient, while weaning too late implies unnecessary expense since the patient will be using medical equipment that is not needed. Traditional methods to determine whether a patient can be weaned are unreliable[3] or extremely expensive, using equipment that is not normally available in most hospitals. Ideally, a physician would like to make these decisions based on variables such as the following, which are easily obtainable from patients: peak negative inspiratory pressure, respiratory rate, unassisted minute ventilation, and tidal volume. The data in 21 weaning trials given in table 3.1 constitute the training set. Of these trials, weaning attempts had been successful in nine instances and unsuccessful in 12. This set was used to train a neural network. For such two-class problems, it is sufficient to choose a network with one output node, whose high value (0.95) indicates that the sample belongs to one class, and a low value (0.05) identifies that the sample belongs to the other class.

The neural network approach successfully solved the desired classification task using a network with one hidden layer. Data was first normalized to make all values lie between 0 and 1, using the transformations

$$x_1 = (\text{NIF} + 60)/50, \qquad x_2 = (\text{VT} - 100)/900, \qquad \text{and} \qquad x_3 = (\text{RR} - 10)/40.$$

A 3-2-1 feedforward network was trained on this data, using parameter values such as learning rate $\eta = 0.9$ and momentum $\mu = 0.1$. The network succeeded in classifying all training data correctly, in less than 2,000 epochs, as shown in table 3.2. The results ob-

---

3. A physician remarked that the current method of making a decision is by checking "whether the patient has a twinkle in his eye"!

Table 3.1
Training set for the respiratory weaning problem. In the notation used, NIF = negative inspiratory pressure (cm. H_2O); VT = tidal volume; and RR = respiratory rate (breaths/minute).

NIF	VT	RR	Weaning Effort	NIF	VT	RR	Weaning Effort
−24	300	24	success	−30	250	30	success
−30	500	17	failure	−42	950	13	success
−23	300	29	success	−12	220	32	failure
−26	265	44	failure	−20	124	33	failure
−18	370	32	failure	−42	750	24	success
−22	350	30	failure	−32	530	21	success
−10	320	29	failure	−40	916	22	success
−60	650	16	success	−30	500	19	success
−20	225	46	failure	−25	412	30	failure
−24	276	38	failure	−28	400	38	failure
−15	270	40	failure				

Adapted with permission from Ashutosh et al., "Prediction criteria for successful weaning from respiratory support: Statistical and connectionist analyses," *Critical Care Medicine*, Vol. 20, No. 9, pp. 1295–1301, ©Williams and Wilkins, 1992.

Table 3.2
Numbers and percentages of correct classification on the training set.

	Predicted Success	Predicted Failure	Total	Correctly Classified
Success	9	0	9	100%
Failure	0	12	12	100%
Total	9	12	21	100%

Adapted with permission from Ashutosh et al., "Prediction criteria for successful weaning from respiratory support: Statistical and connectionist analyses," *Critical Care Medicine*, Vol. 20, No. 9, pp. 1295–1301, ©Williams and Wilkins, 1992.

tained did not vary much with the choice of parameters such as η and μ. There were a few trials in which one training sample remained misclassified even after a few thousand training epochs; this occurred when only one hidden node was used, or when the training tolerance was set to a very low threshold (with desired network outputs for the two classes being 0.99 and 0.01, respectively).

Nine other weaning efforts were made and these data constitute the test set, used only to measure the performance of the trained neural network. In the test set, shown in table 3.3, there were three patients on whom weaning attempts were unsuccessful, and the other six

Table 3.3
Test data, asterisk indicates misclassified case.

NIF	VT	RR	Weaning Effort
−40	465	23	success
−15	450	25	failure
−22	400	41	failure
−28	310	24	failure*
−48	380	24	success
−34	530	28	success
−40	740	19	success
−42	550	27	success
−55	480	19	success

Adapted with permission from Ashutosh et al., "Prediction criteria for successful weaning from respiratory support: Statistical and connectionist analyses," *Critical Care Medicine*, Vol. 20, No. 9, pp. 1295–1301, ©Williams and Wilkins, 1992.

Table 3.4
Numbers and percentages of correct classification on the test set.

	Predicted Success	Predicted Failure	Total	Correctly Classified
Success	6	0	6	100%
Failure	1	2	3	66.7%
Total	7	2	9	88.9%

Adapted with permission from Ashutosh et al., "Prediction criteria for successful weaning from respiratory support: Statistical and connectionist analyses," *Critical Care Medicine*, Vol. 20, No. 9, pp. 1295–1301, ©Williams and Wilkins, 1992.

cases were weaned successfully. The network made one error on the test set, as shown in table 3.4.

3.7.2   Classification of myoelectric signals

Myoelectric signals are electrical signals that correspond to muscle movements in animals, and can be measured on the surface of the skin. This example considers classification of such signals into three groups that translate directly into movements of specific parts of the body. The signal measurements contain significant amounts of noise, due to background electrical activity in nerves unrelated to the movement of the relevant muscles. Hence perfect classification is impossible. Appendix B.2 contains data (332 samples) related to this problem, suitably preprocessed, and with reduced input dimensionality.

Table 3.5
Progress in training a 2-5-3 network on myoelectric signals.

Iteration No.	Fraction of samples misclassified	MSE
100	0.159639	0.213797
200	0.150602	0.189983
300	0.132530	0.172497
400	0.135542	0.170050
500	0.132530	0.168683
600	0.132530	0.168227
700	0.129518	0.167203
800	0.129518	0.167318
900	0.129518	0.167395
1,000	0.126506	0.167376
2,000	0.123494	0.166275
3,000	0.129518	0.165759
4,000	0.123494	0.151863
5,000	0.123494	0.151121
6,000	0.117470	0.151182
7,000	0.111446	0.150595
8,000	0.111446	0.150215
9,000	0.111446	0.149949
10,000	0.111446	0.149668
11,000	0.114458	0.149576
12,000	0.114458	0.149664
13,000	0.111446	0.146705
14,000	0.114458	0.149832
15,000	0.111446	0.147453
16,000	0.114458	0.149184
17,000	0.111446	0.147182
18,000	0.114458	0.147353
19,000	0.114458	0.147297
20,000	0.114458	0.147962

Table 3.5 shows the results of training a 2-5-3 feedforward network on this data. The desired target output tolerance was 0.05, implying that target outputs are 0.95 or 0.05 for each output node. The learning rate chosen was $\eta = 0.9$, and momentum rate was $\alpha = 0.4$. Note that the system error occasionally increases. At the end of 20,000 iterations, 38 samples remain misclassified. Table 3.6 summarizes the performance of the neural network for this data.

3.7.3 Forecasting commodity prices

The time series methodology discussed in chapter 1 is applied to the natural logarithms of the indices of monthly flour prices for Buffalo, Minneapolis, and Kansas City over a period of a hundred months from August 1972 to November 1980, obtained from Tiao

Table 3.6
Performance of a neural network for the myoelectric signals data.

Actual class in which network places sample:	1	2	3
Desired Target Class			
Class 1	75	5	0
Class 2	3	88	9
Class 3	2	19	131

and Tsay (1989). We may treat this data as consisting of three univariate time series, each describing the logarithms of monthly flour prices for one city: $\{x_t : t = 1, 2, \ldots, 100\}$ for Buffalo, $\{y_t : t = 1, 2, \ldots, 100\}$ for Minneapolis, and $\{z_t : t = 1, 2, \ldots, 100\}$ for Kansas City.

A one-hidden-layer feedforward network, with two hidden nodes, was used to model each time series, trained with 90 input data values, ranging from August 1972 to January 1980. In other words, only the values of $x_i, \ldots, x_{i+k}$ were used to predict x_{i+k+1}, where k is the number of input nodes used. Training was conducted for 25,000 to 50,000 epochs, with learning rate $\eta = 0.3$, and momentum $\alpha = 0.6$. Training was followed by output prediction for the next ten time points (for February 1980 to November 1980) using the weights and thresholds generated during training. These predictions were compared with the test data set to judge the performance of the network in terms of MSE(test).

The mean squared errors obtained for separate modeling networks of three different sizes are presented in table 3.7. The values correspond to the mean squared errors observed for (a) the first 90 univariate data items, which correspond to the training data, (b) one-lag, and (c) multilag predictions over the remaining ten univariate data items, for each of the three time series. As the size of the networks is increased, the training performance improves whereas one-lag and multilag performances deteriorate (in terms of MSE(training) and MSE(test) respectively). This suggests that the 4-4-1 and 6-6-1 networks are oversized for the given univariate data and a 2-2-1 network is more suitable for prediction. Thus every data item in each time series is found to be strongly dependent only on the past two values.

Better results are obtained using (for each series) information from all three series, instead of treating each series in isolation. For instance, prediction performance is better if we use a 6-2-1 network trained to predict x_{t+1} from six preceding values (recorded at time points t and $t - 1$ only) from all the three series, i.e., $(x_t, y_t, z_t, x_{t-1}, y_{t-1}, z_{t-1})$. However, performance is poorer if we use a "combined" 6-6-3 network that attempts to predict x_{t+1}, y_{t+1}, as well as z_{t+1} from inputs $(x_t, y_t, z_t, x_{t-1}, y_{t-1}, z_{t-1})$.

Table 3.7
Mean squared errors for separate modeling and prediction.

Network		Buffalo MSE	Minneapolis MSE	Kansas City MSE
2-2-1	Training	0.0034	0.0032	0.0035
	One-lag Testing	0.0044	0.0042	0.0043
	Multilag Testing	0.0045	0.0050	0.0059
4-4-1	Training	0.0034	0.0031	0.0034
	One-lag Testing	0.0098	0.0080	0.0034
	Multilag Testing	0.0100	0.0091	0.0065
6-6-1	Training	0.0028	0.0028	0.0016
	One-lag Testing	0.0121	0.0097	0.0089
	Multilag Testing	0.0176	0.0149	0.0138

Reprinted from *Neural Networks*, Vol. 5, Chakraborty et al., "Forecasting the Behavior of Multivariate Time Series Using Neural Networks," pp. 961–970, Copyright 1992, with kind permission from Elsevier Science, Ltd., The Boulevard, Langford Lane, Kidlington OX5 1GB, UK.

3.7.4 Controlling a gantry crane

Neural networks have been applied to many control problems, such as pole-balancing [Tolat and Widrow (1988)], robot arm control [Guez, Eilbert, and Kam (1988)], truck backing-up [Nguyen and Widrow (1990)], and inverse robot kinematics [Josin, Charney, and White (1988)].

In this section, we discuss a simple application from control systems that uses neural networks for function approximation. A multilayer feedforward network is used to emulate and approximate the direct and inverse transfer function of the gantry crane, a simple time-varying system used to move large parts and assemblies on a factory floor. A cable is attached to the load to be moved, which is then raised and moved (see figure 3.13). The control system is responsible for the horizontal motion of the crane and load, ensuring that

1. the load is moved to a location specified by given coordinates;

2. load motion is well damped; and

3. the system can cope with a wide range of values for load mass and cable length.

Since this is a simple control problem, it is possible to represent the behavior of this system by mathematical formulae. This system can be represented by non-linear differential equations such as $F = M\ddot{X} + m[\ddot{X} + L(\ddot{\theta}\cos\theta - \dot{\theta}^2\sin\theta)] + c_1\dot{X} + c_2(\dot{X} + L\dot{\theta}\cos\theta)$ and $m[L\ddot{\theta} + \ddot{X}\cos\theta] + mg\sin\theta + c_2[L\ddot{\theta} + \ddot{X}\cos\theta] = 0$, where X is the position of the crane, θ is the angle of the cable from the vertical axis, L is the cable length, M is the crane mass, m is the load mass, g is the gravity constant, c_1 is the viscous damping of the

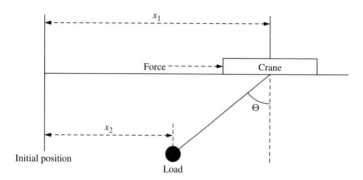

Figure 3.13
Gantry crane system. Reproduced with permission from Proc. IJCNN'91, Singapore, pp. 2410–2413, "Nonlinear System Identification Using Recurrent Networks" by H. Lee et al., ©1991 IEEE.

crane, c_2 is the viscous damping of the load, and F is the force applied to the crane. Dots over variables indicate derivatives with respect to time.

We can obtain expressions for the velocity of the crane $v_1(t + 1)$ and the velocity of the load $v_2(t + 1)$ at time $t + 1$ as functions of $u(t)$, the force applied to the crane's motor, the velocities $v_1(t)$ and $v_2(t)$ at time t, and other parameters. The force measured in terms of voltage applied to the crane's motor and the velocities of crane and load can be measured during the crane's operation. All other parameters of the system are to be realized by the internal representations of neural networks.

To see how well a neural network can learn these non-linear equations, two data sets were created, with 240 data points. Half were used for training networks and half for testing. The voltage at each time point was randomly chosen (ranging from 0 to 200), and the two corresponding velocity measures were generated accordingly. For testing the system, sinusoidal voltage $(\sin(t/3))$ was also used to compare the results in more realistic situations. The values of M, m, L, c_1, and c_2 were chosen arbitrarily. A feedforward network was trained using the backpropagation algorithm. All input values were linearly normalized to range between 0.01 and 0.99.

System identification The feedforward network used for the experiments had four hidden nodes. The inputs to the network were $u(t)$, $v_1(t)$, $v_2(t)$, $v_1(t - 1)$, and $v_2(t - 1)$. In other words, a 4–4–2 neural network was trained to generate (future) outputs $v_1(t + 1)$ and $v_2(t + 1)$. Test results are shown in table 3.8.

Inverse system identification For inverse system identification, the previously generated data set can be used to train and test the networks. In the experiments conducted, a 6-2-1 feedforward network was applied with inputs $v_1(t)$, $v_2(t)$, $v_1(t - 1)$, $v_2(t - 1)$,

Table 3.8
Mean squared errors in system identification by a feedforward net.

Velocities	MSE in training	MSE in test	
		Random input	Sinusoidal input
Crane	0.000364	0.000245	0.000966
Load	0.000560	0.000348	0.000784

Reproduced with permission from Proc. IJCNN'91, Singapore, pp. 2410–2413, "Nonlinear System Identification Using Recurrent Networks" by H. Lee et al., ©1991 IEEE.

$v_1(t - 2)$, and $v_2(t - 2)$ to generate the output $u(t - 1)$, with two nodes in the hidden layer. The mean squared errors obtained were 0.000554 for training data, 0.001168 for random test data, and 0.002168 for sinusoidal test data.

3.8 Conclusion

In this chapter, we have discussed feedforward neural networks with sigmoid node functions, trained by the error backpropagation algorithm. This is the network paradigm so frequently used in practical applications that sometimes the term "neural networks" is (erroneously) construed exclusively to mean such networks.

The main idea underlying backpropagation is gradient descent. Each weight is updated by a small quantity proportional to the negative of the partial derivative of the mean squared error with respect to that weight. Given the simplicity of the rule, it is surprising that a large variety of problems has been successfully solved using this algorithm. Many minor modifications of the backpropagation algorithm have been suggested to improve the speed of training or the quality of solution obtained.

The most general problem solved using backpropagation is many-input many-output function approximation, where each output node in the network corresponds to a dimension of the output vector, and each input node in the network corresponds to a dimension of the input vector. The numbers of hidden layers and nodes are problem-dependent. In a forecasting problem, the output node of the network may indicate the value of a variable to be predicted at time $t + 1$, while the inputs of the network are values of that variable (and possibly other variables) at times $\leq t$. In a two-class classification problem, the output node is intended to have a high value for input patterns from one class, and a low value for input patterns from the other class. In a multiclass classification problem, each output node corresponds to a separate class, and the class to which a pattern is assigned may be indicated by the node with the highest output for that pattern.

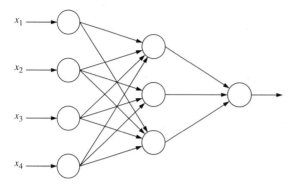

Figure 3.14
A two-layer feedforward neural network with four input nodes.

In the next chapter, we examine variations on the backpropagation algorithm, of which some adapt network size and parameter values on the fly, while others use node functions other than sigmoid functions.

3.9 Exercises

1. Consider the feedforward network with four input nodes, one output node, and three hidden nodes in a single hidden layer, shown in figure 3.14. Express the output of this network as a function of the inputs $(x_1, \ldots, x_4)$ and all the weights, for each of the following node activation functions: (i) ramp function; (ii) step function; (iii) hyperbolic tangent function.

2. Comment on the following statement, regarding networks using sigmoid node functions.

"Any task that can be accomplished by a one-output one-hidden-layer network can also be accomplished by a network containing no hidden node."

3. In a feedforward neural network, it is suggested that the backpropagation weight update rule be changed from

$$\Delta w_{i,j} \propto -\frac{\partial E}{\partial w_{i,j}}$$

to

$$\Delta w_{i,j} \propto -\frac{\partial E / \partial w_{i,j}}{|\partial^2 E / \partial w_{i,j}^2|}.$$

a. Comment on the advantages and disadvantages of the alternate proposal.

b. Write a computer program that implements the proposed modification.

c. Compare the performance of this program with traditional backpropagation, measuring performance in terms of the number of iterations to achieve the same mean squared error for some non-trivial problem.

4. Compare the initial weight selection methods proposed in section 3.4.1. Experiment on some data of moderate difficulty, using these methods, and find which gives the best performance.

5. Describe the modifications to backpropagation (figure 3.5) needed if the network was not strictly feedforward, allowing connections from the input layer to the output layer.

6. Describe the modifications to backpropagation (figure 3.5) needed if the network contained two hidden layers.

7. In the backpropagation algorithm, described in section 3.3, we have used the sigmoid function $1/(1 + \exp(-x))$ to derive the weight changes. Carry out similar calculations, determining the appropriate values for weight changes (Δw), for the following node functions.

a. $S_1(x) = \tanh(x)$

b. $S_2(x) = \begin{cases} 0 & \text{for } x \leq 0 \\ 2x^2 & \text{for } 0 \leq x \leq 1/2 \\ 1 - 2(x-1)^2 & \text{for } 1/2 \leq x \leq 1 \\ 1 & \text{for } x \geq 1 \end{cases}$

8. Consider a neural network with one-dimensional inputs. How does momentum (or neighborhood averaging) affect training when the error surface resembles that of figure 3.15? Answer the question with reference to the initial states of a weight given by S_1, S_2, S_3, and S_4.

9. a. Train and examine the performance of networks of the following sizes, using the backpropagation training algorithm, for the iris data (given in appendix B.1): (1) a 4-1-3 network, (2) a 4-10-3 network, and (3) a 4-2-2-3 network.

b. Train and examine the performance of networks to restricting the task to discriminating only between classes 2 and 3 of the iris data.

c. Train and test a network to predict the petal width based on the other three input parameters for the iris data.

d. Train and test the above networks using Quickprop method, and compare with backpropagation the computational effort needed.

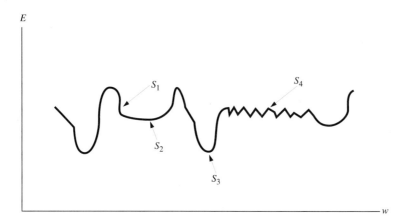

Figure 3.15
The error surface of a neural network; $S_1, \ldots, S_4$ are four possible network states (weights).

10. Show that the maximum number of regions, $R(n, d)$, given by n hyperplanes in d-dimensional space is

$$R(n, d) = \sum_{i=0}^{d} \frac{n!}{i!(n-i)!}.$$

11. A training set for the XOR problem is given in table 3.9.

    a. Prove that a strictly feedforward network with one node in the hidden layer cannot solve the XOR problem.

    b. Show that two hidden nodes are sufficient to solve the XOR problem.

    c. Show that a layered network, shown in figure 3.16, with one hidden node can also solve the XOR problem provided it has direct connections from input nodes to hidden and output nodes, in addition to a connection from the hidden node to the output node.

Table 3.9
XOR training data.

Input		Desired output
0	0	0.01
0	1	0.99
1	0	0.99
1	1	0.01

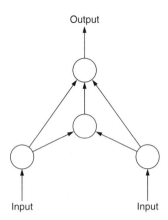

Output

Input   Input

Figure 3.16
A possible network that solves the XOR problem.

12. The "parity" problem is one of the standard benchmarks for classification algorithms. In this problem, n-dimensional bit-vectors with an odd number of 1's are to be separated from n-dimensional bit-vectors with an even number of 1's. For example, the following training set may be available for $n = 4$.

Class I: 1111, 1100, 1001, 0000.

Class II: 1110, 1000, 0111, 0100.

Execute the backpropagation algorithm for the above training set. Also solve the parity problem for $n = 6, 8, 10$, and 20 by generating your own training and test data. The training data should consists of no more than half of all possible 2^n vectors. Examine performance on the training data as well as on the test data (distinct from the training data). For which values of n is reasonable performance obtained?

13. The following sequences represents the value of a variable (the share price of a publicly traded stock) at successive instants. Train, if possible, a feedforward network that is successful in predicting the share price, possibly using information from multiple past values.
21, 21.125, 20.875, 20.75, 20.625, 21.625, 21.5, 21.5, 21.5, 21.5, 21.375, 21.375, 20.75, 20.875, 21.25, 23.25, 23.125, 23, 23.125, 22.3125, 22.625, 23.5

14. Gold prices are given in appendix B.3 for several weeks in 1993. Use the first 75% of the data for training a network. Use the best neural network so obtained to predict the next week's gold price and compare the results with the prices in the test data consisting of the last 25% of the data. Comment on the performance of the network on the test data.

4 Supervised Learning: Multilayer Networks II

No facts are to me sacred; none are profane; I simply experiment, an endless seeker with no Past at my back.
—Ralph Waldo Emerson (1841)

The previous chapter presented backpropagation, probably the most widely used supervised learning algorithm for multilayer networks. Extensive research has been conducted recently, aimed at developing improved supervised learning algorithms for feedforward networks. Some of these new supervised learning algorithms are discussed in this chapter, most being based on gradient descent. The set of algorithms presented here is representative of recent work, but is far from exhaustive.

We first discuss Madalines, which combine many Adalines into a single network. We then present several algorithms that incrementally develop feedforward networks of suitable size, evolving the network architecture to suit the problem. These algorithms facilitate the application of feedforward neural networks to new problems without having to make random guesses about the ideal size and architecture of the network; however, these algorithms have been formulated mostly for classification tasks. We then present recurrent networks that use a generalization of the backpropagation algorithm; these and related networks have been found useful for forecasting and control applications. Finally, we discuss feedforward networks that use non-sigmoid node functions. The first of these uses "radial basis" node functions whose output for a given input pattern increases as a function of the distance between the input pattern and the weight vector associated with the node; such networks have been used in many function approximation tasks. This is followed by a discussion of polynomial networks, useful for applications in which polynomial functions of inputs need to be learned.

4.1 Madalines

A Madaline is a combination of many Adalines. Learning algorithms for Madalines have gone through three stages of development. All three algorithms adhere to the "Minimum Disturbance" principle proposed by Widrow (1962), instead of explicitly computing the gradient of the network error. Nodes whose net input is sufficiently small are selected as candidates for weight changes. The possible result of changing the output of such a node is examined. If the change results in a decrease in network error, then weights of connections leading into that node are changed using the LMS (or similar) algorithm; otherwise, these weights remain unchanged. The magnitude of the weight change may be large enough to force the node output to change, or may be small so that a multitude of such changes are needed to achieve network error reduction. This process is repeated for all input patterns and for all nodes until network error becomes acceptably small.

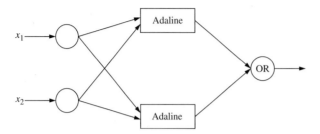

Figure 4.1
A Madaline with an output node that computes the OR logical function.

Madaline I, developed in the 1960s, has an adaptive first layer followed by a logic device (such as AND, OR, or a majority gate) at the second layer. Figure 4.1 depicts a Madaline I consisting of two Adalines and one higher-level node whose output is the logical OR of its inputs. Figure 4.2 describes the *Madaline Rule I* (MRI) training algorithm. The goal is to make the smallest possible perturbation to the network, by modifying the weights on connections leading into some Adaline (hidden node), so as to decrease network error on the current input sample. Note that the Adaline output must change in sign in order to have any effect on the network output. If the net input into an Adaline is large, its output reversal requires a large amount of change in its incoming weights. Therefore, one attempts to find an existing Adaline (hidden node) whose net input is smallest in magnitude, and whose output reversal would reduce network error. This output reversal is accomplished by applying the LMS algorithm to weights on connections leading into that Adaline.

The number of Adalines for which output reversal is necessary (to correct network performance on an input pattern) depends on the choice of the outermost node function. If the outermost node computes the OR of its inputs, then network output can be changed from 0 to 1 by modifying a single Adaline, but changing network output from 1 to 0 requires modifying all the Adalines for which current output is 1. If the outermost node computes the majority function, at most half the Adalines need to be modified to correct network result on a given input pattern. Weights of an Adaline can be changed using the LMS rule or by making a single large modification that will accomplish the desired change in the output of that Adaline.

The *Madaline II* architecture, shown in figure 4.3, improves on the capabilities of Madaline I, by using Adalines with modifiable weights at the output layer of the network, instead of fixed logic devices. Figure 4.4 describes the *Madaline Rule II* (MRII) training algorithm, which is considerably different from backpropagation. The weights are initialized to small random values, and training patterns are repeatedly presented. The algorithm modifies the first hidden layer of Adalines (i.e., connection weights from input nodes to layer number 1), then the second hidden layer (weights from layer 1 to layer 2), and so on,

Algorithm MRI;

  repeat

    Present a training pattern i to the network;

    Compute outputs of various hidden nodes and output node;

    if the pattern is misclassified,

      then

        Sort the Adalines in the network, in the order of
increasing net input magnitude $(|\sum_j w_j i_j|)$;

        Let $S = (A_1, \ldots, A_k)$ be the sorted sequence, omitting
nodes for which $|\sum_j w_j i_j| > \theta$,

        where θ is a predetermined threshold;

        while network output differs from desired output,

        and some nodes in S remain to be examined

        in this iteration, **do**

          if reversing output of the next element $A_j \in S$
can improve network performance,

            then Modify connection weights leading into A_j
to accomplish the output reversal;

        end-if

      end-while

    end-if

  until performance is considered satisfactory or the upper
bound on the number of iterations has been reached.

Figure 4.2
Madaline Rule I training algorithm (MRI).

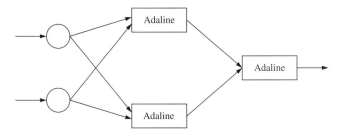

Figure 4.3
High-level structure of a Madaline II with two Adalines at the first level and one Adaline at the second level.

Algorithm MRII;
  repeat
    Present a training pattern *i* to the network;
    Compute outputs of all hidden nodes and the output node;
      Let $h = 1$;
      while the pattern is misclassified
          and $h \leq$ the number of hidden layers, **do**
        Sort the Adalines in layer h, in the order of
          increasing net input magnitude ($|\sum_j w_j i_j|$),
          but omitting nodes for which $|\sum_j w_j i_j| > \theta$,
          where θ is a predetermined threshold;
        Let $S = (A_1, \ldots, A_k)$ be the sorted sequence;
        while network output differs from desired output,
            and S contains nodes not yet examined
            in this iteration, **do**
           if reversing output of the next element $A_j \in S$
             can improve network performance,
           then Modify connection weights leading into A_j
             to accomplish the output reversal;
          end-if;
        end-while
        $h := h + 1$;
      end-while
  until performance is considered satisfactory or the upper
    bound on the number of iterations has been reached.

Figure 4.4
MRII training algorithm.

until the final layer (weights to network output nodes). Adaline weights can be changed by small quantities (using the LMS or α-LMS rule) or by a large quantity.

Note that the Adalines whose weights have already been adjusted can be revisited when new input patterns are presented. Widrow also suggests the possibility of simultaneously adjusting the weights of several Adalines. Since the node functions are not differentiable, there can be no explicit gradient descent, and the algorithm may repeatedly cycle through the same sequence of states.

The MRIII training algorithm was developed by Andes et al. (1988) to train feedforward networks with sigmoid node functions. This algorithm, described in figure 4.5, also follows the minimum disturbance principle using trial adaptations of nodes, instead of assuming the derivative of the node function to be known. Unlike MRII, weights of all nodes

Algorithm MRIII;
  repeat
    Present a training pattern i to the network;
    Compute outputs of hidden nodes and output nodes;
      for $h = 1$ **to** the number of hidden layers, **do**
        for each node k in layer h, **do**
          Let E be the current network error;
          Let network error be E_k if a small quantity $\epsilon > 0$
            is added to the kth node's net input;
          Adjust weights on connections to kth node
            using one of the following update rules:
            $\Delta w = -\eta i (E_k - E)^2 / \epsilon^2$
            or
            $\Delta w = -\eta i E (E_k - E) / \epsilon$
        end-for;
      end-for
  until current network error is considered satisfactory or
    the upper bound on number of iterations has been reached.

Figure 4.5
MRIII training algorithm for a Madaline network.

are adapted in each iteration. If the net input to the kth node is net_k, then the current network error E is compared with the network error E_k that would result if the net input to the kth node had instead been $net_k + \epsilon$, for some small $\epsilon > 0$. One of the following weight adaptation rules is used:

$$\Delta w = -\eta i (E_k - E)^2 / \epsilon^2$$

$$\Delta w = -\eta i E (E_k - E) / \epsilon$$

where i is the current input vector, and η is the learning rate.

The MRIII algorithm has been shown to be mathematically equivalent to backpropagation (Widrow and Lehr, 1990). However, each weight change involves considerably more computation than in backpropagation. MRIII has been advocated for some hardware implementations where the sigmoid node function is inaccurately implemented, so that the mathematically derived gradient is inapplicable. In such cases, MRIII is more useful since it effectively computes an approximation to the gradient, without assuming a specific sigmoid node function. Note that all nodes in each layer are perturbed in each iteration, unlike MRII.

4.2   Adaptive Multilayer Networks

Small networks are more desirable than large networks that perform the same task, for several reasons: training is faster, the number of parameters in the system is smaller, fewer training samples are needed, and the system is more likely to generalize well for new test samples. Unfortunately, there is no easy or general way of determining the smallest possible size of a neural network that will achieve a desired learning task. There are three approaches to building a network of "optimal" size.

1. A large network may be built and then "pruned" by eliminating nodes and connections that can be considered unimportant; this approach is described in section 4.2.1.

2. Starting with a very small network, the size of the network is repeatedly increased by small increments until performance is satisfactory. Algorithms that accomplish this task are described in sections 4.2.2 to 4.2.6. Most of these algorithms have been defined to solve two-class classification problems; extensions of these methods to function approximation and other tasks constitute interesting exercises.

3. A sufficiently large network is trained, and unimportant connections and nodes are then pruned, following which new nodes with random weights are reintroduced and the network is retrained. This process is continued until a network of acceptable size and performance levels is obtained, or further pruning attempts become unsuccessful.

   All these methods are based on sound heuristics that have been shown empirically to work in several cases; however, none is guaranteed to result in an optimal size network.

4.2.1   Network pruning algorithms

Small neural networks that are sufficiently capable of solving a problem can be obtained by training a large network and then repeatedly "pruning" this network until size and performance of the network are both satisfactory. Pruning algorithms use penalties to help determine if some of the nodes and links in a trained network can be removed, leading to a network with better generalization properties. A generic algorithm for such methods is described in figure 4.6.

   The following are some procedures that implement this network pruning methodology.

1. Connections associated with weights of small magnitude may be eliminated from the trained network. Nodes whose associated connections have small magnitude weights may also be pruned.

2. Connections whose existence does not significantly affect network outputs (or error) may be pruned. These may be detected by examining the change in network output when

Train a network large enough to solve the problem at hand;
repeat
    Find a node or connection whose removal does not penalize
    performance beyond desirable tolerance levels;
    Delete this node or connection;
    (Optional:) Retrain the resulting network
until further pruning degrades performance excessively.

Figure 4.6
Generic network pruning algorithm.

a connection weight is changed to 0 or by testing whether $\partial o / \partial w$ is negligible, i.e., if the network outputs change little when a weight is modified.

3. Input nodes can be pruned if the resulting change in network output is negligible. This results in a reduction in relevant input dimensionality by detecting which network inputs are unnecessary for output computation.

4. Lecun, Denker, and Solla (1990) proposed the *optimal brain damage* (OBD) method that attempts to identify which weights can be pruned from the network by examining the second derivatives of the error function contained in the Hessian matrix. In the OBD model, the change in MSE resulting from a small perturbation Δw in any weight w is approximated by

$$\Delta E = \frac{\partial E}{\partial w} \Delta w + \frac{1}{2}(E'')(\Delta w)^2 \tag{4.1}$$

where

$$E'' = \frac{\partial}{\partial w}\left(\frac{\partial E}{\partial w}\right).$$

This expression is obtained by examining two terms from the Taylor series for E, whereas traditional backpropagation examines only the first term in the Taylor series. The *optimal brain surgeon* algorithm, proposed by Hassibi, Stork, and Wolf (1993), additionally examines other second order terms from the Taylor series ($\partial^2 E / \partial w_{i,j} \partial w_{k,l}$) and is hence more general than OBD, but involves more expensive computations.

If a network has already been trained until a local minimum of E has been reached, using an algorithm such as backpropagation, then $\partial E / \partial w \approx 0$, and equation 4.1 simplifies to

$$\Delta E \approx \frac{1}{2}(E'')(\Delta w)^2. \tag{4.2}$$

Pruning a connection corresponds to changing the connection weight from w to 0, i.e., $\Delta w = -w$. The condition for pruning the connection is that the resulting change in error,

$$\Delta E = \frac{1}{2}(E'')(-w)^2 = (E'')w^2/2$$

(from equation 4.2), is small enough. The pruning criterion is hence based on examining whether $(E'')w^2/2$ is below some threshold.

Sometimes, external heuristics indicate how large a network is reasonable for a given task, and these help determine the number of links (and nodes) to be pruned. If a thousand training samples are available, for instance, one may decide *a priori* that no more than 50 weights should persist in the network, so a relatively large network may be trained and then pruned to the desired size, followed by retraining. These methods are especially useful for problems whose solution requires networks with many nodes, although the number of connections needs to be small. Note that a traditional feedforward network fully connects every node in one layer to every node in the succeeding layer, and no external information may be available to dictate which nodes in one layer are actually important for computing the output of a node in the next layer. Multilayer networks in which higher layers have lower connectivity have been proposed by Ghosh and Tumer (1993).

The disadvantage of the pruning approach is that training the original network may still take a large amount of time; also, the network's weights may have converged to a state from which pruning any node or group of connections results in a significant worsening of system performance, so that an optimal size network is not obtained. Therefore, we examine the alternative approach in the following subsections, and discuss several algorithms that adaptively build up larger networks beginning from smaller ones.

4.2.2   Marchand's algorithm

Marchand, Golea, and Rujan (1990) present a training algorithm for a feedforward network with one hidden layer. Each node computes a step function with outputs $\in \{0, 1\}$. Hidden nodes are successively added to the network, such that the $(k + 1)$th hidden node performs some (non-redundant) classification over and above what has been performed by the first k hidden nodes. The description in figure 4.7 is obtained by a slight modification of the algorithm proposed by Marchand, Golea, and Rujan (1990), to fit better with the conventions used in this text. In the description of the algorithm, T_k^+ and T_k^- represent the training samples of two classes that remain to be correctly classified at the kth iteration. At each iteration, a node's weights are trained such that either $|T_{k+1}^+| < |T_k^+|$ or $|T_{k+1}^-| < |T_k^-|$, and $(T_{k+1}^- \cup T_{k+1}^+) \subset (T_k^- \cup T_k^+)$, ensuring that the algorithm terminates eventually at the mth step, when either T_m^- or T_m^+ is empty.

Algorithm Marchand;

$k := 0$;

$T_0^+ :=$ set of training samples of one class, and

$T_0^- :=$ set of training samples of the other class;

while (T_k^+ is nonempty) and (T_k^- is nonempty), **do**

    $k := k + 1$;

    Execute only one of the following two cases:

Case 1:

    Obtain a new (kth) hidden unit such that

        its output is 0 for all patterns currently $\in T_k^+$

        and its output is 1 for at least one of the remaining

        patterns $\in T_k^-$;

    Add this unit to the set of nodes H^-;

    $T_{k+1}^+ = T_k^+$;

    $T_{k+1}^- = \{$all the samples in T_k^- for which the new unit

        generates an output of 0$\}$;

Case 2:

    Obtain a new (kth) hidden unit such that

        its output is 0 for all remaining patterns $\in T_k^-$,

        and its output is 1 for at least one of the remaining

        patterns $\in T_k^+$;

    Add this unit to the set of nodes H^+;

    $T_{k+1}^- = T_k^-$;

    $T_{k+1}^+ = \{$all the samples in T_k^+ for which the new unit

        generates an output of 0$\}$;

end-while.

Figure 4.7
The adaptive network construction algorithm proposed by Marchand, Golea, and Rujan (1990).

Eventually, when this algorithm has been executed until termination, we have two sets of hidden units (H^- and H^+), that together give the correct answers on all samples of each class. A new output unit is chosen, with a connection from each of the nodes in $H^- \cup H^+$, such that the connection from the kth hidden node to the output node carries the weight w_k defined as follows.

$$w_k = \begin{cases} 1/2^k & \text{if the } k\text{th node belongs to } H^+ \\ -1/2^k & \text{if the } k\text{th node belongs to } H^- \end{cases}$$

The above weight assignment scheme ensures that higher weight is given to the earliest generated nodes. If an input sample was correctly classified by the jth node and not by any of the preceding nodes, then

1. the contribution to the weighted sum of hidden node outputs is 0 from hidden nodes numbered 1 to $j - 1$;

2. the contribution to the net from the hidden node numbered j is $1/2^j$ assuming the sample belongs to T_0^+, and $-1/2^j$ otherwise; and

3. the contribution to the net from the hidden nodes numbered $> j$ is $\sum_k \pm 1/2^{j+k}$, whose magnitude is less than $1/2^j$.

Hence the net weighted input to the output node is either positive or negative, depending on the class membership of the sample.

What is the guarantee that one can generate a hidden unit that has the appropriate response at every given step in the algorithm? As long as the given data set is finite, it is always possible to generate a hyperplane that separates at least one sample x from all the rest. A hidden unit can hence be trained to generate one output for this sample x, and another output for all the rest. However, it need not be the case that $x \in T_k^-$; for instance, if all samples in T_k^- are completely "enclosed" by an outer shell containing samples from T_k^+, there exists no hyperplane that separates any sample in T_k^- from all the samples in T_k^+. In that case (case 2 in the while loop of the algorithm), it will certainly be possible to choose a hidden node that separates out one sample in T_k^+ from all samples in T_k^-, instead of the other way around.

EXAMPLE 4.1   We now describe a simple classification problem, *corner isolation*, used to illustrate several network construction algorithms. In this problem, two-dimensional input patterns chosen from $[-1, 1]^2$ need to be separated into two classes. The samples of one class are found near the corners of a square, and the samples of the other class are found everywhere else in the square, as shown in figure 4.8(a). For illustrative purposes, we assume the following set of training patterns, shown in figure 4.8(b).

Class I: $\{(-1, 1), (-1, -1), (1, 1), (1, -1)\}$

Class II: $\{(-1, 0), (0, -1), (0, 1), (1, 0), (0, 0)\}$

The two classes are not linearly separable, and the least number of misclassifications obtainable using an Adaline or the pocket algorithm is three, as indicated in figure 4.8.

We now apply Marchand's algorithm applied to the corner isolation problem. We assume that the desired output is 1 for class I and 0 for class II. The initial training set is

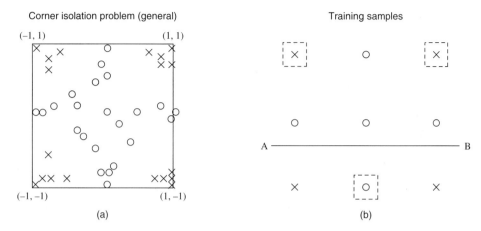

Figure 4.8
The corner isolation problem: (a) general case and (b) training data. The latter figure shows a line AB that may result from applying the pocket algorithm on this data; dashed boxes enclose samples thereby misclassified.

$$T_0^+ = \{(-1, \ 1), \ (-1, \ -1), \ (1, \ 1), \ (1, \ -1)\}$$

$$T_0^- = \{(-1, \ 0), \ (0, \ -1), \ (0, \ 1), \ (1, \ 0), \ (0, \ 0)\}.$$

The sets of hidden nodes, H^+ and H^-, are initially empty. Let the first node chosen correspond to the line with equation $y = x + 1.7$, such that the corresponding hidden node has an output of 1 for the input pattern $(-1, 1)$, and an output of 0 for all other training samples, as illustrated in figure 4.9(a). This node is added to H^+, with a connection weight of 1/2 from this hidden node to the network's output node.

For the next step of the algorithm, the training set is

$$T_1^+ = \{(-1, \ -1), \ (1, \ 1), \ (1, \ -1)\}$$

$$T_1^- = T_0^- = \{(-1, \ 0), \ (0, \ -1), \ (0, \ 1), \ (1, \ 0), \ (0, \ 0)\}.$$

The second node chosen may correspond to the equation $y = x - 1.7$, with the corresponding hidden node having an output of 1 for $(1, -1)$ and an output of 0 for other training samples. This node is also added to H^+, with a connection weight of $(1/2)^2 = 1/4$ from the hidden node to the output node. The resulting state of the network is illustrated in figure 4.9(b). Even though the output of this new node is incorrect for the training sample $(-1, 1)$, note that the first hidden node carries greater weight, so that the net input to the outermost node of the network is $0.5 - 0.25 = 0.25 > 0$ when the pattern $(-1, 1)$ is presented to the network.

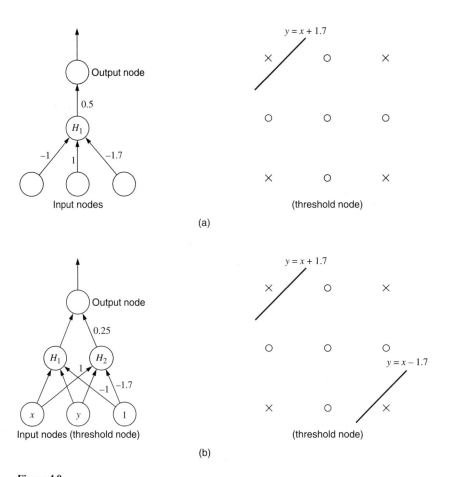

Figure 4.9
Marchand's algorithm applied to the corner isolation problem: (a) state of the network when the first hidden node, H_1, is added; (b) state of the network when the first and second hidden nodes (H_1 and H_2) are added.

For the third hidden node to be added, the training set is

$$T_2^+ = \{(-1, -1), (1, 1)\}$$

$$T_2^- = T_1^- = \{(-1, 0), (0, -1), (0, 1), (1, 0), (0, 0)\}.$$

The trained node chosen may correspond to the equation $y = x + 0.1$, with the hidden node having an output of 1 for $(-1, 0)$ and $(0, 1)$, and an output of 0 for patterns in T_2^+. This node is added to H^-, with a corresponding outer layer weight of $-1/8$, as shown in

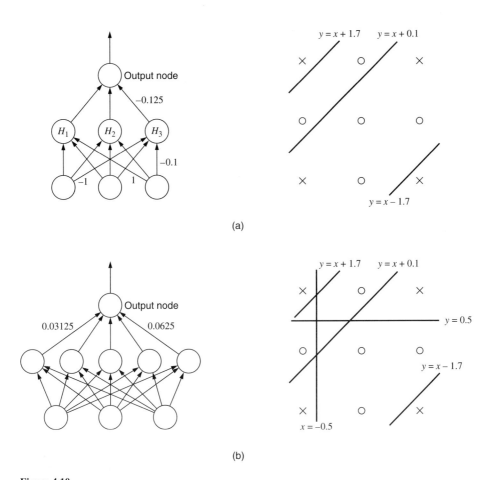

Figure 4.10
Marchand's algorithm applied to the corner isolation problem: (a) with the first three hidden nodes; (b) with all five hidden nodes.

figure 4.10(a). Now $T_3^+ = T_2^+$, and $T_3^- = \{(0, -1), (1, 0), (0, 0)\}$. Two more nodes may be added, resulting in a final network shown in figure 4.10(b).

This example, in which nodes were arbitrarily chosen at each step, illustrates that the algorithm may not derive the smallest sized network for the task: five hidden nodes were used, whereas four would have been sufficient.

4.2.3 Upstart algorithm

Frean (1990) proposed the algorithm described in figure 4.11 for developing a multilayer hierarchical network, successively adding new nodes to the network. The training method

Algorithm Upstart(T_1, T_0);
   T_1 is the set of training samples with desired output 1.
   T_0 is the set of training samples with desired output -1.

   Train a perceptron (a node) α using the pocket algorithm to
   obtain a set of weights that perform as well as possible on
   $T_1 \cup T_0$.

   {The algorithm is terminated if the samples are linearly
   separable, of which a special case is when T_1 or T_0 is empty.}

   If any samples are misclassified by α, **then**
      Let $T_1^+ \subseteq T_1$ and $T_0^+ \subseteq T_0$ be the samples correctly classified
      by α, and $T_1^- \subseteq T_1$, $T_0^- \subseteq T_0$ be the samples misclassified by α.
      Apply the algorithm recursively to develop two networks:
      $N_1 :=$ Upstart(T_1^-, T_0);
      $N_0 :=$ Upstart(T_0^-, T_1);
      Let $MAX := \max_{p \in T_1 \cup T_0} | \sum_k w_k i_k^p |$,
      where w_k is the weight connecting the kth input to α,
      and i_k^p is the kth input of pattern p.
      1. Add a connection with weight $w_{\alpha, N_1} = MAX$ from the
         output node of N_1 to the current node α;
      2. Add a connection with weight $w_{\alpha, N_0} = -MAX$ from the
         output node of N_0 to α.

Figure 4.11
Upstart algorithm; each node in the adaptively evolved network computes a step function whose output $\in \{1, -1\}$.

used to train each node is the pocket algorithm, which misclassifies some of the samples, in general. Frean's algorithm develops additional *subnets* for these misclassified samples. At each step of the algorithm, additional subnets are added closer to the lower levels of a given network, with each subnet operating exclusively on one subset of misclassified samples.

This algorithm is guaranteed to terminate because every recursive call to the Upstart algorithm is invoked with a smaller number of training samples. Assuming a scenario in which the samples from different classes are completely randomly distributed, we would expect that each node successfully classifies at least half the samples, implying that the number of layers in the resulting neural network is at most logarithmic in the number of training samples. Note that the resulting network consists of several layers, and connections exist to a node at layer ℓ only from the nodes at layer $(\ell - 1)$ and layer 0 (inputs). The progress of the algorithm is illustrated in terms of network development in figure 4.12, and data partitioning in figure 4.13.

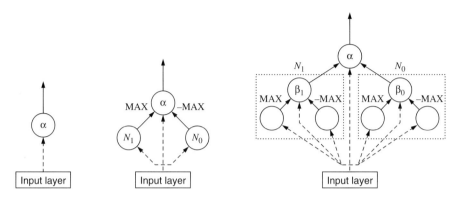

Figure 4.12
Network development using the Upstart algorithm.

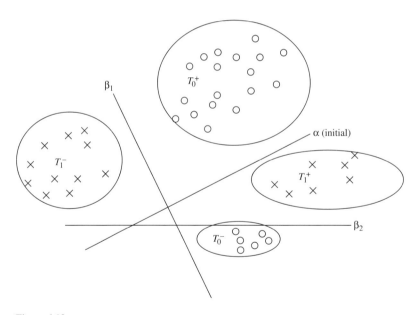

Figure 4.13
Tasks accomplished by each node in the upper layers of the network developed using the Upstart algorithm. Crosses indicate samples with desired output 1, and circles indicate samples with desired output −1.

We now show by induction that the Upstart algorithm is guaranteed to achieve perfect classification (assuming the samples of different classes are separable using some number of hyperplanes). For the induction base, note that the result follows from the correctness of the pocket algorithm if the training samples are linearly separable, of which a special case is when T_0 or T_1 is empty. Under the induction hypothesis that each of N_0 and N_1 achieve perfect classification on the data on which they are invoked, the induction step consists of showing that the larger network consisting of α, N_0, and N_1 achieves perfect classification. This is done by considering different possible cases for any input sample i.

• Let $i \in T_1^+$, i.e., the net input to α must have been positive even before N_0 and N_1 were generated and trained. After training these latter subnets, the contribution to the net input of α from N_0 is $(-\text{MAX})(-1)= \text{MAX}$, since N_0 had been correctly trained. The contribution to the net input of α from N_1 is either MAX or $-\text{MAX}$. In either case, the new net input to α = initial net input $+\text{MAX} \pm\text{MAX} \geq$ initial net input ≥ 0. The output of the entire network is hence correct for all samples in T_1^+. An almost identical argument can be constructed for samples in T_0^+.

• Let $i \in T_1^-$, i.e., the net input to α must have been negative before N_0 and N_1 were generated and trained. After training these latter subnets, the contribution to the net input of α from N_0 is $(-\text{MAX})(-1)= \text{MAX}$, and the contribution from N_1 is MAX. The new net input to α = initial net input $+\text{MAX} +\text{MAX} \geq 0$ since initial net input magnitude is less than MAX. The output of the entire network is hence correct for all samples in T_1^-. An almost identical argument can be constructed for samples in T_0^-.

The Upstart algorithm can be extended to introduce a small network module at a time, instead of a single node (Anton, 1994). This variation is called the "block-start" algorithm and has been found to result in superior performance on some examples.

EXAMPLE 4.2 Upstart algorithm applied to the corner isolation problem   We now illustrate the operation of the Upstart algorithm on the corner isolation described earlier, with the following set of training patterns, shown in figure 4.8.

$T_1 = \{(-1,\ 1),\ (-1,\ -1),\ (1,\ 1),\ (1,\ -1)\}$

$T_0 = \{(-1,\ 0),\ (0,\ -1),\ (0,\ 1),\ (1,\ 0),\ (0,\ 0)\}$

Applying the pocket algorithm results in a node such as that corresponding to the line $x = -0.5$, illustrated in figure 4.14(a).

The misclassified samples are in $T_1^- = \{(1,1),\ (1,-1)\}$ and $T_0^- = \{(-1,0)\}$, while the correctly classified samples are in $T_1^+ = \{(-1,1),\ (-1,-1)\}$ and $T_0^+ = \{(1,0),\ (0,0),$

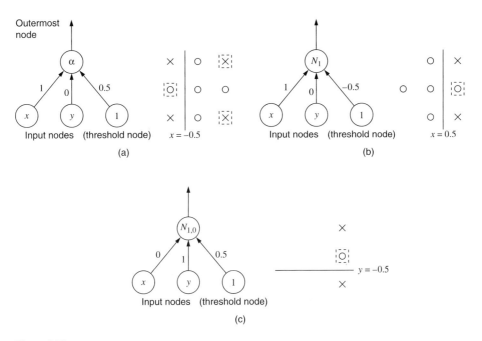

Figure 4.14
Upstart algorithm applied to the corner isolation problem: (a) the outermost node; (b) the first node for N_1; (c) the first node for $N_{1,0}$.

$(0, -1)$, $(0, 1)\}$. The Upstart algorithm is now recursively called, generating the networks $N_1 := \text{Upstart}(T_1^-, T_0)$ and $N_0 := \text{Upstart}(T_0^-, T_1)$.

The problem to be solved by N_1 is illustrated in figure 4.14(b), and one possible choice for the outermost node of this network, obtained by the pocket algorithm, corresponds to the equation $x = 0.5$ with the least number of misclassifications.

For this recursive invocation, $T_0^- = \{(1, 0)\}$ contains one misclassified sample, leading to yet another recursive call $N_{1,0} = \text{Upstart}(\{(1, 0)\}, \{(1, -1), (1, 1)\})$, for which one possible solution obtained by the pocket algorithm corresponds to the equation $y = -0.5$, illustrated in figure 4.14(c).

Since the samples in $N_{1,0}$ were not linearly separable, one more level of recursion is necessitated: $N_{1,0,0} = \text{Upstart}(\{(1, 1)\}, \{(0, 0)\})$, which is finally solved by the equation $y = 0.5$.

Similarly, a sequence of recursive calls occurs for N_0, and the final solution is illustrated in figure 4.15. For the weights on the connections from subnetworks to higher level nodes,

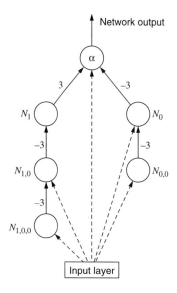

Figure 4.15
Upstart algorithm applied to the corner isolation problem: the entire network.

we choose $MAX = 3$, since $|x| \leq 1$, $|y| \leq 1$, and $|w| \leq 1$ for each weight chosen using the pocket algorithm at various levels of recursion, so that $|w_x x + w_y y + w_0| \leq 3$.

4.2.4 Neural Tree

The "neural tree" approach of Sirat and Nadal (1990) also develops a tree-structured network, but the nodes in the network resemble decision nodes in a decision tree instead of directly modifying the output of a higher level node. Each node in the decision tree can be thought of as asking a yes/no question: the left or right subtree is selected based on the answer (1 or 0). Figure 4.16 illustrates the close resemblance of neural trees with the Upstart algorithm.

   In this algorithm, one perceptron examines only the training samples for which the parent node output is 1, while a sibling node is used to make the best possible decision for the training samples for which the parent node output is 0. We emphasize that the tree is a decision tree, and that the only connections in the neural network sense are from the system inputs to each node; weights to each node are trained using the LMS or pocket algorithm.

   EXAMPLE 4.3 Neural tree algorithm applied to the corner isolation problem   We now illustrate the operation of the neural tree algorithm on the corner isolation problem described

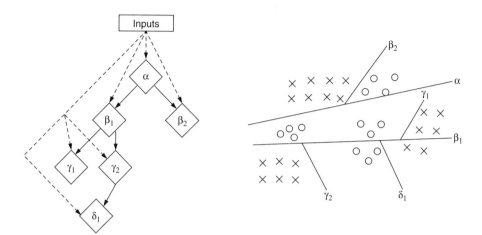

Figure 4.16
Neural tree approach.

earlier, with the following set of training patterns, shown in figure 4.8.

Class I: $\{(-1, 1), (-1, -1), (1, 1), (1, -1)\}$

Class II: $\{(-1, 0), (0, -1), (0, 1), (1, 0), (0, 0)\}$

The first step, applying the pocket algorithm to the entire data, results in a node α similar to that shown in figure 4.14. The left subtree of the neural tree must attempt to separate $B_1 = \{(-1, 0), (-1, -1), (-1, 1)\}$, for which node α generates the output 0, while the right subtree must separate $B_2 = \{(0, 0), (0, -1), (0, 1), (1, 0), (1, 1), (1, -1)\}$, for which node α generates the output 1. The pocket algorithm applied on B_1 results in a node β_1 corresponding to the equation $y = 0.5$, as illustrated in figure 4.17(a), which is unable to separate the samples completely.

The left subtree of the β_1 node must separate $C_1 = \{(-1, 0), (-1, -1)\}$, using a node γ_1, as illustrated in figure 4.17(b) whereas the right child of β_1 has no work left, since the corresponding data set $\{(-1, 1)\}$ contains only samples of a single class. Since the node γ_1 is successful in separating samples from the two classes in C_1, this subtree is not elaborated further.

Similarly, the pocket algorithm cannot classify correctly all samples in B_2, and it is necessary to elaborate the neural decision tree for a few more levels. The final result is indicated in figure 4.18.

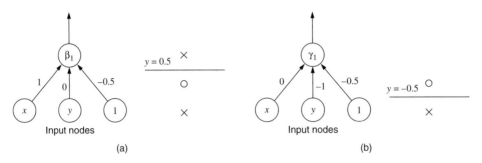

Figure 4.17
Neural tree algorithm applied to the corner isolation problem: (a) Line $y = 0.5$ is represented by the node β_1, which attempts to separate B_1, the subset of the training set for which root node α generates the output 0. (b) Line $y = -0.5$ is represented by the node γ_1, which attempts to separate C_1, the subset of the training set for which node β_1 generates the output 1.

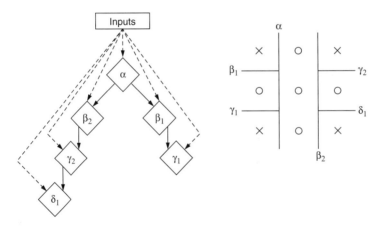

Figure 4.18
Neural tree algorithm applied to the corner isolation problem: the final decision tree.

4.2.5   Cascade correlation

Fahlman and Lebiere (1990) proposed the *cascade correlation* algorithm that allows a network structure to develop according to the requirements of a problem. This algorithm has two important features: (1) the cascade architecture development, and (2) correlation learning. Unlike the upstart algorithm, hidden nodes are added at the outer layers, not the inner layers; unlike the neural tree, the final decision is made only at the outermost nodes, not at the leaves of a tree. Connections from input nodes to outer hidden layer nodes may

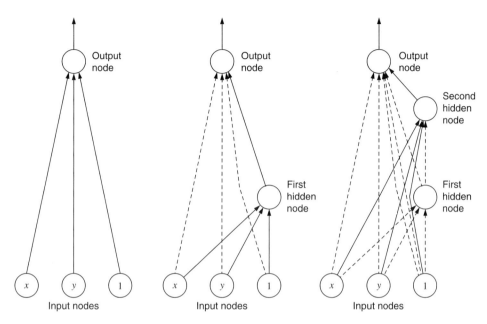

Figure 4.19
Cascade correlation algorithm applied to the corner isolation problem: solid lines indicate connection weights being modified, at different stages in network development.

exist, so that the architecture is not strictly feedforward. Unlike most other algorithms, a correlation measure is used as the training criterion.

In the cascade architecture development process, outer layers of hidden nodes are successively added to a steadily growing layered neural network until performance is judged adequate. The network begins with the input layer and an output layer, and at each step new hidden nodes are introduced between the old hidden nodes and the output layer, as illustrated in figure 4.19. The result of this network growth process is a layered network, with connections to each new node from all input nodes and pre-existing hidden nodes. There are connections from every input node and every hidden node to each output node. Each node may employ a non-linear node function such as the hyperbolic tangent, whose output lies in the closed interval $[-1.0, \ 1.0]$.

Although it is possible to train weights using the LMS rule, Fahlman and Lebiere report better results using the Quickprop learning algorithm (described in chapter 3). When a node is added, its input weights are trained first. Then all the weights on the connections to the output layer are trained while leaving other weights unchanged. Even if the resulting network contains a large number of nodes, the algorithm is much faster than backpropagation, since only a small number of weights are being trained at any given moment. Fahlman and Lebiere also suggest that several different nodes (in a "pool") can be trained simultaneously at a given moment, in parallel, and all but the best discarded.

Weights to each new hidden node are trained to maximize covariance with current network error, i.e., to maximize

$$S(\mathbf{w}_{new}) = \sum_{k=1}^{K} \left| \sum_{p=1}^{P} (x_{new,p} - \bar{x}_{new})(E_{k,p} - \bar{E}_k) \right|$$

where $\mathbf{w}_{new}$ is the vector of weights to the new node from all the pre-existing input and hidden units, $x_{new,p}$ is the output of the new node for the pth input, $E_{k,p}$ is the error of the kth output node for the pth sample before the new node is added, and $\bar{x}_{new}$ and $\bar{E}_k$ are the averages of $x_{new,p}$ and $E_{k,p}$ over the training set.

The use of the absolute value inside the outer summation allows the network to attempt to maximize the magnitude of the hidden node's covariance with each output node error; the sign of $\sum_p (x_p - \bar{x})(E_{k,p} - \bar{E}_k)$ will determine the sign of the weight on the connection from this hidden node to the kth output node. If S is maximized, then we expect that the variations of x_p from $\bar{x}$ will mirror the variations of the errors $E_{k,p}$ from $\bar{E}_k$. By adjusting the weight on the connection to the kth output node, we ensure that the overall error is reduced significantly. S is maximized using a gradient ascent rule, updating each weight $w_i \in \mathbf{w}_{new}$ by the rule

$$\Delta w_i = \eta \frac{\delta S}{\delta w_i} = \eta \sum_k \sum_p S_k (E_{k,p} - \bar{E}_k) f'_p I_{i,p}$$

where $I_{i,p}$ is the kth external input for the pth pattern, S_k is the sign of the correlation between the node's value and the kth network output, η is a learning rate constant, and f'_p is the derivative of the node's activation function with respect to its net input, evaluated at the pth pattern.

EXAMPLE 4.4 Cascade correlation algorithm applied to the corner isolation problem   We now illustrate the operation of the cascade correlation algorithm on the corner isolation problem described earlier and shown in figure 4.8. The hidden nodes were chosen to have sigmoid node functions whose output $\in [-0.5, 0.5]$, with weights trained by the Quickprop algorithm, while the outermost node computed a linear node function. The network performance without any hidden nodes left much to be desired, with four misclassification errors. Addition of the first hidden node reduced the number of misclassified patterns to two, and perfect classification was obtained on adding the second hidden node. The network development process is illustrated in figure 4.19.

4.2.6   Tiling algorithm

The tiling algorithm, proposed by Mézard and Nadal (1989), creates a strictly feedforward network in which connections exist from each layer only to the immediately succeeding layer. Within each new layer, nodes are successively added until every pair of samples of different classes can be differentiated by some node in that layer. Each layer is constructed in such a way that if two samples i_1, i_2 belong to different classes, then some node in the layer produces different outputs for i_1 and i_2. The representations of each such layer are then considered to be "faithful" to the desired task; if this were not the case, subsequent layers of nodes would be incapable of distinguishing between samples of different classes (i.e., there will be two samples of different classes for which the network outputs will be the same).

Each subsequent layer will have fewer nodes than the preceding layer, until there is only one node in the outermost layer for the two-class classification problem. This ensures termination.

The process of adding nodes in a given layer is called "tiling." First, a "master" unit is trained, using the pocket algorithm, to perform the best possible dichotomization on its inputs from the preceding layer. Then, additional "ancillary" units are added one after another, attempting to separate the remaining samples of different classes that could not be separated by the units added so far to that layer. Network development using the tiling algorithm is illustrated in figure 4.20.

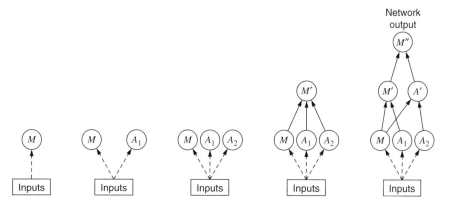

Figure 4.20
The tiling algorithm: progressive development of a three-layer feedforward network. M indicates the master unit in each layer, A', A_1 and A_2 label ancillary units.

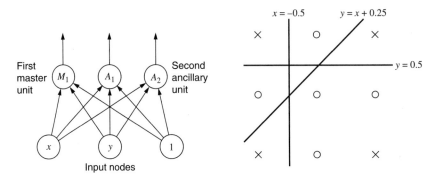

Figure 4.21
Tiling algorithm applied to the corner isolation problem: the first master unit and two ancillary units.

EXAMPLE 4.5 Tiling algorithm applied to the corner isolation problem   We now illustrate the operation of the tiling algorithm on the corner isolation described earlier, with the following set of training patterns, shown in figure 4.8.

Class I: $\{(-1, 1), (-1, -1), (1, 1), (1, -1)\}$

Class II: $\{(-1, 0), (0, -1), (0, 1), (1, 0), (0, 0)\}$

We assume each node is a bipolar threshold unit, associated with a step function whose output $\in \{-1, 1\}$. The master unit for the first layer, if trained by the pocket algorithm, results in the α unit obtained by the neural tree or upstart algorithms, shown in figure 4.14, representing an equation such as $x = -0.5$. The first ancillary unit is then trained to distinguish $\{(-1, 0)\}$ from $\{(-1, -1), (-1, 1)\}$, and to distinguish $\{(1, 1), (1, -1)\}$ from $\{(0, 0), (0, 1), (1, 0), (0, -1)\}$. The pocket algorithm may accomplish part of this task by generating weights corresponding to the equation $y = 0.5$; this node becomes the first ancillary unit A_1 shown in figure 4.21.

The next ancillary units must be trained to separate

- $\{(-1, 0)\}$ from $\{(-1, -1)\}$,
- $\{(1, 1)\}$ from $\{(0, 1)\}$, and
- $\{(1, -1)\}$ from $\{(0, 0), (0, 1), (-1, 0)\}$.

Ancillary unit A_2 that represents the equation $y = x + 0.25$, depicted in figure 4.21, is added to the network but is still unable to complete the task, and the next ancillary unit A_3 must distinguish $\{(1, -1)\}$ from $\{(0, 0), (0, 1), (-1, 0)\}$. The weights of A_3 are adjusted until it represents an equation such as $y = x - 1.5$, which succeeds in this last task.

A new layer of nodes must now be added. The first layer transforms the original two-dimensional training samples into a four-dimensional space, representing the outputs of

M_1, A_1, A_2, and A_3 for each training sample. The transformation is as follows, where the first four samples belong to one class and the rest belong to the other class.

$$(1, 1) \rightarrow (1, 1, 1, -1)$$
$$(1, -1) \rightarrow (1, -1, 1, 1)$$
$$(-1, 1) \rightarrow (-1, 1, -1, -1)$$
$$(-1, -1) \rightarrow (-1, -1, 1, -1)$$

$$(1, 0) \rightarrow (1, -1, 1, -1)$$
$$(0, -1) \rightarrow (1, -1, 1, -1)$$
$$(0, 0) \rightarrow (1, -1, 1, -1)$$
$$(0, 1) \rightarrow (1, 1, -1, -1)$$
$$(-1, 0) \rightarrow (-1, -1, -1, -1)$$

We observe that some samples belonging to the latter class have identical four-dimensional representations; however, no two samples belonging to opposite classes have the same four-dimensional representation. The samples belonging to the two classes are now linearly separable, and a single master unit at the second layer is sufficient to complete the classification task, and no ancillary units are needed in the second layer. The resulting network is shown in figure 4.22.

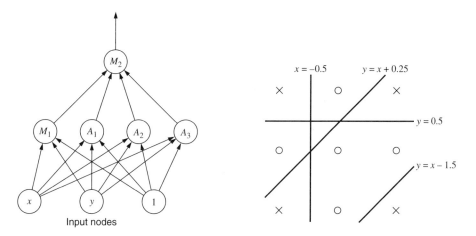

Figure 4.22
Tiling algorithm applied to the corner isolation problem: the final network, with two layers.

4.3 Prediction Networks

Prediction problems constitute a special subclass of function approximation problems, in which the values of variables need to be determined from values at previous instants. In this section, we discuss two classes of neural networks that have been used for prediction tasks: recurrent networks and feedforward networks.

4.3.1 Recurrent networks

Recurrent neural networks contain connections from output nodes to hidden layer and/or input layer nodes, and they allow interconnections between nodes of the same layer, particularly between the nodes of hidden layers. Several kinds of recurrent networks have been proposed, with variations depending upon the nature of the problem addressed. In this section, we study recurrent networks that solve function approximation problems, such as forecasting and control; later chapters describe recurrent network models that have been used for problems such as pattern association and optimization.

Training algorithms for recurrent networks have been presented by several researchers, including Jordan (1986); Rumelhart, Hinton, and Williams (1986); Pineda (1989); Williams and Zipser (1989); and Elman (1990). The procedure proposed by Rumelhart, Hinton, and Williams (1986) is essentially the same as the backpropagation algorithm, and derives from viewing recurrent networks as feedforward networks with a large number of layers. Each layer is thought of as representing a time delay in the network. Using this approach, the fully connected neural network with three nodes, shown in figure 4.23(a), is considered equivalent to a feedforward neural network with k hidden layers, for some value of k, as shown in figure 4.23(b). Since a unique weight is associated with any connection in the recurrent network, connection weights in the "equivalent" feedforward network cannot be completely arbitrary and weights connecting nodes from one layer to the next are identical for all layers of weights, i.e., $w_{i,j}^{(\ell,\ell-1)} = w_{i,j}^{(\ell-1,\ell-2)}$. An alternative training procedure was proposed by Williams and Zipser (1989). The network model relevant for Williams and Zipser's algorithm contains hidden nodes, as illustrated in figure 4.24. The more general procedure, described in figure 4.25, obtains the appropriate weight changes in a natural way.

The basic outline of Williams and Zipser's algorithm is as follows. The net input to the kth node consists of two components: the first is due to the recurrent connections from other nodes, and the second comes from the external inputs to the network.

$$\text{net}_k(t) = \sum_{\ell \in U} w_{k\ell} o_\ell(t) + \sum_{\ell \in I} w_{k\ell} i_\ell(t) = \sum_{\ell \in U \cup I} w_{k\ell} z_\ell(t) \qquad (4.3)$$

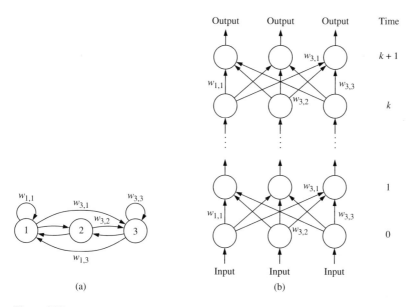

Figure 4.23
(a) Fully connected recurrent neural network with three nodes; (b) Equivalent feedforward version, for Rumelhart's training procedure.

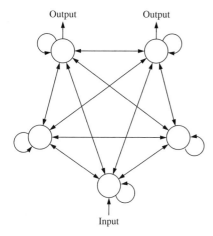

Figure 4.24
Recurrent network with hidden nodes, to which Williams and Zipser's training procedure can be applied.

Algorithm Recurrent Supervised Training;
   Start with randomly chosen weights;
   Let time $t = 0$, and assume the initial condition
   $$\frac{\partial o_k(0)}{\partial w_{i,j}} = 0, \quad \forall\ i, j, k.$$
   while MSE is unsatisfactory and computational bounds are not
      exceeded, **do**
         Compute the output of each node at the next time instant:
         $$o_k(t+1) = f\left(\sum_{\ell \in U \cup I} w_{k,\ell} z_\ell(t)\right)$$
         Compute the error $\sum_k (d_k(t) - o_k(t))^2$,
            for nodes $k \in U$ with a specified target value $d_k(t)$.
         Modify the weights:
         $$\Delta w_{i,j}(t) = \eta \sum_{k \in U} (d_k(t) - o_k(t)) \frac{\partial o_k(t)}{\partial w_{i,j}}$$
         For use in the next iteration, compute
         $$\frac{\partial o_k(t+1)}{\partial w_{i,j}} = f_k'(\text{net}_k(t)) \left[\sum_{\ell \in U \cup I} w_{i,j} \frac{\partial z_k(t)}{\partial w_{i,j}} + \delta_{i,k} z_j(t) \right]$$
         Increment time counter t;
   end-while.

Figure 4.25
Supervised training algorithm for a recurrent network, proposed by Williams and Zipser (1989).

   In equation 4.3, I denotes input nodes, U denotes nodes that generate outputs, $i_\ell(t)$ is the ℓth external input to the network at time t, $o_\ell(t)$ is the output of the ℓth node at time t, and $z(t)$ is used to denote the vector of both external inputs and node outputs. The main difference between the operation of a recurrent network and a feedforward network is that the output of each node depends on the outputs of other nodes at the previous instant

$$o_k(t+1) = f(\text{net}_k(t)) \tag{4.4}$$

where f denotes the node function (e.g., a sigmoid). If d_k is the desired output of the kth node, the performance measure is the usual squared error sum, summing over nodes for which desired output values are specified:

$$E(t) = \sum_k (d_k(t) - o_k(t))^2 = \sum_k e_k(t)^2. \tag{4.5}$$

Weights are updated by performing gradient descent on E,

$$\Delta w_{i,j}(t) = -\eta \frac{\partial E(t)}{\partial w_{i,j}}, \tag{4.6}$$

where η represents the learning rate. Using the chain rule, this weight update simplifies to:

$$\Delta w_{i,j}(t) = \eta \sum_{k \in U} (d_k(t) - o_k(t)) \frac{\partial o_k(t)}{\partial w_{i,j}}. \tag{4.7}$$

The partial derivative of o_k is obtained from equations 4.4 and 4.3 to be

$$\frac{\partial o_k(t+1)}{\partial w_{i,j}} = f_k'(\text{net}_k(t)) \left[\sum_{\ell \in U \cup I} w_{i,j} \frac{\partial z_k(t)}{\partial w_{i,j}} + \delta_{i,k} z_j(t) \right]$$

where $\delta_{i,k}$ denotes the Kronecker delta with $\delta_{i,k} = 1$ if $i = k$, and 0 otherwise. These weight changes are repeatedly applied until the termination criterion is satisfied, in conjunction with the initial condition

$$\frac{\partial o_k(0)}{\partial w_{i,j}} = 0$$

for all possible nodes.

If each node function f is the sigmoid function $\mathcal{S}(u) = (1 + \exp(-u))^{-1}$, then computation is straightforward since the derivative satisfies the equation

$$S'(\text{net}_k(t)) = o_k(t+1)[1 - o_k(t+1)]$$

as in the case of standard backpropagation.

4.3.2   Feedforward networks for forecasting

Simple recurrent networks have been shown to be inadequate for several prediction tasks, possibly because simple gradient descent procedures do not perform well in complex prediction tasks characterized by the existence of many local optima. We now examine other neural networks that have been used successfully for solving some problems in which values for a variable need to be predicted from past values for that variable. The generic network model, shown in figure 4.26, consists of a preliminary preprocessing component that transforms an external input vector $x(t)$ into a preprocessed vector $\bar{x}(t)$ that is supplied to a feedforward network. The feedforward network is trained to compute the desired output value for a specific input $\bar{x}(t)$. Note that $\bar{x}$ and x may be of different dimensionality. The preprocessing component may implement a "short-term memory," and the feedforward network is the "predictor" component, following the terminology of Mozer (1994).

In chapter 3, we discussed an example of a prediction task where $x(t)$ was to be predicted from $x(t-1), x(t-2)$. In this simple case, x at time t consists of a single input

Figure 4.26
Generic neural network model for prediction.

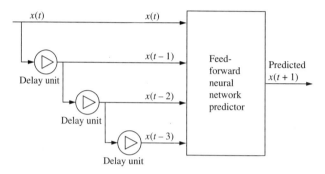

Figure 4.27
Tapped delay-line neural network (TDNN) with three delay elements.

$x(t)$, and $\bar{x}$ at time t consists of the vector $(x(t-1), x(t-2))$ supplied as input to the feedforward network. For this example, preprocessing consists merely of storing past values of the variable and supplying them to the network along with the latest value. Such a model is sometimes called a *tapped delay-line* neural network (TDNN), consisting of a sequence of delay units or buffers, and with the values of variables at recent instants being supplied to the feedforward predictor component. The architecture of this model is depicted in figure 4.27. Weights in the network are often trained by algorithms such as backpropagation and its variants.

Many preprocessing transformations for prediction problems can be described as a convolution of the input sequence with a "kernel" function c_i. If there exists a kernel c_i for each $i = 1, 2, \ldots, n$, then the ith component of the transformed vector is given by the equation

$$\bar{x}_i(t) = \sum_{\tau=0}^{t} c_i(t-\tau)x(\tau). \tag{4.8}$$

The TDNN with d delay elements is a special case of equation 4.8, in which the kernel functions are described by

$$c_i(j) = \begin{cases} 1 & \text{for } j = i \\ 0 & \text{otherwise .} \end{cases}$$

If the input consists of $x(t)$, then the preprocessor produces a $(d+1)$-dimensional vector $(\bar{x}_0(t), \ldots, \bar{x}_d(t))$ where $\bar{x}_i(t) = x(t-i)$, $i = 1, \ldots, d$.

For another class of memories called *exponential trace* memories, $c_i(j) = (1 - \mu_i)\mu_i^j$, where $\mu_i \in [-1, 1]$. In such models, more recent inputs have greater influence than older inputs, and the transformed input variables can be updated by the incremental rule

$$\bar{x}_i(t) = (1 - \mu_i)x_i(t) + \mu_i\bar{x}_i(t-1), \tag{4.9}$$

with $\bar{x}_i(0)$ assumed to equal 0. This rule is a special case of a moving average model known as MA(1) in the statistical literature.

DeVries and Principe (1992) propose a *gamma memory* model that generalizes both the delay-line and exponential models, allowing the user to vary *depth* (the length of time for which information of the past is preserved by the memory model) as well as *resolution* (how well the information regarding specific memory elements can be accurately retrieved by the memory model). The kernel function for discrete-time gamma memories is

$$c_i(j) = \begin{cases} \binom{j}{l_i}(1 - \mu_i)^{l_i+1}\mu_i^{j-l_i} & \text{if } j \geq l_i \\ 0 & \text{otherwise} \end{cases} \tag{4.10}$$

where delay l_i is a non-negative integer and $\mu_i \in [0, 1]$. This model reduces to an exponential memory when $l_i = 0$, and to a delay line memory when μ_i approaches 0. The transformed input variables are updated in gamma memories by the following equation.

$$\bar{x}_{\mu,j}(t) = (1 - \mu)\bar{x}_{\mu,j-1}(t-1) + \mu\bar{x}_{\mu,j}(t-1)$$

with

$$\bar{x}_{\mu,-1}(t) = x(t+1) \text{ for } t \geq 0, \text{ and } \bar{x}_{\mu,j}(0) = 0 \text{ for } j \geq 0. \tag{4.11}$$

Note that new parameters are introduced by these equations, the appropriate choice of which may not be easy to determine.

4.4 Radial Basis Functions

Most node functions considered so far are monotonically non-increasing functions of their net inputs. This is not the best choice for some problems encountered in practice, an example of which is illustrated in figure 4.28, where all samples of one class are clustered together. Although it is possible to solve this problem using a one-hidden-layer feedforward network with sigmoid functions, the nature of the problem calls for a different, simpler solution. With a traditional feedforward network using sigmoid functions, perhaps

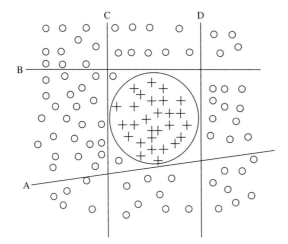

Figure 4.28
Two-class problem with a single cluster; the backpropagation method may implement lines A, B, C, D using four hidden nodes.

four or five hidden nodes may be required for the problem shown in figure 4.28. On the other hand, only one node would be sufficient to discriminate between the two classes if we could use a node function that approximates the circle. This is one motivation for a different class of node functions, especially for higher dimensional problems.

DEFINITION: A function is *radially symmetric* (or is an RBF) if its output depends on the distance of the input sample (vector) from another stored vector. Neural networks whose node functions are radially symmetric functions are referred to as *RBF-nets*.

Each commonly used radial basis function ρ is a non-increasing function of a distance measure u which is its only argument, with $\rho(u_1) \geq \rho(u_2)$ whenever $u_1 < u_2$. Function ρ is applied to the Euclidean distance $u = \|\mu - i\|$, between the "center" or stored vector μ and the input vector i. Vector norms other than the Euclidean distance may also be used, e.g., the generalized distance norm $(\mu_i - x_j)'A'A(\mu_i - x_j)$ for some square matrix A, suggested by Poggio and Girosi (1990). Generalized distance norms are useful, because all coordinates of a vector input may not be equally important. But the main difficulty with this measure is in determining an appropriate A matrix.

In RBF networks, the *Gaussian*, described by the equation

$$\rho_g(u) \propto e^{-(u/c)^2},$$

is the most widely used radially symmetric function. Other radially symmetric functions may also be used, such as Hardy's *inverse quadric*

$\rho_2(u) = (c^2 + u^2)^\beta$, for $\beta < 0$

or the *hyperspheric*

$$\rho_s(u) = \begin{cases} 1 & \text{if } u \le c \\ 0 & \text{if } u > c. \end{cases}$$

The hyperspheric defines a fixed radius within which the output of the node is high, and outside which the node output is low. Our interest is in problems that require the use of many nodes, each of which uses a radially symmetric node function. RBF-nets are generally called upon for use in function approximation problems, particularly for interpolation.

In many function approximation problems, we need to determine the behavior of the function at a new input, given the behavior of the function at training samples. Classical methods of solving such problems often involve linear interpolation. In the simplest case of linear interpolation for one-dimensional input samples, the values of a function f are given at points x_1 and x_2 and we need to determine the value of f at a point x_0 that lies between x_1 and x_2. Interpolation yields

$$f(x_0) = f(x_1) + (f(x_2) - f(x_1))(x_0 - x_1)/(x_2 - x_1)$$

which simplifies to

$$\frac{(D_1^{-1}f(x_1) + D_2^{-1}f(x_2))}{(D_1^{-1} + D_2^{-1})}$$

where D_1 and D_2 are the distances of x_0 from x_1 and x_2, respectively. In general, hyperplane segments connect nearby points, so that the output value corresponding to a new n-dimensional input sample is determined entirely by the P_0 input samples that "surround" it. For interpolation, the new sample lies inside a convex space bounded by these P_0 training samples, since it is expected that the properties of a point can be determined by neighboring points, and that distant points are relatively irrelevant. The output is then of the form

$$\frac{(D_1^{-1}f(\boldsymbol{x}_1) + D_2^{-1}f(\boldsymbol{x}_2) + D_{P_0}^{-1}f(\boldsymbol{x}_{P_0}))}{(D_1^{-1} + D_2^{-1} + \cdots + D_{P_0}^{-1})}$$

where D_p is the Euclidean distance of the new sample from the training sample $\boldsymbol{x}_p$, for $1 \le p \le P_0$, and $f(\boldsymbol{x}_p)$ is the desired output value for input $\boldsymbol{x}_p$. This is illustrated in figure 4.29.

If nodes in an RBF-net with linear radial basis node functions $\rho_0(D) = D^{-1}$ corresponding to each of the training samples $\boldsymbol{x}_p$ for $p = 1, \ldots, P_0$ surround the new input $\boldsymbol{x}$,

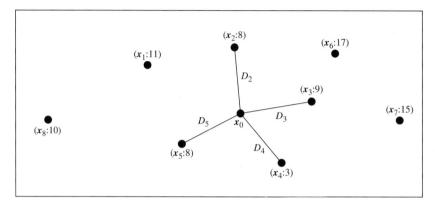

Figure 4.29
An interpolation problem: each input sample x_j is labelled with the function value at that point, e.g., $(x_5 : 8)$ indicates that $f(x_5) = 8$. Distances (D_j's) to x_0 are indicated for several different input samples. Only the four nearest observations participate in the interpolation at x_0; the interpolated value is $(8D_2^{-1} + 9D_3^{-1} + 3D_4^{-1} + 8D_5^{-1})/(D_2^{-1} + D_3^{-1} + D_4^{-1} + D_5^{-1})$.

the output of the network at x is roughly proportional to

$$\frac{1}{P_0} \sum_p d_p \rho_0(\|x - x_p\|), \tag{4.12}$$

where $d_p = f(x_p)$ is the output corresponding to x_p, the pth pattern. In practice, it is difficult to decide precisely which of the training samples do surround the new input. So it is common practice instead to use the output

$$\frac{1}{P} \sum_{p=1}^{P} d_p \rho(\|x - x_p\|),$$

where $d_1, \ldots, d_P$ are the outputs corresponding to the entire set of training samples, and ρ is any radially symmetric function that decreases monotonically with its argument.

When a new sample is presented, the nature of ρ determines how many training samples affect the output of such an RBF-net: if the value of $\rho(u)$ falls rapidly with increasing u, then the only samples that affect network output are those that are closest to the new sample. On one extreme, if each RBF is valued 0 everywhere except in a small neighborhood, then the RBF-net's output may be 0 for most of the samples in the training set. At the other extreme, if each RBF has the same value everywhere, then the network output is always the arithmetic average of training sample outputs.

The choice of the RBF and its parameters may be varied. Functions such as the Gaussian are described by a mean μ and a variance σ^2, of which μ is naturally chosen to be the mean of some training samples, while the variance may be chosen differently for different Gaussians in the network.

When viewed as a network, the equation

$$o = \frac{1}{P} \sum_{p=1}^{P} d_p \rho(\|\boldsymbol{x} - \boldsymbol{x}_p\|)$$

conveys the idea that there are as many nodes as there are training samples, which implies too large a network to be acceptable. It is preferable to have a smaller number of nodes in exchange for some loss of accuracy in generating correct outputs for all training samples. If all samples that generate the same (or similar) outputs are clustered together, one appropriate modification of the above equation is

$$o = \frac{1}{N} \sum_{i=1}^{N} \varphi_i \rho(\|\boldsymbol{\mu}_i - \boldsymbol{x}\|) \tag{4.13}$$

where N is the number of nodes (or clusters), $\boldsymbol{\mu}_i$ is the center of the ith cluster, and φ_i is the desired mean output of all samples of the ith cluster. Note that φ_i may even be a vector of outputs, as in multiclass classification problems. The appropriate value of N is problem-dependent and not easy to obtain. Another difficult task is to find the values of $\boldsymbol{\mu}_i$ and φ_i, i.e., to accomplish the clustering process; we do not know which samples belong to which clusters. Can this information be obtained by a learning procedure?

For a single sample $\boldsymbol{x}_p$ whose output d_p is known, the error measure is

$$E_p = \left(d_p - o_p\right)^2.$$

If the number of nodes N is fixed, our goal can be to learn the values of the parameters

$$w_1 = \frac{\varphi_1}{N}, \ldots, w_N = \frac{\varphi_N}{N}, \boldsymbol{\mu}_1, \ldots, \boldsymbol{\mu}_N,$$

minimizing

$$E = \sum_{p=1}^{P} E_p = \sum_{p=1}^{P} \left(d_p - o_p\right)^2, \tag{4.14}$$

a Euclidean distance measure that can be minimized in some cases by using gradient descent. From equations 4.13 and 4.14 we observe that

$$\frac{\partial E_p}{\partial w_i} = -2(d_p - o_p)\rho(\|\boldsymbol{x}_p - \boldsymbol{\mu}_i\|). \tag{4.15}$$

Similarly, if $\boldsymbol{\mu}_i = (\mu_{i,1}, \ldots, \mu_{i,n})$ describes the coordinates of the ith node of an RBF-net, then

$$\frac{\partial E_p}{\partial \mu_{i,j}} = 2\left(d_p - o_p\right)\left(-w_i \frac{\partial \rho(\|\boldsymbol{x}_p - \boldsymbol{\mu}_i\|)}{\partial(\boldsymbol{x}_i - \boldsymbol{\mu}_i)^2}\right)\frac{\partial(\boldsymbol{x}_p - \boldsymbol{\mu}_i)^2}{\partial \mu_{i,j}}. \tag{4.16}$$

Since a radially symmetric function remains radially symmetric if its argument is raised to any positive power, we simplify the differentiation step by using a function R such that $R(D^2) = \rho(D)$. This enables us to write

$$\frac{\partial \rho(\|\boldsymbol{x}_p - \boldsymbol{\mu}_i\|)}{\partial\left((\boldsymbol{x}_p - \boldsymbol{\mu}_i)^2\right)} = \frac{\partial\left(R(\boldsymbol{x}_p - \boldsymbol{\mu}_i)^2\right)}{\partial((\boldsymbol{x}_p - \boldsymbol{\mu}_i)^2)} = R'((\boldsymbol{x}_p - \boldsymbol{\mu}_i)^2)$$

and this notation, together with $\partial(\boldsymbol{x}_p - \boldsymbol{\mu}_i)^2/\partial \mu_{i,j} = -2(x_{p,j} - \mu_{i,j})$, implies that

$$\frac{\partial E_p}{\partial \mu_{i,j}} = 4w_i\left(d_p - o_p\right)R'((\boldsymbol{x}_p - \boldsymbol{\mu}_i)^2)(x_{p,j} - \mu_{i,j}). \tag{4.17}$$

Gradient descent demands that, to improve performance, the parameters of the network be updated as follows:

$$\Delta w_i = \eta_i(d_p - o_p)\rho(\|\boldsymbol{x}_p - \boldsymbol{\mu}_i\|) \tag{4.18}$$

and

$$\Delta\mu_{i,j} = -\eta_{i,j}w_i(d_p - o_p)R'(\|\boldsymbol{x}_p - \boldsymbol{\mu}_i\|^2)(x_{p,j} - \mu_{i,j}) \tag{4.19}$$

where the learning rates η_i and $\eta_{i,j}$ may be different for each parameter w_i and $\mu_{i,j}$. These gradient descent rules can be applied to minimize the error function for an RBF-net started with any random choice of parameters.

In particular, when the node function is given by a Gaussian, i.e., when $\rho(u) \propto \exp(-u^2/\sigma^2)$, then $R(D) \propto \exp(-D/\sigma^2)$. Consequently,

$$R'(D) \propto (-1/\sigma^2)\exp(-D/\sigma^2),$$

leading to the specific update rules

$$\Delta w_i = \eta_i(d_p - o_p)\exp(-(\|\boldsymbol{x}_p - \boldsymbol{\mu}_i\|)^2/\sigma^2) \tag{4.20}$$

and

$$\Delta\mu_{i,j} = -\eta_{i,j}w_i(d_p - o_p)(x_{p,j} - \mu_{i,j})\exp(-(\|\boldsymbol{x}_p - \boldsymbol{\mu}_i\|)^2/\sigma^2). \tag{4.21}$$

This learning algorithm implies a considerable amount of computation. An alternative approach for a given set of training data, called *partially off-line training*, is to train the RBF-network in two steps.

1. By using any clustering procedure, we can find "best" estimates of cluster centers ($\boldsymbol{\mu}_i$)'s and also a measure of their spread (σ_i)'s.

2. After substituting for each $\boldsymbol{\mu}_i$ and σ_i, all that remains is to find weights (w_i) that minimize the error function E. The gradient descent algorithm described above may be applied to determine only the weights.

Various alternative approaches for obtaining better or faster values of $\boldsymbol{\mu}_i$'s and σ_i's have been proposed in the literature, e.g., by Saha and Keelar (1992). The training of an RBF network can be on-line or partially on-line and partially off-line. Empirical studies such as those by Botros and Alkeson (1993) suggest that off-line training results in faster and better convergence of the network, at least for some frequently used radial basis functions such as the Gaussian.

EXAMPLE 4.6 RBF networks applied to the corner isolation problem   An RBF network with a single outermost decision node and any number of RBF nodes in the hidden layer can be used to solve the corner isolation problem (illustrated in figure 4.8). The solution obtained depends on the number of RBF nodes chosen at the outset. If a single RBF node is used, its weight vector can be located in the center of the square, and the decision node can be a threshold unit implementing a step function that generates an output of -1 if and only if the level of activation of the RBF node is greater than that caused by the corners of the square, as shown in figure 4.30. If four RBF nodes are used, they can be centered at the various corner samples and chosen to have very low variances, with the network output being 1 if and only if one of the RBF units is significantly activated, as shown in figure 4.31. If five RBF nodes are used, on the other hand, they can be centered at the various non-corner samples and chosen to have very low variances, with the network output being 1 if and only if none of the RBF units is significantly activated, as shown in figure 4.32.

Poggio and Girosi (1990) showed that RBF networks are universal approximators, so that an RBF network with a sufficiently large number of nodes can approximate any real multivariate continuous function on a compact set.

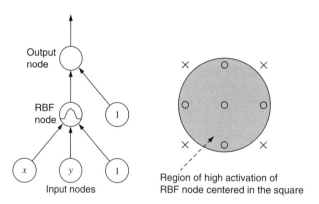

Figure 4.30
RBF networks applied to the corner isolation problem: one RBF node.

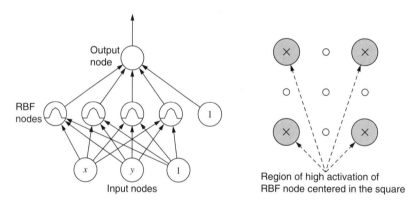

Figure 4.31
RBF networks applied to the corner isolation problem: four RBF nodes.

Platt (1991) has suggested an adaptive network construction algorithm for RBF networks, called the *Resource-Allocation Network*. In this algorithm, when a new input pattern i is supplied to a network, a new RBF node is created in the hidden layer (with $\mu = i$) if i is judged to be sufficiently distant from the centers (μ's) of all existing RBF nodes, and if the network error for i is judged to be unacceptably high.

RBF node functions may be used in conjunction with other learning paradigms, as illustrated in the use of "Growing Cell Structures" for supervised learning, described in chapter 5.

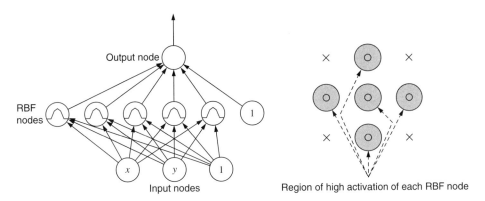

Figure 4.32
RBF networks applied to the corner isolation problem: five RBF nodes.

4.5   Polynomial Networks

The networks examined so far have used node functions that are step functions, sigmoids, or Gaussians. However, many practical problems require computing or approximating functions that are polynomials of the input variables, a task that can require many nodes and extensive training if the aforementioned node functions are employed. For instance, a two-input feedforward network with sigmoid node functions can require considerable training to approximate the function x_1x_2, which is a product of the inputs. This motivates the study of networks whose node functions allow them to directly compute polynomials and functions of polynomials, referred to as *polynomial networks* in this section.

Such a network with a single non-input node is sufficient for a two-class classification task when the surface separating different classes is a quadratic or cubic function, rather than a hyperplane. A polynomial network needed for approximating a quadratic function, for instance, would be much smaller than a network for the same task that contains only sigmoid functions.

The following kinds of polynomial networks have been suggested in the literature:

1. *Higher-order networks* proposed by Giles and Maxwell (1987) contain no hidden layers, but have nodes referred to as *higher-order processing units* that perform complex computations. Such a network is depicted in figure 4.33. A higher-order node applies a non-linear function f (such as a sigmoid) to a polynomial in the input variables, and the resulting node output is

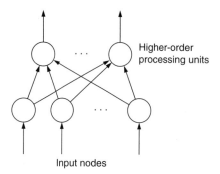

Figure 4.33
Higher-order network with nodes that compute non-linear functions of polynomials of input variables.

$$f\left(w_0 + \sum_{j_1} w_{j_1} i_{j_1} + \sum_{j_1, j_2} w_{j_1, j_2} i_{j_1} i_{j_2} + \dots \sum_{j_1, j_2, \dots, j_k} w_{j_1, j_2, \dots, j_k} i_{j_1} i_{j_2} \dots i_{j_k}\right)$$

where each i_{j_1} is a component of the input vector $\mathbf{i}$. The LMS training algorithm can be applied to train such a network, since it contains no hidden layer.

These networks are considered to be "higher-order," since they (or their subnetworks) compute polynomials whose terms have degree > 1. As in the case of feedforward networks containing sigmoid node functions, these networks are also universal approximators, as implied by a well-known result in real analysis (Rudin, 1964) called the Weierstrass theorem and its generalizations. A special case of the theorem is given below.

THEOREM 4.1 (Weierstrass theorem)   If f is a continuous function on the real interval $[a, b]$, there exists a sequence of real polynomials P_m such that

$$\lim_{m \to \infty} P_m(x) = f(x)$$

uniformly on $[a, b]$.

The main difficulty with higher-order networks is that the number of weights required increases rapidly with the input dimensionality n and polynomial degree k. Even for $k = 2$, the number of weights in the network is quadratic in n. The universal approximation property is lost if we restrict the number of weights by imposing conditions such as $k = 2$ or $k = 3$.

2. *Sigma-pi networks* proposed by Feldman and Ballard (1982) are special cases of higher-order networks, and contain nodes referred to as *sigma-pi* units that apply a non-linear function to sums of weighted products of input variables.

$$f\left(w_0 + \sum_{j_1} w_{j_1} i_{j_1} + \sum_{j_1 \neq j_2} w_{j_1, j_2} i_{j_1} i_{j_2} + \sum_{j_1 \neq j_2 \neq j_3 \neq j_1} w_{j_1, j_2, j_3} i_{j_1} i_{j_2} i_{j_3} + \ldots\right)$$

This model does not allow terms to include powers of input variables, automatically excluding terms such as i_1^2 and $i_1 i_2^2 i_3$. This result can be used to show that sigma-pi networks are not universal approximators.

3. Durbin and Rumelhart (1989) proposed networks with *product units*, each of which computes a product $\Pi_{j=1}^{n} i_j^{p_{j,i}}$, where each $p_{j,i}$ is an integer whose value is to be determined. These networks contain a hidden layer containing some product units and some "ordinary" nodes that apply sigmoids or step functions to their net input. For the ordinary nodes, the weights are adapted during the training process; for the product nodes, weights as well as the exponents p_{ji} (for input variables) are adapted during training. These networks are most appropriate when a function can be expressed in a sum of products form, e.g., for the parity problem when input variables $\in \{-1, 1\}$. The choice of the number of nodes is left to the user, as in other non-adaptive feedforward networks, and the right choice is crucial to the ability of the network to learn successfully. Backpropagation training is used, implying that learning may be slow.

4. A *functional link architecture* (Pao, 1989) conducts linear regression, estimating the weights in $\sum_j w_j \phi_j(i)$, where each "basis function" ϕ_j is chosen from a predefined set of components (such as linear functions, products, and sinusoidal functions). The choice of the right set of components is problem-dependent, and it is not easy to determine *a priori* whether one should use product units or sinusoidal functions for a given problem.

5. *Pi-sigma networks* (PSNs), proposed by Shin and Ghosh (1991), also contain a hidden layer in which each hidden node computes a weighted sum of input components, and the output node computes a product and may also apply a non-linear function such as a sigmoid. Only the weights between the input layer and the hidden layer are adapted during the training process, so that training is much faster than backpropagation. Each hidden node computes the linear function $w_{k,0} + \sum_j w_{k,j} i_j$, and the network output can be expressed as

$$f\left(\prod_k \left(w_{k,0} + \sum_j w_{k,j} i_j\right)\right). \tag{4.22}$$

Figure 4.34 shows a pi-sigma network with three inputs, two nodes in the hidden layer, and one in the output layer, with weights from the hidden layer to the output node fixed at 1.

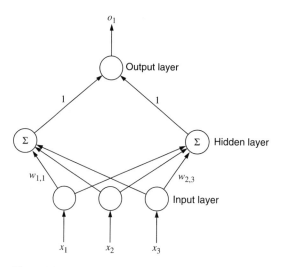

Figure 4.34
A pi-sigma network with three inputs, two nodes in the hidden layer, and one output. Nodes in the hidden layer compute weighted sums while output nodes compute products.

PSNs use fewer weights than higher-order networks, and can be trained quickly using the LMS algorithm. They are not universal approximators, but have been empirically demonstrated to be successful in approximating many smooth functions, in applications such as character recognition.

6. Polynomial networks can also be adaptively developed, growing a network large enough to solve the problem at hand. Shin and Ghosh (1994) proposed *ridge-polynomial networks* (RPNs) with universal approximation capabilities, trained using an adaptive network construction algorithm, and consisting of components that generalize PSNs. A ridge polynomial network computes a function of the form

$$\boldsymbol{i} \cdot \boldsymbol{w}_{1,1} + (\boldsymbol{i} \cdot \boldsymbol{w}_{2,1})(\boldsymbol{i} \cdot \boldsymbol{w}_{2,2}) + \ldots + (\boldsymbol{i} \cdot \boldsymbol{w}_{N,1}) \cdots (\boldsymbol{i} \cdot \boldsymbol{w}_{N,N}) \qquad (4.23)$$

where each input vector $\boldsymbol{i}$ includes the fixed component $i_0 = 1$ and each weight vector includes the corresponding threshold weight. Nodes corresponding to successive terms in equation 4.23 are introduced one after another, with corresponding weights trained as in the case of PSNs. New nodes are introduced if the current network's MSE is unsatisfactory, as long as computational bounds are not exceeded. RPNs are closely related to a statistical method known as *projection pursuit* regression.

4.6 Regularization

Many of the algorithms discussed in this chapter can be unified under the umbrella of *regularization theory*, proposed by Tikhonov (1963). The regularization method of solving problems involves optimizing a function $E + \lambda |P|^2$, where E is the original cost (or error) function, P is a "stabilizer" that incorporates *a priori* problem-specific requirements or constraints, and λ is a constant that controls the relative importance of E and P. Shin and Ghosh (1994) and Mao and Jain (1993) survey applications of regularization theory to neural networks.

Regularization can be implemented either explicitly or implicitly. For example, regularization is explicitly specified by algorithms that introduce terms such as $\lambda \sum_j w_j^2$ (to penalize large magnitude weights) into the cost function being minimized. The training algorithm or the function being optimized is changed, penalizing networks whose "complexity" is high.

• A weight decay term may be introduced into the generalized delta rule, so that the weight change

$$\Delta w = -\eta(\partial E / \partial w) - \lambda w$$

depends on the negative gradient of the mean squared error as well as the current weight. This favors the development of networks with smaller weight magnitudes, and may be considered a special case of the weight change rule

$$\Delta w = -\eta(\partial E / \partial w) - \lambda(\partial C(w) / \partial w)$$

where $C(w)$ is a function of w that attempts to capture the cost associated with using a weight w.

• "Smoothing" penalties may be introduced into the error function, e.g., terms proportional to $|\delta^2 E / \delta w_i^2|$ and other higher-order derivatives of the error function. Such penalties prevent a network's output function from having very high curvature, and may prevent a network from overspecializing on the training data to account for outliers in the data,

Examples of implicit regularization appear in algorithms such as those that introduce artificial noise into training data or connection weights. Reed, Oh, and Marks (1992) have shown that training networks with artificially perturbed data (using Gaussian noise) is equivalent to using a stabilizer that imposes a smoothness constraint on the derivative of the squared error function with respect to the input variables. Similarly, adding random noise to weights during training has been shown by Mao and Jain (1993) to impose a smoothness constraint on the derivatives of the squared error function with respect to the weights. Poggio and Girosi (1990) have shown that radial basis function networks constitute a special case of networks that accomplish regularization.

In section 4.2, we examined various algorithms that attempt to develop a network of the "correct" size for a problem. Barron (1991) posed this as a regularization task in which the stabilizer represents the complexity of the network, a function of the number of parameters and training patterns. In other words, network development is seen as the task of minimizing a combination of the mean squared error and network complexity, with network complexity being a function of the effective number of parameters in a network, shown by Moody (1992) often to be smaller than the number of weights.

4.7   Conclusion

In this chapter, we have presented several variations on the network and learning algorithm discussed in chapter 3.

1. The weight update procedure can be changed from gradient descent, as in Madalines, discussed in section 4.1. Madaline training algorithms measure the error when a node's output is perturbed, in order to determine which weight must change to reduce the error, and in which direction.

2. As discussed in section 4.2, network connectivity, size, and parameters such as momentum and learning rate can be modified on the fly, instead of using arbitrarily predetermined values.

3. The nature of the network architecture may itself be modified to contain cycles, as in recurrent networks discussed in section 4.3.1, which have been used in automatic control and forecasting applications. Section 4.3.2 discusses the general methodology of applying feedforward networks to forecasting problems.

4. The nature and purpose of each node function can be changed, as in the radial basis function networks discussed in section 4.4, which use a radially symmetric node function instead of a sigmoid function.

5. The function of the weights and hidden nodes may be modified, as in various polynomial networks whose nodes compute products and sums of weighted inputs, as discussed in section 4.5.

6. Cost functions may be introduced into the learning rules to reduce network complexity, a special case applying regularization theory, discussed in section 4.6.

4.8 Exercises

1. How may Marchand's algorithm be modified to work for multiclass problems?

2. Modify equations 4.18 and 4.19 to obtain gradient descent rules for RBF-nets whose desired outputs are vectors d_i rather than scalars d_i.

3. Find the update rules for RBF-nets that use each of the following radial basis function.

   a. $\rho_1(d) = 1/d$

   b. $\rho_2(d) = (c^2 + d^2)^\beta$ for $\beta < 0$

   c. $\rho_3(d) = \exp(-d/c)^2$

4. The output of a pi-sigma network is given by equation 4.22 where f is the usual sigmoid function, $f(u) = \left(1 + \exp(-u)\right)^{-1}$.

   a. Derive the expression for the mean squared error, for the training set $\{(x_i, d_i) : i = 1, \ldots, P\}$, where d_i denotes the desired output for the input vector x_i.

   b. Derive the weight update rule based on application of gradient descent to the minimization of the mean squared error function.

   c. Extend the pi-sigma network for problems where the output is a vector, not a scalar.

5. Answer the above question for the sigma-pi network of Feldman and Ballard in which each node's output is

$$f\left(w_0 + \sum_{j_1} w_{j_1} i_{j_1} + \sum_{j_1 \neq j_2} w_{j_1, j_2} i_{j_1} i_{j_2}\right)$$

where f is a sigmoid function.

6. Are there any quadratic functions that cannot be learnt by a pi-sigma network?

7. What is the maximum number of steps required for Marchand's algorithm to converge?

8. Apply each of the following algorithms to the function approximation problem for which training data are given in appendix B.5, and compare the results in terms of the amount of computation and size of network required to obtain the same mean squared error.

   a. backpropagation

   b. cascade correlation

   c. Madaline Rule III

   d. RBF network

   e. pi-sigma network

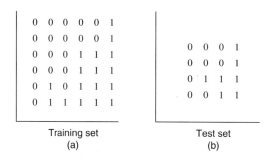

<table>
<tr><td>0</td><td>0</td><td>0</td><td>0</td><td>0</td><td>1</td></tr>
<tr><td>0</td><td>0</td><td>0</td><td>0</td><td>0</td><td>1</td></tr>
<tr><td>0</td><td>0</td><td>0</td><td>1</td><td>1</td><td>1</td></tr>
<tr><td>0</td><td>0</td><td>0</td><td>1</td><td>1</td><td>1</td></tr>
<tr><td>0</td><td>1</td><td>0</td><td>1</td><td>1</td><td>1</td></tr>
<tr><td>0</td><td>1</td><td>1</td><td>1</td><td>1</td><td>1</td></tr>
</table>

Training set
(a)

<table>
<tr><td>0</td><td>0</td><td>0</td><td>1</td></tr>
<tr><td>0</td><td>0</td><td>0</td><td>1</td></tr>
<tr><td>0</td><td>1</td><td>1</td><td>1</td></tr>
<tr><td>0</td><td>0</td><td>1</td><td>1</td></tr>
</table>

Test set
(b)

Figure 4.35
Training set consisting of elements of two classes in a two-dimensional space.

9. Describe the behavior of Marchand's algorithm on the two-dimensional data given in figure 4.35(a), where 1 and 0 represent observations from two different classes. Evaluate and comment on the trained network's performance on the test set given in figure 4.35(b). How would you modify Marchand's algorithm so that its performance on test data is likely to be comparable to the performance on training data, assuming all training and test data samples are drawn randomly from the same data distribution?

10. Solve the above problem for the Upstart, neural tree, and cascade correlation algorithms.

11. Appendix B.3 contains daily gold prices for several weeks in 1993. Use the first 75% of the data for training a recurrent network with five nodes. Use the best neural network so obtained to predict the following week's gold price, and compare the results with the prices in the test data consisting of the last 25% of the data. Comment on the performance of the network on the test data. Compare the performance of the recurrent network with the performance of a feedforward network trained by backpropagation algorithm.

5 Unsupervised Learning

That all knowledge begins with experience, there is indeed no doubt . . . but although our knowledge originates with experiences, it does not all arise out of experience.
—Immanuel Kant

A three-month-old child receives the same visual stimuli as a newborn infant, but can make much more sense of them, and can recognize various patterns and features of visual input data. These abilities are not acquired from an external teacher, and illustrate that a significant amount of learning is accomplished by biological processes that proceed "unsupervised" (teacherless). Motivated by these biological facts, the artificial neural networks discussed in this chapter attempt to discover special features and patterns from available data without using external help. Such networks use unsupervised learning algorithms to address tasks such as the following.

1. Some problems require an algorithm to cluster or to partition a given data set into disjoint subsets ("clusters"), such that patterns in the same cluster are as alike as possible, and patterns in different clusters are as dissimilar as possible. The application of a clustering procedure results in a partition (function) that assigns each data point to a unique cluster. A partition may be evaluated by measuring the average squared distance between each input pattern and the centroid of the cluster in which it is placed.[1]

$$E = \sum_{\text{clusters}} \sum_{\text{patterns}} ||(\text{pattern} - \text{cluster centroid})||^2 / (\text{number of patterns})$$

In neural networks used for clustering, the weights from the input layer to each output node constitute the *weight vector* of that node, identified with the centroid of one cluster (or subcluster) of input patterns. In some clustering problems, it is desirable to place a pattern in a cluster whose centroid is far from that pattern. Several different nodes may then be associated with each non-uniform or asymmetric cluster, such as those shown in figure 5.1(b).

Terminology varies in the literature on networks used for clustering, and the weight vector associated with a node is sometimes referred to as a *prototype, cluster centroid, cluster mean*, or *reference vector*.

---

1. A related criterion, not used in neural networks, examines the sum of the squared distances between patterns in the same cluster,

$$E = \sum_{C_\ell} \sum_{i_j \in C_\ell} \sum_{i_k \in C_\ell} ||i_j - i_k||^2,$$

where C_ℓ ranges over all clusters.

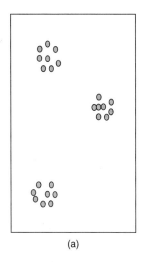 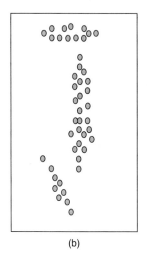

          (a)   (b)

Figure 5.1
Different kinds of clustering problems: (a) uniform, symmetric clusters; (b) asymmetric clusters. Patterns may
not belong to the cluster whose centroid is nearest.

2. *Vector quantization* is another task closely related to clustering, also solved using unsupervised learning methods. Input space is to be divided into several connected regions,
called *Voronoi regions*. Each region is represented using a single vector, called a *codebook vector*. Every point in the input space belongs to one of these regions, and is mapped
to the corresponding (nearest) codebook vector. The set of codebook vectors is a compressed form of the information represented by input data vectors, since many different
input data vectors may be mapped to the same codebook vector. Figure 5.2 gives an example of such a division of a two-dimensional space into Voronoi regions, called a Voronoi
diagram (or "tessellation"). Note that the boundaries of regions are obtained by sketching
the perpendicular bisectors of the lines joining neighboring codebook vectors. Although
vector quantization can also be viewed as an association task (discussed in chapter 6), the
neural network algorithms for this task implement unsupervised learning to accomplish explicit minimization of the distance between input pattern and output pattern, and are thus
distinguished from the association networks.

3. Sometimes it is necessary to obtain a concise description of large amounts of data
drawn from a probability distribution. Such a description may consist of a set of points in
the data space, such that the distribution of these points is an approximation of the original
distribution. In this context, unsupervised learning consists of extracting this set of points,
which need not be a subset of the data points originally provided. In some cases, a small

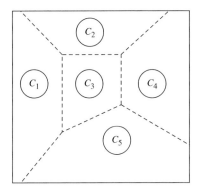

Figure 5.2
Voronoi diagram, with five Voronoi regions, with codebook vectors $C_1, \ldots, C_5$.

region in data space may contain a disproportionately large number of data points (in the original distribution), as in the case of figure 5.3(a). In such cases, several such points within the same region would be included in the concise approximate description of the distribution, as shown in figure 5.3(b), whereas a clustering algorithm would extract only a single point to represent that cluster.

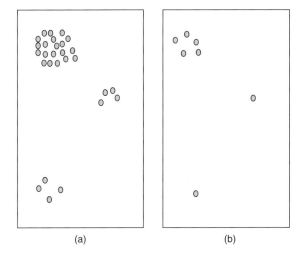

                  (a)   (b)

Figure 5.3
Clustering vs. probability density approximation: (a) a distribution containing three clusters whose densities differ; (b) an approximation of the same probability distribution.

4. When assigning patterns to different clusters, one would like to ensure that patterns belonging to different clusters can be distinguished by some *features*. If most members of a population have roughly the same values for a feature, that feature is no longer important in distinguishing between members of that population. For instance, hair color may not be an interesting feature to distinguish different humans living in Timbuktu if most people there have the same hair color, but it becomes an interesting feature if there is considerable variation in hair color of different individuals. The goal of *feature extraction* is to find the most important features, i.e., those with the highest variation (in the population under consideration).

An important side-effect of feature extraction is the reduction of input dimensionality, allowing computation with a smaller number of inputs than the original input dimensionality. For example, in a program that needs to work with input patterns that describe people, a very large amount of computation may be called for if the inputs consist of the entire set of parameters that can be used to describe people. However, if preprocessing can determine that only the ratio of the height and weight is relevant to the task under consideration, then computation can be carried out after each individual is described only in terms of this parameter, reducing input dimensionality to 1. Preprocessing methods must first extract this feature from input data that may consist of a large number of parameters such as height, weight, age, and blood sugar level. Another advantage of dimensionality reduction is improvement in generalizability. For a fixed-size training set, using more input dimensions does not necessarily provide additional discriminatory information. An increase in input dimensionality while the size of the training sample remains fixed is outweighed by a decrease in accuracy of the parameters.

In this chapter, we present several neural networks that conduct unsupervised learning for achieving the above goals. Each node of the network represents an important aspect of the data used for learning. In some cases, each node's weight vector is in the same vector space as the input data, and each input sample is associated with the nearest weight vector (with the smallest Euclidean distance). Such networks have been used for clustering, approximating probability distributions, and compressing voluminous input data into a small number of codewords. In other cases, each node computes a function of the inputs such that each output value for this node represents the extent to which the corresponding input vector contains an important feature of the input data. Such networks perform feature extraction and accomplish dimensionality reduction.

Extensions of unsupervised learning algorithms to supervised learning tasks are also discussed in this chapter. Unsupervised learning and clustering have been active areas of research in statistics, and many neural networks bear close relations with well-known statistical methods, which are briefly described in this chapter along with the networks.

5.1   Winner-Take-All Networks

In this section, we describe networks that conduct unsupervised learning using very simple methods that are essential to more complex models as well. Section 5.1.1 describes networks that compute distances, section 5.1.2 describes networks with inhibitory connections that can be used to determine the "winner" node with the highest level of activation, and section 5.1.3 combines these mechanisms with a learning rule that adapts network weights.

5.1.1   Hamming networks

Distance computations and comparisons are essential in most neural networks that conduct unsupervised learning. Hence the first network to be discussed in this context accomplishes the simple task of distance computation, by a neural mechanism that we have already encountered: summing the weighted inputs to a node. The particular distance measure that is computed is the *Hamming distance*, the number of differing bits in two bit vectors.

The *Hamming network*, shown in figure 5.4, contains an input layer and an output layer. Weights on links between the two layers represent the components of stored input patterns.

Let $\{i_p : p = 1, \ldots, P\}$ denote the set of binary "stored" vectors of dimensionality n,

$$i_p = \begin{pmatrix} i_{p,1} \\ \vdots \\ i_{p,n} \end{pmatrix}$$

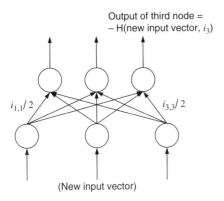

Figure 5.4
A network to calculate Hamming distances between stored vectors and input vectors. H(new input vector, i_3) denotes the Hamming distance between the new input vector and i_3.

where $i_{p,j} \in \{-1, 1\}$ for each $j = 1, \ldots, n$, and $p = 1, \ldots, P$. The input (first) layer of the two-layer network contains n nodes, and the output (second) layer of the network contains P nodes. The connection from the jth input node to the pth output node carries a weight $w_{p,j} = i_{p,j}/2$. Each upper level node is also associated with a threshold $\theta = -(n/2)$. The weight matrix W and threshold vector Θ are given by

$$
W = \frac{1}{2} \begin{pmatrix} i_1^T \\ \vdots \\ i_P^T \end{pmatrix}, \quad \Theta = \begin{pmatrix} -\frac{n}{2} \\ \vdots \\ -\frac{n}{2} \end{pmatrix}.
$$

When a new input vector i is presented to this network, its upper level nodes generate the output

$$
o = Wi + \Theta = \frac{1}{2} \begin{pmatrix} i_1 \cdot i - n \\ i_2 \cdot i - n \\ \vdots \\ i_P \cdot i - n \end{pmatrix}
$$

where $i_p \cdot i$ represents the dot product $\sum_k i_{p,k} i_k$.

Given W and Θ, each network output represents the negative of the Hamming distance between a stored pattern and an input pattern. The following example illustrates this property.

EXAMPLE 5.1   Suppose we wish to store three vectors $i_1 = (1, -1, -1, 1, 1)$, $i_2 = (-1, 1, -1, 1, -1)$, $i_3 = (1, -1, 1, -1, 1)$. The two layers of this Hamming net will have five and three nodes respectively. The 3×5 weight matrix W and threshold vector Θ are given below.

$$
W = \frac{1}{2} \begin{pmatrix} i_1^T \\ i_2^T \\ i_3^T \end{pmatrix} = \frac{1}{2} \begin{pmatrix} 1 & -1 & -1 & 1 & 1 \\ -1 & 1 & -1 & 1 & -1 \\ 1 & -1 & 1 & -1 & 1 \end{pmatrix}, \quad \Theta = \frac{1}{2} \begin{pmatrix} -5 \\ -5 \\ -5 \end{pmatrix}
$$

When an input vector such as $i = (1, 1, 1, -1, -1)$ is presented to this network, nodes in the second layer of this network generate the following outputs.

$$
(\frac{1}{2} \times 1) - (\frac{1}{2} \times 1) - (\frac{1}{2} \times 1) + (\frac{1}{2} \times -1) + (\frac{1}{2} \times -1) - \frac{5}{2} = -4
$$

$$
(-\frac{1}{2} \times 1) + (\frac{1}{2} \times 1) - (\frac{1}{2} \times 1) + (\frac{1}{2} \times -1) + (\frac{1}{2} \times 1) - \frac{5}{2} = -3
$$

$$
(\frac{1}{2} \times 1) - (\frac{1}{2} \times 1) + (\frac{1}{2} \times 1) - (\frac{1}{2} \times 1) + (\frac{1}{2} \times 1) - \frac{5}{2} = -2
$$

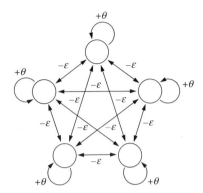

Figure 5.5
Maxnet: a simple competitive network.

These are negatives of Hamming distances between the stored vectors and the input vector i.

We can determine which stored pattern is nearest to a new input pattern by taking the maximum of the outputs of the different nodes in the second layer. This can be accomplished by attaching a *maxnet*, described below, on top of the second layer of the Hamming network.

5.1.2 Maxnet

A "maxnet" is a recurrent one-layer network that conducts a competition to determine which node has the highest initial input value. Its architecture is illustrated in figure 5.5.

The primary mechanism is an iterative process in which each node receives inhibitory inputs from all other nodes via "lateral" (intra-layer) connections. Weights can be chosen so that a single node whose value is initially the maximum can eventually prevail as the only active or "winner" node, while the activation of all other nodes subsides to zero. The simplest neuron model that accomplishes this is a lower-bounded variation of the identity function, with $f(net) = \max(0, net)$. For the network of figure 5.5, the network tasks can be accomplished by the choices of self-excitation weight $\theta = 1$ and mutual inhibition magnitude $\epsilon \leq 1/(\text{number of nodes})$.

It is assumed that all nodes update their outputs simultaneously (synchronously). The weighted input from the current node is treated just like the weighted inputs from other nodes, in that the whole function examines

$$net = \sum_{i=1}^{n} w_i x_i.$$

EXAMPLE 5.2   For the nodes in the network of figure 5.5, if the initial activation values of the five nodes were (0.5, 0.9, 1, 0.9, 0.9), and if $\theta = 1$ and $\epsilon = 1/5$, the output of the first node falls to $\max(0, 0.5 - \frac{1}{5}(0.9 + 1.0 + 0.9 + 0.9)) = 0$, the outputs of the second, fourth, and fifth nodes fall to $\max(0, 0.9 - \frac{1}{5}(0.5 + 1.0 + 0.9 + 0.9)) = 0.24$, and the output of the third node falls to $\max(0, 1.0 - \frac{1}{5}(0.5 + 0.9 + 0.9 + 0.9)) = 0.36$, all in a single iteration. So the new output vector is (0, 0.24, 0.36, 0.24, 0.24). In subsequent iterations, this successively changes to (0, 0.072, 0.216, 0.072, 0.072), then to (0, 0, 0.1728, 0, 0), which is the stable set of node outputs and subject to no further changes. Only three iterations were needed to choose the winner, even though the winner's initial output (1.0) was fairly close to that of other competing nodes (0.9).

Why is it necessary to use a maxnet for the algorithmically straightforward task of choosing the maximum of n numbers? Apart from neural plausibility and the desire to perform every task using neural networks, it can be argued that the maxnet allows for greater parallelism in execution than the algebraic solution, since every computation is local to each node rather than being controlled by a central coordinator.

5.1.3   Simple competitive learning

The Hamming net and maxnet are not of much practical use by themselves, but assist in the task of determining the node whose weight vector is nearest to an input pattern. The maxnet contains a single layer, with no separate connections modulating input from the outside world. The Hamming net assumes binary input and output vectors, which we now generalize to real-valued vectors. In this section, we present a simple competitive network model, consisting of an input layer with n nodes and an output layer with m nodes. Each node in the first layer is connected to each node in the output layer, as shown in figure 5.6, and $w_{j,\ell}$ refers to the weight on the connection from the ℓth input node to the jth output node, for $\ell = 1, \ldots, n; \quad j = 1, \ldots, m$. Nodes in the output layer (sometimes referred to as a "Kohonen layer") are interconnected with inhibitory connections, as in a maxnet. The number of nodes in the output layer are fixed; only their connection weights vary.

An appropriate weight update rule is used by the learning algorithm to determine the connection weights from the input nodes to the competitive layer. The choice of the weight update rule depends on what one would like to learn from the input patterns. Given that the overall purpose of the network is to assign a unique upper-layer node for each input pattern, a reasonable criterion is that each output node should "represent" the input patterns to be associated with that node. Note that the jth node in the competitive layer is completely described by the vector of weights to it from the input nodes, $\boldsymbol{w}_j = (w_{j,1}, \ldots, w_{j,n})$. Each such *weight vector* (or "prototype") has the same dimensionality as each input vector, and a distance measure may be used to estimate how "similar" an input vector is to the weight

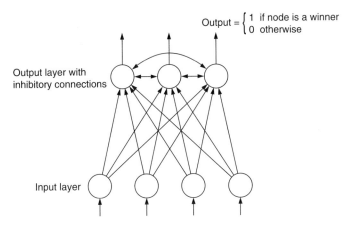

Output = $\begin{cases} 1 & \text{if node is a winner} \\ 0 & \text{otherwise} \end{cases}$

Output layer with
inhibitory connections

Input layer

Figure 5.6
Simple competitive learning network.

Algorithm Simple Competitive Learning;
   Initialize all weights to random values;
   repeat
       • (Optional:) Adjust the learning rate $\eta(t)$;
       • Select an input pattern i_k from the training set;
       • Find node $j*$ whose weight vector w_{j*} is closest to i_k;
       • Update each weight $w_{j*,1}, \ldots, w_{j*,n}$ using the rule:
         $\Delta w_{j*,\ell} = \eta(t)(i_{k,\ell} - w_{j*,\ell})$, **for** $\ell \in \{1, \ldots, n\}$
   until network converges or computational bounds are exceeded.

Figure 5.7
Simple competitive learning algorithm.

vector associated with a node. The weight update rule is formulated such that the weight vector associated with each node is as near as possible to all the input samples for which the node is the winner of the competition.

Figure 5.7 describes the simple competitive learning algorithm, applied to the training set $\{i_1, \ldots, i_P\}$, where each $i_\ell = (i_{\ell,1}, \ldots, i_{\ell,n})$. Initially, all connection weights are assigned randomly, with values between 0 and 1. When an input vector i_ℓ is presented to the network, the jth processing unit calculates the distance $d(w_j, i_\ell)$ of i_ℓ from w_j for each $j = 1, \ldots, m$. A competition occurs to find the "winner" among nodes in the outer layer, defined as the node j^* whose weight vector is nearest to the input vector, i.e.,

$$d(w_{j*}, i_\ell) \leq d(w_j, i_\ell) \text{ for } j \in \{1, \ldots, m\}.$$

The Euclidean distance measure is often used, with $d(\boldsymbol{w}_j, \boldsymbol{i}_\ell) = \sqrt{\sum_{\ell=1}^{n}(i_{\ell,k} - w_{jk})^2}$. If normalized weights and inputs are used, i.e., $||\boldsymbol{w}_j|| = 1$, for all weight vectors $j = 1, \ldots, m$ and $||\boldsymbol{i}_\ell|| = 1$, $\ell = 1, \ldots, P$ for all patterns in the training set, then the squared Euclidean distance $d^2(\boldsymbol{w}, \boldsymbol{i})$ simplifies to $2 - 2\sum_\ell w_\ell i_\ell = 2 - 2\boldsymbol{i} \cdot \boldsymbol{w}$. This distance will be minimum when the dot product $\boldsymbol{i} \cdot \boldsymbol{w}$ takes its maximum value. Consequently, for the special case of normalized vectors, an input vector $\boldsymbol{i}$ is closest to $\boldsymbol{w}_{j*}$ if the net input $\sum_\ell w_\ell i_\ell$ is largest, i.e.,

$$\boldsymbol{w}_{j*} \cdot \boldsymbol{i} = \max_{j}\{\boldsymbol{w}_j \cdot \boldsymbol{i}\}.$$

Hence a maxnet can be used to minimize distance.

Connection weights of the winner node, j^*, are modified so that the weight vector $\boldsymbol{w}_j^*$ moves closer to $\boldsymbol{i}_\ell$, while the other weights remain unchanged. This is the "winner-take-all" phase. The weight update rule can be described as

$$\boldsymbol{w}_j(\text{new}) = \boldsymbol{w}_j(\text{old}) + \eta(\boldsymbol{i}_\ell - \boldsymbol{w}_j(\text{old})) \times \delta_{j,\ell} \qquad (5.1)$$

where

$$\delta_{j,\ell} = \begin{cases} 1 & \text{if the } j\text{th node is "winner" for input } \boldsymbol{i}_\ell \\ 0 & \text{otherwise} \end{cases}$$

and the learning rate, η, is a predetermined constant.

The process of weight adjustment brings the winning node's weight vector closer to those training samples that fall within its zone of attraction. It can be shown that in the limiting case, i.e., if and when further changes in weights are insignificant with each training pattern presentation, each weight vector $\boldsymbol{w}_j$ converges (moves successively closer) to

$$\boldsymbol{w}_j = \frac{1}{\sum_\ell \delta_{j,\ell}} \sum_\ell \boldsymbol{i}_\ell \delta_{j,\ell},$$

which represents the average of all those input vectors $\boldsymbol{i}_\ell$ for which $\boldsymbol{w}_j$ is the winner.

In a minor variation of equation 5.1, the learning rate η may be a non-increasing function of time, i.e., $\eta(t + 1) \leq \eta(t)$. With this modification, later corrections in weights are smaller, resulting in faster convergence of the network.

We now present an example to illustrate the simple competitive learning process, and comment on various issues raised regarding its implementation, termination criteria, and quality of results obtained.

EXAMPLE 5.3   Let the training set T consist of 6 three-dimensional vectors, $\boldsymbol{i}_1, \ldots, \boldsymbol{i}_6$.

$T = \{i_1 = (1.1, 1.7, 1.8),\ i_2 = (0, 0, 0),\ i_3 = (0, 0.5, 1.5),$

$\qquad i_4 = (1, 0, 0),\ i_5 = (0.5, 0.5, 0.5),\ i_6 = (1, 1, 1)\}$

We begin with a network containing three input nodes and three processing units (output nodes), A, B, C. The connection strengths of A, B, C are initially chosen randomly, and are given by the weight matrix

$$W(0) = \begin{pmatrix} w_1: & 0.2 & 0.7 & 0.3 \\ w_2: & 0.1 & 0.1 & 0.9 \\ w_3: & 1 & 1 & 1 \end{pmatrix}.$$

To simplify computations, we use a learning rate $\eta = 0.5$ and update weights (using equation 5.1). In the calculations that follow, fractions are shown rounded to the first decimal place, for ease of presentation, unless the second decimal happens to be 5 (as in 0.15). We compare squared Euclidean distances to select the winner; $d^2_{j,\ell} \equiv d^2(w_j, i_\ell)$ refers to the squared Euclidean distance between the current position of the processing node j from the ℓth pattern.

$t = 1$:   Sample presented: $i_1 = (1.1, 1.7, 1.8)$. Squared Euclidean distance between A and i_1: $d^2_{1,1} = (1.1 - 0.2)^2 + (1.7 - 0.7)^2 + (1.8 - 0.3)^2 = 4.1$. Similarly, $d^2_{2,1} = 4.4$ and $d^2_{3,1} = 1.1$.

C is the "winner" since $d^2_{3,1} < d^2_{1,1}$ and $d^2_{3,1} < d^2_{2,1}$. A and B are therefore not perturbed by this sample whereas C moves halfway towards the sample (since $\eta = 0.5$). The resulting weight matrix is

$$W(1) = \begin{pmatrix} w_1: & 0.2 & 0.7 & 0.3 \\ w_2: & 0.1 & 0.1 & 0.9 \\ w_3: & 1.05 & 1.35 & 1.4 \end{pmatrix}.$$

$t = 2$:   Sample presented: $i_2 = (0, 0, 0)$. $d^2_{1,2} = 0.6$, $d^2_{2,2} = 0.8$, $d^2_{3,2} = 4.9$, hence A is the winner. The weights of A are updated. The resulting weight matrix is

$$W(2) = \begin{pmatrix} w_1: & 0.1 & 0.35 & 0.15 \\ w_2: & 0.1 & 0.1 & 0.9 \\ w_3: & 1.05 & 1.35 & 1.4 \end{pmatrix}.$$

Since only one weight vector changes in each sample presentation, we show only the changed vectors in the following snapshots of execution of simple competitive learning.

$t = 3$:   Sample presented: $i_3 = (0, 0.5, 1.5)$. $d^2_{2,3} = 0.5$ is least, hence B is the winner and is updated. The resulting weight vector is

$w_2: (0.05,\quad 0.3,\quad 1.2)$.

$t = 4$:   Sample presented: $i_4 = (1, 0, 0)$. $d_{1,4}^2 = 1$, $d_{2,4}^2 = 2.4$, $d_{3,4}^2 = 3.8$, hence A is the winner and is updated.

$w_1 : (0.55, \quad 0.2, \quad 0.1)$

$t = 5$: $i_5 = (0.5, 0.5, 0.5)$ is presented, winner A is updated: $w_1(5) = (0.5, 0.35, 0.3)$.

$t = 6$: $i_6 = (1, 1, 1)$ is presented, winner C is updated: $w_3(6) = (1, 1.2, 1.2)$.

$t = 7$: i_1 is presented, winner C is updated: $w_3(7) = (1.05, 1.45, 1.5)$.

$t = 8$:   Sample presented: i_2. Winner A is updated to $w_1(8) = (0.25, 0.2, 0.15)$.

$t = 9$:   Sample presented: i_3. Winner B is updated to $w_1(9) = (0, 0.4, 1.35)$.

$t = 10$:   Sample presented: i_4. Winner A is updated to $w_1(10) = (0.6, 0.1, 0.1)$.

$t = 11$:   Sample presented: i_5. Winner A is updated to $w_1(11) = (0.55, 0.3, 0.3)$.

$t = 12$:   Sample presented: i_6. Winner C is updated and $w_3(12) = (1, 1.2, 1.25)$. At this state the weight matrix is

$$W(12) = \begin{pmatrix} w_1: & 0.55 & 0.3 & 0.3 \\ w_2: & 0 & 0.4 & 1.35 \\ w_3: & 1 & 1.2 & 1.25 \end{pmatrix}.$$

The following observations are relevant to this example.

• Node A becomes repeatedly activated by the samples i_2, i_4, and i_5, node B by i_3 alone, and node C by i_1 and i_6. The centroid of i_2, i_4, and i_5 is $(0.5, 0.2, 0.2)$, and convergence of the weight vector for node A towards this location is indicated by the progression

$$(0.2, 0.7, 0.3) \rightarrow (0.1, 0.35, 0.15) \rightarrow (0.55, 0.2, 0.1) \rightarrow (0.5, 0.35, 0.3) \rightarrow$$

$$(0.25, 0.2, 0.15) \rightarrow (0.6, 0.1, 0.1) \rightarrow (0.55, 0.3, 0.3) \cdots.$$

• The high value of η, causing substantial modification of a node position (as seen in terms of the centroid of the cluster) with every sample presentation, is one reason the convergence is not smooth. If $\eta = 1$, in fact, convergence will never occur because the node position will be completely changed to that of the activating pattern. If $\eta = 0.01$, on the other hand, hundreds of sample iterations will be necessary, since changes in node position are very small at each sample presentation.

• The network is sensitive to the choice of the exact distance metric used. For instance, if the Manhattan distance $d(x, y) = \sum_\ell |x_\ell - y_\ell|$ is used instead of the Euclidean distance, node B would be chosen instead of node A at the presentation of the second sample $(0, 0, 0)$ in the example discussed above. Thus, instead of $W(2)$ shown earlier, we would obtain

$$W(2)' = \begin{pmatrix} \boldsymbol{w}_1: & 0.2 & 0.7 & 0.3 \\ \boldsymbol{w}_2: & 0.05 & 0.05 & 0.45 \\ \boldsymbol{w}_3: & 1.05 & 1.35 & 1.4 \end{pmatrix}.$$

• The initial values of the node positions played some role in determining which node is activated by which samples. If, for instance, we had chosen

$$W(0) = \begin{pmatrix} \boldsymbol{w}_1: & 0 & 0 & 0 \\ \boldsymbol{w}_2: & 0 & 0 & 5 \\ \boldsymbol{w}_3: & 0 & 5 & 0 \end{pmatrix}$$

then B and C would not be activated by any samples, and A would converge to the centroid of all six samples. Using three nodes is hence no guarantee that three clusters will be obtained by the network. If two of the initial node positions were almost identical, the network might result in "splitting" a cluster into two parts and assigning them to these two nodes, e.g., if we had chosen

$$W(0) = \begin{pmatrix} \boldsymbol{w}_1: & 0 & 0 & 0 \\ \boldsymbol{w}_2: & 1.01 & 1.01 & 1.01 \\ \boldsymbol{w}_3: & 1 & 1 & 1 \end{pmatrix}$$

and the sample presentations were as before, in the sequence $(i_1, i_2, i_3, \ldots)$, then A would converge to the centroid of samples i_2, i_3, i_4, and i_5 while B would move towards i_1 and C would move towards i_6. This would be different from the network computations in example 5.3 where i_1 and i_6 were considered to be in the same cluster.

• The result of network computations also depends on the sequence in which samples are presented to the network, especially when the learning rate η is not very small. For instance, if $\eta = 0.5$ and if the initial weight matrix is

$$W(0) = \begin{pmatrix} \boldsymbol{w}_1: & 0 & 0 & 0 \\ \boldsymbol{w}_2: & 0.6 & 0.5 & 0.5 \\ \boldsymbol{w}_3: & 1 & 1 & 1 \end{pmatrix}$$

and a sample $i_1 = (0.7, 0.7, 0.7)$ is presented to the network, followed by $i_2 = (0.8, 0.8, 0.8)$, then node B is most highly activated by both samples. However, if the sample $i_2 = (0.8, 0.8, 0.8)$ is presented before the sample $i_1 = (0.7, 0.7, 0.7)$ is presented, then node C is most highly activated by these samples. If the other samples in the data set are $i_3 = (0, 0, 0)$ and $i_4 = (0.9, 0.9, 0.9)$, then the sequence of presentations $i_1, i_2, i_3, i_4, i_1, i_2, \ldots$ results in three clusters, with A converging to i_3, B converging to i_4, and C converging to the remaining two inputs. On the other hand, the sequence of presentations $i_2, i_1, i_3, i_4, i_2, i_1, \ldots$ results in two clusters, with A converging to i_3, B not moving at all, and C converging to the other three samples.

After an early phase in which different nodes may be winners for the same sample in different iterations, the network stabilizes and the same nodes continue to be the winners for the same input patterns. Towards the latter part of this phase, each weight vector is approximately the centroid of all the samples for which it is the winner. However, weight vectors will continue to change at every sample presentation unless the sample presented coincides with a weight vector.

When should computations be terminated? The use of a small amount of "memory" helps, although this is not biologically plausible. If the net change in each node position is zero, when an entire epoch of sample presentations is completed, we may conclude that no further useful computations can be carried out by the network; to use this principle, each node can store its position at the beginning of the previous epoch, and compare this with its position at the beginning of the next epoch.

We may also use memory to reduce some of the redundant computations of the network in the later phases. If the node activated by each sample remains the same as the node activated by that sample at the immediately preceding epoch, we may conclude that the network has stabilized, and that the same nodes will continue to be activated in the following iterations as well. This can be detected by storing (with each node) the identification labels of the samples with which it was associated in the preceding epoch. A small amount of non-neural computation can be used to find the centroid of those samples, which is then stored as the weight of the relevant node. Such methods assume a fixed set of training samples that are repeatedly presented to the network; the competitive learning algorithm discussed in this section makes no such assumption.

To interpret the competitive learning algorithm as a clustering process is attractive, but the merits of doing so are debatable, as illustrated by example 5.4.

EXAMPLE 5.4   Let the input space be one-dimensional, with the following five input patterns: 0, 2, 3, 5, 6. Assume that the competitive layer of the network contains three nodes. One possible distribution of the weight vectors that may result from the competitive learning rule discussed above is

$$w_1 = (1), w_2 = (4), w_3 = (6).$$

If the network is interpreted as a clustering scheme, then samples 0 and 2 are placed in the cluster corresponding to w_1, samples 3 and 5 are placed in the cluster corresponding to w_2, and sample 6 is placed in the third cluster. This is contrary to the obvious clustering scheme that combines 2 and 3 into one cluster, 5 and 6 into another, and places 0 in a third cluster. Perhaps the difficulty is not with the interpretation of the network as a clustering scheme, but lies with the inherent difficulty of the clustering problem.

The simple competitive learning algorithm updates weight vectors in such a way as to conduct stochastic gradient descent on the *quantization error* defined by

Algorithm k-means Clustering;

   Initialize k prototypes $(w_1, \ldots, w_k)$, e.g., by identifying them
   with distinct randomly chosen input vectors:
   $w_j = i_\ell$, $j \in \{1, \ldots, k\}$, $\ell \in \{1, \ldots, P\}$.
   Each cluster C_j is associated with prototype w_j.

   repeat
   - **for** each input vector i_ℓ, where $\ell \in \{1, \ldots, P\}$, **do**
       Place i_ℓ in the cluster C_{j*} with nearest prototype
       w_{j*}, with $|i_\ell - w_{j*}| \leq |i_\ell - w_j|$, $j \in \{1, \ldots, k\}$
       end-for;
   - **for** each cluster C_j, where $j \in \{1, \ldots, k\}$, **do**
       Update the prototype w_j to be the centroid of all
       samples currently in C_j, so that $w_j = \sum_{i_\ell \in C_j} i_\ell / |C_j|$
       end-for;
   - Compute the total quantization error:

$$E = \sum_{j=1}^{k} \sum_{i_\ell \in C_j} |i_\ell - w_j|^2$$

   until E no longer decreases, or cluster membership no longer changes.

Figure 5.8
k-means clustering algorithm.

$$\sum_p |i_p - \mathbb{W}(i_p)|^2$$

where $\mathbb{W}(i_p) \in \{w_1, \ldots, w_n\}$ is the weight vector nearest to i_p, such that

$$|i_p - \mathbb{W}(i_p)| \leq |i_p - w_j|, \text{ for all } w_j \in \{w_1, \ldots, w_n\}.$$

The competitive learning algorithm discussed above may be viewed as a clustering algorithm by considering each node's weight vector (prototype) as representing the centroid of a cluster. The clustering scheme suggested by such a network is one in which an input pattern is associated with cluster j if the jth node is the winner of the competition when this input pattern is presented. Simple competitive learning is then seen to be closely related to a statistical procedure called "k-means clustering," described in figure 5.8, devised by MacQueen (1967). The main difference between the two procedures is that simple competitive learning updates the winning weight vector by a small quantity as soon as an input pattern is presented, whereas k-means clustering computes the precise cluster centroids after a complete epoch of presentation of all input vectors.

k-means clustering is one example of a "partitional" clustering procedure, in which we start with an initial partition and repeatedly move patterns from one cluster to another

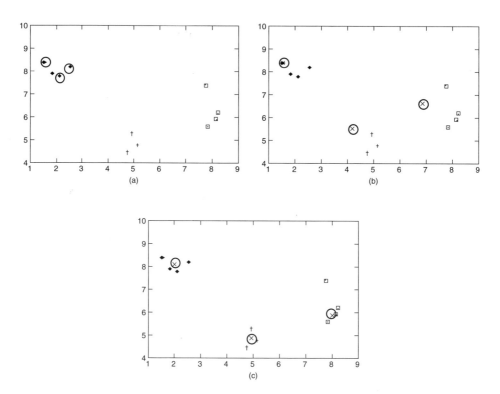

Figure 5.9
Example of k-means clustering: (a) Initial cluster centers (within circles) are the first three observations of the training set; (b) In one iteration, cluster centers have moved towards the other observations of the training set; (c) Final result, after two iterations.

until the result is considered satisfactory. Figure 5.9 shows an example of applying the k-means algorithm to obtain three well-separated clusters in two-dimensional space. In this example, convergence to the correct partition required only two iterations, even though the initial cluster centers were very close to each other.

The number of clusters k is assumed to be fixed in k-means clustering as well as in simple competitive learning. For a given problem, the right choice of k may not be obvious. Note that the quantization error is zero if each point is a separate cluster, that is, $k =$ number of data points; but this accomplishes nothing. To emphasize the need for a small number of clusters, a penalty term proportional to the number of clusters could be added to the mean squared error. Clustering can then be performed by varying the number of clusters (k), and selecting one with a minimum combined sum (mean squared error + $k \times$ cost per cluster), analogous to the regularization methods discussed in chapter 4.

The k-means algorithm is fast, and has been shown by Salim and Ismail (1984) to converge, i.e., to result in a state in which each prototype changes little, assuming that successive vectors presented to the algorithm are drawn by independent random trials from the input data distribution.[2] However, the k-means algorithm can get trapped in local minima of the quantization error. Similar properties are shared by the simple competitive learning algorithm. Unfortunately, the quantization error often has a large number of local minima, and the quality of solutions obtained by these methods may be far from optimal.

5.2   Learning Vector Quantizers

Unsupervised learning and clustering can be useful preprocessing steps for solving classification problems. A learning vector quantizer (LVQ) is an application of winner-take-all networks for such tasks, and illustrates how an unsupervised learning mechanism can be adapted to solve supervised learning tasks in which class membership is known for every training pattern.

Each node in an LVQ is associated with an arbitrarily chosen class label. The number of nodes chosen for each class is roughly proportional to the number of training patterns that belong to that class, making the assumption that each cluster has roughly the same number of patterns. The update rule in an LVQ is slightly different from that of the simple competitive learning rule for winner-take-all networks. The new rule may be paraphrased as follows.

When pattern i from class $C(i)$ is presented to the network, let the winner node j^* belong to class $C(j^*)$. The winner j^* is moved towards the pattern i if $C(i) = C(j^*)$ and away from i otherwise.

The algorithm is presented in figure 5.10; this algorithm is referred to as LVQ1, to distinguish it from more recent variants of the algorithm. In the LVQ1 algorithm, the weight update rule uses a learning rate $\eta(t)$ that is a function of time t, such as $\eta(t) = 1/t$ or $\eta(t) = a[1 - (t/A)]$ where a and A are positive constants and $A > 1$. This allows the network to "converge" to a state in which the weight vectors are stable and change little with further input sample presentations.

EXAMPLE 5.5   This example illustrates the result of running the LVQ1 algorithm on the same input samples and with the same initial weight vectors used to illustrate the simple competitive learning rule in example 5.3.

---

2. Such an assumption is not required for convergence of the similar quantization algorithms proposed by Lloyd (1957); Gray, Kieffer, and Linde (1979); and others.

Algorithm LVQ1;
   Initialize all weights to random values in the range [0,1];
   repeat

      Adjust the learning rate $\eta(t)$;
      for each input pattern i_k in the training set, **do**
         find node j^* whose weight vector w_{j^*} is closest to i_k;
         for $\ell = 1,\ldots,n$, **do**
            Update the weight $w_{j^*,\ell}$ as follows:
            if the class label of node j^* equals
               the desired class of i_k,
              then $\Delta w_{j^*,\ell} = \eta(t)(i_{k,\ell} - w_{j^*,\ell})$
              else $\Delta w_{j^*,\ell} = -\eta(t)(i_{k,\ell} - w_{j^*,\ell})$
         end-for
      end-for

   until network converges or computational bounds are exceeded.

Figure 5.10
LVQ1 algorithm.

The data are cast into a classification problem by arbitrarily associating the first and last samples with Class 1, and the remaining samples with Class 2. Thus the training set is: $T = \{(i_1; 1), (i_2; 0), \ldots, (i_6; 1)\}$ where $\{i_1 = (1.1, 1.7, 1.8),\ i_2 = (0, 0, 0),\ i_3 = (0, 0.5, 1.5),\ i_4 = (1, 0, 0),\ i_5 = (0.5, 0.5, 0.5),\ \text{and}\ i_6 = (1, 1, 1)\}$. The initial weight matrix is

$$W(0) = \begin{pmatrix} w_1: & 0.2 & 0.7 & 0.3 \\ w_2: & 0.1 & 0.1 & 0.9 \\ w_3: & 1 & 1 & 1 \end{pmatrix}.$$

Since there are twice as many samples in Class 2 as in Class 1, we label the first node (w_1) as associated with Class 1, and the other two nodes with Class 2. Let $\eta(t) = 0.5$ until $t = 6$, then $\eta(t) = 0.25$ until $t = 12$, and $\eta(t) = 0.1$ thereafter. In the calculations that follow, fractions are shown rounded to the second decimal place, for ease of presentation, although more accurate values are actually used in calculating the next set of weights. It is sufficient to mention the change in a single weight vector in each weight update iteration of the network, instead of writing out the entire weight matrix.

1. Sample i_1, winner w_3 (distance 1.07), w_3 changed to (0.95, 0.65, 0.60).

2. Sample i_2, winner w_1 (distance 0.79), w_1 changed to (0.30, 1.05, 0.45).

3. Sample i_3, winner w_2 (distance 0.73), w_2 changed to (0.05, 0.30, 1.20).

4. Sample i_4, winner w_3 (distance 0.89), w_3 changed to (0.97, 0.33, 0.30).

5. Sample i_5, winner w_3 (distance 0.54), w_3 changed to (0.74, 0.41, 0.40).

6. Sample i_6, winner w_3 (distance 0.88), w_3 changed to (0.61, 0.12, 0.10).

7. Sample i_1, winner w_1 (distance 1.70), w_1 changed to (0.50, 1.21, 0.79).

8. Sample i_2, winner w_3 (distance 0.63), w_3 changed to (0.45, 0.09, 0.08).

9. Sample i_3, winner w_2 (distance 0.36), w_2 changed to (0.04, 0.35, 1.27).

10. Sample i_4, winner w_3 (distance 0.56), w_3 changed to (0.59, 0.07, 0.06).

11. Sample i_5, winner w_3 (distance 0.63), w_3 changed to (0.57, 0.18, 0.17).

12. Sample i_6, winner w_1 (distance 0.58), w_1 changed to (0.62, 1.16, 0.84).

13. Sample i_1, winner w_1 (distance 1.20), w_1 changed to (0.67, 1.21, 0.94).

14. Sample i_2, winner w_3 (distance 0.62), w_3 changed to (0.51, 0.16, 0.15).

15. Sample i_3, winner w_2 (distance 0.27), w_2 changed to (0.03, 0.37, 1.30).

16. Sample i_4, winner w_3 (distance 0.53), w_3 changed to (0.56, 0.14, 0.14).

17. Sample i_5, winner w_3 (distance 0.51), w_3 changed to (0.55, 0.18, 0.17).

18. Sample i_6, winner w_1 (distance 0.40), w_1 changed to (0.71, 1.19, 0.94).

$$\vdots \quad \vdots \quad \vdots \quad \vdots \quad \vdots$$

151. Sample i_1, winner w_1 (distance 0.57), w_1 changed to (1.05, 1.37, 1.42).

152. Sample i_2, winner w_3 (distance 0.58), w_3 changed to (0.46, 0.17, 0.17).

153. Sample i_3, winner w_2 (distance 0.02), w_2 changed to (0.00, 0.49, 1.48).

154. Sample i_4, winner w_3 (distance 0.58), w_3 changed to (0.52, 0.15, 0.15).

155. Sample i_5, winner w_3 (distance 0.50), w_3 changed to (0.52, 0.18, 0.18).

156. Sample i_6, winner w_1 (distance 0.56), w_1 changed to (1.04, 1.33, 1.38).

157. Sample i_1, winner w_1 (distance 0.57), w_1 changed to (1.05, 1.37, 1.42).

158. Sample i_2, winner w_3 (distance 0.58), w_3 changed to (0.46, 0.17, 0.17).

159. Sample i_3, winner w_2 (distance 0.02), w_2 changed to (0.00, 0.49, 1.48).

160. Sample i_4, winner w_3 (distance 0.58), w_3 changed to (0.52, 0.15, 0.15).

161. Sample i_5, winner w_3 (distance 0.50), w_3 changed to (0.52, 0.18, 0.18).

162. Sample i_6, winner w_1 (distance 0.56), w_1 changed to (1.05, 1.33, 1.38).

Note that associations between input samples and weight vectors stabilize by the second cycle of pattern presentations, although the weight vectors continue to change, converging approximately to the centroids of associated input samples in 150 iterations.

In a variation called the LVQ2 learning algorithm, the following learning rule is used instead, with an emphasis on adjusting the boundaries between adjacent classes. This algorithm adapts weight vectors only under special circumstances.

If, among the two nodes with weight vectors w_1, w_2 nearest to the input pattern (i), only one node belongs to the desired class, and both weight vectors are at comparable distances from i. In other words, if $Class(w_1) = Class(i) \neq Class(w_2)$ and

$$\min\left(\frac{||w_1 - i||}{||w_2 - i||}, \frac{||w_2 - i||}{||w_1 - i||}\right) > c$$

where c is a constant (with a suggested value ≈ 0.7) then w_1 is moved closer to the presented pattern, and w_2 is moved farther from the presented pattern, using an update rule similar to that of LVQ1.

5.3   Counterpropagation Networks

A counterpropagation neural network is a multilayer feedforward network that uses a training methodology that combines supervised and competitive unsupervised learning techniques in an innovative way that is significantly different from backpropagation. This hybrid network model was developed by Hecht-Nielsen (1987) and further studied by Huang and Lippmann (1988). It has been used successfully for function approximation, hetero-association, and data compression, and its training occurs much faster than backpropagation. In the rest of this section, we discuss details of two variations of counterpropagation neural networks, referred to as *forward-only* and *full* counterpropagation.

Forward-only counterpropagation   The architecture of the forward-only counterpropagation network, shown in figure 5.11, consists of an input layer, a hidden layer, and an output layer. Connections exist from every input node to every hidden node, and from every hidden node to every output node. Additionally, unlike feedforward networks, every hidden node is also connected to other hidden nodes, as in the case of the simple competitive winner-take-all learning network models discussed in section 5.1.3.

The major difference between counterpropagation and backpropagation is in the training algorithm that modifies weights. In backpropagation, the error signal and corresponding weight modification are propagated backwards from the output layer to the input layer. Different training samples may exert opposite forces in increasing or decreasing the same weight, and the net effect is that weight changes are often of extremely small magnitude in networks with learning rates small enough to have some assurance of converging to a local minimum of the mean squared error. Some of the adaptive algorithms discussed in chapter 4 (such as the Tiling algorithm) remedy this difficulty by modifying all weights on connections from input layer to the first hidden layer, then modifying the weights to

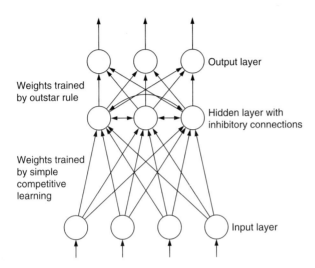

Figure 5.11
Architecture of the forward-only counterpropagation neural network.

successively next layers while leaving previously trained weights unchanged. A similar philosophy is followed in forward-only counterpropagation. Weights to the hidden layer are completely trained using an unsupervised learning algorithm, followed by training the weights to the output layer while leaving the previously trained weights unchanged. Thus, as described in figure 5.12, forward-only counterpropagation consists of two phases, each of which uses separate time-varying learning rates ($\eta^{(1)}(t)$ and $\eta^{(2)}(t)$).

1. In the first phase, hidden layer nodes are used to divide the training set into clusters containing similar input patterns. The learning rule is identical to that of the simple competitive learning algorithm discussed in section 5.1.3, with the difference that the learning rate $\eta^{(1)}(t)$ is steadily reduced. Consequently, weights change much less in later iterations of this phase of the algorithm, stabilizing the first layer of weights such that the same hidden layer node continues to be the winner for similar input patterns. Inhibitory interconnections among hidden layer nodes are used to conduct a competition for winners when training patterns are presented at the input layer. At the end of the first phase, each hidden node represents a cluster centroid or the codebook vector corresponding to one Voronoi region in the input space.

2. In the second phase, the primary task is to adjust the connection strengths from the hidden nodes to the output nodes, using a gradient descent rule and with steadily decreasing learning rate $\eta^{(2)}(t)$. This is done using a variant of the delta rule proposed by Grossberg

Algorithm Forward-only Counterpropagation;

  Phase 1:

    1. Initialize weights $\in (0,1)$ randomly, and learning rate $\eta^{(1)}$;

    2. **repeat**

        • **for** $p = 1, \ldots, P$, **do** :

           (a) Calculate the distance of i_p from all hidden nodes, i.e., calculate $D_k = \sum_{j=1}^{n}(w_{k,j} - i_{p,j})^2$, for $k = 1, \ldots, K$.

           (b) Find a winner k^* such that $D_{k^*} \leq D_k$; for $k = 1, \ldots, K$.

           (c) Update weights $w_{k^*,\ell}$; for $\ell = 1, \ldots, n$ using the rule:
$$w_{k^*,\ell}(\text{new}) = (1 - \eta^{(1)})w_{k^*,\ell}(\text{old}) + \eta^{(1)}i_{p,\ell};$$

        end-for;

        • Decrease $\eta^{(1)}$, e.g., by a small constant;

    until performance is satisfactory or computational bounds are exceeded;

  Phase 2:

    1. Fix $\eta^{(1)}$ at current level (from Phase 1) and initialize $\eta^{(2)}$;

    2. **repeat**

        • **for** $p = 1, \ldots, P$, **do** :

           (a) Calculate $D_k = \sum_{j=1}^{n}(w_{k,j} - i_{p,j})^2$, the distance between i_p and the kth hidden layer node, for $k = 1, \ldots, K$.

           (b) Find a winner k^* such that $D_{k^*} \leq D_k$, $k = 1, \ldots, K$.

           (c) Adjust weights as follows:
$$w_{k^*,\ell}(\text{new}) = (1 - \eta^{(1)})w_{k^*,\ell}(\text{old}) + \eta^{(1)}i_{p,\ell}; \text{ for } \ell = 1, \ldots, n.$$
$$v_{k^*j}(\text{new}) = (1 - \eta^{(2)})v_{k^*,\ell}(\text{old}) + \eta^{(2)}_{p,j}d_{p,j}; \text{ for } j = 1, \ldots, m$$

        end-for;

        • Decrease $\eta^{(2)}$, e.g., by a small constant;

    until performance is satisfactory or computational bounds are exceeded.

Figure 5.12
Forward-only counterpropagation algorithm.

(1977, 1982), called the "outstar" learning rule, in which all weights fanning *out* of a single hidden node are modified simultaneously. When an input pattern is presented to the network, a competition is conducted among the hidden nodes, and only the connections from the winner node to the output nodes are modified. The change in each weight is proportional to the difference between the desired node output value and the weight

$$\Delta w_{j*,\ell} = \eta^{(2)}(t)(d_\ell - w_{j*,\ell})$$

where $j*$ is the winning hidden node. Note that d_ℓ, the desired output of the ℓth node in the higher layer, is available for each training sample. Small corrections may also be made to the first layer weights even during the second phase to enable the system to evolve with time, using a small learning rate $\eta^{(1)}(t) > 0$.

After training is complete, the forward-only counterpropagation network is used as follows. Given an input vector, the network is used to find the hidden node whose weight vector matches best with the input vector. The output pattern generated by this network is identical to the vector of weights leading out of the winner hidden node. In this respect, this method is like a table lookup. The difference from the usual table lookup is that the weight vectors are obtained by the training algorithm, rather than in an *ad hoc* manner.

Full counterpropagation   The high-level architecture of the full counterpropagation neural network is given in figure 5.13, and illustrates how it extends the forward-only counterpropagation neural network. The main difference between the full and forward-only counterpropagation neural networks is that the former treats both i_p and d_p without any special preference; both function similarly in finding the winner cluster node of the hidden layer. The full counterpropagation neural network is designed to function in both directions

1. to predict i_p, given d_p, and

2. to predict d_p, given i_p.

As in forward counterpropagation, the training set consists of many patterns: $\{(i_p, d_p) : p = 1, \ldots, P\}$, and the network is trained in two phases. Initially, all four sets of the weights ($w^{(1)}, w^{(2)}, v^{(1)}, v^{(2)}$ in figure 5.13) are assigned random values between 0 and 1. The first phase adjusts the $w^{(1)}$–weights and $w^{(2)}$–weights, associated with connections leading into the hidden nodes. This part of the training algorithm is similar to the first phase of the forward-only algorithm except that i_p and d_p are both used in this process. The main purpose of the second phase is to adjust the $v^{(1)}$–weights and $v^{(2)}$–weights, associated with connections leading away from the hidden nodes. When training is completed, the network can be used in either direction: to predict i_p from d_p, or d_p from i_p.

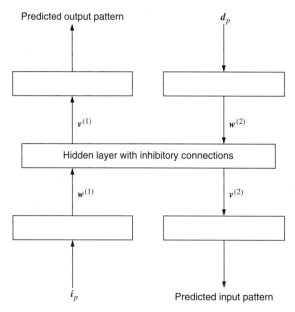

Figure 5.13
Architecture of the full counterpropagation neural network.

In a variation of the counterpropagation networks, the restriction of using only one (winner) node can be modified. Instead of using only the winner node, all hidden nodes participate in predicting a value in proportion to their distance from the input. These distances can be considered to indicate the probabilities of membership of an input pattern to various clusters.

5.4 Adaptive Resonance Theory

Adaptive resonance theory (ART) models are neural networks that perform clustering, and can allow the number of clusters to vary with problem size. The major difference between ART and other clustering methods is that ART allows the user to control the degree of similarity between members of the same cluster by means of a user-defined constant called the vigilance parameter. ART networks have been used for many pattern recognition tasks, such as automatic target recognition and seismic signal processing. The first version of ART was "ART1," developed by Carpenter and Grossberg (1988). Subsequently, several other modifications of this algorithm have been proposed by these researchers and their collaborators. ART networks use at least two layers of nodes with feedforward connections (from input to output nodes) as well as feedback connections (from output to input nodes). Each outer layer node can be visualized as representing a *prototype* or cluster centroid. The first layer contains as many nodes as the size of the pattern vector; and the second layer has a variable number of nodes representing the number of clusters.

"Resonance" refers to the process used to match a new input vector to one of the cluster prototypes stored in the network; signals travel repeatedly between the output layer and the input layer as in a BAM network, discussed in the next chapter. The system is "adaptive" in allowing for the addition of new cluster prototypes to a network.

ART networks associate patterns with prototypes. The first layer receives and holds the input patterns, and the second layer responds with a pattern associated with the given input pattern. If this returned pattern is sufficiently similar to the input pattern, then there is a match. But if the difference is substantial, then the layers communicate with each other until a match is discovered; otherwise, a new cluster of patterns is formed around the new input vector.

ART networks undergo unsupervised learning; the connection weights change over time as new patterns are presented to the system. There is no distinction between the training phase and the operational phase, and training data are not distinguished from test data. The same pattern is presented to the network several times, and a pattern may move from one cluster to another until the network stabilizes. At each successive presentation, network weights are modified. In a stable network, weights no longer change, and each input pattern activates the same prototype in successive presentations. On the presentation of a new input pattern that is considerably different from existing prototypes, a new prototype (outer layer node) may be introduced, thereby increasing network size. The number of clusters to which these networks associate input patterns can thus increase over time.

In the rest of this section, we study in greater detail a simple version of ART called the ART1 model. The architecture of an ART1 network is illustrated in figure 5.14. ART1 restricts all inputs to be binary valued. A high-level description of the ART1 unsupervised learning algorithm is given in figure 5.15.

The initial weights are assigned as follows.

$$b_{j,\ell} = \frac{1}{1+n} \quad \text{and} \quad t_{\ell,j} = 1 \quad \text{for} \quad \ell = 1, \ldots, n; \; j = 1, \ldots, m$$

When samples are presented, ART1 learns the "bottom-up" weights $\{\ldots, b_{j,\ell}, \ldots\}$ (from the input layer to the output layer) and "top-down" weights $\{\ldots, t_{\ell,j}, \ldots\}$ (from the output layer to the input layer). In general, weights are unequal, $b_{j,\ell} \neq t_{\ell,j}$. When a new input vector x is presented to the network, it is communicated to the second layer via upward connections carrying bottom-up weights. At this layer, $y_j = \sum_\ell b_{j,\ell} x_\ell$ represents the output value of the jth node in the second layer; y_j represents the similarity between

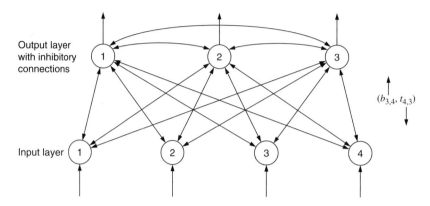

Figure 5.14
ART1 network.

Algorithm ART1;
    Initialize each top-down weight $t_{\ell,j}(0) = 1$;
    Initialize each bottom-up weight $b_{j,\ell}(0) = \frac{1}{n+1}$;
    while the network has not stabilized, **do**
        1. Present a randomly chosen pattern $x = (x_1, \ldots, x_n)$ for learning;
        2. Let the active set A contain all nodes; calculate
            $y_j = b_{j,1}\, x_1 + \cdots + b_{j,n}\, x_n$ for each node $j \in A$;
        3. **repeat**
            (a) Let j^* be a node in A with largest y_j, with ties being
                broken arbitrarily;
            (b) Compute $s* = (s_1^*, \ldots, s_n^*)$ where $s_\ell^* = t_{\ell,j^*}\, x_\ell$;
            (c) Compare similarity between $s*$ and x with the given
                vigilance parameter ρ:

                if $\dfrac{\sum_{\ell=1}^{n} s_\ell^*}{\sum_{\ell=1}^{n} x_\ell} \le \rho$ **then** remove j^* from set A

                else associate x with node j^* and update weights:

$$b_{j^*,\ell}(\text{new}) = \frac{t_{\ell,j^*}(\text{old})\, x_\ell}{0.5 + \sum_{\ell=1}^{n} t_{\ell,j^*}(\text{old})x_\ell}$$

                $t_{\ell,j^*}(\text{new}) = t_{\ell,j^*}(\text{old})x_\ell$

        until A is empty or x has been associated with some node j;
        4. If A is empty, then create a new node whose weight vector
            coincides with the current input pattern x;
    end-while.

Figure 5.15
Algorithm for updating weights in ART1.

the prototype vector $\boldsymbol{b}_j = (b_{j,1}, \ldots, b_{j,n})$ and the input vector. A competitive activation process occurs among nodes that are in the current "active" list A; the node in A with highest $\sum_\ell b_{j,\ell} x_\ell$ wins, and the corresponding cluster is declared to match $\boldsymbol{x}$ best. The maxnet can be used to find j^* such that $y_{j^*} = \max\{y_1, \ldots, y_m\}$.

Since even the best match may not be close enough to satisfy an externally chosen threshold, the final decision (whether the attempted match succeeds) depends on a *vigilance* parameter. If the winner is y_{j^*}, then a tentative decision is taken to associate the input vector with the j^*th cluster. The j^*th node in the second layer produces the n-dimensional vector $\boldsymbol{s}^*$ with components $s_\ell^* = t_{\ell,j^*} x_\ell$ using the top-down weights. The input vector $\boldsymbol{x}$ and $\boldsymbol{s}^*$ are compared. If the proportion of "ON" bits in $\boldsymbol{x}$ that are also in $\boldsymbol{s}^*$ exceeds a threshold ρ, called the *vigilance parameter*, i.e.,

$$\sum_\ell \frac{t_{\ell,j^*} x_\ell}{\|\boldsymbol{x}\|} > \rho$$

then the match with the j^*th node is judged acceptable, the weights $t_{1,j^*}, \ldots, t_{n,j^*}$ and $b_{j^*,1}, \ldots, b_{j^*,n}$ are modified to make the node output $\boldsymbol{s}^*$ resemble $\boldsymbol{x}$ to a greater extent, and computation proceeds with the next input pattern.

If the vigilance test fails, the j^*th cluster is removed from the "active" set of nodes A, and does not participate in the remainder of the process of assigning $\boldsymbol{x}$ to an existing cluster. The above process (of determining the best match from the active set A) is repeated until A is empty or until a best match has been found that satisfies the vigilance criterion. If A is empty and no satisfactory match has been found, a new output node (cluster prototype) is created with connections that carry top-down weights t identical to $\boldsymbol{x}$.

EXAMPLE 5.6   Consider a set of vectors $\{(1, 1, 0, 0, 0, 0, 1), (0, 0, 1, 1, 1, 1, 0), (1, 0, 1, 1, 1, 1, 0), (0, 0, 0, 1, 1, 1, 0),$ and $(1, 1, 0, 1, 1, 1, 0)\}$ to be clustered using the ART1 algorithm. Let the vigilance parameter be $\rho = 0.7$.

We begin with a single node whose top-down weights are all initialized to 1, i.e., $t_{\ell,1}(0) = 1$, and bottom-up weights are set to $b_{1,\ell}(0) = \frac{1}{8}$. Here $n = 7$ and initially $m = 1$. Given the first input vector, $(1, 1, 0, 0, 0, 0, 1)$, we compute

$$y_1 = \frac{1}{8} \times 1 + \frac{1}{8} \times 1 + \frac{1}{8} \times 0 + \cdots + \frac{1}{8} \times 0 + \frac{1}{8} \times 1 = \frac{3}{8},$$

and y_1 is declared the uncontested winner. Since

$$\frac{\sum_{\ell=1}^7 t_{\ell,1} x_\ell}{\sum_{\ell=1}^7 x_\ell} = \frac{3}{3} = 1 > 0.7,$$

the vigilance condition is satisfied and the updated weights are

$$b_{1,\ell}(1) = \begin{cases} \frac{1}{0.5+3} = \frac{1}{3.5} & \text{for } \ell = 1, 2, 7; \\ 0 & \text{otherwise.} \end{cases}$$

Likewise,

$$t_{\ell,1}(1) = t_{\ell,1}(0)x_\ell.$$

These equations yield the following weight matrices.

$$B(1) = \begin{bmatrix} \frac{1}{3.5} & \frac{1}{3.5} & 0 & 0 & 0 & 0 & \frac{1}{3.5} \end{bmatrix}^T$$

$$T(1) = \begin{bmatrix} 1 & 1 & 0 & 0 & 0 & 0 & 1 \end{bmatrix}^T$$

Now we present the second sample $(0, 0, 1, 1, 1, 1, 0)$. This generates $y_1 = 0$, but the uncontested winner fails to satisfy the vigilance threshold since $\sum_\ell t_{\ell,1}x_\ell / \sum_\ell x_\ell = 0 < 0.7$. A second node must hence be generated, with top-down weights identical to the sample, and bottom-up weights equal to 0 in the positions corresponding to the zeroes in the sample, and remaining new bottom-up weights $= 1/(0.5 + 0 + 0 + 1 + 1 + 1 + 1 + 0)$. The new weight matrices are

$$B(2) = \begin{bmatrix} \frac{1}{3.5} & \frac{1}{3.5} & 0 & 0 & 0 & 0 & \frac{1}{3.5} \\ 0 & 0 & \frac{1}{4.5} & \frac{1}{4.5} & \frac{1}{4.5} & \frac{1}{4.5} & 0 \end{bmatrix}^T$$

and

$$T(2) = \begin{bmatrix} 1 & 1 & 0 & 0 & 0 & 0 & 1 \\ 0 & 0 & 1 & 1 & 1 & 1 & 0 \end{bmatrix}^T.$$

When the third vector $(1, 0, 1, 1, 1, 1, 0)$ is presented to this network,

$$y_1 = \frac{1}{3.5} \text{ and } y_2 = \frac{4}{4.5}$$

are the node outputs, and the second node is the obvious winner. The vigilance test suc-ceeds, because $\sum_{\ell=1}^7 t_{\ell,2} x_\ell / \sum_{\ell=1}^7 x_\ell = \frac{4}{5} \geq 0.7$. The second node's weights are hence adapted, with each top-down weight being the product of the old top-down weight and the corresponding element of the sample $(1, 0, 1, 1, 1, 1, 0)$, while each bottom-up weight is obtained on dividing this quantity by $0.5 + \sum_\ell t_{\ell,2} x_\ell = 4.5$. Note that this results in no change to the weight matrices, so that $B(3) = B(2)$ and $T(3) = T(2)$. Thus, weights are unchanged by the presentation of a sample whose bits subsume the node's top-down weights, if the vigilance test succeeds.

When the fourth vector $(0, 0, 0, 1, 1, 1, 0)$ is presented to this network,

$$y_1 = \frac{1}{3.5} \text{ and } y_2 = \frac{3}{4.5}$$

are the node outputs, and the second node is the obvious winner. The vigilance test succeeds, because $\sum_{\ell=1}^{7} t_{\ell,2} x_\ell / \sum_{\ell=1}^{7} x_\ell = \frac{3}{3} \geq 0.7$. The second node's weights are hence adapted, with each top-down weight being the product of the old top-down weight and the corresponding element of the sample $(0, 0, 0, 1, 1, 1, 0)$, while each bottom-up weight is obtained on dividing this quantity by $0.5 + \sum_\ell t_{\ell,2} x_\ell = 3.5$. The resulting weight matrices are

$$B(4) = \begin{bmatrix} \frac{1}{3.5} & \frac{1}{3.5} & 0 & 0 & 0 & 0 & \frac{1}{3.5} \\ 0 & 0 & 0 & \frac{1}{3.5} & \frac{1}{3.5} & \frac{1}{3.5} & 0 \end{bmatrix}^T, \quad T(4) = \begin{bmatrix} 1 & 1 & 0 & 0 & 0 & 0 & 1 \\ 0 & 0 & 0 & 1 & 1 & 1 & 0 \end{bmatrix}^T.$$

This example illustrates that the numbers of non-zero bits in weight vectors decrease as a result of the presentation of an input pattern whose ON bit-positions are a proper subset of the ON bit-positions of the top-down weights of a node.

When the fifth vector $(1, 1, 0, 1, 1, 1, 0)$ is presented to this network,

$$y_1 = \frac{2}{3.5} \text{ and } y_2 = \frac{3}{4.5}$$

are the node outputs, and the second node is the obvious winner. The vigilance test fails, because $\sum_{\ell=1}^{7} t_{\ell,2} x_\ell / \sum_{\ell=1}^{7} x_\ell = \frac{3}{5} < 0.7$. The active set A is hence reduced to contain only the first node, which is the new winner (uncontested). The vigilance test fails with this node as well, with $\sum_\ell t_{\ell,1} x_\ell / \sum_{\ell=1}^{7} x_\ell = \frac{2}{5} < 0.7$. A third node is hence created, and the resulting weight matrices are

$$B(5) = \begin{bmatrix} \frac{1}{3.5} & \frac{1}{3.5} & 0 & 0 & 0 & 0 & \frac{1}{3.5} \\ 0 & 0 & 0 & \frac{1}{3.5} & \frac{1}{3.5} & \frac{1}{3.5} & 0 \\ \frac{1}{5.5} & \frac{1}{5.5} & 0 & \frac{1}{5.5} & \frac{1}{5.5} & \frac{1}{5.5} & 0 \end{bmatrix}^T, \quad T(5) = \begin{bmatrix} 1 & 1 & 0 & 0 & 0 & 0 & 1 \\ 0 & 0 & 0 & 1 & 1 & 1 & 0 \\ 1 & 1 & 0 & 1 & 1 & 1 & 0 \end{bmatrix}^T.$$

We now cycle through all the samples again. This is generally performed in random order, but we opt for the same sequence as in the earlier cycle, to minimize confusion regarding how samples are chosen in each step. When the first vector $(1, 1, 0, 0, 0, 0, 1)$ is presented, $y_1 = 3/3.5$, $y_2 = 0$, and $y_3 = 2/5.5$, so that the first node is the winner, the vigilance threshold is clearly exceeded, but no change occurs in the weight vectors since the sample presented is identical to the top-down weight vector. When the second vector $(0, 0, 1, 1, 1, 1, 0)$ is presented, $y_1 = 0$, $y_2 = 3/3.5$, and $y_3 = 3/5.5$, the second node is the winner, which satisfies the vigilance threshold; again, no change occurs in the weight vectors. When the third vector $(1, 0, 1, 1, 1, 1, 0)$ is presented, $y_1 = 1/3.5$, $y_2 = 3/3.5$, and $y_3 = 4/5.5$, the second node is the winner. This time, however, the vigilance threshold is not satisfied since $\sum_{\ell=1}^{7} t_{\ell,3}\,x_\ell / \sum_{\ell=1}^{7} x_\ell = \frac{3}{5} < 0.7$. The active set is reduced to $A = \{1, 3\}$, and the third node is the winner since $y_3 > y_1$; the vigilance threshold is now satisfied, since $\sum_{\ell=1}^{7} t_{\ell,3}\,x_\ell / \sum_{\ell=1}^{7} x_\ell = \frac{4}{5} \geq 0.7$, and the weight matrices are modified to the following.

$$
B(8) = \begin{bmatrix} \frac{1}{3.5} & \frac{1}{3.5} & 0 & 0 & 0 & 0 & \frac{1}{3.5} \\ 0 & 0 & 0 & \frac{1}{3.5} & \frac{1}{3.5} & \frac{1}{3.5} & 0 \\ \frac{1}{4.5} & 0 & 0 & \frac{1}{4.5} & \frac{1}{4.5} & \frac{1}{4.5} & 0 \end{bmatrix}^T, \quad
T(8) = \begin{bmatrix} 1 & 1 & 0 & 0 & 0 & 0 & 1 \\ 0 & 0 & 0 & 1 & 1 & 1 & 0 \\ 1 & 0 & 0 & 1 & 1 & 1 & 0 \end{bmatrix}^T
$$

Now, when the fourth vector is presented, the second node is the winner, and also passes the vigilance test, though this causes no change in the weights. When the fifth vector is presented, the second node is the initial winner, but fails the vigilance test; the third node is the new winner, but no further weight changes occur. Subsequent presentations of the samples do not result in further changes to the weights, and $T(8)$ represents the prototypes for the given samples. The network has thus stabilized.

This example illustrates that

1. samples may switch allegiance: a sample previously activating node 2 now activates node 3.

2. when the initial winner in the competition (with highest y_ℓ) fails the vigilance test, another node may subsequently satisfy the vigilance test.

3. top-down weights are modified by computing intersections with the input vector, so that the number of 1's gradually decreases or remains the same. That is also the reason for initializing each top-down weight to 1.

Minor variations in weight updates, choice of initial weights, and vigilance test have been suggested in the literature for the basic algorithm given in figure 5.15.

1. Each bottom-up weight is assigned some common value such that $0 < b_{j,\ell} < \frac{L}{(L-1+n)}$ where L (typically 2 or 3) is a preassigned positive integer. Likewise, given two preassigned positive integers B and D such that $D \geq B \geq 1$, the top-down weights are chosen such that

$$\frac{B-1}{D} < t_{\ell,j} < 1.$$

The bottom-up weight updates depend on L, with

$$b_{j,\ell} = \frac{L\,x_\ell}{L - 1 + \sum_{\ell=1}^{n} x_\ell},$$

and the top-down weights are updated as before.

2. An additional check can be performed to determine the appropriateness of membership of a given pattern to a cluster. Instead of working with a set of bottom-up and top-down weights, we consider prototypes representing clusters. Suppose $w_j = (w_{j,1}, \ldots, w_{j,n})$ denotes the prototype of the jth cluster, $j = 1, \ldots, m$. Given a pattern $x = (x_1, \ldots, x_n)$, the similarity of active prototypes is found by examining the value of

$$\frac{\sum_{\ell=1}^{n} w_{j,\ell}\, x_\ell}{\beta + \sum_{\ell=1}^{n} w_{j,\ell}},$$

where β is a preassigned positive constant. Let the best matching prototype be labeled j^*. If it is sufficiently similar to x, i.e.,

$$\frac{\sum_{\ell=1}^{n} w_{j^*,\ell}\, x_\ell}{\beta + \sum_{\ell=1}^{n} w_{j^*,\ell}} > \frac{\sum_{\ell=1}^{n} x_\ell}{\beta + \rho},$$

for vigilance threshold $\rho > 0$, then we examine whether

$$\frac{\sum w_{j^*,\ell}\, x_\ell}{\sum_{\ell=1}^{n} x_\ell} > \rho.$$

Only if both of these conditions are satisfied is x associated with cluster j^* and the prototype of the winning cluster is modified.

The learning methods (weight determination procedure) of later versions of ART (such as ART2) follow the same principles as ART1, but are more complicated. With all of these algorithms, given a sufficient number of nodes, "outliers" that ought not to belong to any cluster will also be assigned separate nodes.

5.5 Topologically Organized Networks

The development of topologically organized networks is motivated by an attempt to understand how biological neurons come to organize themselves to achieve various tasks such as pattern recognition, in the absence of any instruction regarding the desired goals for each neuron. Von der Malsburg (1973) and Willshaw and von der Malsburg (1976) showed how a simple learning procedure is sufficient for the organization of some essential properties of neurons, without assuming genetic predetermination of detailed neural organization. Amari (1980) proposed a simple model with modifiable excitatory and inhibitory connections, and showed how topographical self-organization can be achieved, with frequently excited parts of the input nerve field being mapped to large areas of the output nerve field. The most commonly used topologically organized network is the model proposed by Kohonen (1982), referred to as the *self-organizing map* (SOM), *topology-preserving map*, or *self-organizing feature map* (SOFM). These phrases and abbreviations are frequently used to refer to Kohonen's model alone, even though some other related network models also conduct self-organization and develop maps. The following subsections discuss the SOM model proposed by Kohonen, its properties, and subsequent modifications of this model.

5.5.1 Self-organizing maps

The self-organizing map (SOM), proposed by Kohonen, combines a competitive learning principle with a topological structuring of nodes such that adjacent nodes tend to have similar weight vectors. Competitive learning requires inhibitory connections among all nodes; topological structuring implies that each node also has excitatory connections to a small number of nodes in the network. The topology is specified in terms of a neighborhood relation among nodes.

The learning algorithm ensures that the most highly activated node (winner of the competition) as well as its neighbors move towards a sample presented to the network. The networks are self-organizing in that nodes tend to attain weight vectors that capture characteristics of the input vector space, with the neighborhood relation translating into proximity in Euclidean space, even if the initial values of weight vectors are arbitrary. In clustering, the weight vectors associated with nodes in these networks are interpreted as cluster centroids. In the context of vector quantization, each weight vector is a codebook vector to which input vectors may be mapped. In approximating probability distributions, the number of nodes with weight vectors in a given region (in input vector space) is roughly proportional to the number of input vectors in that region.

The SOM learning algorithm is described in figure 5.16. As in winner-take-all networks, the first layer of an SOM is the input layer, and each node in the second layer is the winner for all input vectors in a region of input space. The second layer contains output nodes with many intra-layer connections set up according to a predetermined topology such as a grid (in which each node has four neighbors), as shown in figure 5.17. Each jth output node has connections from all input nodes, with connection strengths given by the n-dimensional vector $w_j = \{w_{j,1}, \ldots, w_{j,n}\}$. These weights are initially assigned random values, and their values change during the learning process, with each weight vector moving towards the centroid of some subset of input patterns. The number of nodes should be larger than the maximum number of possible clusters for the problem, but smaller than the number of training samples. As before, the output of each processing node represents "proximity" of the node to the input vector.

The SOM training algorithm updates the winner node and also nodes in its topological vicinity, when an input pattern is presented. The only criterion is the topological distance between nodes: there is no other excitatory "weight" between the winner node and other nodes in its topological vicinity. The neighborhood $\mathcal{N}_j(t)$ contains nodes that are within

Algorithm Self-Organize;
- Select network topology to determine which nodes are adjacent to which others;
- Initialize weights to small random values;
- Initialize current neighborhood distance $D(0)$ to a positive integer;
- **while** computational bounds are not exceeded, **do**
  1. Select an input sample i_ℓ;
  2. Compute the square of the Euclidean distance of i_ℓ from the weight vector (w_j) associated with each output node:
     $\sum_{k=1}^n (i_{\ell,k}(t) - w_{j,k}(t))^2$;
  3. Select the output node $j*$ with minimum $\sum_{k=1}^n (i_{\ell,k}(t) - w_{j,k}(t))^2$;
  4. Update weights to all nodes within a topological distance of $D(t)$ from $j*$, using the update rule
     $w_j(t+1) = w_j(t) + \eta(t)(i_\ell(t) - w_j(t))$,
     where $0 < \eta(t) \le \eta(t-1) \le 1$;
  5. Increment t;
  end-while.

Figure 5.16
Learning algorithm for Kohonen's topology-preserving network (SOM).

a topological distance of $D(t)$ from node j at time t, where $D(t)$ decreases with time, as shown in figures 5.17 and 5.18. Note that $D(t)$ does not refer to Euclidean distance in input space; it refers only to the length of the path connecting two nodes for the prespecified topology chosen for the network.

Weights change at time t at a rate $\eta(t)$ which decreases with time. For instance, the sequence of such changes with time may be as follows (as depicted in figure 5.17).

$0 \le t < 10$, $\eta(t) = 0.10$, $D(t) = 4$, $\mathcal{N}_j(t)$ contains all nodes at a distance ≤ 4 from j;

$10 \le t < 20$, $\eta(t) = 0.08$, $D(t) = 3$, $\mathcal{N}_j(t)$ contains all nodes at a distance ≤ 3 from j;

$20 \le t < 30$, $\eta(t) = 0.06$, $D(t) = 2$, $\mathcal{N}_j(t)$ contains all nodes at a distance ≤ 2 from j;

$30 \le t < 40$, $\eta(t) = 0.04$, $D(t) = 1$, $\mathcal{N}_j(t)$ contains all nodes at a distance ≤ 1 from j;

$40 \le t$, $\eta(t) = 0.02$, $D(t) = 0$, $\mathcal{N}_j(t)$ contains only j.

If j is the winner node, $\mathcal{N}_j(t) = \{j\} \cup \{$neighbors of j at time $t\}$, and i is the input vector presented to the network at time t, then the weight change rule is

$$w_\ell(t+1) = \begin{cases} w_\ell(t) + \eta(t)(i - w_\ell(t)), & \text{if } \ell \in \mathcal{N}_j(t) \\ w_\ell(t), & \text{if } \ell \notin \mathcal{N}_j(t). \end{cases} \qquad (5.2)$$

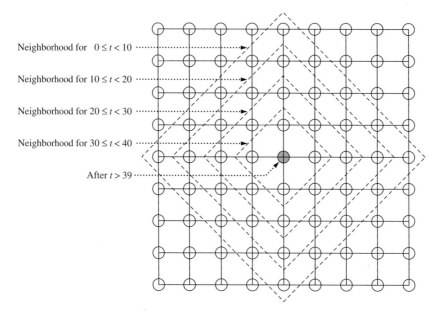

Neighborhood for $0 \le t < 10$ ········

Neighborhood for $10 \le t < 20$ ········

Neighborhood for $20 \le t < 30$ ········

Neighborhood for $30 \le t < 40$ ········

After $t > 39$ ········

Figure 5.17
Time-varying neighborhoods of a node in an SOM network with grid topology: $D(t) = 4$ for $0 \le t < 10$, $D(t) = 3$ for $10 \le t < 20$, $D(t) = 2$ for $20 \le t < 30$, $D(t) = 1$ for $30 \le t < 40$, and $D(t) = 0$ for $t \ge 40$.

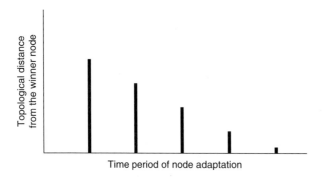

Figure 5.18
Shrinkage of the neighborhood of the winner node in topologically organized SOM networks, as time increases.

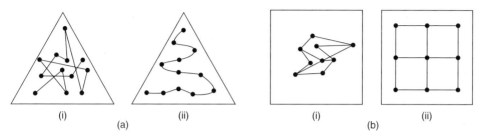

Figure 5.19
Weight vectors (in the input space) before and after the SOM learning algorithm is applied, (a) using a one-dimensional linear network topology for two-dimensional input data uniformly distributed in a triangular region; and (b) using a two-dimensional grid network topology for two-dimensional input data uniformly distributed in a rectangular region. Weight vectors are initially located randomly, as shown in (a)(i) and (b)(i). By the end of the learning process, the weights become "ordered," as shown in (ii) of each example.

As a result of the application of the SOM learning algorithm, nodes eventually become "ordered," and neighboring nodes (in the topology) become associated with weight vectors that are near each other in the input space. This property is shown in figure 5.19 where inputs (not shown in the figure) are uniformly distributed [in triangular space in (a) and rectangular space in (b)]. Initially, the output nodes are also randomly distributed in the input space, but the nodes are expected to align themselves at the end of the training process, as shown in figure 5.19(a)(ii) and (b)(ii).

EXAMPLE 5.7   We use the same training set T and a network with the same three randomly chosen nodes A, B, and C as in example 5.3 used to illustrate the simple competitive learning algorithm (in section 5.1.3). For illustrative purposes, we assume that the network has a linear topology, with node A (associated with weight vector w_A) adjacent to nodes B and C (with weight vectors w_B and w_C, respectively).

Note that this topology is independent of the precise weight vectors chosen initially for the nodes. The training set $T = \{i_1 = (1.1, 1.7, 1.8), \ i_2 = (0, 0, 0), i_3 = (0, 0.5, 1.5), \ i_4 = (1, 0, 0), \ i_5 = (0.5, 0.5, 0.5), \ i_6 = (1, 1, 1)\}$. The initial weight vectors are given by

$$W(0) = \begin{pmatrix} w_A: & 0.2 & 0.7 & 0.3 \\ w_B: & 0.1 & 0.1 & 0.9 \\ w_C: & 1 & 1 & 1 \end{pmatrix}.$$

Let $D(t) = 1$ for one initial round of training set presentations (until $t = 6$), and $D(t) = 0$ thereafter. As in the LVQ example, let $\eta(t) = 0.5$ until $t = 6$, then $\eta(t) = 0.25$ until $t = 12$, and $\eta(t) = 0.1$ thereafter.

$t = 1$: Sample presented: $i_1 = (1.1, 1.7, 1.8)$.
  Squared Euclidean distance between A and i_1: $d_{A1}^2 = (1.1 - 0.2)^2 + (1.7 - 0.7)^2 + (1.8 - 0.3)^2 = 4.1$. Similarly, $d_{B1}^2 = 4.4$ and $d_{C1}^2 = 1.1$.
  C is the "winner" since $d_{C1}^2 < d_{A1}^2$ and $d_{C1}^2 < d_{B1}^2$.
  Since $D(t) = 1$ at this stage, the weights of both C and its neighbor A are updated according to equation 5.2. For example,

$$w_{A,1}(1) = w_{A,1}(0) + \eta(1) \cdot (x_{1,1} - w_{A,1}(0)) = 0.2 + (0.5)(1.1 - 0.2) = 0.65$$

The resulting weight matrix is

$$W(1) = \begin{pmatrix} w_A: & 0.65 & 1.2 & 1.05 \\ w_B: & 0.1 & 0.1 & 0.9 \\ w_C: & 1.05 & 1.35 & 1.4 \end{pmatrix}.$$

Note that the weights attached to B are not modified since B falls outside the neighborhood of the winner node C.

$t = 2$: Sample presented: $i_2 = (0, 0, 0)$. $d_{A2}^2 = 3$, $d_{B2}^2 = 0.8$, $d_{C2}^2 = 4.9$, hence B is the winner. The weights of both B and its neighbor A are updated. The resulting weight matrix is

$$W(2) = \begin{pmatrix} w_A: & 0.325 & 0.6 & 0.525 \\ w_B: & 0.05 & 0.05 & 0.45 \\ w_C: & 1.05 & 1.35 & 1.4 \end{pmatrix}.$$

$t = 3$: Sample presented: $i_3 = (0, 0.5, 1.5)$. $d_{A3}^2 = 1.1$, $d_{B3}^2 = 1.3$, $d_{C3}^2 = 1.7$, hence A is the winner. The weights of A and its neighbors B, C are all updated. The resulting weight matrix is

$$W(3) = \begin{pmatrix} w_A: & 0.16 & 0.55 & 1.01 \\ w_B: & 0.025 & 0.275 & 0.975 \\ w_C: & 0.525 & 0.925 & 1.45 \end{pmatrix}.$$

$t = 4$: Sample presented: $i_4 = (1, 0, 0)$. $d_{A4}^2 = 2$, $d_{B4}^2 = 1.9$, $d_{C4}^2 = 3.2$, hence B is the winner; both B and A are updated.

$$W(4) = \begin{pmatrix} \boldsymbol{w}_A: & 0.58 & 0.275 & 0.51 \\ \boldsymbol{w}_B: & 0.51 & 0.14 & 0.49 \\ \boldsymbol{w}_C: & 0.525 & 0.925 & 1.45 \end{pmatrix}.$$

$t = 5$:   Sample presented: $\boldsymbol{i}_5$. A is the winner. All nodes are updated.

$$W(5) = \begin{pmatrix} \boldsymbol{w}_A: & 0.54 & 0.39 & 0.50 \\ \boldsymbol{w}_B: & 0.51 & 0.32 & 0.49 \\ \boldsymbol{w}_C: & 0.51 & 0.71 & 0.975 \end{pmatrix}.$$

$t = 6$:   Sample presented: $\boldsymbol{i}_6$. C is the winner; both $\boldsymbol{w}_C$ and $\boldsymbol{w}_A$ are updated.

$$W(6) = \begin{pmatrix} \boldsymbol{w}_A: & 0.77 & 0.69 & 0.75 \\ \boldsymbol{w}_B: & 0.51 & 0.32 & 0.49 \\ \boldsymbol{w}_C: & 0.76 & 0.86 & 0.99 \end{pmatrix}.$$

$t = 7$: η is now reduced to 0.25, and the neighborhood relation shrinks, so that only the winner node is updated henceforth. Sample presented: $\boldsymbol{i}_1$. C is the winner; only $\boldsymbol{w}_C$ is updated.

$\boldsymbol{w}_C$:   (0.84 1.07 1.19).

$t = 8$:   Sample presented: $\boldsymbol{i}_2$. B is winner and $\boldsymbol{w}_B$ is updated.

$\boldsymbol{w}_B$:   (0.38 0.24 0.37).

$t = 9$:   Sample presented: $\boldsymbol{i}_3$. C is winner and $\boldsymbol{w}_C$ is updated.

$\boldsymbol{w}_C$:   (0.63 0.93 1.27).

$t = 10$:   Sample presented: $\boldsymbol{i}_4$. B is winner and $\boldsymbol{w}_B$ is updated.

$\boldsymbol{w}_B$:   (0.53 0.18 0.28).

$t = 11$:   Sample presented: $\boldsymbol{i}_5$. B is winner and $\boldsymbol{w}_B$ is updated.

$\boldsymbol{w}_B$:   (0.53 0.26 0.33).

$t = 12$:   Sample presented: $\boldsymbol{i}_6$. Weights of the winner node A are updated.

$\boldsymbol{w}_A$:   (0.83 0.77 0.81).

$t = 13$:   Now η is further reduced to 0.1.

Sample presented: i_1. Weights of the winner node C are updated.

w_C : (0.68 1.00 1.32).

$t = 14$:   Sample presented: i_2. Weights of the winner node B are updated.

w_B : (0.47 0.23 0.30).

$t = 15$:   Sample presented: i_3. Winner is C and w_C is updated. At this stage, the weight matrix is given by

$$W(15) = \begin{pmatrix} w_A : & 0.83 & 0.77 & 0.81 \\ w_B : & 0.47 & 0.23 & 0.30 \\ w_C : & 0.61 & 0.95 & 1.34 \end{pmatrix}.$$

At the beginning of the training process, the Euclidean distances between various nodes were given by

$$|w_A - w_B| = 0.85, \quad |w_B - w_C| = 1.28, \quad |w_A - w_C| = 1.22.$$

The training process increases the relative distance between non-adjacent nodes (B, C), while the weight vector associated with A remains roughly in between B and C, with

$$|w_A - w_B| = 1.28, \quad |w_B - w_C| = 1.75, \quad |w_A - w_C| = 0.80.$$

The above example illustrates the extent to which nodes can move during the learning process, and how samples switch allegiance between nodes, especially in the early phases of computation. Computation continues in this manner until the network stabilizes, i.e., the same nodes continue to be the winners for the same input patterns, with the possible exception of input patterns equidistant from two weight vectors.

If the neighborhood relation is always trivial (containing only the winner node), as in the simple competitive learning algorithm of section 5.1.3, the initial arbitrary choice of node positions may have a significant deleterious effect. For instance, when 8 three-dimensional samples at the corners of the unit cube are presented, and one node is initially in the cube while all others are far away, the node inside the cube continues to be the winner for all samples, while the other nodes do not move at all. If the neighborhood relation for the inner node does include other nodes, however, then those nodes will be pulled towards the cube. Whether they will succeed in moving close enough to be winners for some samples depends on their initial positions and the length of time for which $D(t) > 0$.

For many problems, the quality of solutions improves by using a time-varying neighborhood relation. If the neighborhood relation is static (not changing with time), the performance of the SOM network is similar to simple competitive learning for noisy data. The presence of noise contributes to the development of more "robust" networks, so that the algorithm can avoid getting trapped in some of the local optima of the relevant energy function. The SOM algorithm with steadily shrinking neighborhood relations has been shown to perform better than networks with static neighborhood functions. There is an analogy to "simulated annealing" (outlined in section 6.4 and discussed in chapter 7): the probability of reaching a global optimum is maximized by steadily reducing one or both of the following quantities.

1. The amount of noise (described by the temperature parameter in annealing, that determines the probability of taking "uphill" steps)

2. The number of nodes perturbed by the presentation of an input sample vector (in the neighborhood of the winner node)

The SOM learning algorithm can also be extended for supervised learning tasks, in a manner similar to learning vector quantizers (LVQ) based on simple competitive learning, discussed in section 5.2. For this purpose, we invoke a variant of LVQ that maintains a topological relation between nodes and updates nodes in a neighborhood whose size decreases with time. The rest of the algorithm is identical to the LVQ algorithm.

5.5.2 Convergence*

Theoretical convergence results are clearly established only for one-dimensional topological maps (trained by Kohonen's SOM algorithm) in one-dimensional input space, and address whether the network reaches an ordered configuration that preserves distance relationships between input patterns. A one-dimensional configuration of nodes, in which the ℓth node (with weight vector w_ℓ) of the network is connected to the $(\ell + 1)$th node, is ordered if

$$|r - s| < |r - q| \quad \Leftrightarrow \quad |w_r - w_s| < |w_r - w_q|$$

where r, s, q are node labels and w_r, w_s, w_q are the weights corresponding to those nodes. The weights are one-dimensional, so that we can treat them as scalar numbers, not vectors. An example of the result of ordering is illustrated in figure 5.20.

For topological maps in one-dimensional space, if the neighborhood relation satisfies certain properties, Kohonen (1982), Ritter and Schulten (1986), and others have shown that an ordered configuration is stationary and stable. Erwin, Obermayer, and Schulten (1992) have shown that this state will be reached with probability 1 as long as the neighborhood function is positive-valued, normalized, and decreasing with distance, proving that there exists a sequence of patterns that will lead the network into the ordered configuration. However, for some sequences of input pattern presentations (e.g., if patterns

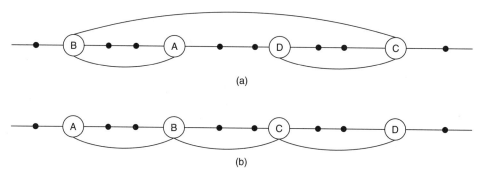

Figure 5.20
Emergence of an "ordered" map. The dark circles represent data points in one-dimensional space, and nodes are identified as A, B, C, and D, with connections indicating linear topology. Figure (a) depicts initial positions of nodes before applying SOM learning algorithm, and figure (b) shows final positions of nodes, with topologically adjacent nodes having similar weights.

are presented in a fixed sequence), then the one-dimensional Kohonen network may not converge to an ordered state. The network may instead settle into a state in which topologically adjacent nodes may be physically distant from each other in the weight space.

One may view an SOM's execution as consisting of two phases, where nodes are more "volatile" in the first phase, searching for niches to move into, with the second "sober" phase consisting of nodes settling into cluster centroids in the vicinity of positions found in the earlier phase. If the nodes are already well ordered, with topological neighbors being in nearby positions in the data space, then the weight update rule does perform gradient descent on an energy function analogous to that of the k-means clustering algorithm, from which convergence of the algorithm follows, as shown by Luttrell (1989). In other words, the sober (second) phase converges, though the emergence of an ordered map depends on the result of the volatile (first) phase.

Convergence of multidimensional self-organizing maps to ordered states is much less certain. Lo and Bavarian (1991) have shown that a topologically ordered configuration is reachable using the SOM update rule for multidimensional networks, but Erwin, Obermayer, and Schulten (1992) have argued that an ordered configuration may not be an absorbing state, i.e., the network may move out of such an ordered configuration. For the general case, Erwin, Obermayer, and Schulten (1992) have shown that there cannot be any energy function on which the SOM weight update rule performs gradient descent.

EXAMPLE 5.8   [Erwin, Obermayer, and Schulten (1992)]: Let a two-dimensional network initially be in its ordered configuration with four nodes connected as a square lattice with weight vectors w_0, w_1, w_2, w_3, and located at the vertices of a unit square. If input patterns

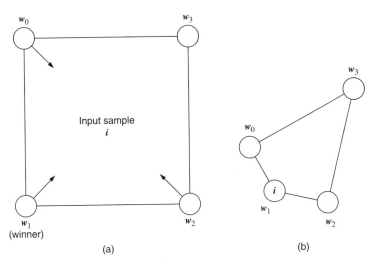

Figure 5.21
A self-organizing network in which the weight vectors (w_0, w_2) of topologically non-adjacent nodes move closer to each other than to the weight vector of an adjacent node (w_3), on repeated presentation of an input sample for which w_1 is the winner: (a) initial positions of weight vectors; (b) final positions of weight vectors.

are repeatedly chosen near the center of the square but slightly closer to one node w_1 [e.g., for input patterns $(0.5 - \epsilon, \ 0.5 - \epsilon)$, for small $\epsilon > 0$], and a non-empty neighborhood relation is used for updating weight vectors of nodes, then the nodes previously at w_0 and w_2 will eventually move closer to each other than to node w_3, as shown in figure 5.21(b). The final network is thus not in an ordered configuration, since topologically adjacent nodes are farther from each other than topologically non-adjacent nodes.

Despite the absence of conclusive theoretical proofs, the SOM and its variants have been a useful tool in practice, very often converging quickly to maps that are reasonably well ordered even in high-dimensional problems.

5.5.3 Extensions

The topology-preserving map and its learning algorithm have biological justification, and have been developed following the discovery of various map-like structures connecting neurons in animal brains. Several extensions to the SOM have been developed for computational efficiency, in order to obtain better solutions to various unsupervised learning problems. A few of these extensions are outlined in this section.

Conscience An important modification to SOM and other competitive learning algorithms attempts to limit the number of samples for which any node can be the winner.

This mechanism, proposed by DeSieno (1988), is called "conscience": the intention is that no node becomes too greedy in grabbing patterns, irrespective of the poor positioning of the other nodes. The conscience mechanism can be implemented by maintaining with each (jth) node the frequency $freq_j$ with which that node emerges as the winner of each competition. Each node updates its current frequency of activation whenever a sample is presented, increasing it if this node is the winner, and decreasing it otherwise. The conscience mechanism may be implemented as follows.

1. The mechanism proposed by DeSieno uses a combination of distance and current frequency to determine the winner. The winner is chosen as that node for which $d(w, x) + g(freq_j)$ is minimum, where g is a monotonically increasing function. DeSieno uses a linear function, $g(freq_j) = c(freq_j - 1/m)$, where c is a positive constant and m is the number of nodes competing to be the winner. This resembles the regularization approach discussed in chapter 4.

2. Another possible implementation temporarily deactivates a node whose frequency exceeds a predetermined limit that depends on P/m where P is the number of patterns and m is the number of nodes; then, competition (for subsequent presentation of patterns to the network) is conducted only among other nodes that are not deactivated. Eventually, some of the samples previously associated with the deactivated node may become closer to other nodes that have moved while the former node was deactivated.

Even if many of the nodes are initially positioned far away from most of the patterns, the conscience mechanism allows their weight vectors to move eventually towards the patterns, unlike the SOM.

Hierarchical SOMs   Traditional "hierarchical" clustering algorithms develop a tree of clusters, in which the root corresponds to the entire data space, and each node corresponds to a cluster, whose subclusters are associated with children of that node. In "bottom-up" hierarchical clustering algorithms, smaller (lower level) clusters are first formed from input data, and successively merged together to result in larger (higher level) clusters. "Top-down" hierarchical clustering algorithms, on the other hand, start with all the points belonging to one cluster, and successively refine each cluster into two or more clusters.

Hierarchical methods can also be used in the context of neural networks applied for clustering tasks. For instance, elongated, ellipsoid, and arbitrarily-shaped clusters occur in some applications. The simple SOM is inadequate for these clustering tasks since it attempts to minimize Euclidean distance between samples and weight vectors of nodes, generating symmetric clusters in which every dimension of the input space receives the same importance. This problem can be solved by a multilayer self-organizing map (MSOM), introduced by Lampinen (1993). In an MSOM, the outputs of the first SOM are fed into the second SOM as inputs. The first layer clusters together all similar elements of the training set, but this similarity is confined to circular symmetry in the original space. The second layer of nodes manages to combine these circular clusters together into arbitrary shapes in the desirable cluster. This approach can be viewed as a "bottom-up" hierarchical clustering algorithm. The MSOM can be used to form clusters of arbitrary shapes and forms, including elongated clusters.

An approach similar to a top-down hierarchical clustering algorithm was formulated by Luttrell (1992). This adaptive algorithm starts with a small number of nodes, and repeatedly applies the SOM learning rule until no further improvement is obtained. The number of nodes in the network steadily increases, and each application of the SOM learning algorithm attempts to add new nodes to the existing network. This algorithm uses small neighborhoods, with only a few topological neighbors of the winner being updated at any given time. Each new node is inserted halfway between two existing nodes. High-level clusters obtained at early phases of the algorithm are partitioned into subclusters in later phases of the algorithm.

Growing cell structures   Fritzke (1993) proposed a network model called *growing cell structures* (GCS), in which the number of nodes changes as samples are presented to the network; this results in a flexible network model which is able to approximate some probability distributions better than the SOM. GCS networks maintain a hyper-tetrahedral topology of fixed dimensionality; for example, in figure 5.22, the topology consists of triangles, which are hyper-tetrahedral in two-dimensional space. The choice of neighbors may be modified as the network evolves, tracking changes in the nature of the problem. A "signal counter" (τ_j) is associated with each (jth) node, and estimates the proportion of samples currently associated with a cluster located at a given node.

There are three main components of the GCS algorithm.

NODE ADAPTATION   When an input sample i is presented to the network, a competition is conducted as in simple competitive learning to determine the winner j^*. Its signal counter τ_{j^*} is incremented, while the signal counters associated with all nodes decay: $\Delta\tau_\ell = -\eta\tau_\ell$, for each ℓ. The winner j^* and *only* its immediate neighbors (adjacent to j^* in the topology) are adapted, the former to a greater extent than the latter.

$$\boldsymbol{w}_{j^*}(t+1) = \boldsymbol{w}_{j^*}(t) + \eta^*(\boldsymbol{i}(t) - \boldsymbol{w}_{j^*}(t))$$

$$\boldsymbol{w}_j(t+1) = \boldsymbol{w}_j(t) + \eta(\boldsymbol{i}(t) - \boldsymbol{w}_j(t)) \text{ with } \eta < \eta^*, \text{ if } j \text{ is adjacent to } j^*$$

NODE INSERTION   After a fixed number of node adaptations, a new node ℓ_{new} is added to take over some of the "load" of the node ℓ with largest signal counter value. To achieve this, ℓ_{new} must be located in the neighborhood of ℓ, but not too close to ℓ (since it is

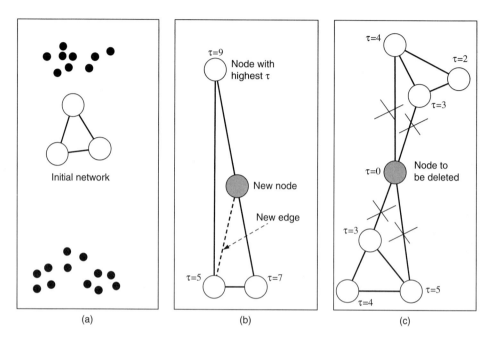

Figure 5.22
Growing cell structures network with triangular topology, applied to a two-dimensional data distribution. (a) Data distribution and initial network. (b) Snapshot of network structure after initial nodes have adapted to suitable locations, when a new node is being added; the broken line denotes a new connection needed to maintain the triangular topology. (c) Node deletion at a later stage, accompanied by deletion of associated connections. The resulting network consists of two disconnected components.

desirable for ℓ_{new} and ℓ to be the winners for different sets of samples). If ℓ has a neighbor ℓ_{near} that is physically close to ℓ, then it would not be desirable to situate ℓ_{new} between ℓ and ℓ_{near}. The GCS algorithm finds the neighbor ℓ_{far} of ℓ that is *farthest* (in Euclidean distance) from ℓ, and positions the new node ℓ_{new} exactly in between ℓ_{far} and ℓ. This is illustrated in figure 5.22(b). The set of neighbors of ℓ now includes ℓ_{new} instead of ℓ_{far}. Neighbors of ℓ_{new} are ℓ, ℓ_{far}, and others to preserve the hyper-tetrahedral topology of the network, chosen from the neighbors of ℓ and ℓ_{far} (whose neighborhood relations are also updated when ℓ_{new} is added to the network). The signal counter values for the neighbors of ℓ_{new} decrease as a result of adding ℓ_{new} to the system. The decrease in counter value for node ℓ is roughly proportional to the fraction of the volume of the Voronoi region of ℓ lost to ℓ_{new} by ℓ. The initial counter value for the new node ℓ_{new} is the sum of the decreases in counter values for its neighbors.

NODE DELETION   Nodes whose counter values are too low are deleted from the network, along with all connections incident on such nodes, as illustrated in figure 5.22(c). This is accompanied by the deletion of isolated nodes with no other neighbors. These deletions may destroy the topological structure of the network, in which each node has a fixed number of neighbors; Fritzke suggests removing other nodes to re-establish the structure. This may result in massive purges in the network.

In a typical application of GCS, the network grows and shrinks repeatedly. Convergence depends on the choice of parameters and criteria for insertion, deletion, and termination of the algorithm.

Instead of the signal counter value, one may use any general *resource* value whose interpretation depends on the task to be performed by the network. For a clustering task, the resource may measure the quantization error, i.e., the sum of the distances from a winner vector to all the samples to which it is the winner.

GCS networks have also been used for supervised learning, using networks that contain a hidden layer and an output layer. Each hidden node computes a Gaussian function of its net input, whereas output nodes use a sigmoid node function. When a sample is presented, the difference of the target output vector and the actual output vector provides an error signal that is used to update the resource value τ_j. More specifically, the resource value of the current best matching unit j is updated by $\delta\tau_j = \sum_{\ell=1}^{m}(o_\ell - d_\ell)^2$ if the network is intended for a function approximation problem, where o_ℓ is the activation of the ℓth output node. For a classification problem, the update rule is $\delta\tau_j = 1$ if the sample is correctly classified and $\delta\tau_j = 0$ otherwise. The weight vector for each hidden node is obtained using unsupervised GCS with a cluster of samples. Weights to output nodes are modified using the delta rule,

$$\delta w_{\ell,j} = \eta(d_\ell - o_\ell)y_j,$$

where d_ℓ is the desired output for that node, η is the learning rate, and y_j is the output of the jth hidden layer node.

5.6   Distance-Based Learning

Kohonen's SOM and its extensions (outlined above) have two aspects: (a) there is a predefined network topology, and (b) nodes other than the winner are updated. In this section, we study unsupervised learning algorithms that have the second property, but not the first. These algorithms are applicable for problems in which extracting a feature map is not important, and a topological organization of the nodes is not necessary.

Updating nodes other than the winner is useful in developing more robust networks, which outperform simple competitive learning. In the absence of a topological relationship among nodes, the criterion used by these algorithms is the Euclidean distance between any node and the input vector presented to the network. When the criterion is formulated as a differentiable function, it may be possible to construct an energy function on which the algorithm conducts gradient descent; this allows convergence results to be stated about the algorithm.

5.6.1   Maximum entropy

The maximum entropy clustering algorithm, proposed by Rose, Gurevitz, and Fox (1990), can be viewed as an unsupervised neural network learning algorithm. In this algorithm, all weight vectors are affected by the presentation of each input vector. The amount of change in each weight vector is a non-linear function of the distance between the input vector and the weight vector. All weight vectors are drawn closer to the input vector, but weight vectors far from the input vector are modified to a smaller extent than weight vectors close to the input vector. The magnitude of the change in each weight vector also depends on a "temperature" parameter (T), as in Boltzmann machines (cf. chapters 6 and 7). The weight update rule is of the following form:

$$\Delta w_j = \eta(i - w_j)\frac{\exp(-|i - w_j|^2/T)}{\sum_\ell \exp(-|i - w_\ell|^2/T)}$$

where η is the learning rate, i is the input vector, and w_j is the weight vector associated with the jth node. Temperature is lowered steadily, so that only the weight vectors close to the input vector have significant updates in later phases of the algorithm.

5.6.2   Neural gas

Martinetz, Berkovich, and Schulten (1993) proposed the *neural gas* algorithm, in which all weight vectors are affected by each sample presentation by an amount that depends on the distance between the weight vector and the input vector. Nodes are "ranked" by their proximity to the input vector, and the magnitude of the weight change depends on such a rank. If $W = (w_1, \ldots, w_n)$ is the set of weight vectors, and i is the input vector presented to the network, then the *rank* denoted by $k_j(i, W)$ is defined as the number of weight vectors $\in W$ whose distance from i is smaller than the distance from i to w_j. The adaptation step used by the neural gas algorithm for modifying the weight vector w_j is

$$\Delta w_j = \eta(i - w_j)h(k_j(i, W)), \quad j \in \{1, \ldots, N\}$$

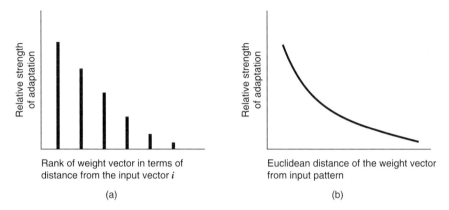

Rank of weight vector in terms of   Euclidean distance of the weight vector
distance from the input vector i from input pattern

            (a)   (b)

Figure 5.23
Weight adaptation rules for (a) the neural gas learning rule and (b) the maximum entropy algorithm. The ordinate
(y-axis) denotes the relative strength of adaptation, measured in terms of $|\Delta w_j|/|i - w_j|$.

where $i - w_j$ is the vector distance, $\eta \in [0, 1]$ is the learning rate, and h is a monotonically
decreasing function with $h(0) = 1$. One non-linear choice of h is defined by

$$h(x) = h_\lambda(x) = e^{-x/\lambda},$$

where $\lambda > 0$ is called the *decay* constant. When $\lambda \approx 0$, the neural gas update rule becomes
very similar to the winner-take-all adaptation rule of the simple competitive learning
algorithm.

In practice, if the weight vectors of many nodes are in the vicinity of an input pattern, the
simple competitive learning rule updates only one node (the winner node), SOM updates
the winner and its topological neighbors, maximum entropy updates all, and neural gas
makes significant updates to only a small number of them. The difference between the
neural gas and maximum entropy update rules is illustrated in figure 5.23; these may be
contrasted with the topological update rule of SOM, shown in figure 5.18.

The neural gas weight update rule conducts stochastic gradient descent on the following
function:

$$\frac{1}{2C(\lambda)} \sum_{j=1}^{N} \int_i P(i) h_\lambda(k_j(i, w))(i - w_j)^2 \, di$$

where $C(\lambda)$ is a normalization factor, and i ranges over the input vector space. For best
results, the decay constant λ is decreased with time, with large initial value and small
final value, analogous to the temperature parameter in simulated annealing (discussed in
chapters 6 and 7).

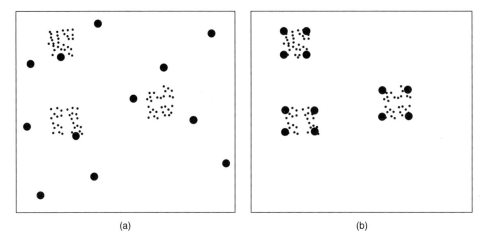

Figure 5.24
The neural gas algorithm applied to a clustering problem, with all data points contained in several small square-shaped regions. The network contains four times as many nodes as the number of regions. (a) Initial node positions; (b) positions of nodes after applying the neural gas algorithm.

Martinetz, Berkovich, and Schulten (1993) show that the density of the weight vectors is non-linearly proportional to the density of data points, for the stationary state of the network. They have empirically observed that the neural gas algorithm performs better than each of Kohonen's SOM, a statistical clustering algorithm (k-means clustering), and maximum entropy algorithms, on a large clustering problem of which a simplified version is illustrated in figure 5.24.

However, the neural gas algorithm is slower since each adaptation step is complicated and involves sorting the weight vectors by distance from each presented input sample, as opposed to the simple competitive learning rule, which only needs to determine the winner of a competition.

5.7   Neocognitron

The *neocognitron*, illustrated in figure 5.25, is a multilayer feedforward neural network model developed by Fukushima (1980, 1987) for visual pattern recognition, trained using a competitive learning procedure. The input images are two-dimensional arrays, and the final result of pattern recognition indicates which high-level feature or shape has been found in the entire input image, activating the appropriate output node. The network uses a hierarchy of many modules, with each module extracting features from the previous mod-

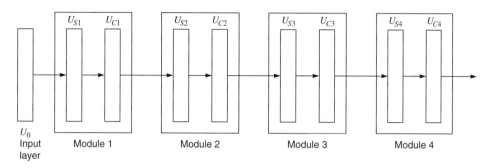

Figure 5.25
The neocognitron network.

ule. A neocognitron with three to four modules has been used successfully for handwritten character recognition problems, with one output node corresponding to each alphabetic character.

Each network module consists of two layers of nodes, as shown in figures 5.25 and 5.26. The first layer in each module is known as the S–layer, while the second is called the C–layer. Each node in the S–layer searches for the presence of a feature in a specific region of the input image (U_0 in figure 5.25). For a character recognition problem, for instance, one S–layer node may search for a vertical line segment in the top-left corner of the input image, while another may search for a horizontal line segment in the lower-left corner of the input image. Each C–layer node corresponds to one relatively position-independent feature, and receives inputs from a subset of S–layer nodes for that feature (in that module). For instance, one C–layer node may determine whether a vertical line segment occurs anywhere in the image.

Modules that are closer to the input layer (lower in the hierarchy) are trained before those that are farther from the input layer (higher in the hierarchy), e.g., in the sequence Module 1, Module 2, etc.

Only the input weights to the S–nodes can be modified during training. The "receptive field" of each C–node (subset of S–nodes in a module from which inputs are provided to a C–node) must be fixed by the user before training begins. Lower level modules use smaller receptive fields. Higher level modules represent complex position-independent features that depend on the detection of simpler features in preceding layers.

A competitive learning rule similar to the SOM is used in training weights to S–nodes. Since each S–layer contains many nodes that detect identical features (at different locations), only one such node is trained for each feature, and later replicated.

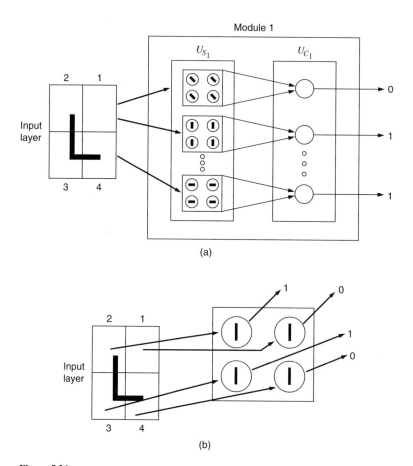

(a)

(b)

Figure 5.26
Some details of the connections between the input layer and the first module of a neocognitron: (a) Nodes of each type in the *S*-layer receive inputs from each of four regions (quadrants) of the input space. If any one of the four *S*-nodes detects the pattern that it is responsible for, then the corresponding output of the *C*-layer node is 1. (b) A vertical line segment is present in the second and third quadrants of the input space; consequently the associated nodes of the *S*-layer generate outputs that equal 1, whereas the outputs of the other two nodes equal 0.

206

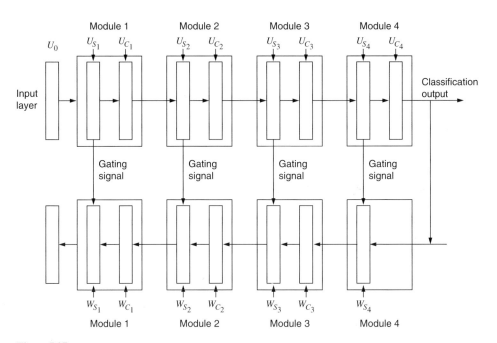

Figure 5.27
The selective-attention neural network.

Selective-attention neural network Fukushima (1990) also proposed a variation of the neocognitron with forward and backward connections, called the selective-attention network. The function of the forward connections is very similar to those in the neocognitron. The reverse connections are a complete copy of the forward connections, but wired to run in reverse (see figure 5.27). The purpose of this parallel network is to allow the system to identify those active elements of the input layer, U_0, due to whose presence the forward part of the network had concluded that the currently detected pattern was present. The reverse flow of information originates from the active node in the last layer of the forward part of the network.

Unlike the simpler neocognitron, the selective-attention network has an "active" input layer. The reverse connections can turn off some of the units in this layer by inhibitory signals. Thus the reverse signals have the effect of suppressing those portions of the input image that did not contribute to the activation of the currently active node in the last layer. To shift the attention of the network to another pattern, it is necessary to suppress briefly the active node in the output layer and allow some other node to become active. That node then reinforces its output by reverse inhibitory signals.

The position-independent pattern recognition capability of the neocognitron works against the task of identifying specific parts of the input image as responsible for the final output. Recall that a node in a C–layer becomes active if any one of the S–nodes in its receptive field becomes active. In the reverse direction, the C–layer receives its input from the next higher module in the hierarchy, e.g., W_{C_2} from W_{S_3}. But any S–node feeding into this C–node (in the forward direction) could have caused that C–node to become active. Therefore, to help identify the appropriate S–node, the S–nodes in the forward path send gating signals to S–nodes in the reverse direction module.

5.8 Principal Component Analysis Networks

Principal component analysis is a well-known statistical procedure that can be used to derive important features by reducing the dimensionality of a given input vector without losing information. The features of interest may not be explicitly available, and must be derived from the available attributes of individuals. Although infinitely many new candidate "features" can be derived by applying various mathematical functions to available attributes, there are many problems in which interesting features can be obtained merely by examining linear combinations of available attributes of individuals.

If we are interested in obtaining the smallest number of such features, these features should be linearly independent, identifying aspects of the population that are significantly different for different samples, rather than those aspects that vary little over the population. We may think of various features as being orthogonal geometrical transformations. For example, consider the task of reducing each three-dimensional observation $x = (x_1, x_2, x_3)$ to two-dimensional features. Let $w_1 = [a\ b\ c]$ and $w_2 = [p\ q\ r]$ be 2 three-dimensional vectors. The following transformation produces a two-dimensional vector y.

$$y = \begin{bmatrix} y_1 \\ y_2 \end{bmatrix} = \begin{bmatrix} a & b & c \\ p & q & r \end{bmatrix} \begin{bmatrix} x_1 \\ x_2 \\ x_3 \end{bmatrix} = \begin{bmatrix} ax_1 + bx_2 + cx_3 \\ px_1 + qx_2 + rx_3 \end{bmatrix}$$

y is the new description of x in a two-dimensional feature space. The elements y_1 and y_2 of the two-dimensional vector y are values of the new features. The row vectors $[a\ b\ c]$ and $[p\ q\ r]$ are orthogonal if their dot product is zero, i.e., $ap + bq + cr = 0$. We may assume without loss of generality that these vectors have unit length (Euclidean norm), i.e., $\sqrt{a^2 + b^2 + c^2} = \sqrt{p^2 + q^2 + r^2} = 1$. Normalization can be achieved by dividing each vector by its length. If the rows of

$$W = \begin{bmatrix} a & b & c \\ p & q & r \end{bmatrix}$$

are orthonormal, i.e., orthogonal and of unit length, then

$$WW^T = \begin{bmatrix} 1 & 0 \\ 0 & 1 \end{bmatrix},$$

the identity matrix. W^T is thus the pseudo-inverse of W, a property independent of the number of orthonormal features and their dimension.

We now generalize this idea. If W is a transformation that results in the least loss of "information" in mapping n-dimensional vectors x to m-dimensional vectors y, where $m < n$, then applying the inverse transformation W^T to y should result in an n-dimensional vector that is as close to the original vector as possible, i.e., $||x - W^T W x||$ should be minimized. This criterion should hold for all vectors in the population under consideration. Hence the performance of W over all vectors is maximized if W is chosen to minimize $\mathcal{E}||x - W^T W x||^2$, where $\mathcal{E}$ denotes the expected value. In practical problems, the entire population is unavailable or is too large to conduct computations with; only a training set $T = \{x_1, x_2, \ldots, x_N\}$ is available. The above goal is hence approximated by finding W that minimizes

$$\sum_{i=1}^{N} ||x_i - W^T W x_i||^2.$$

Principal component analysis is a procedure that performs this task, extracting the desired number of orthonormal features with maximum variability. The procedure first constructs the variance-covariance matrix $S(T)$ of the training set T, and exploits the following mathematical result (relevant definitions are given in appendix A.2).

Let b be any vector such that $||b|| = 1$. Then the variance of $b \cdot x$, where $x \in T$, is maximized when b is chosen to be the eigen-vector of $S(T)$ that corresponds to the largest magnitude eigen-value of $S(T)$.

If n-dimensional samples are being mapped to one-dimensional space, then this result tells us that variance is maximized by choosing the relevant eigen-vector as the feature. By extension of this result, if m features are desired, then the principal component analysis procedure maximizes variance by selecting the m eigen-vectors of $S(T)$ that correspond to the m largest eigen-values.

EXAMPLE 5.9   Let T be a training set containing 5 three-dimensional vectors given by $T = \{(1.3, 3.2, 3.7), (1.4, 2.8, 4.1), (1.5, 3.1, 4.6), (1.2, 2.9, 4.8), (1.1, 3.0, 4.8)\}$. The associated mean vector is $(1.3, 3.0, 4.4)$. We first subtract the mean (vector) from each of the five patterns in T, so that the new mean vector is $(0, 0, 0)$. The new input vectors are $x_1 = (0, 0.2, -0.7), x_2 = (0.1, -0.2, -0.3)$, and so on. The covariance matrix is given by

$$S = \frac{1}{5} \begin{pmatrix} 0.10 & 0.01 & -0.11 \\ 0.01 & 0.10 & -0.10 \\ -0.11 & -0.10 & 0.94 \end{pmatrix}.$$

The eigen-values of this matrix are $\gamma_1 = 0.965$, $\gamma_2 = 0.090$, and $\gamma_3 = 0.084$. The associated eigen-vectors are $(-0.823, -0.542, -0.169)$, $(0.553, -0.832, -0.026)$, and $(-0.126, -0.115, 0.985)$, respectively. For $m = 1$, we consider the largest magnitude eigen-value 0.965 and this gives $W = W_1$ where

$$W_1 = (-0.823 \; -0.542 \; -0.169).$$

For $m = 2$, we choose $\gamma_1 = 0.965$ and $\gamma_2 = 0.090$, and the associated $W = W_2$, where

$$W_2 = \begin{pmatrix} -0.823 & -0.542 & -0.169 \\ 0.553 & -0.832 & -0.026 \end{pmatrix}.$$

In this example, we note that $\gamma_1/(\gamma_1 + \gamma_2 + \gamma_3) = 0.965/1.139 = 0.84$. An interpretation of this fraction is that about 84% of the variation in the training set can be explained by a single eigen-vector. In other words, if we map an input vector x into the one-dimensional feature, $y_1 = W_1 x$, this feature alone captures 84% of the characteristics of the input patterns. To obtain more than 84% of the characteristics, we may use W_2 and reduce the three-dimensional x vector into a two-dimensional space, with $y = W_2 x$.

The above mathematical formulation is the basis of principal component analysis-based neural networks. The neural network structure is simple, with connections only from n input nodes to m output nodes, as shown in figure 5.28, where n is the input dimensionality and $m < n$ is the desired number of principal components.

The jth output node calculates the sum $y_j = \sum_{i=1}^{n} w_{ji} x_i$ for $j = 1, \ldots, m$. In this neural network implementation, the key concern is how to adjust the weights so that they represent principal components. The initial values of all weights are randomly assigned. Several update rules have been suggested, all of which follow the same matrix equation:

$$\Delta W_\ell = \eta_\ell y_\ell x_\ell^T - K_\ell W_\ell$$

where x_ℓ and y_ℓ are the input and output vectors, η_ℓ is the learning rate, and W_ℓ is the weight matrix at the ℓth iteration. K_ℓ is a matrix whose choice depends on the specific algorithm, such as the following.

1. $K_\ell = y_\ell y_\ell^T$, suggested by Williams (1985)
2. $K_\ell = 3\mathbb{D}(y_\ell y_\ell^T) + 2L(y_n y_n^T)$, suggested by Oja and Karhunen (1985)
3. $K_\ell = \mathbb{L}(y_\ell y_\ell^T)$, suggested by Sanger (1989)

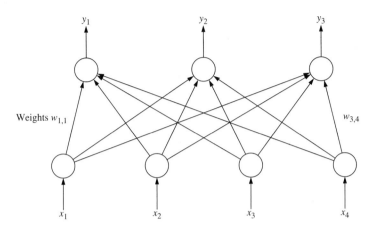

Figure 5.28
A one-layer neural network for principal component analysis.

where $\mathbb{D}(A)$ represents a matrix whose diagonal entries are equal to the entries in A and all other entries are zero, and $\mathbb{L}(A)$ represents a matrix whose entries above and including the main diagonal are zero, while other entries are the same as that of A. For example,

$$\mathbb{D}\begin{bmatrix} 1 & 2 \\ 3 & 4 \end{bmatrix} = \begin{bmatrix} 1 & 0 \\ 0 & 4 \end{bmatrix} \text{ and } \mathbb{L}\begin{bmatrix} 1 & 2 \\ 3 & 4 \end{bmatrix} = \begin{bmatrix} 0 & 0 \\ 3 & 0 \end{bmatrix}.$$

EXAMPLE 5.10   To see how this neural network approach works, we consider the data in the previous example and find the first principal component. Note that we must use the x observations, whose mean is the zero vector. For this simple problem, the network shown in figure 5.29 will suffice. For convenience, we choose a constant learning rate $\eta_\ell = 1.0$ for all values of ℓ, and arbitrarily select initial values of w_1, w_2, and w_3 equal to 0.3, 0.4, and 0.5, respectively.

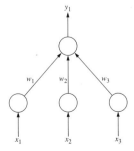

Figure 5.29
A neural network that generates the first principal component.

For the first input $x_1 = (0, 0.2, -0.7)$, $y = (0.3, 0.4, 0.5) \cdot (0, 0.2, -0.7) = 0.27$. Using Williams' suggested value of K_ℓ, the updated equation results in

$$\Delta W = \left(-0.27(0.00, 0.20, -0.70) - (-0.27)^2(0.30, 0.40, 0.50) \right).$$

This modifies the weight vector to

$$W = (0.30, 0.40, 0.50) + \Delta W = (0.278, 0.316, 0.652).$$

The next input to the network is $x_2 = (0.1, -0.2, -0.3)$ for which the associated $y = -0.231$. Thus

$$\Delta W = \left(-0.231(0.10, -0.20, -0.30) - (-0.231)^2 (0.278, 0.316, 0.651) \right)$$

and the new weight vector is

$$W = (0.278, 0.316, 0.652) + \Delta W = (0.240, 0.346, 0.687).$$

Subsequent presentations of x_3, x_4, and x_5 change the weight matrix (in this case, a vector) W to $(0.272, 0.351, 0.697)$, $(0.238, 0.313, 0.751)$, and $(0.172, 0.293, 0.804)$, respectively.

This process is repeated, cycling through the input vectors $x_1, \ldots, x_5$. By the end of the second iteration, the weight vector becomes $(-0.008, 0.105, 0.989)$, and at the end of the third iteration, it changes to $(-0.111, -0.028, 1.004)$. The weight adjustment process continues in this manner, resulting in the first principal component.

The above principal component analysis has some limitations, because only a linear composition of elements in x is used to extract the m features; better features may be extractable by employing non-linear functions of x. Karhunen and Jontsensalo (1993) have extended principal component analysis to non-linear mappings. They minimize $\mathcal{E}\left\{||x - W^T S(Wx)||^2\right\}$ where S is a non-linear function with scalar arguments, extended to apply to vector arguments

$$S \begin{pmatrix} y_1 \\ \vdots \\ y_m \end{pmatrix} = \begin{pmatrix} S(y_1) \\ \vdots \\ S(y_m) \end{pmatrix}.$$

In other words, the same function S applies to all coordinates of the input vector. Karhunen and Jontsensalo suggest a neural network implementation of this non-linear principal component analysis, using a gradient descent technique, for cases when S is continuous, monotonically increasing, odd function, i.e., $S(-y) = -S(y)$.

5.9   Conclusion

Biological neural networks are capable of learning to recognize patterns by abstracting what is common to many different instances of similar data. The driving force in this learning process is the similarity among various patterns, not an external reinforcement nor the relationships between various input dimensions. This chapter has presented various artificial neural network procedures that accomplish such tasks.

We first examined simple competitive learning networks that modify the weights of connections to a single node, when an input pattern is presented. ART networks allow the number of nodes to increase, and also utilize a user-specified threshold to determine the degree of success in matching an input pattern and the best matching prototype represented by a node. Self-organizing feature maps arrange their nodes using a topological structure, and accomplished unsupervised learning in such a way that neighboring nodes (in the topology) respond similarly to input patterns. We have also examined networks that extract important features of input data, analogous to principal component analysis. Principal component analysis networks accomplish feature extraction of a different kind than clustering, determining features that are linear combinations of input dimensions, in such a way as to preserve the maximum possible information that distinguishes input samples.

Figure 5.30 illustrates a comparison of the results of applying k-means clustering, the self-organizing map, and growing cell structures network, for 46 two-dimensional input patterns. For this example, all three methods result in clusters that are exactly the same for data in the second and third quadrants, but differ considerably in forming the other two clusters. The k-means clustering algorithm attempts to construct larger size clusters, whereas the self-organizing maps may construct clusters with a single input pattern. Results obtained using these clustering procedures depend on the initial values and the sequence in which input patterns are presented.

Unsupervised learning algorithms have also been used for supervised learning tasks. LVQ networks, for instance, modify the simple competitive learning procedure for classification tasks. Counterpropagation networks combine the competitive learning procedure with a table lookup to generate output patterns from input patterns. The neocognitron is a complex multilayer network for pattern recognition tasks in which some components are trained using an unsupervised learning algorithm.

Algorithms such as LVQ, counterpropagation, and supervised GCS are likely to be useful for classification tasks if the training data consists of readily identifiable clusters. Such algorithms can be misled by noisy training data, e.g., some weight vectors (prototypes) may be frozen near training samples erroneously classified in input data. Network models and algorithms (such as backpropagation) in which nodes divide space into large regions

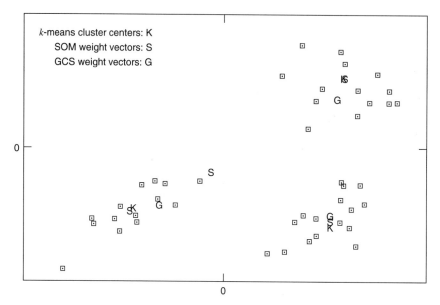

Figure 5.30
Results obtained by applying a Kohonen's self-organizing map (four nodes in grid topology), growing cell structures (three nodes in triangular topology), and k-means clustering (with $k = 3$) algorithm, on a two-dimensional input distribution. The prototypes (weight vectors) obtained are shown using symbols S, G, and K, respectively.

generalize better for noisy training data and in classification problems where there is no obvious cluster formation.

5.10   Exercises

1.   a. Suggest a modification of maxnet that conserves non-zero outputs at all nodes whose initial outputs exceed 0.8. For example, for input vector $(0.8, 0.9, 0.6)$ the desired output of the network should be $(0.8, 0.9, 0.0)$.

    b. Suggest a modification of maxnet that preserves the value of the node with highest output while reducing others to 0.

2. What are the results obtained using the network of figure 5.5 if the initial node output vectors are (0.5, 0.9, 1, 1, 0.9)? What would be a more desirable value? Suggest a modification of maxnet that gives this desirable answer.

3. Consider the maxnet algorithm. What would happen if the mutual inhibition magnitude exceeds 1/(number of nodes)?

4. In an SOM, what are the conditions under which almost coincident nodes will move away from each other? Conversely, under what conditions will they move closer to each other?

5. Under what conditions, if at all, would an SOM network be unable to stabilize to a state in which the same nodes were the winners for the same samples?

6. Consider a hardware implementation of an SOM in which nodes are processors that may fail, giving unreliable or fluctuating outputs. What would be the effect of the failure of a node (a) during the learning process, and (b) after learning is complete?

7. The neural gas algorithm uses a ranking scheme that requires sorting various nodes in the order of increasing distance from an input vector. Implement the following modifications to improve its performance, and examine the quality of the resulting solutions and improvements in computational requirements.

a. Instead of sorting and ranking all nodes, find and rank only three nodes whose weight vectors are nearest the input vector, and make weight updates only to these nodes.

b. Select a node randomly, and adapt only those nodes whose weight vectors are nearer than this node to the input vector, using the neural gas node adaptation rule.

c. Select a node randomly, and adapt only those nodes whose weight vectors are nearer than this node to the input vector, ignoring the "rank" of nodes.

8. Appendix B.5 contains sample data for the three-dimensional version of the Corners problem discussed in chapter 4. For this data, develop and compare the performance and learning times of neural networks using (a) the LVQ1 algorithm, and (b) forward-only counterpropagation.

9. When would you expect the LVQ2 algorithm to outperform LVQ1? Compare the results of applying LVQ2 and LVQ1 for the three-dimensional Corners problem, in terms of computation time and quality of results.

10. For the same three-dimensional input data from the Corners problem (in appendix B.5), apply the topology-preserving SOM algorithm and observe the result of using

a. neighborhoods whose size is fixed;

b. neighborhoods that shrink rapidly (from the whole network to just the winner node);

c. neighborhoods that shrink very gradually.

11. For the same three-dimensional input data from the Corners problem (in appendix B.5), apply the topology-preserving SOM algorithm and observe the result of using

    a. learning rate fixed at 0.1 throughout the training process;

    b. learning rate that decreases rapidly (from 1.0 to 0.01);

    c. learning rate that decreases gradually.

12. Apply the simple competitive learning algorithm using (i) three nodes and (ii) four nodes to the following data.

$\{(1.1, 1.7, 1.8, 3.9),\ (0.1, 0.5, 0.5, 0.4),\ (3.1, 2.7, 2.8, 3.9),\ (1.4, 1.6, 1.7, 4.1),\ (1.1, 1.7, 1.8, 3.7),\ (1.4, 0.9, 1.6, 3.9),\ (0.2, 0.7, 0.6, 0.5),\ (0.8, 1.3, 1.5, 3.9),\ (0.4, 0.7, 0.8, 0.9),\ (2.1, 3.7, 0.8, 2.1),\ (2.3, 2.8, 0.3, 1.7),\ (2.2, 3.9, 0.7, 1.5),\ (2.0, 4.9, 0.6, 1.8),\ (1.9, 4.5, 0.8, 1.9),\ (1.8, 4.7, 1.1, 9.0)\}$

Perform two different experiments with each network, presenting data in

    a. the sequence in which they were presented above;

    b. a random sequence.

Compute the total quantization error for each experiment.

13. Perform the above experiments for various random initializations of weight vector elements, choosing each weight value randomly from the interval

    a. (0, 1),

    b. (0, 100),

    c. (0, 0.1),

    d. (0.9, 1.0).

14. Apply the ART1 algorithm to the following data.

$\{(1, 1, 1, 1, 1, 1),\ (1, 1, 1, 0, 0, 0),\ (0, 0, 0, 1, 1, 1),\ (0, 0, 0, 0, 0, 0),\ (1, 1, 0, 0, 0, 0),\ (0, 0, 1, 1, 1, 1),\ (1, 0, 1, 0, 0, 0)\}$

15. Comment on the role of the vigilance parameter in ART1. What would be the effect of making it decrease with time? How may the ART1 algorithm be modified, adapting the vigilance parameter depending on network progress? What would be the advantage of introducing a vigilance parameter into the SOM (topology-preserving) learning algorithm?

6 Associative Models

Man cannot make principles, he can only discover them.
—Thomas Paine (1794)

This chapter discusses neural networks useful in association problems. Association is the task of mapping patterns to patterns. An associative memory is one in which the stimulus of an incomplete or corupted pattern leads to the response of a stored pattern that corresponds in some manner to the input pattern. For instance, the appropriate word and its meaning would have been retrieved by a reader of the previous sentence, despite the fact that a word was spelled incorrectly; we may think of the human brain as retrieving the correct word in response to the associated incorrectly spelled word. This is in sharp contrast to traditional computer memories that map address to data; for instance, when a variable x is used in a computer program containing an expression such as $x + 1$, the name x is used to refer to the address of a specific location in memory, and the contents of that location are retrieved (and used in computation).

It is believed that human memory is stored in the form of complex interconnections between various neurons. In artificial neural networks that play the role of associative memory, data is collectively stored in the form of a memory or weight matrix, which is used to generate the output that should correspond to a given input. The process of developing the weight matrix is referred to as *learning* or *storing* the desired patterns, while *retrieval* or *recall* refers to the generation of an output pattern when an input pattern is presented to the network.

There are two kinds of association tasks, *hetero-association* and *auto-association*, briefly described in chapter 1. Hetero-association involves mapping input vectors to output vectors that range over a different vector space. For instance, an English-to-Spanish translation system performs hetero-association, mapping English words to Spanish words. In auto-association, both input vectors and output vectors range over the same vector space. For instance, a spelling corrector maps possibly incorrectly spelled words to correctly spelled words in the same language.

Character recognition is an important practical application of auto-associative neural networks. The task is to reproduce a clear, noise-free pattern at the outputs when the input vectors are noisy versions of the required output patterns. In figure 6.1, for instance, the upper image at the left is an input array of "pixels," where each pixel value $\in \{0, 1\}$. This particular image is not identical to any of the images (of numerals) previously stored in the associative memory or network.

This example illustrates the following.

1. The input pattern may have considerable noise (e.g., a pixel that is 1 in the appropriate stored pattern is valued 0 in the input pattern).

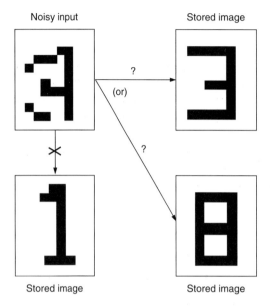

Noisy input   Stored image

Stored image   Stored image

Figure 6.1
A noisy input image that must be auto-associated with one of the desired output images that represent different numerals. The input pattern resembles numerals "3" and "8," but not "1."

2. There may be several alternative output patterns to which an input pattern could be mapped by the auto-associator.

3. There are some output patterns to which an input pattern should clearly not associate.

Character recognition involves auto-association, since output vectors are merely noise-free versions of the input vectors. The number of output patterns is sometimes called the "memory size" of the auto-associator, and each output pattern is sometimes referred to as a "memory," and sometimes as an "attractor." Each output pattern may be considered analogous to a magnet that exerts an attractive force on the input pattern, and the successful attractor is often the one that is closest to the input pattern. Some research on auto-associative neural networks stems from analogies to "spinglasses" in physics [Hertz, Krogh, and Palmer (1990)].

Most of the models discussed in this chapter are based on variations of Hebb's rule, which establishes the relationship between connection weights and correlations among input attributes. It is therefore appropriate to restate the fundamental observations of Hebb (1949) about the modification of synaptic strengths among biological neurons.

When one cell repeatedly assists in firing another, the axon of the first cell develops synaptic knobs (or enlarges them if they already exist) in contact with the soma of the second cell.

Given an input pattern, some systems accomplish association in a single step. Such non-iterative, "one-shot" procedures for association are discussed in the next section. The rest of the chapter describes iterative models with better error-correction capabilities, in which node states may be updated several times. Eventually, the network outputs "stabilize" at an output pattern, i.e., the state update rule does not further modify any node states.

Section 6.2 contains a description and analysis of the widely used Hopfield network model for auto-association, in which node activations are repeatedly modified until a stored pattern is retrieved. Both *discrete* and *continuous* Hopfield models are discussed. In the discrete models, node outputs are chosen from $\{1, 0\}$ or $\{-1, 1\}$; either representation can be obtained from the other, using transformations $x \rightarrow (2x - 1)$ and $y \rightarrow (y + 1)/2$. In the continuous models, each node output is chosen from an interval of real numbers. This is followed by a discussion of a related auto-association network called the "brain-state-in-a-box," in section 6.3. Section 6.4 discusses the Boltzmann machine, in which node updates are made stochastically, and the related mean field annealing procedure. Iterative networks for hetero-association are discussed in section 6.5.

The examples in this chapter use the following notational convention, in the interest of readability. Vectors that occur in narrative text will be written as parenthesized lists of numbers separated by commas, e.g., $(1, -1)$, but these vectors will be written as columns in equations that involve matrix multiplication, e.g., $\begin{pmatrix} 1 \\ -1 \end{pmatrix}$, since each n-dimensional vector can be considered a matrix with n rows and one column.

6.1 Non-iterative Procedures for Association

This section addresses "one-shot" association, in which the desired output pattern is generated from the input pattern by a single iteration of a neural network. By contrast, in the neural network models discussed later in this chapter, nodes repeatedly change their values until their output values stabilize; this may require many time cycles. In this section, we explore whether the same effect can be achieved by defining the weights and state change rules in such a way that all the nodes change their values exactly once, using *non-iterative* procedures for association. We first discuss the application of Hebb's law to develop associative "matrix memories," and then discuss methods of minimizing recall error.

For full generality, we consider the problem of hetero-association, using a two-layer network developed using the training set

$$T = \{(i_p, d_p) : p = 1, \ldots, P\} \tag{6.1}$$

where i_p is an n-dimensional vector whose components $i_{p,\ell} \in \{-1, 1\}$ for $\ell = 1, \ldots, n$, and d_p is an m-dimensional vector whose components $d_{p,j} \in \{-1, 1\}$ for $j = 1, \ldots, m$. $\mathcal{I}$ represents the matrix whose columns are input patterns i_p, and $\mathcal{D}$ represents the matrix whose columns are desired output patterns d_p. I denotes the identity matrix of appropriate dimensionality. We now develop computation rules such that presenting the input pattern i_p at the first layer of the network leads to the instant generation of the appropriate output vector at the second layer.

In the context of an artificial neural network whose nodes correspond to different components of input (i) and desired output (d) patterns, Hebb's observations can be translated into a weight update rule such as

$$\Delta w_{j,k} \propto i_{p,k}\, d_{p,j}.$$

Often, all the input and output patterns are available at once, and a lengthy training procedure (that involves repeated weight updates) can be replaced by a direct calculation of weights such as

$$w_{j,k} \propto \sum_{p=1}^{P} i_{p,k}\, d_{p,j}.$$

The exact form of the weight update or calculation rule depends on the node function and network model used.

Matrix associative memories   A *matrix associative memory* consists of a single weight matrix W. The first step in computing the output vector is to transform the input vector $X^{(1)}$ by pre-multiplication with the weight matrix

$$y = W X^{(1)}.$$

If the desired output pattern is bivalent, with node values ranging over $\{-1, 1\}$, then each element of the output vector $X^{(2)}$ is obtained by applying the signum function to each coordinate of y, i.e.,

$$X_j^{(2)} = \text{sgn}(y_j), \text{ for } j = 1, \ldots, m.$$

Direct application of Hebb's rule results in a weight matrix W whose elements $w_{j,k}$ can be computed by the rule

$$w_{j,k} = \frac{1}{P} \sum_{p=1}^{P} i_{p,k}\, d_{p,j}. \tag{6.2}$$

In this formulation, each $w_{j,k}$ measures the correlation between the kth component of the input vectors and the jth component of the associated output vectors. For bivalent output patterns, we are interested only in the sign of each component of $\mathbf{y}$. Therefore, the multiplier $1/P$ in equation 6.2 can safely be omitted, and we may instead rewrite equation 6.2 using a matrix multiplication,

$$W = \sum_{p=1}^{P} \boldsymbol{d}_p [\boldsymbol{i}_p]^T = \mathcal{D}\mathcal{I}^T, \tag{6.3}$$

where $[\boldsymbol{i}_p]^T$ is the transpose of $\boldsymbol{i}_p$. In other words,

$W =$ (matrix whose columns are output vectors) $\times$ (matrix whose rows are input vectors).

In using a matrix associative memory for recall, the result of multiplying W with a new input vector $\boldsymbol{i}$ may result in an output vector that differs from the patterns intended to be stored in the memory. Such a resulting output vector is called a "spurious" output pattern. Non-iterative procedures have low error-correction capabilities, and a spurious pattern often results when the memory is stimulated by an input pattern that differs even slightly from the input patterns used to build W.

EXAMPLE 6.1   Consider a hetero-association problem in which both input and output patterns are two-dimensional. A matrix associative memory must be defined to associate the input vector $(1, 1)$ with output vector $(-1, 1)$, and the input vector $(1, -1)$ with output vector $(-1, -1)$.
   The weight matrix is

$$W = \begin{pmatrix} -1 & -1 \\ 1 & -1 \end{pmatrix} \begin{pmatrix} 1 & 1 \\ 1 & -1 \end{pmatrix} = \begin{pmatrix} -2 & 0 \\ 0 & 2 \end{pmatrix}. \tag{6.4}$$

When the network with this weight matrix is stimulated by the original input pattern $(1,1)$, the resulting output pattern is

$$\mathbf{y} = WX^{(1)} = \begin{pmatrix} -2 & 0 \\ 0 & 2 \end{pmatrix} \begin{pmatrix} 1 \\ 1 \end{pmatrix} = \begin{pmatrix} -2 \\ 2 \end{pmatrix}, \tag{6.5}$$

and application of signum function on $\mathbf{y}$ gives $X^{(2)}$ whose transpose is $(-1, 1)$. Note that $X^{(2)}$ is the correct output pattern associated with the input pattern $(1, 1)$. If the stimulus is a new input pattern $(-1, -1)$, for which no stored association exists, the resulting output pattern is

$$\mathbf{y} = WX^{(1)} = \begin{pmatrix} -2 & 0 \\ 0 & 2 \end{pmatrix} \begin{pmatrix} -1 \\ -1 \end{pmatrix} = \begin{pmatrix} 2 \\ -2 \end{pmatrix}, \tag{6.6}$$

which generates the output $(1, -1)$. This is a new spurious output pattern that does not correspond to one of the stored patterns.

The above example illustrates that spurious output patterns may be generated by matrix associative memories.

Least squares procedure   The weight matrix of the preceding section was defined using Hebb's law as $W = \sum_{p=1}^{P} d_p[i_p]^T$. Alternatively, the weight matrix, W, can be obtained by using the criterion of minimizing the error

$$E = \sum_{p=1}^{P} ||d_p - X_p^{(2)}||^2,$$

where $X_p^{(2)} = Wi_p$ is the output pattern generated by the network when stimulated by the input pattern i_p. The *least squares procedure* (or Widrow-Hoff rule) may be used to derive the weight matrix Ω that minimizes mean squared error. When an input pattern $i_p = (i_{p,1}, \ldots, i_{p,n})$ is presented to the network, the resulting output $\Omega\, i_p$ must be as close as possible to the desired output pattern d_p, where $p \in \{1, \ldots, P\}$. Hence Ω must be chosen to minimize the mean square error defined by

$$E = \sum_{p=1}^{P} ||d_p - \Omega\, i_p||^2 \tag{6.7}$$

$$= \sum_{p=1}^{P} [(d_{p,1} - \sum_{j} \Omega_{1,j} i_{p,j})^2 + \cdots + (d_{p,m} - \sum_{j} \Omega_{m,j} i_{p,j})^2]. \tag{6.8}$$

Since E is a quadratic function whose second derivative is positive, we obtain the weights that minimize E by differentiating E with respect to $\Omega_{j,\ell}$ for all values of ℓ, j, and solving the equation $\partial E / \partial \Omega_{j,\ell} = 0$. Solving the equation

$$\frac{\partial E}{\partial \Omega_{j,\ell}} = -2 \sum_{p=1}^{P} \left(d_{p,j} - \sum_{k=1}^{n} \Omega_{j,k}\, i_{p,k} \right) i_{p,\ell} = 0,$$

we obtain

$$\sum_{p=1}^{P} d_{p,j}\, i_{p,\ell} = \sum_{p=1}^{P} \sum_{k=1}^{n} \Omega_{j,k}\, i_{p,k}\, i_{p,\ell}$$

$$= \sum_{k=1}^{n} \Omega_{j,k} \left(\sum_{p=1}^{P} i_{p,k}\, i_{p,\ell} \right).$$

The right-hand side of the above equation is seen to be the matrix product of the jth row of Ω with the ℓth column of $\left(\sum_{p=1}^{P} i_p[i_p]^T\right)$. Collectively, the set of all such equations obtained above (for $j \in \{1, \ldots, m\}$, $\ell \in \{1, \ldots, n\}$) can be combined into a single matrix equation:

$$\left(\sum_{p=1}^{P} d_p\, i_p^T\right) = \Omega \sum_{p=1}^{P} i_p\, i_p^T.$$

Whenever the matrix $\left(\sum_{p=1}^{P} i_p[i_p]^T\right)$ is invertible, the weight matrix that minimizes mean squared error is given by

$$\Omega = \left(\sum_{p=1}^{P} d_p[i_p]^T\right)\left(\sum_{p=1}^{P} i_p[i_p]^T\right)^{-1}. \tag{6.9}$$

The least squares method is seen to "normalize" the Hebbian weight matrix $\sum_{p=1}^{P} d_p\, i_p^T$ using the inverse of $\sum_{p=1}^{P}(i_p[i_p]^T)$. If $\mathcal{I}$ is the matrix whose columns are input patterns, and $\mathcal{D}$ is the matrix whose columns are the corresponding desired output patterns, equation 6.9 can be rewritten as

$$\Omega = \mathcal{D}\mathcal{I}^T(\mathcal{I}\mathcal{I}^T)^{-1}. \tag{6.10}$$

Unfortunately, this approach is not helpful for auto-association tasks, since $\Omega = \mathcal{I}\mathcal{I}^T(\mathcal{I}\mathcal{I}^T)^{-1}$ is then the identity matrix I that trivially auto-associates each vector with itself.

Optimal linear associative memory (OLAM)   Equation 6.10 may be generalized to problems in which $\mathcal{I}\mathcal{I}^T$ does not have an inverse, using the notion of a *pseudo-inverse*. Every matrix A has a unique pseudo-inverse, defined to be a matrix A^* that satisfies the following conditions.

$$AA^*A = A$$
$$A^*AA^* = A^*$$
$$A^*A = (A^*A)^T$$
$$AA^* = (AA^*)^T$$

The *optimal linear associative memory* (OLAM), proposed by Wee (1968), is obtained by the natural generalization of equation 6.10 to cases where $(\mathcal{I}\mathcal{I}^T)$ has no inverse, using the weight matrix defined in terms of the pseudo-inverse of $\mathcal{I}$:

$$\Omega = \mathcal{D}\left[\mathcal{I}\right]^*. \tag{6.11}$$

In particular, when $\mathfrak{I}$ is a set of orthonormal unit vectors, i.e.,

$$i_p \cdot i_{p'} = \begin{cases} 1 & \text{if } p = p' \\ 0 & \text{otherwise} \end{cases}$$

for all $p, p' \in \{1, \ldots, P\}$, we find that $\mathfrak{I}\left[\mathfrak{I}\right]^T = I$, the identity matrix, and also $\left[\mathfrak{I}\right]^T \mathfrak{I} = I$, so that each of the four conditions defining the pseudo-inverse are satisfied when $\left[\mathfrak{I}\right]^T = \left[\mathfrak{I}\right]^*$. Then, the weight matrix

$$W = \mathcal{D}\left[\mathfrak{I}\right]^* = \mathcal{D}\left[\mathfrak{I}\right]^T . \tag{6.12}$$

This is a special case of OLAM, and is equivalent to classical linear regression and the linear associative memory proposed by Anderson (1972). In general, however, OLAM makes no orthonormality assumption. For auto-association, $\mathfrak{I} = \mathcal{D}$, so that $\Omega = \mathfrak{I}\left[\mathfrak{I}\right]^*$.

Note that each component in the transformed vector $y = \Omega x = \mathfrak{I}\left[\mathfrak{I}\right]^* x$, where x is any given vector of appropriate dimensions, is a linear combination with weights depending upon the inputs $\mathfrak{I}$. The vector y is the *projection* of x on the space *spanned* by $\mathfrak{I}$; otherwise, error E could have been reduced by modifying y in the direction of the space *spanned* by $\mathfrak{I}$. This concept is illustrated in figure 6.2 for a three-dimensional vector x projected on the plane generated by the x_1 and x_2 axes.

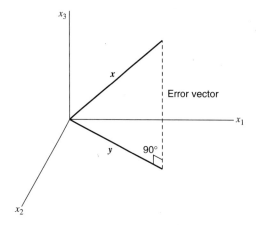

Figure 6.2
y is the projection of x on the space spanned by the x_1 and x_2 axes.

EXAMPLE 6.2 We examine the hetero-association problem in which three input/output patterns are $(1, 1, 1; -1, 1)$, $(1, -1, 1; -1, -1,)$, $(-1, 1, 1; 1, -1)$. For this data set the input and output matrices are

$$\mathcal{J} = \begin{pmatrix} 1 & 1 & -1 \\ 1 & -1 & 1 \\ 1 & 1 & 1 \end{pmatrix} \text{ and } \mathcal{D} = \begin{pmatrix} -1 & -1 & 1 \\ 1 & -1 & -1 \end{pmatrix}.$$

The inverse of $\mathcal{J}[\mathcal{J}]^T$ exists, so that

$$\Omega = \mathcal{D}[\mathcal{J}]^T (\mathcal{J}[\mathcal{J}]^T)^{-1}$$

$$= \begin{pmatrix} -1 & -1 & 1 \\ 1 & -1 & -1 \end{pmatrix} \begin{pmatrix} 1 & 1 & 1 \\ 1 & -1 & 1 \\ -1 & 1 & 1 \end{pmatrix} \begin{pmatrix} 0.50 & 0.25 & 0.25 \\ 0.25 & 0.50 & 0.25 \\ 0.25 & 0.25 & 0.50 \end{pmatrix}$$

$$= \begin{pmatrix} -1 & 0 & 0 \\ 0 & 0 & -1 \end{pmatrix}.$$

Consequently, the associated output pattern for $(-1, -1, -1)$ is generated on premultiplying it by Ω. The resulting output is $(-1, 1)$.

In the following example, we encounter a situation where the inverse of the desired matrix does not exist; however, this does not influence our ability to obtain an output vector.

EXAMPLE 6.3 We examine the hetero-association problem in which four input/output patterns are $(1, 1, -1; -1, -1)$, $(1, -1, -1; 1, -1,)$, $(-1, -1, 1; 1, 1)$, $(-1, 1, 1; -1, 1)$. For this data set, the input and output matrices are

$$\mathcal{J} = \begin{pmatrix} 1 & 1 & -1 & -1 \\ 1 & -1 & -1 & 1 \\ -1 & -1 & 1 & 1 \end{pmatrix} \text{ and } \mathcal{D} = \begin{pmatrix} -1 & 1 & 1 & -1 \\ -1 & -1 & 1 & 1 \end{pmatrix}.$$

In this case,

$$\mathcal{J}[\mathcal{J}]^T = \begin{pmatrix} 4 & 0 & -4 \\ 0 & 4 & 0 \\ -4 & 0 & 4 \end{pmatrix}$$

whose inverse does not exist. However, its pseudo-inverse is given by

$$\left(\mathcal{J}[\mathcal{J}]^T\right)^* = \begin{pmatrix} 0.25 & 0.00 & 0.00 \\ 0.00 & 0.25 & 0.00 \\ 0.00 & 0.00 & 0.00 \end{pmatrix}.$$

Finally,

$$\Omega = \mathcal{D}[\mathfrak{I}]^T \begin{pmatrix} 0.25 & 0.00 & 0.00 \\ 0.00 & 0.25 & 0.00 \\ 0.00 & 0.00 & 0.00 \end{pmatrix}$$

$$= \begin{pmatrix} -1 & 1 & 1 & -1 \\ -1 & -1 & 1 & 1 \end{pmatrix} \begin{pmatrix} 1 & 1 & -1 \\ 1 & -1 & -1 \\ -1 & -1 & 1 \\ -1 & 1 & 1 \end{pmatrix} \begin{pmatrix} 0.25 & 0.00 & 0.00 \\ 0.00 & 0.25 & 0.00 \\ 0.00 & 0.00 & 0.00 \end{pmatrix}$$

$$= \begin{pmatrix} 0 & -1 & 0 \\ -1 & 0 & 0 \end{pmatrix}.$$

Given an input vector, say $(1, 1, -1)$, the output is generated by premultiplication by the above matrix so that the output is given by

$$\begin{pmatrix} 0 & -1 & 0 \\ -1 & 0 & 0 \end{pmatrix} \begin{pmatrix} 1 \\ 1 \\ -1 \end{pmatrix} = \begin{pmatrix} -1 \\ -1 \end{pmatrix}.$$

Noise extraction   Given a set of vectors $\mathfrak{I}$, any vector x of the appropriate dimensionality can be written as the sum of two components, of which one is a projection onto the vector space spanned by $\mathfrak{I}$, and the other is an "error" or noise component orthonormal to this space. We can thus write

$$x = Ix = Wx + (I - W)x = \hat{x} + \tilde{a} = \sum_{i=1}^{m} c_i i_i + \tilde{a} \tag{6.13}$$

where $\hat{x}$ is the projection of x onto the vector space spanned by $\mathfrak{I}$, and the remainder $\tilde{a}$ is referred to as the *noise component*. Matrix multiplication by W thus projects any vector onto the space of the stored vectors, whereas matrix multiplication by $(I - W)$, the novelty filter [Kohonen (1988)], extracts the noise component. Since the goal is to recover a given stored vector from a possibly noisy input vector, it is necessary to minimize the noise component $\tilde{a}$. It is hoped that each element of the noise component is small and can be corrected by applying the signum function on each element of x.

Noise is suppressed if the number of patterns being stored is less than the number of neurons in layer 1; otherwise, the noise may be amplified. This is a major limitation on the number of patterns that can be stored in a network of given size.

Non-linear transformations   A linear transformation was used in all of the above procedures; the output vector $X^{(2)}$ was obtained by a matrix multiplication followed by applying the signum function. This may be generalized to non-linear transformations such as

$$X^{(2)} = \begin{pmatrix} X_1^{(2)} \\ \vdots \\ X_m^{(2)} \end{pmatrix} = f(WX^{(1)}) \triangleq \begin{pmatrix} f(w_{1,1}X_1^{(1)} + \cdots + w_{1,n}X_n^{(1)}) \\ \vdots \\ f(w_{m,1}X_1^{(1)} + \cdots + w_{m,n}X_n^{(1)}) \end{pmatrix},$$

where f is some differentiable nonlinear function. For such problems, minimization of error E with respect to each weight $w_{j,\ell}$ (via the least squares approach) requires the following system of $m \times n$ equations to be solved.

$$\frac{\partial E}{\partial w_{j,\ell}} = \sum_{p=1}^{P}(d_{p,j} - X_{p,j}^{(2)})f'\left(\sum_{k=1}^{n} w_{j,k}\,\boldsymbol{i}_{p,\ell}\right)\boldsymbol{i}_{p,\ell} = 0 \tag{6.14}$$

for $\ell = 1, \ldots, n$; $j = 1, \ldots, m$; and where $X_{p,j}^{(2)} = f\left(\sum_{k=1}^{n} w_{j,k}\,\boldsymbol{i}_{p,\ell}\right)$ and f' denotes the derivative of f with respect to its argument. This system of equations is not linear in W, and cannot often be solved using non-iterative procedures. However, any reasonable iterative procedure for solving this matrix system of equation provides the weight matrix W, which, in turn, can be used to solve the problem of hetero-association.

6.2   Hopfield Networks

In this section, we present one of the neural network models most commonly used for auto-association and optimization tasks, referred to as the Hopfield network. Hopfield networks are auto-associators in which node values are iteratively updated based on a local computation principle: the new state of each node depends only on its net weighted input at a given time. The network is fully connected, as shown in figure 6.3, and weights are determined by the Hebbian principle. Unlike certain other networks, no lengthy training procedure is needed for determining the weight matrix of a Hopfield network. The main computational expense is in allowing the system to undergo a large number of state

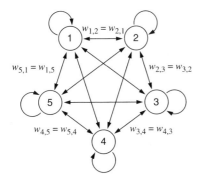

Figure 6.3
Hopfield network with five nodes.

transitions before converging to a stable state, but even this number is much smaller than the number of iterations often needed in training feedforward networks.

Work on this model (and related models) has been carried out by many researchers, such as Amari (1971), Anderson (1972), Kohonen (1972), Nakano (1972), Cohen and Grossberg (1973), and Little (1974). However, the name by which the networks are commonly known stems from a paper by John Hopfield (1982) that sparked substantial interest in these networks.

We first present discrete models with binary node outputs, and then proceed to continuous models in which nodes take values in a real interval.

6.2.1   Discrete Hopfield networks

For simplicity, we first assume that input (and output) patterns are discrete vectors whose elements $\in \{-1, 1\}$. One node in the network corresponds to each input (and output) dimension. Each node applies a step function to the sum of external inputs and the weighted outputs of other nodes, resulting in an output of either $+1$ or -1. Node output values may change when an input vector is presented, until the state of the network converges to an attractor. The models described above are discrete-time models, since we assume that computation proceeds in "jumps": the values for the time variable range over natural numbers, not real numbers. Where possible, the notation explicitly considers time.

Let $T = \{i_1, \ldots, i_P\}$ be the "training set" of n-dimensional patterns to be stored. We use $x_{p,j}(t)$ to indicate the value generated by the jth node at time t, when the pth input pattern activates the network; $w_{k,j}$ is the weight of the connection from the jth node to the kth node. $I_{p,k}$ denotes the external input to the kth node of the network for the pth input vector; this external input can be assumed to include any threshold term needed in a specific network. The first subscript p may be omitted from $x_{p,k}$ and $I_{p,k}$ when irrelevant.

The node output function is described by

$$x_{p,k}(t+1) = \text{sgn}\left(\sum_{j=1}^{n} w_{k,j} x_{p,j}(t) + I_{p,k}\right) \tag{6.15}$$

where "sgn" represents the signum function,[1] defined here as $\text{sgn}(x) = 1$ if $x \geq 0$ and $\text{sgn}(x) = -1$ if $x < 0$.

---

1. Some sources use a slightly different definition of the signum function with $\text{sgn}(0) = 0$, suggesting that node output is 0 if net input is 0, in a Hopfield network. Some researchers instead leave the node value unchanged if the net input is 0, i.e.,

$$x_{p,k}(t+1) = x_{p,k}(t) \text{ if } \left(\sum_{j=0}^{n} w_{k,j} x_{p,j}(t) + I_{p,k}\right) = 0.$$

Another assumption in the traditional Hopfield model is that of asynchronicity: at every time instant, precisely one node's output value is updated. The network dynamics are more accurately described as follows.

Select a node $k \in \{1, \ldots, n\}$ to be updated;

$$x_{p,\ell}(t+1) = \begin{cases} x_{p,\ell}(t) & \text{if } \ell \neq k \\ \text{sgn}\left(\sum_{j=1}^{n} w_{\ell,j} x_{p,j}(t) + I_{p,\ell}\right) & \text{if } \ell = k. \end{cases} \tag{6.16}$$

The selection of a node for updating may be random. For any progress to be made, it is necessary that the same node is not chosen persistently, and that different nodes in the system have the opportunity to change states; this property is called "fairness" in the context of computer networks and communication protocols. Often, the selection is made in a cyclic manner, updating one node after another.

Asynchronicity is to be distinguished from "non-synchronicity" (absence of synchronous behavior), which merely implies that not all nodes are updated simultaneously. For example, a model in which all the even-numbered nodes are updated in one step, followed by simultaneous updates of all the odd-numbered nodes, i.e.,

$$x_{p,\ell}(t+1) = \begin{cases} x_{p,\ell}(t) & \text{if } (\ell + t) \text{ is even} \\ \text{sgn}\left(\sum_{j=1}^{n} w_{\ell,j} x_{p,j}(t) + I_{p,\ell}\right) & \text{if } (\ell + t) \text{ is odd} \end{cases}$$

describes a non-synchronous model that is not strictly asynchronous.

In the alternate synchronous model, proposed by Little (1974), all nodes are updated simultaneously at every time instant. Consequently, the following equation holds for *every* node in the network:

$$x_{p,\ell}(t+1) = \text{sgn}\left(\sum_{j=1}^{n} w_{\ell,j} x_{p,j}(t) + I_{p,\ell}\right).$$

However, there is no guarantee that synchronous updates will lead to convergent behavior, as illustrated by figure 6.4; cyclic behavior may result when two nodes update their values simultaneously, each attempting to move towards a different attractor. The network may then repeatedly shuttle between two network states. It has been shown that any such cycle consists of only two states and hence can be detected easily.

The Hopfield network can be used to retrieve a stored pattern when a corrupted version of the stored pattern is presented. Returning to the physical analogy, the discrete-time

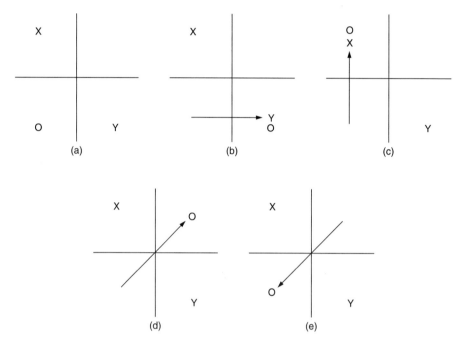

Figure 6.4
Asynchronous vs. synchronous dynamics: X and Y are two attractors, and the circle denotes the network state, whose initial value is equidistant from both attractors, as shown by figure (a). Asynchronous computation instantly leads to *one* of the attractors, as shown in figures (b) and (c); the choice of the attractor may be random. In synchronous computation, however, the object moves in both directions to a non-attractor position, shown in figure (d), from where it moves to the position shown in figure (e), and then repeatedly moves back and forth between these two positions without terminating.

asynchronous Hopfield model implies that an object being pulled in different directions (by various magnetic attractors) successively moves in small jumps along one input dimension at a time toward an attractor, hopefully the nearest one. The Hopfield network can also be used to "complete" a pattern when parts of the pattern are missing. For instance, when node inputs $\in \{1, -1\}$, an external input or initial node activation of 0 may be construed to mean that the corresponding element's value is initially unknown.

EXAMPLE 6.4   Consider a four-node Hopfield network whose weights store two patterns, $(1, 1, 1, 1)$ and $(-1, -1, -1, -1)$, respectively. Correlation between every pair of nodes is perfect: a node is ON if and only if every other node is expected to be ON. Hence each weight $w_{\ell,j} = 1$, for $\ell \neq j$, and we assume $w_{j,j} = 0$ for all j.

Let a corrupted input pattern such as $(1, 1, 1, -1)$ be supplied to the network, i.e., $I_1 = I_2 = I_3 = 1$ and $I_4 = -1$; these also specify the initial values for node outputs. Assume that the second node is randomly selected for possible update. Its net input is $w_{2,1}x_1 + w_{2,3}x_3 + w_{2,4}x_4 + I_2 = 1 + 1 - 1 + 1 = 2$. Since $\text{sgn}(2) = 1$, this node's output remains at 1. If the fourth node is selected for possible update, its net input is $1 + 1 + 1 - 1 = 2$, and $\text{sgn}(2) = 1$ implies that this node changes state to 1. No further changes of state occur from this network configuration $(1, 1, 1, 1)$. Thus, the network has successfully recovered one of the stored patterns from the corrupted input vector.

If the input vector is $(1, 1, -1, -1)$, then both stored patterns are equally distant, but only one is preferred because the node function yields 1 when the net input is 0. If the second node is selected for updating, its net input is 0, hence state is not changed from 1. If the third node is selected for updating, its net input is 0, hence state is changed from -1 to 1. Subsequently, the fourth node also changes state, resulting in the network configuration $(1, 1, 1, 1)$.

If the input pattern is $(1, 0, -1, -1)$, and the second node is selected for updating, its net input is $w_{1,2}x_1 + w_{3,2}x_3 + w_{4,2}x_4 + I_2 = 1 - 1 - 1 + 0 = -1 < 0$, implying the updated node output is -1 for this node. Subsequently, the first node also switches state to -1, resulting in the network configuration $(-1, -1, -1, -1)$.

Even if the input pattern is $(0, 0, 0, -1)$, with most of the initial inputs unknown, the network succeeds in switching states of three nodes, resulting in the stored pattern $(-1, -1, -1, -1)$. Thus, a significant amount of corruption, noise, or missing data can be successfully handled in problems with a small number of stored patterns.

Energy function What do the Hopfield network dynamics accomplish? What is the assurance that computations using network state update rules terminate eventually? These questions are addressed below by describing an "energy" or cost function minimized by the Hopfield network using gradient descent, roughly analogous to the error (MSE) function minimized by the weight update rules in backpropagation.

For auto-association problems, the desired output vector for a given sample consists of the nearest stored attractor pattern. Since the training samples are to be the attractors, the desired outputs for these are themselves. The attractors are implicitly stored using the weights of the network. Each weight roughly measures the correlation between node values for all the attractor patterns. If $w_{\ell,j}$ is positive and large, then we expect that the ℓth and jth nodes are frequently ON or OFF together in the attractor patterns. In other words, with large positive $w_{\ell,j}$, we expect that $\sum_{p=1}^{P}(i_{p,\ell}\, i_{p,j})$ is positive and large. Similarly, $w_{\ell,j}$ is negative and large when the ℓth and jth nodes frequently have opposite activation values for different attractor patterns, i.e., $\sum_{p=1}^{P}(i_{p,\ell}\, i_{p,j})$ is negative and large.

This discussion suggests that $w_{\ell,j}$ should be proportional to $\sum_{p=1}^{P}(i_{p,\ell}\, i_{p,j})$. In cases of strong positive or negative correlation, $w_{\ell,j}$ and $\sum_{p}(i_{p,\ell}\, i_{p,j})$ have the same sign, hence $\sum_{p=1}^{P} w_{\ell,j}(i_{p,\ell}\, i_{p,j})$ is always positive. In general, the self-excitation term $w_{j,j}$ is chosen to be non-negative, for each j. If interpreted as a correlation term, we would expect $w_{j,j}=1$. But in many networks described in the literature, $w_{j,j}$ is constrained to be 0.

The above argument applies to all the weights in the network. Hence, summing over all pairs of nodes in the network, $\sum_{\ell}\sum_{j} w_{\ell,j} i_{p,\ell} i_{p,j}$ is positive and large for each attractor pattern. This remains the case even when the network is presented with a new input pattern that is not an attractor, but only a slightly corrupted version of the same. But if the network is presented with an input vector i that is distant from all the attractor patterns, then we expect that the node correlations present in the attractors are absent in the new pattern, so that $\sum_{\ell}\sum_{j} w_{\ell,j} i_{\ell} i_{j}$ is low or negative. Therefore, the first candidate term for the energy function is

$$-\left(\sum_{\ell}\sum_{j} w_{\ell,j} x_{\ell} x_{j}\right).$$

When this term is minimized, varying x_{ℓ} and x_{j}, it is expected that the final values of various node outputs are very close to one of the attractor patterns.

It is not sufficient that the final network output pattern is close to an attractor: we also desire that it should be as close as possible to the input vector. For example, when presented with a corrupted image of the numeral 3, we do *not* want the system to generate an output corresponding to the numeral 1, as shown in figure 6.1. If nodes have non-zero external inputs (I_{ℓ}), this motivates using another term $-\sum_{\ell} I_{\ell} x_{\ell}$ in the energy expression; $I_{\ell} x_{\ell}$ is positive if and only if the input and output values are the same for the ℓth node in the network, hence the desire to minimize $(-\sum_{\ell} I_{\ell} x_{\ell})$. In this way, we obtain the following expression for the "energy" function, E, to be minimized by modifying various x_{ℓ} values.

$$E = -a\sum_{\ell}\sum_{j} w_{\ell,j} x_{\ell} x_{j} - b\sum_{\ell} I_{\ell} x_{\ell} \qquad (6.17)$$

where a, b are arbitrary positive values. The values $a=1/2$ and $b=1$ correspond to reduction in energy whenever a node update occurs, as described below.

Even in models in which each I_{ℓ} is chosen to be 0, we can ensure that the network settles into a state close to the input pattern, by initializing node inputs $x_{\ell}(0)$ to the input pattern values. A variation of the Hopfield model supplies external input only at the beginning of the activation process, so that the state of the network at any time depends only on the preceding state, not on the external input. Such a model can be encompassed by generalizing $I_{p,\ell}$ to be a time-varying function $I_{p,\ell}(t)$, and choosing $I_{p,\ell}(0) = $ initial input, but $I_{p,\ell}(t) = 0$ for $t > 0$. Alternatively, we may omit external inputs completely, with $I_{p,\ell} = 0$, and instead force each initial node output $x_j(0)$ to equal the initial external input.

E is called a Lyapunov function, and we are assured that running the Hopfield net (in asynchronous mode) in such a way as to perform gradient descent on the energy function will eventually result in convergence to a stable state (which may or may not be one of the desired attractors). We now examine the gradient descent process, implemented by the node state update rule.

Energy minimization   Let the kth node be selected for updating at time t. When E is as defined in equation 6.17 and the node update rule is as described in 6.16, the resulting change of energy is

$$\Delta E(t) = E(t+1) - E(t)$$
$$= -a \sum_\ell \sum_{j \neq \ell} w_{\ell,j} \left[x_\ell(t+1) x_j(t+1) - x_\ell(t) x_j(t) \right] - b \sum_\ell I_\ell (x_\ell(t+1) - x_\ell(t)),$$

i.e.,

$$\Delta E(t) = -a \sum_{j \neq k} \left((w_{k,j} + w_{j,k})(x_k(t+1) - x_k(t)) x_j(t) \right) - b I_k (x_k(t+1) - x_k(t)),$$

because $x_j(t+1) = x_j(t)$ for every node $(j \neq k)$ not selected for updating at this step in an asynchronous computation. Hence,

$$\Delta E(t) = -\left[a \sum_{j \neq k} (w_{k,j} + w_{j,k}) x_j(t) + b I_k \right] \left(x_k(t+1) - x_k(t) \right).$$

This quantity must be negative if the state change is to decrease energy. This leads to the weight change criterion that $(x_k(t+1) - x_k(t))$ and $(a \sum_{j \neq k}(w_{k,j} + w_{j,k}) x_j(t) + b I_k)$ must have the same sign. The weights are chosen to be proportional to correlation terms, i.e., $w_{\ell,j} = \sum_{p=1}^{P} i_{p,\ell} i_{p,j} / P$. Hence $w_{j,k} = w_{k,j}$, i.e., the weights are symmetric, and for the choice of the constants $a = 1/2$, $b = 1$, the above expression simplifies to

$$\Delta E(t) = -\left(\sum_{j \neq k} w_{j,k} x_j(t) + I_k \right) (x_k(t+1) - x_k(t)) \qquad (6.18)$$

$$= -\text{net}_k(t) \Delta x_k(t), \qquad (6.19)$$

where $\text{net}_k(t) = \left(\sum_{j \neq k} w_{j,k} x_j(t) + I_k \right)$ is the net input to the kth node at time t.

Equation 6.19 suggests the natural gradient descent rule: in order to reduce energy, the chosen (kth) node examines its net input and decides to flip its state if and only if

$$\text{net}_k(t) \cdot \Delta x_k(t) > 0.$$

This computation rule can be summarized for each node as

Change state of a node if current state differs from the sign of the net input.

So if the kth node is chosen to be updated at time t, and $x_k(t) = 1$, the change to $x_k(t+1) = -1$ will be made if and only if $\text{net}_k(t) < 0$. Otherwise $x_k(t+1) = x_k(t) = 1$. Similarly, if $x_k(t) = -1$, the change to $x_k(t+1) = +1$ will be made if and only if $\text{net}_k(t) > 0$, and otherwise no state change results.

What remains is the precise choice of weights in the network, so as to implement the mutual correlations between pairs of nodes in the system. As described earlier, a straightforward choice is

$$w_{j,\ell} = \sum_{p=1}^{P} (i_{p,\ell}\, i_{p,j})/P, \qquad (6.20)$$

where $i_{p,\ell}$ is the ℓth element of the pth attractor (or stored target pattern).

So far we have described a rule that changes the state of a randomly selected node and argued that the Hopfield network moves to states with non-increasing energy levels. Repeated applications of the rule described above results in a "stable state" in which all nodes stop changing their current values.

There is no guarantee that the stable state reached in this manner will always correspond to one of the desired attractor states. Spurious states that correspond to local minima of the energy function often occur in practical applications, especially in problems whose state variables have discrete ranges.

EXAMPLE 6.5   This example illustrates the possibility of spurious patterns being stored in a Hopfield network. We again consider a network with four nodes, but this time the patterns to be stored are $(1, 1, -1, -1)$, $(1, 1, 1, 1)$ and $(-1, -1, 1, 1)$, respectively. The first and second nodes have perfect correlation, i.e., have exactly the same values in every stored pattern, hence $w_{1,2} = 1$. The same holds for the third and fourth nodes, so that $w_{3,4} = 1$. The first and third nodes agree in one stored pattern but disagree in the other two stored patterns, hence

$$w_{1,3} = \frac{\text{(number of agreements)} - \text{(number of disagreements)}}{\text{number of patterns}} = \frac{1-2}{3} = -1/3.$$

Similarly, $w_{1,4} = w_{2,3} = w_{2,4} = -1/3$. To see how this network performs, consider the following cases.

• If the input vector is $(-1, -1, -1, -1)$, and the fourth node is selected for possible node update, its net input is $w_{1,4}x_1 + w_{2,4}x_2 + w_{3,4}x_3 + I_4 = (-1/3)(-1) + (-1/3)(-1) + (-1) + (-1) = -4/3 < 0$, hence the node does not change its state. The same holds for every node in the network, so that the network configuration remains at $(-1, -1, -1, -1)$, a spurious pattern that was not one of the patterns originally stored in the network.

• If the input vector is $(-1, -1, -1, 0)$, representing the case when the fourth input value is missing, and the fourth node is selected for possible node update, its net input is $w_{1,4}x_1 + w_{2,4}x_2 + w_{3,4}x_3 + I_4 = (-1/3)(-1) + (-1/3)(-1) + (-1) + (0) = -1/3 < 0$, and the node changes state to -1, resulting in the spurious pattern $(-1, -1, -1, -1)$ mentioned above.

• If the input vector is $(-1, 0, 0, -1)$, and the fourth node is selected for possible node update, its net input is $w_{1,4}x_1 + w_{2,4}x_2 + w_{3,4}x_3 + I_4 = (-1/3)(-1) + (0) + (0) + (-1) = -2/3 < 0$, implying that no state change occurs. The same holds for the first node. For the third node, the net input is $w_{1,3}x_1 + w_{2,3}x_2 + w_{3,4}x_4 + I_3 = (-1/3)(-1) + 0 + (-1) + 0 = -2/3 < 0$, so that it changes state to -1, and the current network configuration is $(-1, 0, -1, -1)$. If the second node is now chosen for possible node update, its net input is negative, hence we again reach the spurious pattern $(-1, -1, -1, -1)$.

EXAMPLE 6.6 In this example, we consider an application of Hopfield neural network for auto-association. Images of four different objects are shown in figure 6.5. In order to store these objects for later recall, we treat each image as a 19×19 pixel array, as shown in figure 6.6. From this pixel array, we obtain a 19×19 matrix of zeroes and ones, with a 1 in the (ℓ, j)th coordinate if the corresponding pixel of the input image is dark; otherwise the (ℓ, j)th entry of the matrix has a 0. These images are stored in the form of associative memory in a network with 19×19 neurons whose connection weights are obtained by the usual Hebbian learning, resulting in a weight matrix whose elements are given by equation 6.20.

To recall any of the stored images, we present one of the stored image representations (a 19×19 array of zeroes and ones), and the trained network retrieves the correct image. We now examine a more interesting question: Will this network be able to recall the correct

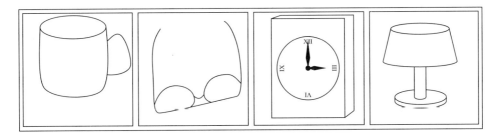

Figure 6.5
Four images stored in a Hopfield network associative memory.

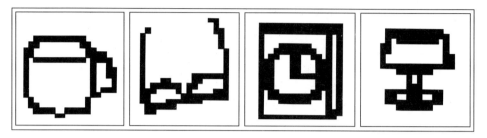

Figure 6.6
Binary representation of the objects shown in figure 6.5.

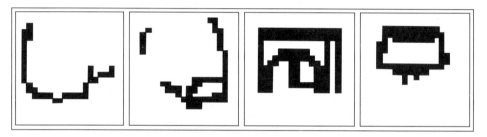

Figure 6.7
Distorted versions of the objects shown in figure 6.6.

stored image when the network is stimulated by a distorted version of a stored image? Many such experiments were conducted, and some of the distorted versions are shown in figure 6.7. In each case, as long as the total amount of distortion is less than 30% of the number of neurons, the network was able to recover the correct image. The network was successful in reproducing the correct stored memories even when big chunks of each image were darkened (filled with ones), or lightened (filled with zeroes).

Such remarkable retrieval performance could occur because we have stored only four objects in a large network (number of nodes equals $19 \times 19 = 361$). Poorer performance would be expected if the network was smaller, or if the number of stored objects was much larger than 4.

The assumption of full connectivity (existence of connections from every node to every other node) is a drawback of a Hopfield network: a million parameters (weights) are needed for a thousand-node network. Problems of such high dimensionality may occur in image-processing applications, where each node may correspond to one pixel in an image.

The performance of Hopfield nets depends considerably on the number of target attractor patterns that are to be stored. The following subsection contains a discussion of the storage capacity of discrete networks, i.e., the number of patterns that can be stored and retrieved successfully.

6.2.2 Storage capacity of Hopfield networks*

The performance of Hopfield nets depends considerably on the number of target attractor patterns that are to be stored. In this section, we consider some results that provide a "rule of thumb" that relates the number of nodes and the number of patterns that can be stored and retrieved successfully in a fully connected discrete Hopfield network.

The *storage capacity* of a neural network refers to the quantity of information that can be stored in a network in such a way that it can be retrieved without error. One among several possible measures of storage capacity is

$$C = \frac{\text{number of stored patterns}}{\text{number of neurons in the network}}.$$

If a network is not fully connected, then another measure of capacity may be more appropriate, such as

$$C_w = \frac{\text{number of stored patterns}}{\text{number of connection weights in the network}}.$$

For a Hopfield network, these two measures are closely related, since a Hopfield network with n neurons has roughly n^2 connection weights.

We find several different upper bounds on the capacity of a Hopfield network, in the neural network literature. This is because the capacity of the network depends on several factors, such as the connection weights, the characteristics of the stored patterns, and the difference between the stimulus patterns and stored patterns. For instance, instead of the general scheme of obtaining a weight matrix via the Hebbian rule, it may be more appropriate in some problems to obtain a different set of weights that are more suitable for the given set of patterns to be stored and retrieved. In the latter case, an optimal collection of weights that are not necessarily symmetric can be chosen in an $n(n-1)$-dimensional space and may thus increase the storage capacity of the network.

In the following discussion, we describe some results pertinent to the capacity of a Hopfield network used for association. We consider the case in which the training set contains P vectors $(i_1, \ldots, i_P)$ where each $i_p = (i_{p,1}, \ldots, i_{p,n})$ is an n-dimensional vector of bipolar values $\in \{1, -1\}$. These n-dimensional vectors are randomly selected and stored in a distributed manner using the connection weights

$$w_{\ell,j} = c \sum_{p=1}^{P} i_{p,\ell}\, i_{p,j}. \tag{6.21}$$

In this equation, the precise magnitude of the constant $c > 0$ is irrelevant, since node updates depend only on the sign of the net input, not the precise value. For convenience in the calculations that follow, we use $c = 1/n$.

During auto-association or the test phase, we provide a stimulus and hope that the network will successfully retrieve a stored vector. In particular, it should be possible to retrieve each stored pattern when the stimulus is identical to the pattern to be retrieved. For a network with n nodes, how large can P be, so that the network responds to every stored vector i_ℓ by correctly retrieving the same vector i_ℓ? The following theorem answers this question [Amit (1989)].

THEOREM 6.1   The maximum capacity of a Hopfield neural network is bounded above by $c = (1/4 \ln n)$, where n is the number of nodes in the network. In other words, if we define

$$\beta = \text{Prob.}\big[\ell\text{-th bit of } p\text{-th stored vector is correctly}$$

$$\text{retrieved for all } \ell = 1, 2, \ldots, n, \text{ and all } p = 1, \ldots, P\big],$$

then $\lim_{n \to \infty} \beta = 1$ whenever $P < n/(4 \ln(n))$.

Proof   We first evaluate the probability of correct retrieval for the first bit of the first stored vector. For stimulus i_1, the output of the first node is given by $o_1 = \sum_{j=2}^{n} w_{1,j} i_{1,j}$, which after substitution for $w_{1,j}$ from equation 6.21 is

$$o_1 = \frac{1}{n} \sum_{j=2}^{n} \sum_{p=1}^{P} i_{p,1} i_{p,j} i_{1,j}.$$

This output will be correctly decoded if $o_1 i_{1,1} > 0$, since each $i_{\ell,j} \in \{-1, 1\}$ and each node is endowed with the signum (sgn) function. For convenience in calculations we examine the probability that $o_1 i_{1,1}/n > 0$. However,

$$o_1 i_{1,1} = \frac{1}{n} \sum_{j=2}^{n} \sum_{p=1}^{P} i_{p,1} i_{p,j} i_{1,j} i_{1,1}$$

$$= \frac{1}{n} \left[\sum_{j=2}^{n} i_{1,1} i_{1,j} i_{1,j} i_{1,1} + \sum_{j=2}^{n} \sum_{p=2}^{P} i_{p,1} i_{p,j} i_{1,j} i_{1,1} \right]$$

$$= \frac{n-1}{n} + \frac{1}{n} \sum_{j=2}^{n} \sum_{p=2}^{P} i_{p,1} i_{p,j} i_{1,j} i_{1,1}$$

$$= \frac{n-1}{n} + Z = 1 + Z - \frac{1}{n}$$

where $Z = (1/n) \sum_{j=2}^{n} \sum_{p=2}^{P} i_{p,1} i_{p,j} i_{1,j} i_{1,1}$, because $i_{\ell,j}^2 = 1$ for all values of ℓ and j. By assumption, i_ℓ's are randomly selected to be -1 or 1. In other words, they are stochastically independent of each other, implying that

$$\mathcal{E}(i_{\ell,j}) = 0$$

$$\mathcal{E}(i_{\ell,j} i_{\ell'j'}) = \begin{cases} 1 & \text{if } \ell = \ell', \ j = j' \\ 0 & \text{otherwise} \end{cases}$$

where $\mathcal{E}(\cdot)$ denotes the expected value of its argument.

Due to these properties, it follows that $\mathcal{E}(Z) = 0$ and the variance of Z is $(P-1)(n-1)/n^2$ which approximates to P/n for large n and P. By the central limit theorem [see page 229 in Feller (1957)], Z would be distributed as a Gaussian random variable with mean 0 and variance $\sigma^2 \approx (P/n)$. Hence its density function is given by $(2\pi P/n)^{-1/2} \exp(-nx^2/2P)$ and the probability

$$\text{Prob}[Z > a] = \int_a^\infty (2\pi P/n)^{-1/2} \exp(-nx^2/2P) dx.$$

Returning to the probability of correct retrieval of the first bit, we note that

$$\varphi = \text{Prob}[o_1 i_{1,1} > 0] = \text{Prob}[1 + Z - \frac{1}{n} > 0] \approx \text{Prob}[Z > -1]$$

and in view of the Gaussian distribution of Z,

$$\varphi = \frac{\sqrt{n}}{\sqrt{2\pi P}} \int_{-1}^\infty e^{-(nx^2/2P)} dx$$

$$= \frac{\sqrt{n}}{\sqrt{2\pi P}} \int_{-\infty}^1 e^{-\left(\frac{nx^2}{2P}\right)} dx$$

since the density function of Z is symmetric.

If (n/P) is very large, then it can be shown [cf. Feller (1957), page 166] that

$$\varphi \approx 1 - \sqrt{\frac{P}{2\pi n}} \exp\left(-\frac{n}{2P}\right). \tag{6.22}$$

So far, we have approximated the probability that the first bit of the first stored pattern will be correctly retrieved. Note that φ does not contain terms such as $i_{1,1}$ and $w_{1,j}$. In other words, the same probability expression applies for all bits of all patterns. Therefore, the probability of correct retrieval of all bits of all stored patterns is given by $\beta = (\varphi)^{nP}$ which can be approximated by

$$\beta \approx \left(1 - \sqrt{\frac{P}{2\pi n}} \exp(-\frac{n}{2P})\right)^{nP}$$

$$\approx 1 - nP\sqrt{\frac{P}{2\pi n}} \exp(-\frac{n}{2P})$$

if P/n is a small real number. In particular, if we take $P/n = 1/(2\alpha \ln n)$, for some $\alpha > 0$, then

$$\exp(-\frac{n}{2P}) = \exp(-\frac{2\alpha \ln n}{2}) = n^{-\alpha},$$

which converges to zero as $n \to \infty$. Therefore, for large values of n,

$$nP\sqrt{\frac{P}{2\pi n}} \exp(-\frac{n}{2P}) \approx \frac{n^{2-\alpha}}{(2\alpha \ln n)^{3/2}\sqrt{2\pi}}$$

which converges to zero as long as $\alpha \geq 2$. This concludes the proof of the theorem.

In the above discussion, we have calculated the probability of correct retrieval of all bits of all patterns and then argued for its convergence to 1. But correct retrieval of all bits of all patterns is a harsh condition. The above argument ignores the fact that Hopfield networks are able to correct some of the errors in the process of iterative evaluations. Hence a better bound would be obtained by considering the possibility of correcting errors during the iterative evaluations.

The final association of an input vector is made after several iterations: a node evaluates its output several times. Hopfield network dynamics are not deterministic: the node to be updated at any given time is chosen randomly. In two different runs, different sequences of choices of nodes to be updated may lead to different stable states, even if the initial network inputs are the same. Consequently, an appropriate analysis of the network is obtained using a stochastic method. A stochastic version of the Hopfield neural network is implemented as follows.

Given the cumulative input net_ℓ arriving at node ℓ, the output of the node is $+1$ with probability $(1 + \exp(-2\beta \text{net}_\ell))^{-1}$, and -1 with probability $(1 - (1 + \exp(-2\beta \text{net}_\ell))^{-1})$.

In other words, the output of the ℓth node does not depend only upon the sign of the input net_ℓ: a stochastic decision is made. For such a network, Hertz, Krogh, and Palmer (1990) have shown that retrieval of stored patterns will be effective if the number of stored patterns is $P < 0.138\,n$.

In example 6.6, only four input patterns were stored using a Hopfield network with 19×19 nodes. Theorem 6.1 suggests that we should be able to store approximately $(19 \times 19)/4$

$\ln(19 \times 19)$ or 16 objects that can be retrieved without significant errors. In a realistic situation, we may be able to store as many as $0.138 \times 19 \times 19 \approx 50$ input patterns in a network of size 19×19, with the associated Hopfield network continuing to perform reasonably well.

6.2.3 Continuous Hopfield networks

The Hopfield models considered so far assume discrete, bivalent node outputs, so that the number of possible states is finite. However, there are many problems where it is necessary or more convenient for node outputs to range over the real numbers, e.g., where each node output can take any value between -1 and 1. This necessitates use of the *continuous* Hopfield network model, with the following changes to the discrete model discussed earlier.

1. Node outputs need not belong to a small discrete set of values. Accordingly, the node function must not be a step function, but must instead be a continuous function.

2. Time is continuous, i.e., each node constantly examines its net input and updates its output.

3. Changes in node outputs must be gradual, implying that in an infinitesimal amount of time, only an infinitesimal change can occur in a node's output. This is a major departure from the discrete model: instead of a node update rule of the form $\Delta x_\ell = f$ (net weighted input), the new update rule must be of the form $(\delta x_\ell / \delta t) = f$ (net weighted input). In this section, we assume that the change in output of the ℓth node at time t is given by the equation

$$\frac{\delta x_\ell(t)}{\delta t} = \frac{x_\ell(t + \delta t) - x_\ell(t)}{\delta t} = \eta \, f\left(\sum_j w_{j,\ell} x_j(t) + I_\ell\right)$$

where $x_j(t)$ is the output of the jth node at time t, and the learning rate η is a small positive constant whose magnitude governs the speed of convergence. In the model discussed in this section, we assume that f is the hyperbolic tangent.

4. Node outputs are often assumed to be bounded, and saturate at some values as the net input approaches $\pm\infty$. This assumption is useful for ease of implementation, assurance of convergence, as well as biological plausibility. In this section, we assume that each node's output at each instant must belong to the closed interval $[-1, 1]$, i.e., $-1 \le x_\ell \le 1$ for the ℓth node. The modified node update rule is effectively the following.

$$\frac{\delta x_\ell(t)}{\delta t} = \begin{cases} 0, & \text{if } x_\ell = 1 \text{ and } f(\sum_j w_{j,\ell} x_j(t) + I_\ell) > 0 \\ 0, & \text{if } x_\ell = -1 \text{ and } f(\sum_j w_{j,\ell} x_j(t) + I_\ell) < 0 \\ \eta f(\sum_j w_{j,\ell} x_j(t) + I_\ell) & \text{otherwise} \end{cases} \qquad (6.23)$$

Given such network dynamics, the proof of convergence of computations follows the same method as for the discrete Hopfield model. An energy function with a lower bound is constructed, and it is shown that every change made in a node's output decreases energy, assuming asynchronous dynamics. The logical choice for the energy function E is similar to that of the discrete Hopfield network, a special case of equation 6.17:

$$E = -(1/2) \sum_{\ell} \sum_{j \neq \ell} w_{\ell,j} x_\ell(t) x_j(t) - \sum_{\ell} I_\ell x_\ell(t). \tag{6.24}$$

E is minimized as the values of $x_1(t), \ldots, x_n(t)$ vary with time t. For a given choice of weights and external inputs, E has a lower bound if the values of $x_1(t), \ldots, x_n(t)$ have upper and lower bounds, as is assured by equation 6.23.

Since $(1/2) w_{\ell,j} x_\ell x_j + (1/2) w_{j,\ell} x_j x_\ell = w_{\ell,j} x_\ell x_j$ for symmetric weights, we have

$$\frac{\delta E}{\delta x_\ell(t)} = -\left(\sum_j w_{\ell,j} x_j + I_\ell \right). \tag{6.25}$$

The Hopfield net update rule, from equation 6.23, requires

$$\frac{\delta x_\ell}{\delta t} > 0 \text{ if and only if } f\left(\sum_j w_{j,\ell} x_j + I_\ell \right) > 0. \tag{6.26}$$

Whenever f is a monotonically increasing function (such as tanh), with $f(0) = 0$,

$$f\left(\sum_j w_{j,\ell} x_j + I_\ell \right) > 0 \text{ if and only if } \left(\sum_j w_{j,\ell} x_j + I_\ell \right) > 0. \tag{6.27}$$

From equations 6.25, 6.26, and 6.27, we can conclude that

$$\frac{\delta x_\ell}{\delta t} > 0 \text{ if and only if } \left(\sum_j w_{j\ell} x_\ell + I_\ell > 0 \right), \text{ i.e., } \frac{\delta E}{\delta x_\ell} < 0.$$

This implies that

$$\left(\frac{\delta x_\ell}{\delta t} \right) \left(\frac{\delta E}{\delta x_\ell} \right) < 0, \text{ for each } i.$$

Hence

$$\frac{\delta E}{\delta t} = \sum_\ell \left(\frac{\delta x_\ell}{\delta t} \right) \left(\frac{\delta E}{\delta x_\ell} \right) < 0.$$

This result implies that the continuous Hopfield network update rule is assured to decrease energy, assuming that the node function f is monotonically increasing with $f(0) = 0$.

For the discrete Hopfield network, this would have been sufficient to show that computation terminates, since (a) each node update reduces a lower-bounded energy function, (b) the number of possible states is finite, and (c) the number of possible node updates is limited. But for the continuous Hopfield model, node output magnitudes cannot be arbitrarily large. If node outputs are allowed to increase or decrease without bound, then energy may decrease indefinitely. Therefore, the bounds $(-1, 1)$ on the node values imposed by equation 6.23 are needed to ensure termination.

EXAMPLE 6.7   Consider a two-node continuous Hopfield network, with the initial node output values $x_1 = 1$ and $x_2 = 1$, no bias weights or external inputs, and the hyperbolic tangent node function.

• Let the weights be $w_{1,2} = w_{2,1} = 1$. If there is no bound on the node values, each node influences the other, increasing its node value using equation 6.23. This process continues without limit, so that

$$\lim_{t \to \infty} x_1(t) = \lim_{t \to \infty} x_2(t) = \infty.$$

• Consider a different set of weights, with $w_{1,2} = w_{2,1} = -1$. Both nodes simultaneously update their states, resulting in a decrease of both node values, so that

$$\lim_{t \to \infty} x_1(t) = \lim_{t \to \infty} x_2(t) = 0.$$

By contrast, the analogous discrete Hopfield model with asynchronous dynamics leads instantly to either the state $x_1 = 1, x_2 = -1$ or $x_1 = -1, x_2 = 1$.

Several slightly different formulations of the continuous Hopfield model can be found in the literature. In the original paper by Hopfield (1984), for instance, the energy function has an additional term to allow modeling the electrical resistance of a neural membrane model. The update rule is sometimes expressed in terms of changes occurring in the net input to a node instead of a node output (x_ℓ); both formulations are equivalent.

While the continuous Hopfield net model is a powerful generalization of the discrete model, the size of the state space increases drastically and the energy function is hence likely to have many more local minima than is the case for the discrete model.

Cohen-Grossberg theorem   The dynamics of the continuous Hopfield network (as well as many of its variants) constitute a special case of the following theorem due to Cohen and Grossberg (1973), which gives sufficient conditions for a network to converge asymptotically to a stable state. In the notation used, u_ℓ denotes the net input to the ℓth node, and

f_ℓ is its node function. The function a_j corresponds to the rate of change. The function b_j is arbitrary, and corresponds to an additional "loss" term used in some versions of the Hopfield model.

THEOREM 6.2   Let $a_j(u_j) \geq 0$, $(df_j(u_j)/du_j) \geq 0$, where u_j is the net input to the jth node in a neural network with symmetric weights $w_{j,\ell} = w_{\ell,j}$, whose behavior is governed by the following non-linear differential equation.

$$\frac{du_j}{dt} = a_j(u_j) \left[b_j(u_j) - \sum_{i=1}^{N} w_{j,\ell}\, f_\ell(u_\ell) \right], \quad \text{for } j = 1, \ldots, n$$

Then, there exists an energy function E for which $(dE/dt) \leq 0$ for $u_j \neq 0$, i.e., the network dynamics lead to a stable state in which energy ceases to change.

6.3   Brain-State-in-a-Box Network

The "Brain-State-in-a-Box" (BSB) neural network model is similar to and predates the Hopfield network, and was introduced by Anderson et al. (1972). It can be used for auto-association tasks, and can also be extended to hetero-association with two or more layers of nodes. In this section, we present details of the auto-associator BSB model.

A BSB network is fully connected, with as many nodes as the dimensionality n of the input space. Unlike the discrete Hopfield network, all nodes are updated simultaneously, and the nodes take values in the continuous range from -1 to $+1$. Unlike the continuous Hopfield network, the node function used is a ramp function

$$f(\text{net}) = \min(1,\ \max(-1,\ \text{net}))$$

which is bounded, continuous, and piecewise linear, as shown in figure 6.8. In the operation of this network, each node changes its state according to the following equation.

$$x_\ell(t+1) = f\left(\sum_{j=1}^{n} w_{\ell,j} x_j(t) \right) \tag{6.28}$$

where $x_\ell(t)$ is the state of the ℓth node at time t. Some formulations of equation 6.28 fix the self-excitation parameter $w_{\ell,\ell}$ to equal 1.

Equation 6.28 may be described by saying that an initial activation of the network is steadily amplified by positive feedback, subject to the constraint that node activations saturate at 1 or -1. Each node's activation belongs to the closed interval $[-1,\ 1]$, so that

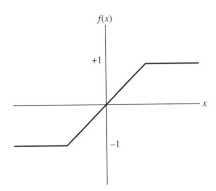

Figure 6.8
The ramp function, which takes values between −1 and +1.

the state of the network always remains inside an *n*-dimensional "box" (hypercube), giving rise to the name of the network, "Brain-State-in-a-Box."

The ramp node function leads to an interesting behavior in network operation, where the state of the network steadily moves from an arbitrary point inside the box towards one side of the box, and then crawls along the side of the box to reach a corner of the box (vertex of the hypercube). The network in figure 6.9(a) contains three nodes, connected by weights 1/3, 1/3, and 1, respectively. Each possible bipolar pattern corresponds to one vertex of the cube shown in figure 6.9(b). When supplied with initial stimulus *A*, the state of the network may first be modified until it reaches *B*, a point on one of the faces of the cube, and further modifications lead to the final state *C*, which corresponds to one of the stored patterns.

As in the Hopfield network, the connections between nodes are Hebbian, representing correlations between node activations, and can be obtained by iterative or non-iterative computations. The non-iterative procedure assumes a fixed set of training patterns, with the weight associated with the connection from the *j*th node to the ℓth node obtained using the equation

$$w_{\ell,j} = \frac{1}{P} \sum_{p=1}^{P} (i_{p,\ell} \, i_{p,j}), \tag{6.29}$$

for all values of ℓ and *j*, where $i_{p,\ell}$ is the ℓth component of the *p*th training pattern, *P* is the number of training patterns, and training patterns are bipolar, so that each $i_{p,j} \in \{-1, 1\}$. In the iterative training procedure, training patterns are repeatedly pre-

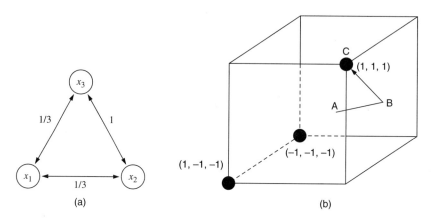

Figure 6.9
State change trajectory in a Brain-State-in-a-Box: (a) the network, with three nodes; (b) three stored patterns, indicated by darkened circles. The state of the network changes from initial stimulus A to B, and then along a face of the cube to C (a stored pattern).

sented to the network, and the weights successively modified using the weight update rule

$$\Delta w_{\ell,j} = \eta i_{p,j}\left(i_{p,\ell} - \sum_k w_{\ell,k} i_{p,k}\right), \text{ for } p = 1, \ldots, P, \tag{6.30}$$

where $\eta \geq 0$ is a prespecified positive constant. Equation 6.30 indicates that the weight change is proportional to $i_{p,j}$ as well as the difference between the desired value $i_{p,\ell}$ and the current computed value $\sum_k w_{\ell,k} i_{p,k}$. This rule corresponds to gradient descent on the error

$$E = \sum_{p=1}^{P}\sum_{\ell=1}^{n}\left(i_{p,\ell} - \sum_k w_{\ell,k} i_{p,\ell}\right)^2 \tag{6.31}$$

with respect to $w_{\ell,k}$'s. The weight update rule in 6.30 is applied repeatedly for each pattern until the error $\sum_\ell (i_{p,\ell} - \sum_k w_{\ell,k} i_{p,k})^2$ becomes negligible. When training is completed, we expect that $\sum_p \Delta w_{\ell,j} = 0$, implying that

$$\sum_p i_{p,j}\left(i_{p,\ell} - \sum_k w_{\ell,k} i_{p,k}\right) = 0,$$

i.e.,

$$\sum_p (i_{p,j}\, i_{p,\ell}) = \sum_p i_{p,j} \sum_k (w_{\ell,k}\, i_{p,k}),$$

an equality satisfied when

$$i_{p,\ell} = \sum_k (w_{\ell,k}\, i_{p,k}).$$

The trained network is hence "stable" for the trained patterns, i.e., presentation of a stored pattern does not result in any change in the network.

Weights can be calculated dynamically, as patterns to be learnt arrive sequentially over time. But once the weights are learnt, i.e., the training is complete, these weights remain fixed during the network application phase. In the latter phase, the equation 6.28 is repeatedly invoked, beginning from the given input state, until the output converges or an upper bound on the number of iterations is reached.

EXAMPLE 6.8   Consider a network with three nodes, where each node corresponds to one input dimension. The state of the network is represented by a three-dimensional cube (box), some of whose vertices correspond to stored patterns. If the training set consists of the three patterns

$$\{(1, 1, 1),\ (-1, -1, -1),\ (1, -1, -1)\},$$

as shown in figure 6.9, the network connections carry the following Hebbian weights:

$$w_{1,2} = w_{2,1} = (1 + 1 - 1)/3 = 1/3,$$

$$w_{1,3} = w_{3,1} = (1 + 1 - 1)/3 = 1/3,$$

and

$$w_{2,3} = w_{3,2} = (1 + 1 + 1)/3 = 1.$$

• If an input pattern $(0.5, 0.6, 0.1)$ is presented to this network, and the update rule of equation 6.28 is used, then the next state of the network is described by

$$\left(f\left(0.5 + \frac{0.6}{3} + \frac{0.1}{3}\right),\ f\left(0.6 + \frac{0.5}{3} + 0.1\right),\ f\left(0.1 + 0.6 + \frac{0.5}{3}\right)\right)$$

$$= (0.73,\ 0.97,\ 0.97)$$

where f is the ramp function described earlier. Note that the second and third nodes begin to exhibit identical states, since $w_{2,3} = 1$. At the next time step, the network state changes to

$$\left(f\left(0.73 + \frac{0.97}{3} + \frac{0.97}{3}\right),\ f\left(0.97 + \frac{0.73}{3} + 0.97\right),\ f\left(0.97 + \frac{0.73}{3} + 0.97\right)\right)$$

$$= (1,\ 1,\ 1),$$

which corresponds to one of the stored patterns.

• Instead, if the input pattern presented to this network is $(0.5, 0.6, -0.7)$, then the next state of the network is described by

$$\left(f\left(0.5 + \frac{0.6}{3} - \frac{0.7}{3} \right), f\left(0.6 + \frac{0.5}{3} - \frac{0.7}{3} \right), f\left(-0.7 + \frac{0.5}{3} + 0.6 \right) \right)$$

$$= (0.47, \ 0.07, \ 0.07).$$

At the next time step, the network state changes to

$$\left(f\left(0.47 + \frac{0.07 + 0.07}{3} \right), f\left(0.07 + \frac{0.47}{3} + 0.07 \right), f\left(0.07 + \frac{0.47}{3} + 0.07 \right) \right)$$

$$= (0.52, 0.3, 0.3).$$

Eventually, the network does converge to the stable memory $(1, 1, 1)$ even in this case.

• If the input pattern presented is $(0, 0, 0)$, however, the state of the network does not change.

• If the input pattern presented is $(0, 0.5, -0.5)$, the state of the network changes instantly to $(0, 0, 0)$, and does not change thereafter.

The BSB network in the above example converges to one of the stored memories even if the input pattern presented corresponds to a vertex of the box that is not a stored memory, e.g., the input pattern $(1, -1, 1)$ leads the network to the state $(1, 1, 1)$. As in the case of Hopfield networks, spurious attractors (that are not stored patterns) may exist, towards which the network state may migrate when some input patterns are presented. If a three-dimensional BSB network was intended to store only the two patterns

$$\{(1, 1, 1), \ (1, -1, -1)\},$$

with weights

$w_{1,2} = w_{2,1} = (1 - 1)/2 = 0,$

$w_{1,3} = w_{3,1} = (1 - 1)/2 = 0,$

and $w_{2,3} = w_{3,2} = (1 + 1)/2 = 1,$

then the input pattern $(-1, -1, -1)$ is a spurious attractor, being unchanged by the network.

The execution of the BSB network minimizes the Lyapunov energy function

$$-\sum_{\ell} \sum_{j} w_{\ell,j} x_\ell x_j,$$

carrying out a gradient descent on this function when the weight matrix W [whose (ℓ, j)th element is $w_{\ell,j}$] is symmetric and positive definite (i.e., all eigen-values of W are positive). However, if we allow all nodes to be updated simultaneously, then the network may remain stuck at the origin (the center of the box or hypercube). If the weight matrix is "diagonal-dominant," with

$$w_{j,j} \geq \sum_{\ell \neq j} w_{\ell,j} \text{ for each } j \in \{1, \ldots, n\},$$

then every vertex of the box (hypercube) is a stable memory. In general, the stability of memories as well as the number of spurious attractors tends to increase with increases in the values of the self-excitatory weights $w_{j,j}$.

The hetero-associative version of the BSB network contains two layers of nodes; connections are from the input layer to the output layer, and the connection from the jth node of the input layer to the ℓth node of the output layer carries the weight

$$w_{\ell,j} = \frac{1}{P} \sum_{p=1}^{P} i_{p,j} d_{p,\ell}.$$

The BSB network has been used by Anderson et al. (1990) for clustering radar pulses, distinguishing meaningful signals from noise in a radar surveillance environment where a detailed description of the signal sources is not known *a priori*.

6.4   Boltzmann Machines

Discrete Hopfield networks have serious limitations in memory capacity. Ackley, Hinton, and Sejnowski (1985) have generalized Hopfield networks to *Boltzmann machines* that contain hidden nodes. This significantly improves storage capacity. The nodes in this network change state stochastically, resulting in a node state distribution known in statistical physics as the Boltzmann distribution, from which the Boltzmann machine receives its name.

In discrete Hopfield networks, node states are changed using an update rule such as $x_i(t+1) = \text{sgn}(\sum_j w_{i,j} x_j(t))$, where the weights are determined by Hebbian learning or directly by examining correlations among input variables. But a Boltzmann machine architecture includes hidden nodes and the patterns to be stored give no direct information about the weights between hidden and "visible" (non-hidden) nodes. A learning process is therefore invoked to determine these weights.

The Boltzmann machine uses a stochastic learning algorithm, such that the weights have a good chance of moving to their optimal values. Their initial values are randomly chosen. Principles of *simulated annealing* are invoked to change the state of a hidden node from -1 to 1 or from 1 to -1 to minimize the energy function defined earlier for Hopfield networks. The details of simulated annealing are discussed in chapter 7, but a high-level description will suffice for the present: an external parameter called *temperature*, τ, is steadily lowered, and each node is allowed to change state with a probability that depends on $(\Delta E/\tau)$, where ΔE is the energy change that results from the state change and E is as defined in the Hopfield network. As in the case of the Hopfield network, a node is randomly chosen for state change; the current value is altered to measure the change ΔE. A state change that results in decreasing energy is immediately accepted, but even if the state change increases energy, the state change is accepted with probability proportional to $1/(1 + \exp(-\Delta E/\tau))$.

A large number of such state changes are allowed to occur at each temperature. If such a system is allowed to reach equilibrium at any temperature τ, the ratio of the probabilities of two states a, b with energies E_a and E_b will be given by $P(a)/P(b) = \exp(E_b - E_a)/\tau$. Such a probability distribution is called the *Boltzmann distribution*. This distribution is independent of the path followed in reaching equilibrium and independent of the initial state. Note that the difference in log-probabilities is proportional to the energy difference.

Details of a commonly used version of the Boltzmann machine learning algorithm are described in figure 6.10. This algorithm assumes that input and output nodes can be distinguished, and the task addressed is to predict values of output nodes from those of input nodes. In the auto-association case, there are no separate input and output nodes, so that no nodes are "clamped" in the second phase of the algorithm. "Clamping" nodes refers to forcing those node outputs to remain at values available from the training patterns, so that only the other nodes are allowed to change state.

The Boltzmann machine weight change rule can be shown to conduct gradient descent on a measure called *relative entropy* or *cross-entropy*,

$$H(P, P') = \sum_s P_s \ln(P_s/P'_s)$$

where s is a variable that ranges over all possible network states, P_s is the probability of network state s when the visible nodes are clamped, and P'_s is the probability of network state s when no nodes are clamped. $H(P, P')$ is an asymmetric distance measure that compares the probability distributions P and P'; note that $H(P, P') = 0$ when $P = P'$, the desired goal of the Boltzmann machine training algorithm.

Several ways of using the trained Boltzmann machine have been suggested. One possibility is the Hopfield network model: an input pattern is presented, and all nodes change

Algorithm Boltzmann;
  while weights continue to change
    and computational bounds are not exceeded, **do**
      Phase 1:
        for each training pattern, **do**
          Clamp all input and output nodes;
          ANNEALING: **for** temperature τ ranging over a
                          finite set of decreasing values, **do**
            for a time period that increases with τ, **do**
              Change each hidden node state with
              a probability proportional to
              $\min(1, \ 1/(1 + \exp(-\Delta E/\tau)))$;
            end-for;
          end-for;
          Update $\{\ldots p_{i,j}\ldots\}$, the equilibrium probabilities
            with which node pairs are ON or OFF
            simultaneously (after annealing);
        end-for;

      Phase 2:
        for each training pattern, **do**
          Clamp all input nodes;
          ANNEALING: **for** temperature τ ranging over a
                          finite set of decreasing values, **do**
            for a time period that increases with τ, **do**
              Change each output and hidden node
              state with probability proportional
              to $\min(1, \ 1/(1 + \exp(-\Delta E/\tau)))$;
            end-for;
          end-for;
          Update $\{\ldots p'_{i,j}\ldots\}$, the equilibrium probabilities
            with which node pairs are ON or OFF
            simultaneously (after annealing);
        end-for;

      Modify each weight $w_{i,j}$ by the quantity
        $\Delta w_{i,j} = \eta(p_{i,j} - p'_{i,j})$, where η is a small constant;
  end-while.

Figure 6.10
Boltzmann machine learning algorithm.

state in such a manner as to reduce energy, so that the new node output corresponds to the sign of the net weighted input to that node. However, the initial states of the hidden nodes are undetermined, therefore the resulting network outputs are unpredictable. The other extreme is to carry out a complete simulated annealing process on the network states; this would result in the system reaching a global optimum of the energy function, which may have nothing in common with the input pattern for which the associated stored pattern needs to be retrieved.

Hartman (1991) suggested an intermediate solution: If a (possibly corrupted) input pattern is presented to the network, the visible input nodes are initially clamped, and the network is annealed from a high temperature to an intermediate temperature. This is expected to lead the network to the vicinity of a local minimum of the energy function near the input pattern. The visible nodes are then unclamped, and annealing continues from the current (intermediate) temperature until a sufficiently low temperature (≈ 0) is reached, allowing some of the visible node states also to be modified, correcting errors that may have been present in the input pattern. The rate at which temperature decreases is called the *cooling rate*, which must be extremely slow to assure convergence to global minima of E, as described in section 7.3. In practice, annealing cannot be allowed to occur at the slow rates demanded by theory, hence faster annealing rates are often used, losing the theoretical guarantee of convergence to global optima. Ackley, Hinton, and Sejnowski (1985) also noted that this approach may fail when the best solution is a deep, narrow, isolated minimum.

EXAMPLE 6.9   Ackley, Hinton, and Sejnowski (1985) applied the Boltzmann machine to *Encoder-Decoder* problems of various sizes. The 4-2-4 version of the Boltzmann machine, shown in figure 6.11, is described below. In this instance of the problem, four-dimensional binary input vectors are presented to the network at its input nodes, and the output nodes must reproduce these vectors, but there is no direct connection between input nodes and output nodes. Two hidden nodes mediate, and weights between the input layer and the hidden layer, as well as weights between the hidden layer and the output layer, must be "learnt" by the system using the Boltzmann machine learning algorithm. The following learning cycle was used by Ackley, Hinton, and Sejnowski.

1. In the estimation of $p_{i,j}$, a noisy clamping mechanism was used, with P(On$\rightarrow$Off) = 0.15, and P(Off$\rightarrow$On) = 0.05. Annealing was conducted, running the network for two time units at temperature 20, two time units at temperature 15, two time units at temperature 12, and four time units at temperature 10, where each time unit was defined as the time required for each node to be given one chance to change its state, on average.

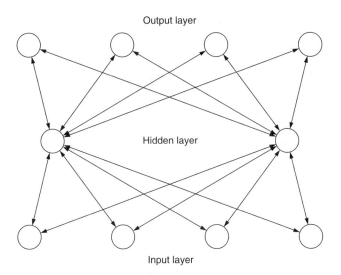

Output layer

Hidden layer

Input layer

Figure 6.11
Boltzmann machine architecture for the 4-2-4 encoder-decoder problem.

2. Estimation of $p'_{i,j}$ was conducted using the same annealing schedule.

3. Weights were updated using a fixed weight step of ± 2, depending on the sign of $(p_{i,j} - p'_{i,j})$.

A weight decay mechanism was used to keep weights low.

The Boltzmann machine uses the weight change rule $\Delta w_{i,j} = \eta(p_{i,j} - p'_{i,j})$; this may be modified, incrementing or decrementing each weight by a fixed quantity depending on whether $p_{i,j} > p'_{i,j}$. The original weight change rule for the Boltzmann machine, described by Ackley et al., used values for $p_{i,j}$ that represented the probability with which the ith and jth nodes were "ON" simultaneously; greater success has been reported in later versions of the algorithm by using values for $p_{i,j}$ that represented the probability with which the ith and jth nodes had the same value, which also includes cases when the two nodes are "OFF" simultaneously.

The Boltzmann machine is a much more powerful system than the Hopfield network, owing to its use of hidden nodes and stochastic updates. However, the main difficulty with the Boltzmann machine is that its learning algorithm is extremely slow: a large number of observations of state variables have to be made at many temperatures before computation concludes. This problem is addressed in *mean field annealing*, a modification of the Boltzmann machine discussed below.

6.4.1 Mean field annealing

Peterson and Anderson (1987) proposed the *mean field annealing* algorithm, improving on the speed of execution of the Boltzmann machine by using a "mean field" approximation. For instance, if f is a function of two variables, the average value of $f(x, y)$ is approximated by $f(\mathcal{E}(x), \mathcal{E}(y))$, the result of applying f to the average values of x, y. This approximation is applied in the weight change rule of the Boltzmann machine, as follows.

Recall that the Boltzmann machine's weight update rule is $\Delta w_{\ell,j} = \eta(p_{\ell,j} - p'_{\ell,j})$, where η is a small constant, and $p_{\ell,j} = \mathcal{E}(x_\ell x_j)$ when the visible nodes are clamped, while $p'_{\ell,j} = \mathcal{E}(x_\ell x_j)$ when no nodes are clamped. This rule is modified in mean field annealing to

$$\Delta w_{\ell,j} = \eta(q_\ell q_j - q'_\ell q'_j),$$

where q_ℓ represents the average output of the ℓth node when the visible nodes are clamped, and q'_ℓ represents the average output of the ℓth node when no nodes are clamped.

For the Boltzmann distribution, the ℓth node takes the value 1 at temperature τ with probability

$$1/(1 + \exp(-\sum_j w_{\ell,j} x_j/\tau)),$$

and the value -1 with probability

$$1 - [1/(1 + \exp(-\sum_j w_{\ell,j} x_j/\tau))],$$

so that the average output is given by

$$q_\ell = \left(\frac{1}{(1 + \exp(-\sum_j w_{\ell,j} x_j/\tau))}\right) - \left(1 - \frac{1}{(1 + \exp(-\sum_j w_{\ell,j} x_j/\tau))}\right)$$

$$= \tanh\left(\sum_j w_{\ell,j} x_j/\tau\right).$$

Again, since node output x_j is a random variable, the mean field approximation suggests replacing x_j in the above equations by its expected value $\mathcal{E}(x_j)$, so that

$$q_\ell = \tanh\left(\sum_j w_{\ell,j}\mathcal{E}(x_j)/\tau\right).$$

The rest of the mean field annealing algorithm is identical to that of the Boltzmann machine. These approximations result in large improvements in the speed of execution of the Boltzmann machine. Although convergence of the weight values to global optima is not assured, the literature describes many applications where satisfactory results have been obtained using mean field annealing.

6.5 Hetero-associators

A hetero-associator or a generalized associative memory is a mapping from a set of input patterns to a different set of output patterns. In this section, we study some simple iterative hetero-associative neural network models, containing two layers of nodes. Many of these models and their variants are described by Kosko (1992) in greater detail.

Certain hetero-association tasks can be performed using a feedforward network in conjunction with a lookup table. For instance, consider the hetero-association task of translating English word inputs into equivalent Spanish word outputs. A simple feedforward network trained by backpropagation may be able to assert that a particular word supplied as input to the system is the 125th word in the dictionary. The desired output pattern may be obtained by composing the feedforward network function $f : \Re^n \longrightarrow \{C_1, \ldots, C_k\}$ with a lookup table mapping $g : \{C_1, \ldots, C_k\} \longrightarrow \{P_1, \ldots, P_k\}$ that associates each "address" C_i with a pattern P_i, as shown in figure 6.12.

However, training the corresponding feedforward network could be computationally expensive. Hetero-association is most frequently performed using neural net models that have much more in common with Hopfield networks, with weights determined by a Hebbian principle, e.g., using equation 6.2. In such models, the first-layer node activations correspond to input patterns, and the second-layer node activations correspond to output patterns to which the network must associate these input patterns. Node values in the output layer are updated by applying a node function f to the net input flowing into this node from the input layer. If the input patterns are binary, then this node function f must be a step function.

$$x_\ell^{(2)}(t+1) = f\left(\sum_j w_{\ell,j} x_j^{(1)}(t) + \theta_\ell\right) \tag{6.32}$$

The update rule in equation 6.32 corresponds to a non-iterative pattern association step, with no error correction. There are several alternatives that may be followed in order to make the network produce an output pattern that belongs to a set of stored memories.

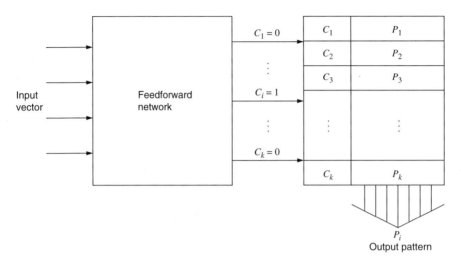

Figure 6.12
Association between input and output patterns using feedforward network and simple memory (at most one C_i is
"ON" for any input vector presentation).

- Perform iterative auto-association within the input layer, resulting in an input pattern that
belongs to a predetermined set of stored patterns, before feeding the result into the second
layer of the hetero-associator network. This scheme is illustrated in figure 6.13.

- Generate the output pattern corresponding to the non-iterative node update rule, multiplying the input pattern with the weight matrix, and then perform iterative auto-association
within the output layer, resulting in a final output pattern that belongs to a predetermined
set of stored patterns. This scheme is illustrated in figure 6.14.

- **Bidirectional associative memory** (BAM): There are no intra-layer connections in this
model. Generate a pattern at the second layer using a rule similar to the non-iterative node
update rule, multiplying the first-layer pattern with the weight matrix W and then passing
it through the signum activation function

$$x_\ell^{(2)}(t+1) = f\left(\sum_j w_{\ell,j} x_j^{(1)}(t) + \theta_\ell^{(2)}\right).$$

$$(6.33)$$

Then generate the first-layer pattern that ought to correspond to the just-generated output
pattern, using a similar state change rule.

$$x_\ell^{(1)}(t+2) = f\left(\sum_j w_{\ell,j} x_j^{(2)}(t+1) + \theta_\ell^{(1)}\right)$$

$$(6.34)$$

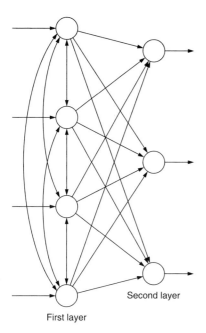

Figure 6.13
Auto-association in first layer, followed by weight matrix mapping into second layer.

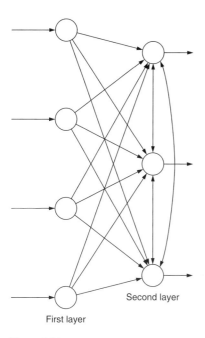

Figure 6.14
Weight matrix mapping from first layer into second layer, followed by auto-association in second layer.

257

The new pattern generated at a layer may not be identical to the pattern previously at that layer. Hence the process is repeated, successively updating both layers of nodes in each iteration, until the network stabilizes, i.e., until

$$x_\ell^{(1)}(t+2) = x_\ell^{(1)}(t), \text{ and } x_\ell^{(2)}(t+2) = x_\ell^{(2)}(t).$$

This scheme is illustrated in figure 6.15 and has been studied extensively by Kosko (1988).

We now study BAM models in greater detail. As in the case of Hopfield nets, weights in a BAM can be chosen to be Hebbian (correlation) terms: the (symmetric) weight between two nodes represents the frequency with which they are simultaneously ON or simultaneously OFF in the pairs of patterns to be stored in the BAM. Given a training set $T = \{(i_p, d_p) : p = 1, \ldots, P\}$, the weights are

$$w_{\ell,j} = \sum_{p=1}^{P} i_{p,j} d_{p,\ell} / P \qquad (6.35)$$

where P is the number of pattern-pairs stored in the BAM. Sigmoid node functions can be used in continuous BAM models. A BAM is said to be *bivalent* if each node activation value is restricted to $\{0, 1\}$ (or to $\{+1, -1\}$), and each node applies a step function to its net input.

EXAMPLE 6.10   We construct a BAM with four nodes in the first layer, two nodes in the second layer, and symmetric weights. The goal is to establish the following three associations between four-dimensional and two-dimensional patterns.

$(+1, +1, -1, -1) \rightarrow (+1, +1)$

$(+1, +1, +1, +1) \rightarrow (+1, -1)$

$(-1, -1, +1, +1) \rightarrow (-1, +1)$

The nature of the associations is such that the weights can be obtained by the Hebbian rule. For instance,

$$w_{1,1} = \frac{\left(\sum_{p=1}^{3} i_{p,1} d_{p,1}\right)}{3} = 1.$$

Likewise, one can show that $w_{1,2}$ is also equal to 1. All other weights are equal to $-1/3$, for example,

$$w_{1,3} = \frac{\left(\sum_{p=1}^{3} i_{p,3} d_{p,1}\right)}{3} = \frac{(-1 \times 1) + (1 \times 1) + (1 \times -1)}{3} = -\frac{1}{3}$$

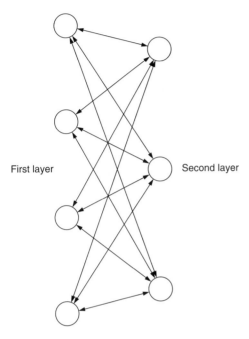

Figure 6.15
Bidirectional associative memory (BAM).

All eight weights so obtained constitute the weight matrix

$$W = \begin{pmatrix} 1 & 1 & -1/3 & -1/3 \\ -1/3 & -1/3 & -1/3 & -1/3 \end{pmatrix}.$$

When an input vector such as $\boldsymbol{i} = (-1, -1, -1, -1)$ is presented at the first layer, $x_1^{(1)} = i_1 = -1$, and, similarly, $x_2^{(1)} = x_3^{(1)} = x_4^{(1)} = -1$, and the BAM computation rules imply that $x_1^{(2)} = \text{sgn}(x_1^{(1)}w_{1,1} + x_2^{(1)}w_{1,2} + x_3^{(1)}w_{1,3} + x_4^{(1)}w_{1,4}) = \text{sgn}(-1 - 1 + 1/3 + 1/3) = \text{sgn}(-4/3) = -1$ and $x_2^{(2)} = \text{sgn}(x_1^{(1)}w_{2,1} + x_2^{(1)}w_{2,2} + x_3^{(1)}w_{2,3} + x_4^{(1)}w_{2,4}) = \text{sgn}(1/3 + 1/3 + 1/3 + 1/3) = \text{sgn}(4/3) = 1$. Thus the output pattern generated is $(-1, 1)$, one of the stored output patterns. In response to these activations for the second-layer nodes, the corresponding first-layer pattern generated is $(-1, -1, 1, 1)$, following computations such as

$$x_1^{(1)} = \text{sgn}(x_1^{(2)}w_{1,1} + x_2^{(2)}w_{2,1}) = \text{sgn}(-1 - 1/3) = -1.$$

Computation has stabilized since this first-layer pattern causes no further change in the second-layer pattern, and vice versa.

Other variants of node update rules have also been used in BAM models. For instance, the "additive" model separates out the effect of the previous activation value and the external input I_ℓ for the node under consideration, using the following state change rule:

$$x_\ell^{(2)}(t+1) = a_\ell x_\ell^{(2)}(t) + b_\ell I_\ell + f\left(\sum_{j\neq\ell} w_{\ell,j} x_j^{(1)}(t)\right). \tag{6.36}$$

The parameters a_i, b_i are frequently chosen from $\{1, 0\}$. If the BAM is discrete, bivalent, as well as additive, then node updates at the second layer are performed according to the following equation:

$$x_i^{(2)}(t+1) = \begin{cases} 1, & \text{if } [a_i x_i^{(2)}(t) + b_i I_i + \sum_{j\neq i} w_{i,j} x_j^{(1)}(t)] > \theta_i \\ 0, & \text{otherwise,} \end{cases}$$

where θ_i is the threshold for the ith node. A similar expression is used for the first-layer updates. BAM models have been shown to converge using a Lyapunov function such as the signal-energy function (L_1), defined as follows:

$$L_1 = -\sum_\ell \sum_j x_\ell^{(1)}(t) x_j^{(2)}(t) w_{\ell,j}. \tag{6.37}$$

This energy function can be modified, taking into account external node inputs I_ℓ^k as well as thresholds $\theta_\ell^{(k)}$ for nodes:

$$L_2 = L_1 - \sum_{k=1}^{2} \sum_{\ell=1}^{N(k)} x_\ell^{(k)} (I_\ell^k - \theta_\ell^{(k)}), \tag{6.38}$$

where $N(k)$ denotes the number of nodes in the kth layer. As in the case of Hopfield nets, there is no guarantee that the system stabilizes to a desired or nearest output pattern when presented with an input pattern.

The previous discussion of synchrony and asynchrony (cf. section 6.2) is applicable to BAM models. Stability is not assured for synchronous computations. However, stability is assured with inter-layer asynchrony, even if all the nodes in one layer change state simultaneously. This allows a greater amount of parallelism than Hopfield networks.

When a new input pattern is presented, the rate at which the system stabilizes depends on the proximity of the new input pattern to a stored pattern, and not on the number of patterns stored. The number of patterns that can be stored in a BAM is limited by network size, as in the case of Hopfield networks and matrix associative memories.

Importance factor   In some applications, certain pattern-pairs being stored in the BAM are known to be more important than others. In the human memory, for instance, certain name-face associations are stored much better than others, depending on the significance attached to them. This may be accomplished in a BAM by attaching an "importance factor" (σ_p) to each pattern $\boldsymbol{i}_p$ being used to modify the BAM weights. If σ_p represents the relative importance of the pth pattern-pair, then the new weight definition is

$$w_{j,i} = w_{i,j} = \sum_{p=1}^{P} \left(\sigma_p \, i_{p,i} \, d_{p,j} \right). \tag{6.39}$$

Human memory exhibits a decay effect, and events that have occurred a long time ago are more difficult to recall. This analogy suggests that instead of being a constant, the importance factor may be chosen to vary with time. This can be implemented by using a monotonically decreasing function for each importance factor. For example,

$$\sigma_p(t) = (1 - \epsilon)\sigma_p(t - 1), \tag{6.40}$$

or

$$\sigma_p(t) = \max(0, \sigma_p(t - 1) - \epsilon) \tag{6.41}$$

are possible methods to use to decrease the weight of importance factors over time, where a small positive constant $\epsilon < 1$ represents the rate at which forgetting occurs. When an old pattern is presented anew, its importance factor increases. This mechanism is useful if new pattern-pairs are continuously being learned by the BAM, i.e., different events are encoded at different instants. In other words, if pattern-pair $(\boldsymbol{i}_p, \boldsymbol{d}_p)$ is the pair added to the training set at time t, then

$$w_{i,j}(t) = (1 - \epsilon)w_{i,j}(t - 1) + \sigma_p(t - 1)i_{p,j} \, d_{p,i} \tag{6.42}$$

where $(1 - \epsilon)$ is the attenuation factor. Note that the time sequence in which weights are updated is completely different from the time sequence in which the memory is being used to retrieve specific pattern-pairs. Weights are updated when new pattern-pairs need to be encoded, possibly more than one such pattern-pair with each weight update, whereas node values are updated depending on the current set of weights, when a specific pattern-pair is to be accessed. Alternatively, the rate at which memory fades may be fixed to a global clock:

$$w_{i,j}(t) = (1 - \epsilon)w_{i,j}(t - 1) + \sum_{p=1}^{v(t)} \sigma_p(t - 1)i_{p,j} \, d_{p,i} \tag{6.43}$$

where $v(t) \geq 0$ is the number of new patterns being stored at time t. There may be many instants at which $v(t) = 0$, i.e., no new patterns are being stored, but existing memory continues to decay.

6.6 Conclusion

The biologically inspired Hebbian learning principle has been the focus of another important stream of artificial neural network research. In chapters 2, 3, and 4, the question addressed was: how do we modify connection weights in such a way as to minimize error, in a context where such error can be measured for some training samples? By contrast, the networks discussed in this chapter address a different question: how can we make connection weights represent the similarities and differences inherent in various attributes or input dimensions of available data? No extensive slow "training" phase is required in using these networks, but the number of state changes executed before the network stabilizes (when an input vector is presented) is of the order of the number of nodes in the networks.

Given that each node represents an input dimension, associative learning reinforces the magnitudes of connections between correlated nodes. The prototypical task for which such networks can be used is that of retrieving the correct output pattern, given a corrupted input pattern. In auto-association, the input pattern space and output space are identical; these spaces are distinct in hetero-association tasks. Hetero-associative systems may be bidirectional, with a vector from either vector space being generated when a vector from the other vector space is presented. These tasks can be accomplished using one-shot, non-iterative procedures, as well as iterative mechanisms that repeatedly modify the weights as new samples are presented to the system. Several variants of such networks have been discussed.

A biologically inspired variant of Hebbian learning is *differential* Hebbian learning (not discussed in this chapter due to the paucity of practical applications), proposed by Kosko (1986) and Klopf (1987). In this learning algorithm, changes in a weight $w_{i,j}$ are caused not by the amount of stimulation at each node, but by the change in the stimulation of the ith node by the jth node, at the time the output of the ith node changes. Furthermore, the weight change is governed not just by the current change in the activation of the jth node, but by the sum of such changes over a period of time.

The systems discussed here are limited in the "memories" or number of pattern associations that can be stably stored in the networks. If the desired number of memories is small, perfect retrieval is possible even when the input stimulus is significantly noisy or corrupted. However, such networks often store spurious memories that were not intended to be stored by the network developer. In chapter 7, we will examine the use of some of these network models for a completely different task: optimization.

6.7 Exercises

1.   a. Show that for a matrix A, if (AA^T) is invertible, then $A^T(AA^T)^{-1}$ satisfies the four conditions defining the pseudo-inverse.

b. Is the generalized inverse unique for every matrix?

2. Consider an auto-associative OLAM network with weight matrix W.

a. If the number of nodes equals the number of patterns to be stored, what is $\tilde{a}$, and what is $\hat{x}$ (in equation 6.13) for this network?

b. If the number of nodes is one less than the number of patterns to be stored, what is $\tilde{a}$, and what is $\hat{x}$? Consider a special case with two nodes and three patterns.

c. Show that W is idempotent, i.e., $W = WW$.

d. Show that every vector in W is orthogonal to every vector in $I - W$.

3.   a. Let x be a pattern stored in a bivalent Hopfield network. Let y be another bivalent pattern, each of whose components is opposite in sign to the corresponding component of x, i.e., $y_i = -x_i$ for each i. Will y also be a stable attractor in the same network (i.e., will the network generate the same output pattern y when y is presented to the network)? Why?

b. Consider a bivalent Hopfield network with four nodes that stores the patterns $(1, 1, 1, 1)$ and $(1, 1, -1, -1)$. What other patterns are stable attractors in this network?

4. The following weight matrices describe the connection weights of two-node recurrent networks. Describe the behavior of each network when stimulated by various possible patterns.

a.

$$W_1 = \begin{pmatrix} 0 & 1 \\ -1 & 0 \end{pmatrix}$$

b.

$$W_2 = \begin{pmatrix} 1 & 0 \\ 0 & 1 \end{pmatrix}$$

c.

$$W_3 = \begin{pmatrix} 1 & -1 \\ -1 & 1 \end{pmatrix}$$

d.

$$W_4 = \begin{pmatrix} 0 & -1 \\ -1 & 0 \end{pmatrix}$$

5. Morse code messages consist of "dots" and "dashes."

   a. Construct a Hopfield network to associate 3×3 input images with dots and dashes.

   b. How many spurious attractors does this network have, i.e., how many patterns other than dots and dashes are stable attractors?

   c. How many input errors can this network withstand, i.e., how much can the image of a dot (or dash) be corrupted while still allowing the network to retrieve a dot (or dash)?

6. In character recognition problems, we can work with small images or large images that have the same features. How large a Hopfield network would be needed to store images corresponding to the characters {H, O, P, F, I, E, L, D}? What is the expected performance of the network, with respect to the presence of spurious attractors and the amount of noise (corruption) in the input images that can be tolerated?

7. a. Is the Lyapunov measure L_2 (in equation 6.38) bounded? If yes, what are the upper and lower bounds? Does L_2 decrease whenever a single node in a BAM changes state?

   b. In a discrete bivalent BAM, a node changes state from 1 to 0 only when its net weighted input is less than its threshold. Similarly, a node changes state from 0 to 1 when its net input exceeds its threshold. Under this condition, show that L_2 decreases whenever a single node in a BAM changes state.

   c. Will L_2 decrease if any number of nodes in the same layer change state simultaneously?

   d. Will L_2 decrease if any number of nodes in the BAM change state simultaneously?

   e. Which of the above results hold if node outputs are not discrete values, but are outputs of sigmoidal functions?

8. a. Implement the decaying BAM model for a set of pattern-pairs that constantly change, e.g.,

   $$X_{j,k}^{(2)}(t+1) = (1-\epsilon) \cdot X_{j,k}^{(2)}(t).$$

   b. Can the dynamics of this decaying BAM model be associated with a Lyapunov energy function that decreases with time?

9. Apply the Boltzmann machine model to identify the presence of vertical and horizontal inclined lines. The network has nine binary inputs, corresponding to positions in a 3×3 binary input image, and two outputs, of which the first (or second) is "ON" if a vertical (or horizontal) line is present in the input image. Compare the performance of the Boltzmann machine with mean field annealing, and with a BAM network for the same task.

10. The "mirror image" problem consists of generating a binary pattern in which bits are "ON" whenever the corresponding bit in the input pattern is "OFF," and vice versa. Apply the BAM network model with nine nodes in each layer to solve this problem, for a 3×3 input image. Which other networks would be appropriate for this task?

7 Optimization Methods

Long walks and especially hill-climbing are very difficult for me in a world where universal gravitation persists.
—Gregor Mendel (on account of his portliness)

This chapter presents several neural and non-neural optimization methods. In many interesting problems, optimal solutions cannot be guaranteed by reasonably fast algorithms whose space and time requirements are bounded by polynomial functions of the problem size. The algorithms we present do not guarantee optimal solutions, aiming instead to find near-optimal solutions in much less time than that required to find optimal solutions.

Optimization problems may be solved by choosing an algorithm to conduct *state space search*. The state space for a problem is a set of states, where each state consists of one possible assignment of values to each variable relevant to the problem. A generic state space search algorithm is defined in figure 7.1. Each algorithm can be described by identifying how each of the components of the generic algorithm is implemented.

The state space depends on the representation chosen. A "feasible" solution is a candidate solution that is acceptable without further modification. Problems often contain constraints that restrict the feasible solution space to be significantly smaller than the entire search space. Many algorithms that solve optimization problems attempt to minimize an "energy" function E that combines the cost or performance criteria (describing the quality of a candidate solution) with penalty functions that implement constraints needed to ensure feasibility. Infeasible solutions should have higher energies than feasible solutions, and the better of two feasible solutions should have lower energy.

A global optimum is a candidate solution whose quality is better than or equal to the quality of every other candidate solution. A local optimum is a candidate solution whose quality cannot be improved by any single move, i.e., its neighbors in the state space are of lower quality. Changing the move set or the representation can lead to a change in the number and position of local optima. Since most algorithms lead to local optima, it is desirable to ensure that every local optimum of the energy function is a feasible solution.

Algorithm Search;
  Initialize a state;
  while termination criteria are not satisfied, **do**
    Generate a move from the current state;
    Decide whether the move is to be accepted;
    Update the current state using the move;
  end-while.

Figure 7.1
A generic state space search algorithm.

EXAMPLE 7.1   Consider the task of minimizing the function $3x^2 + y^2 + z^2$ subject to two restrictions: (1) $x + y + z = 9$ and (2) x, y, z are integers. Three possible choices for the state space are

• the set of 3-tuples of integers that satisfy $x + y + z = 9$.

• the set of all 3-tuples of integers: in this case one may add a penalty function such as $10,000(x + y + z - 9)^2$ to the function being optimized, penalizing choices of values for x, y, z that do not satisfy $x + y + z = 9$.

• the set of all 3-tuples of real numbers that satisfy $x + y + z = 9$: in this case, a penalty function could be of the form $1,000[(x - \lfloor x \rfloor)^2 + (y - \lfloor y \rfloor)^2 + (z - \lfloor z \rfloor)^2]$, where $\lfloor x \rfloor$ is the largest integer $\leq x$.

It is not always clear which of such choices is best. For instance, the first among the above possibilities, which ensures that every state is a feasible solution, may make it harder to reach an optimal solution, although the search space is smaller.

Section 7.1 describes how Hopfield networks (discussed in chapter 6) may be used to solve optimization problems. Hopfield networks implement a gradient descent or *hill-climbing* search method. A hill-climbing algorithm is one that only accepts moves (state change) that improve solution quality, i.e., decrease energy. The termination criterion consists of stopping when no possible move results in a state with lower energy. Alternatively, only moves that can lower energy are generated, and the move-generation process may be fine-tuned to ensure that energy is decreased as much as possible in any accepted move.

As suggested in earlier chapters, gradient descent and hill-climbing techniques suffer from the handicap that they are susceptible to getting stuck in local optima. Later sections of this chapter present search methods with random or stochastic features, which are better able to escape from local optima, possibly accepting moves to states that are worse than the current state. These are not neural network algorithms, and do not require the presence of nodes or connections. Their resemblance to neural networks, and the reason for discussing them here, is that they are numerical methods that generally rely on local information and computations rather than on centralized processing. Methods such as *simulated annealing* and *evolutionary algorithms* often obtain better solutions than gradient descent or hill-climbing. Simulated annealing, briefly mentioned in chapter 6, allows the system to escape from local optima using moves that worsen solution quality, with some probability that decreases with time. The following paragraph motivates evolutionary computation, which conducts a search in a *population* of candidate solutions rather than by steadily improving upon a single candidate solution.

Observations about nature reveal that increasingly fit organisms evolve in a fixed environment, and that organisms are able to adapt to a changing environment. Each organism or species evolves with time, so that the survival capabilities of later generations are better than those of earlier generations, with this change becoming more pronounced over a large number of generations or when drastic changes occur in the environment. We may view this evolutionary process as conducting a search for the organism with survival capabilities best suited to the environment. Each possible organism (either at the level of its externally observable features or at the level of its genetic structure) can be viewed as a candidate solution for the optimization problem of maximizing the survival capabilities of organisms. This is a powerful paradigm, discussed in section 7.5 from the viewpoint of applying evolutionary optimization properties from nature to combinatorial optimization problems.

7.1 Optimization using Hopfield Networks

Hopfield and Tank (1985) proposed solving optimization problems using the neural network models discussed in chapter 6, using an analogy between the network's energy function and a cost function to be minimized. The main task of the neural network developer is to translate the problem-specific cost function into a quadratic form, from which network weights can be extracted. An appropriate representation must be developed, relating problem parameters to node output values. Some decisions are left to the designer (e.g., how to assign relative importance when there are multiple problem-specific constraints). After the weights are determined, the network nodes are initialized with values chosen randomly from the appropriate set ($\{0, 1\}$ or $\{-1, 1\}$) for the discrete model and appropriate interval ([0, 1] or [-1, 1]) for the continuous model. This initial set of node values constitutes a candidate solution for the optimization problem, which is successively modified by changing node values asynchronously, conducting gradient descent on the energy function until no further node state changes can decrease energy.

In chapter 6, Hopfield networks were applied to auto-association problems; certain patterns (referred to earlier as memories or attractors) are stored using the weights of the network, and the presentation of a corrupted pattern is followed by repeated state changes to the nodes of the network until the node states stabilize to an attractor pattern. In applying Hopfield networks to optimization problems, the attractors are not stored memories or desirable patterns; instead, each attractor is a candidate solution to the optimization problem that lies at a local minimum of the energy function. The purpose of the network is to search for and *find* satisfactory suboptimal solutions, not to *select* one out of a known set of patterns.

This scheme has an obvious drawback, as do all gradient descent procedures: the network may converge to a local optimum of the energy function, instead of the global optimum. The quality of the solution found by the Hopfield network depends significantly on the initial state of the network. For some problems, clever choices of initial states (node activation values) may increase the likelihood of reaching a good solution. Since there is no reason to attempt to reach a local optimum that is close to the initial network configuration, there is no reason for node updates to depend on external inputs, nor for a self-excitatory term in the node update rule. For most problems, bias or threshold values can be specified in order to completely describe the constraints inherent in the problem. Thus, when the ith node is selected for updating, the typical node update rule for discrete binary optimization problems is

$$x_\ell(t+1) = \text{sgn}\left(\sum_{j=0,\, j\neq\ell}^{m} w_{\ell,j} x_j(t) \right) \tag{7.1}$$

where $x_0 \equiv 1$, so that $w_{\ell,0}$ represents the bias or threshold. Similarly, the update rule frequently used for continuous optimization problems is

$$\delta x_\ell(t) = \eta\, g\left(\sum_{j=0\, j\neq\ell}^{m} w_{\ell,j} x_j(t) \right) \tag{7.2}$$

where $\eta > 0$ is a small constant and g is the node transfer function. Node values in discrete optimization problems are often chosen from the set $\{0, 1\}$, not from $\{-1, 1\}$; 0 implies that a particular node is in the "OFF" state, and 1 implies that the node is in the "ON" state.

The limitations of Hopfield networks in solving optimization problems have been explored by Gee, Aiyer, and Prager (1993). We now illustrate this methodology by presenting three applications of Hopfield networks to optimization problems.

7.1.1   Traveling salesperson problem

The *traveling salesperson problem* (TSP) is historically among the first optimization problems to be solved using Hopfield neural network models. The early results described by Hopfield and Tank (1985) are important primarily in initiating attempts to solve a large number of other optimization problems using similar methods.

In an instance of the TSP, we are given a set of cities and a symmetric distance matrix that indicates the cost of direct travel from each city to every other city. The goal is to find the shortest circular *tour*, visiting each city exactly once, so as to minimize the total travel cost, which includes the cost of traveling from the last city back to the first city. In a four-city problem, for instance, D-B-A-C represents the travel plan that takes the salesperson from D to B, from B to A, from A to C, and finally from C to D again. The cost of this tour is hence the sum of the distances traversed in each travel segment. The number of possible tours is extremely large even for problems containing a small number of cities, and finding the optimal tour (guaranteed to be of shortest length) is an "NP-complete" task requiring enormous amounts of computational time, irrespective of the algorithm used. The Hopfield network, hence, attempts only to find sub-optimal tours.

Each tour for an n-city TSP can be expressed in terms of an $n \times n$ matrix M whose xth row describes the xth city's location in the feasible solution. In a four-city tour, for instance, the row $(0, 1, 0, 0)$ in the matrix corresponds to the city in second position. Matrices M_1 and M_2, below, describe two solutions for the four-city TSP, A-B-C-D and D-B-A-C, respectively.

$$M_1 = \begin{bmatrix} A: & 1 & 0 & 0 & 0 \\ B: & 0 & 1 & 0 & 0 \\ C: & 0 & 0 & 1 & 0 \\ D: & 0 & 0 & 0 & 1 \end{bmatrix}, \quad M_2 = \begin{bmatrix} A: & 0 & 0 & 1 & 0 \\ B: & 0 & 1 & 0 & 0 \\ C: & 0 & 0 & 0 & 1 \\ D: & 1 & 0 & 0 & 0 \end{bmatrix}.$$

This binary representation suggests that an n-city TSP can be solved by a Hopfield network if we use n sets of n nodes, each set representing a city's location in the tour. Each node in the network corresponds to one element in the matrix, and it is convenient to allow each node's output to take values from $\{0, 1\}$. A candidate solution is *feasible* (or is a *valid* tour) if it is a permutation of the given cities. The energy function contains terms corresponding to the cost of a travel plan (sum of intercity distances) as well as terms contributed by constraints needed to ensure that solutions are feasible, as discussed below.

1. Each city can occur in only one position in the tour. Hence, precisely one element must equal 1 in each row of the matrix M that represents a feasible solution. Other elements in each row must equal 0. The constraint can be expressed as

$$\sum_{j=1}^{n} M_{x,j} = 1 \quad \text{for} \quad x \in \{1, \dots, n\}.$$

Thus, the energy function to be minimized contains a term proportional to

$$\sum_{x=1}^{n} \left(1 - \sum_{j=1}^{n} M_{x,j}\right)^2.$$

2. Precisely one city can occur in any position in the tour. Therefore, in each column of M, precisely one element must equal 1, and every other element must equal 0, implying that

$$\sum_{x=1}^{n} M_{x,j} = 1 \quad \text{for} \quad j \in \{1, \dots, n\}$$

Hence, the energy function to be minimized contains a term proportional to

$$\sum_{j=1}^{n} \left(1 - \sum_{x=1}^{n} M_{x,j} \right)^2 .$$

Let an $(n \times n)$ square matrix C denote the "cost matrix" of the traveling salesperson problem for n cities, $n > 0$, where the element $C_{x,y}$ (in the xth row, yth column of C) denotes the cost of traveling from city x to city y. The energy function contains terms corresponding to $C_{x,y}$, the cost associated with traveling directly from city x to city y, whenever x and y are adjacent in a candidate tour, i.e., when $M_{x,i} = 1$ and $M_{y,i\pm 1} = 1$ for any i. Since each node output value is either 0 or 1, we can add the following terms to the energy function, for every pair of distinct cities x, y.

$$\sum_{i=1}^{n} C_{x,y} \, M_{x,i} \left(M_{y,i+1} + M_{y,i-1} \right)$$

Combining the cost and constraint terms, the following energy function E is obtained, using λ_1 and λ_2 as weighting constants for the penalty terms, to be chosen appropriately.

$$E = \frac{1}{2} \sum_{i=1}^{n} \sum_{x} \sum_{y \neq x} C_{x,y} \, M_{x,i} \left(M_{y,i+1} + M_{y,i-1} \right)$$

$$+ \left[\lambda_1 \sum_{x} \left(1 - \sum_{i} M_{x,i} \right)^2 + \lambda_2 \sum_{i} \left(1 - \sum_{x} M_{x,i} \right)^2 \right] \tag{7.3}$$

A Hopfield network implementation of this problem, minimizing E, is possible because E is quadratic in the $M_{x,i}$'s. Each node of the network corresponds to one element of the matrix M, and its output value $\in \{0, 1\}$. Between nodes that correspond to $M_{x,i}$ and $M_{y,j}$, the connection weight is the negative of the coefficient of the quadratic term $M_{x,i}M_{y,j}$ in the expression for E in equation 7.3, obtained after straightforward simplification. The coefficients of the linear terms $M_{x,i}$ in the same expression yield the thresholds of the neural network, since each linear term $C_{x,i}M_{x,i}$ in the right-hand side of equation 7.3 may be considered equivalent to $C_{x,i}M_0M_{x,i}$, where $M_0 \equiv 1$. Instead of using λ_1 and λ_2, one may equivalently write the net input to the (x, i)th node, used to determine if the node should change state, as

$$-\sum_y C_{x,y}M_{y,i\pm1} - a\sum_{j\neq i}M_{x,j} - b\sum_{y\neq x}M_{y,i} + c, \tag{7.4}$$

where a, b, c are positive constants to be determined by the network developer.

We now discuss a specific instance of a traveling salesperson problem with six cities, {CHI, DET, PHI, WDC, DEN, NYC}, illustrated in figure 7.2. The goal is to find a sequential tour of cities with the shortest total length, including the length of the edge from the sixth city in the tour to the first city in the tour. The geographical distances between various cities, indicated by edges in figure 7.2, are represented by the cost matrix in table 7.1.

A discrete Hopfield network was implemented to solve this instance of TSP. The network contained a two-dimensional array of 36 nodes, whose (x, i)th entry was 1 if the city

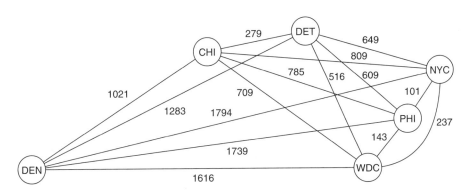

Figure 7.2
A six-city traveling salesperson problem (distances shown in miles).

Table 7.1
Cost matrix of a six-city TSP problem; costs are distances between the cities.

	CHI	DET	NYC	WDC	DEN	PHI
CHI	0	279	809	709	1021	785
DET	279	0	649	516	1283	609
NYC	809	649	0	237	1794	101
WDC	709	516	237	0	1616	143
DEN	1021	1283	1794	1616	0	1739
PHI	785	609	101	143	1739	0

x occurred in the ith position of the tour, and 0 otherwise. For ease of computation, the cost matrix was linearly normalized (dividing all lengths by 1800) so that all edge lengths were in the closed interval $[0, 1]$. The network was randomly initialized, and nodes were selected randomly for updating.

Each node (x, i), selected for updating, was updated as follows. If node (y, j) corresponds to a city adjacent to (x, i) in the tour such that $|i - j| = 1$ or 5, and if node (y, j) is currently ON (with value 1), then the net input to (x, i) is decremented by $C_{x,y}$, the negated normalized distance (cost) between x and y. If node (x, j) is currently ON, where $i \neq j$, then the net input to (x, i) is decremented by a constant a. If node (y, i) is currently ON, where $x \neq y$, then the net input to (x, i) is decremented by a constant b. The net input to (x, i) is also incremented by an external input (or bias), fixed at a constant c.

Relative values of a, b and c determined whether a feasible solution was achieved. Experiments conducted such that a, b are smaller than c generated infeasible solutions, in which two elements in a row (or column) of the network were both ON. Feasible solutions were generated when a, b were larger than c. In most cases, however, the solutions generated by the Hopfield network were of poor quality, with the average tour length ≈ 5058 (in ten experiments). The best tour among these was PHI $-$ WDC $-$ DET $-$ CHI $-$ DEN $-$ NYC, with a tour length of 3854. Note that the optimal tour length is 3809 for this instance of TSP, with the best tour being PHI $-$ WDC $-$ DEN $-$ CHI $-$ DET $-$ NYC.

The network state in each experiment was repeatedly modified, beginning from the initial state, until every node's net input has the same sign as its output. This required about 100 node state changes on the average, leading to a local minimum of the energy function, likely to be a feasible solution nearest to the initial network state.

The feasible solution space size is smaller than $6! = 720$, the number of permutations of six cities.[1] But since this instance of the TSP was encoded into a 36-node network, the system searches for local optima in a search space of size 2^{36}, which are not the local optima in the feasible solution space. The choice of the parameters of the network (penalty factors) was such that it could guarantee only that the result was a feasible solution, not that the result was a good quality tour.

As reported by Wilson and Pawley (1988), Hopfield networks do not often lead to good quality solutions for TSP, and this application is thus primarily of historical importance.

---

1. The actual feasible solution space size equals 60, much smaller than the number of permutations of six cities, since many distinct permutations represent equivalent tours. For instance, moving the first city of the tour to the end of the tour results in an equivalent tour, e.g., $ABCDEF$, $BCDEFA$, $CDEFAB$, ..., $FABCDE$ are all equivalent. Hence the state space may be reduced by fixing the first city arbitrarily, and considering only permutations that begin with that city. Similarly, reversing a tour yields an equivalent tour, e.g., $ABCDEF$ and $FEDCBA$ are equivalent, whenever the cost matrix is symmetric. Hence we may arbitrarily label cities with numbers and restrict search to those permutations in which the second city's label is smaller than the last city's label.

Lin et al. (1994) have compared the results obtained using several variants of the energy function, using a continuous Hopfield network model. The energy function presented in this section, initially proposed by Abe (1989), converged fastest, and produced feasible solutions in about 90% of the trials; best solution qualities were obtained using a somewhat more complex energy function proposed by Aiyer, Niranjan, and Fallside (1990), which was slower but also produced feasible solutions in about 90% of the trials.

7.1.2 Solving simultaneous linear equations

A continuous Hopfield network with n nodes can be used to find solutions to a system of n linear equations in n unknowns $x_1, \ldots, x_n$, with real coefficients and constant terms.

$$
\begin{aligned}
a_{1,1}x_1 + a_{1,2}x_2 + \ldots + a_{1,n}x_n + a_{1,n+1} &= 0 \\
a_{2,1}x_1 + a_{2,2}x_2 + \ldots + a_{2,n}x_n + a_{2,n+1} &= 0 \\
&\vdots \\
a_{n,1}x_1 + a_{n,2}x_2 + \ldots + a_{n,n}x_n + a_{n,n+1} &= 0
\end{aligned}
\tag{7.5}
$$

The network attempts to minimize the energy function $E = \frac{1}{2}\sum_{\ell=1}^{n}(\sum_{j=1}^{n} a_{\ell,j}x_j + a_{\ell,n+1})^2$ [see Chakraborty et al. (1991)]. The network dynamics are governed by the differential equation

$$
\frac{du_p}{dt} = -\frac{\partial}{\partial x_p}E(x_1, x_2, \ldots x_n)
\tag{7.6}
$$

$$
x_p = g_p(u_p), \qquad 1 \leq p \leq n
$$

where $u_p = \sum_j w_{p,j}x_j$ is the net input to the pth neuron in the network and x_p is its output. In this application, the function g_p is a linear input-output transfer function for the pth neuron. Simplifying the first equation, we get

$$
\frac{du_p}{dt} = -\sum_{j=1}^{n}\left(\sum_{\ell=1}^{n} a_{\ell,p}a_{\ell,j}\right)x_j - \sum_{\ell=1}^{n} a_{\ell,n+1}a_{\ell,p}, \qquad 1 \leq p \leq n.
\tag{7.7}
$$

The dynamic behavior of the pth neuron in the network is described by the equation

$$
\frac{du_p}{dt} = -\sum_{j=1}^{n} w_{p,j}x_j + I_p, \qquad 1 \leq p \leq n.
\tag{7.8}
$$

From equations 7.7 and 7.8 we get $w_{p,j} = \sum_{\ell=1}^{n} a_{\ell,p}a_{\ell,j}$ and $I_p = -\sum_{\ell=1}^{n} a_{\ell,n+1}a_{\ell,p}$. Note that $w_{p,j} = w_{j,p}$, i.e., coupling coefficients are symmetric, and hence the energy function would decrease monotonically with network iterations.

For systems with infinitely many solutions, the network converges very quickly (often within 100 iterations) to a solution that corresponds to the minimum of E that is nearest to the random initial output configuration. For systems with no solution, the energy function fails to approach zero even after a very large number of iterations.

For systems with unique solutions, convergence times depend on the system of equations and network parameters. In some cases, the time taken for large systems of equations was found to be actually less than the time for smaller systems, even though each network iteration for the larger systems involved more computation. For most other algorithms, an increase in the number of unknowns implies that the time taken for getting a solution will increase. For a system of equations with $n = 300$, the network converged in 58,911 iterations to produce a system error of 0.000021, where system error is defined as the normalized root mean square error,

$$\frac{\sqrt{2E/n}}{\frac{1}{n}\sum_{\ell=1}^{n}|a_{\ell,n+1}|}.$$

When the coefficients of the system of equations had very large magnitude, both the first and second derivatives of the inputs (with respect to time) had very large magnitudes, and so the discrete approximations turned out to be grossly inaccurate. This problem was circumvented by multiplying some or all of the equations by constants that would scale down both the coefficients and the constant terms in those equations.

7.1.3 Allocating documents to multiprocessors

Given a multiprocessor system and a number of documents, each of which is known to belong to some preallocated "cluster," a Hopfield network can be used to distribute documents among various processors as evenly as possible while minimizing communication cost. Communication cost can be minimized by minimizing the average distance between different processors containing documents that belong to the same cluster. In other words, the energy function must contain a cost term for every pair of documents in the same cluster that are allocated by the network to different processors. Load balance is achieved by adding a cost term whenever the number of documents on a processor differs from the expected average (number of documents/number of processors). Every document must be allocated to exactly one processor, a constraint satisfied by adding cost measures similar to those for TSP. Two solutions of this NP-complete problem are proposed in Al-Sehibani et al. (1995).

Discrete Hopfield network   Let d be the number of documents, P the number of processors, N the number of document clusters, and $m(q)$ the number of documents in the qth cluster. Let $c_{j,i} = c_{i,j}$ be the cost of sending unit data from processor i to processor j.

A discrete Hopfield network can be constructed with an array of $P \times d$ nodes. Each node activation is shown with three indices, of which the first identifies the processor and the last two identify the document, e.g., $x_{i,j,q} = 1$ if document j of the qth cluster is assigned to the ith processor, and 0 otherwise. The energy function to be minimized can be written as

$$E = F + k_1 \sum_{i=1}^{P} \left(\frac{d}{P} - \sum_{q=1}^{N} \sum_{j=1}^{m(q)} x_{i,j,q} \right)^2 + k_2 \sum_{q=1}^{N} \sum_{j=1}^{m(q)} \left(1 - \sum_{i=1}^{P} x_{i,j,q} \right)^2,$$

where k_1 and k_2 are the penalty factors associated with the two constraints, and

$$F = \frac{1}{2} \sum_{q=1}^{N} \sum_{i=1}^{P} \sum_{i'=1}^{P} \sum_{j=1}^{m(q)} \sum_{j'=1}^{m(q)} x_{i,j,q} x_{i',j',q} c_{i,i'}$$

is the average cluster distance to be minimized by the network. Nodes with the same cluster index q are connected by symmetric connections with weight $w_{x_{i,j,q},x_{i',j'q}} = c_{i,i'}$, nodes with the same processor index i are connected by symmetric connections with weight $w_{x_{i,j,q},x_{i,j',q'}} = 2k_1$, and nodes with the same cluster and document indices are connected by symmetric connections with weight $w_{x_{i,j,q},x_{i',j,q}} = 2k_2$. Every node has a threshold of $2k_1 d / P + k_1 - k_2$.

Continuous Hopfield network   The previous approach has the disadvantage of using too many neurons, since the size of the network is proportional to the number of documents. We reformulate the neural network as a two-dimensional $N \times P$ array of neurons, where the first dimension represents the clusters and the second dimension represents the processors, and each node output value $x_{i,j} \in [0, 1]$ represents the proportion of documents in the ith cluster allocated to the jth processor.

As before, the energy function contains terms representing the average cluster distance, along with the load balancing and unique assignment constraints. The average cluster distance is

$$F = \frac{1}{2} \sum_{i=1}^{N} \sum_{j=1}^{P} \sum_{k=1}^{P} x_{i,j} x_{i,k} m^2(i) c_{j,k},$$

whereas other constraints are as before: each processor should have the same load, i.e.,

$$\sum_{i=1}^{N} x_{i,j} m(i) \approx (d/P)$$

for every processor, and all documents are assigned to unique processors in each cluster, i.e., $\sum_{j=1}^{P} x_{i,j} = 1$ for every cluster. The total energy function to be minimized is

$$E = F + k_1 \sum_{j=1}^{P} \left(\frac{d}{P} - \sum_{i=1}^{N} x_{i,j} m(i) \right)^2 + k_2 \sum_{i=1}^{N} \left(1 - \sum_{j=1}^{P} x_{i,j} \right)^2 .$$

For this example, a sigmoid function $x_{i,j} = g(u_{i,j}) = 0.5(1 + \tanh(\lambda u_{i,j}))$ was chosen for the activation function of neurons, where $u_{i,j}$ denotes the net input of neuron $x_{i,j}$, and λ is a gain parameter that controls the slope of the transfer function. The dynamics of the network are governed by $(\partial u_{i,j}/\partial t) = -(\partial E/\partial x_{i,j})$, where $(\partial E/\partial x_{i,j})$ is easily obtained from E given above, i.e.,

$$\frac{\partial E}{\partial x_{i,j}} = \sum_{k=1}^{P} x_{i,k} m(i)^2 c_{j,k} + 2k_1 \sum_{l=1}^{N} x_{lj} m(i) m(l)$$

$$+ 2k_2 \sum_{k=1}^{P} x_{i,k} - 2k_1 \frac{d}{P} m(i) - 2k_2.$$

Thus the dynamics of the system can be described by

$$\frac{\partial u_{i,j}}{\partial t} = \sum_{l=1}^{N} \sum_{k=1}^{P} w_{(i,j),(l,k)} x_{l,k} + I_{i,j},$$

where

$$w_{(i,j),(l,k)} = -m(i)^2 c_{j,k} \delta_{i,l} - 2k_1 m(i) m(l) \delta_{j,k} - 2k_2 \delta_{i,l},$$

$$I_{i,j} = 2k_1 \frac{d}{P} m(i) + 2k_2,$$

and $\delta_{i,j} = 1$ if $i = j$, and $\delta_{i,j} = 0$ otherwise. Since $g(u_{i,j})$ is a monotonically increasing function, $\partial E/\partial t$ is either negative or zero, and it is easy to verify that the energy does not increase with any node update made according to the Hopfield network dynamics.

In a feasible solution, we expect each row-sum $\sum_j x_{i,j} = 1$, hence node activation values are normalized, with each $x_{i,j}$ modified to $x_{i,j}/\sum_j x_{i,j}$, which represents the fraction of documents in cluster i allocated into processor j. Multiplying this fraction by the number of documents in cluster i and rounding the result to the nearest integer yields $m_{i,j}$, the number of documents of cluster i allocated to processor j.

Performance   Both the discrete and continuous Hopfield models were tested by attempting document allocation for each of two multiprocessor architectures, a 16-1 mesh and a 16-node hypercube. In each case, testing was done for problems with an equal number of

Table 7.2
Load imbalance and average cluster distances using Hopfield networks for multiprocessor document allocation.

	Load imbalance				Average distance			
	Equal clustering		Unequal clustering		Equal clustering		Unequal clustering	
Number of documents	64	256	64	256	64	256	64	256
Disc-mesh	3.70	8.35	4.80	12.00	1.56	3.47	1.94	4.17
Disc-hyper	2.16	2.66	3.35	4.00	1.09	1.17	1.88	1.94
Cont-mesh	1.10	1.15	1.48	1.63	0.63	0.56	0.70	0.65
Cont-hyper	1.10	1.10	1.28	1.33	0.63	0.57	0.66	0.58

documents per cluster as well as problems with an unequal number of documents per cluster. Performance is compared in terms of the average cluster distance and load imbalance, measured as the standard deviation of load among various processors.

The performance results are presented in table 7.2. Better quality results were obtained using the continuous Hopfield model, and the difference in performance increased with the number of documents. The continuous model also gave good results on much larger data sets (up to 25,600 documents), for which the discrete Hopfield network had excessively high computational requirements. However, the discrete Hopfield model was faster when the number of documents was small.

7.2 Iterated Gradient Descent

Iterated gradient descent involves executing a gradient descent procedure (e.g., a Hopfield network for optimization)[2] many times, and selecting the best result obtained in these attempts. Random initialization precedes each attempt at gradient descent (or search *path*), so that each path is independent of the other paths. Each move generates a state that is a "neighbor" of the state to which the move is applied. Only moves that lower energy are accepted. Each attempt at gradient descent terminates when no moves that lower energy can be generated.

Pursuing several paths increases the probability of reaching a global optimum. Let p be the probability that any search path results in a state that is not the global optimum. If n

---

2. For discrete optimization problems, the function to be optimized may be discontinuous or have no definable gradient. Our discussion extends to such problems, when we substitute the phrase "hill-climbing" for "gradient descent," interpreted to mean "repeatedly make a move that improves solution quality."

different search paths are explored, the probability of achieving the global optimum (in at least one search path) using iterated gradient descent is $1 - p^n$. If the energy function has N randomly distributed optima of which only one is a global optimum, then we assume $p = (N-1)/N$, in the absence of any other information. In order to be assured of reaching the global optimum with at least 90% probability, we require

$$(1 - ((N-1)/N)^n) \geq 0.9,$$

i.e., one must choose $n > 1/(\log_{10} N - \log_{10}(N-1))$. For $N = 10$, this would imply that $n > 21$ independent search paths are needed to reach the global minimum with 90% probability; for $N = 100$, the corresponding $n > 229$; and for $N = 1,000$, the corresponding $n > 2,301$. Thus, the number of trials needed appears to increase linearly with the number of local optima. Though problem-dependent, it is not uncommon for the number of required trials (n) to increase exponentially with the number of variables in the system.

7.3   Simulated Annealing

In hill-climbing (or gradient descent), a move in the direction that appears to be the best at the time is made; but in a problem that has many hills we may not be climbing the right hill. In response to this, Kirkpatrick et al. (1983) suggest an alternative approach that captures essential features of the metallurgical process of *annealing*.

In annealing, a metal or alloy is very slowly cooled and maintained at each intermediate temperature until some kind of an equilibrium is achieved. Higher temperatures correspond to greater kinetic energy of the particles in the metal, which means the existing structure may change more easily at high temperatures; even an optimal structure that has already been reached may be perturbed at high temperatures. The best structures are stably obtained at very low temperatures, but rapidly cooling a metal can result in a brittle structure. The cooling process is hence slow and carefully controlled, resulting in better structural properties.

Annealing can be viewed as solving an optimization problem, maximizing strength and minimizing brittleness, by generating a structure with least energy. *Simulated annealing* is a probabilistic algorithm that uses a similar method to solve difficult combinatorial optimization problems for which gradient descent yields inadequate answers. An energy (or cost) function is defined, which is to be minimized by the algorithm. A candidate move is generated from the current state, and the system must decide whether to "accept" that move, based upon the current temperature and the resulting energy change. This process of move generation and acceptance decision is repeated for a long time, steadily lowering

Algorithm Simulated Annealing;
  Initialize;
  repeat
    repeat
      generate new-state by perturbing current-state;
      if random[0,1] < exp((E(current-state)-E(new-state))/T)
      then current-state := new-state;
      if E(current-state) < E(best-so-far)
        then best-so-far := current-state;
    until quasi-equilibrium has been reached;
    Decrease temperature as dictated by the cooling rate;
  until temperature is small enough;
  return best-so-far.

Figure 7.3
The simulated annealing algorithm.

the temperature parameter. This mechanism enables a system to transcend small energy barriers, thereby moving from one valley in the energy landscape to another.

The simulated annealing algorithm, described in figure 7.3,[3] consists of an outer loop in which the temperature is periodically lowered, and an inner loop in which moves are generated and accepted, as described below.

1. **Move-generation**: In every move, the simulated annealing algorithm often explores states that are proximate (or neighbors) to the current state. For instance, if each state is a bit-vector, then a single move consists of modifying a single component of the bit-vector, so that 10011 is immediately reachable from 10111, but not from 11111. This move-set fully connects all states, and every state is reachable from every state in some number of steps. In some problems, different immediate neighbors are reachable with different "selection" probabilities. For instance, if a bit-vector represents a sequence of yes/no decisions, where the latter bits in the vector represent less serious decisions that can be made more easily, then a move from 10011 to 10010 may be selected with greater probability than a move from 10011 to 10001. This selection probability does not depend on temperature or cost criteria.

2. **Move-acceptance**: Moves that decrease energy are always accepted, as in gradient descent. In addition, moves that increase energy are also accepted with an *acceptance*

---

3. Traditional formulations of simulated annealing include an additional "Boltzmann constant" by which the temperature is multiplied, ignored here since it can be absorbed directly into the temperature parameter.

probability $(\exp(E(\text{current state}) - E(\text{new state}))/T)$ that depends on temperature and energy difference resulting from the move. The higher the temperature, the higher the move acceptance probability. This is analogous to the metallurgical annealing process, in which a structure can be modified more easily (or a particle can move to a higher energy level) at higher temperatures than at lower temperatures. In many problems, temperature represents the magnitude of "noise" in the environment; a system may change its state or hypotheses more easily at higher noise levels. The probability of making a move is also higher when the energy difference between the new state and the current state is small, and vice versa.

If allowed to run long enough at any temperature, the inner loop of the algorithm leads to a Boltzmann distribution of states:

$$\text{Probability (the current state has energy } e_\ell) = \frac{\exp(-e_\ell/T)}{\sum_j \exp(-e_j/T)},$$

irrespective of initial state, assuming that every state is reachable from every state in a finite number of moves. All states are equally likely at high temperatures, while states with low energies have much higher probabilities at low temperatures. The inner loop of simulated annealing is hence terminated when the system reaches "quasi-equilibrium," i.e., the probability of being in a state depends only on its energy. Testing whether the system is in quasi-equilibrium can require much computation. A practical alternative is merely to allow the system to run at each temperature for a duration of time that depends on the temperature, with the durations being longer at lower temperatures.

The outer loop of the simulated annealing algorithm steadily lowers temperature, allowing the system to reach quasi-equilibrium at each temperature. Ideally, when the distribution of system states settles into the Boltzmann distribution at temperature 0, the system reaches a global optimum with probability 1. The "cooling rate" refers to the rate at which temperature is lowered.

Simulated annealing draws its strength from the following asymptotic convergence result, proved by Geman and Geman (1984).

THEOREM 7.1   If the initial temperature T_0 is sufficiently large, and if the temperature in the kth step of simulated annealing $\geq T_0/\log(1 + k)$ for every k, then the simulated annealing algorithm minimizes the energy function with probability 1.

This theoretical result provides a sufficient condition for reaching a global optimum of the energy function. Unfortunately, this result implies extremely large computational requirements, since the temperature must be lowered extremely slowly in order to achieve the global optimum with probability approaching 1. If (non-global) local optima exist, there is no guarantee of reaching a global optimum in a finite number of steps. Many researchers instead use *exponential cooling*, with the temperature in the kth step obtained as a product of the previous temperature and a constant (< 1, frequently chosen to be > 0.8). The resulting faster algorithm, sometimes referred to as *simulated quenching*, is not guaranteed to yield global optima.

Instead of using an extremely slow cooling rate, the following alternatives may be pursued.

1. Execute several iterations of the simulated annealing procedure with a fast cooling rate, applying gradient descent at the end of each run; select the best result obtained in these iterations.

2. Perform annealing many times, steadily decelerating the cooling schedule, and apply gradient descent at the end of each annealing process. This process is continued as long as the solution quality improves from one annealing cycle to the next (slower) annealing cycle.

EXAMPLE 7.2   In the problem of graph partitioning, the goal is to divide the nodes of a given graph into two equal-sized groups in such a way as to minimize the total cost (number of edges between the two groups). This problem is known to be NP-complete; no deterministic polynomial-time algorithm is known to exist to solve this problem. We illustrate the graph partitioning problem with the graph given in figure 7.4.

A partition of a graph with n nodes may be represented by a binary n-bit sequence with an entry for each node indicating in which group that node is placed. For instance, 100011

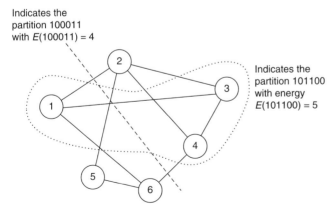

Figure 7.4
Two possible partitions for a six-node graph.

indicates that the second, third, and fourth nodes are in one group (labeled 0), while all other nodes are in the other group (labeled 1). The requirement that groups of nodes be of equal size implies the constraint that there are as many zeroes as ones in any solution vector.

An energy function for this problem is the number of edges between the two groups. For instance, $E(100011) = 4$, whereas $E(101100) = 7$. This shows that we prefer the solution (100011), yet the move to a higher energy state could be made with probability $p = e^{(4-7)/T}$.

For efficiency, it is desirable that moves must be easy to compute and that they result in small changes to the current state. An example move-set for this problem is that of exchanging two 0/1 nodes, i.e., simultaneously changing a single 0-bit to 1 and a single 1-bit to 0. States obtainable from 100011 by this move set are 010011, 001011, 000111, 110001, 101001, 100101, 110010, 101010, and 100110.

Assume that the current state is 010011, with energy $E(010011) = 6$. If the move generated is to the state 100011, it will always be accepted, since $E(100011) = 4 < E(100011) = 6$. But if the generated move is to 100110 whose energy is 8, then the probability of acceptance of this move will be given by the expression $e^{(6-8)/T} = e^{-2/T}$, which depends on the current temperature T. For instance, if $T = 50$, then the acceptance probability is $e^{-2/T} = e^{-2/50} = 0.96$; if $T = 10$, then the acceptance probability is $e^{-2/10} = 0.82$, and if $T = 1$, then the acceptance probability is $e^{-2} = 0.13$.

This example illustrates that a move to a lower energy state is made with probability 1, whereas a move to a higher energy state is made with a probability that is higher for higher temperatures.

Several minor variations of simulated annealing have been discussed in the literature, such as *adaptive simulated annealing*, proposed by Ingber (1993). Another variant, called threshold annealing, suggested by Dueck and Scheuer (1990), avoids the generation of random numbers, and accepts every move for which $\exp(-\Delta E/T)$ exceeds a fixed value such as 0.5.

Korst and Aarts (1989) suggested the application of simulated annealing to optimization problems using Hopfield network architectures. Problem representations and weights are chosen in a manner exactly same as in Hopfield networks; in addition, self-excitatory connections may be present, i.e., it is possible that $w_{\ell,\ell} \neq 0$. A 1-1 correspondence is defined between solutions and configurations of the network. In the Hopfield network representations for optimization problems, not all states of the network satisfy all of the problem constraints, e.g., some network states may imply that some cities in a traveling salesperson problem are visited more than once or not at all. However, connection patterns and strengths are chosen such that all local minima of the cost or energy function correspond to feasible solutions. The last phase of the annealing algorithm is conducted at a temperature ≈ 0, so that it is guaranteed that the final network state is a feasible solution.

7.4   Random Search

Among the simplest random search methods is the *generate-and-test* approach, which repeatedly generates a random feasible state, and compares its cost with that of the best solution obtained so far. If the new solution is better, then it is stored as the best solution encountered so far. This process is repeated until computational bounds are exceeded.

Any "reasonable" systematic scheme should do better than this generate-and-test method. In a problem with m binary variables, the state space contains 2^m states, and the probability of reaching a global optimum (if unique) in n trials is $1 - (1 - 2^{-m})^n$. Therefore, for a problem with ten variables, the number of trials needed to reach the global minimum with 90% probability is $n > 2,356$, which exceeds the state space size ($2^{10} = 1,024$).

Better results can be obtained for most problems by improving the "generate" step of the generate-and-test method. Under the hypothesis that good quality solutions are to be found in the neighborhood of other good quality solutions, the new candidate solution may be generated in the vicinity of the better solutions found so far. Instead of being generated from anywhere in the search space with equal probability, the candidate solution is biased to be generated with greater probability near the better solutions found so far. The algorithm will be less prone to be trapped in a local optimum if we explore new candidate solutions in the vicinity of several of the better solutions found so far, rather than the best solution alone.

The resulting *iterative focusing* algorithm is described in figure 7.5 and illustrated in figure 7.6. The algorithm steadily shrinks the size of the *focus-regions* from which successive candidate solutions are generated, in a manner analogous to the decrease in the temperature parameter of the simulated annealing algorithm. This algorithm conducts nondeterministic search, examining multiple regions of the search space, and leads naturally to the evolutionary computation methods discussed in the next section.

EXAMPLE 7.3   Consider the traveling salesperson problem (TSP) for six cities, shown in figure 7.2. Initially, the following three tours are randomly generated and evaluated.

(NYC, WDC, DET, PHI, CHI, DEN),

(WDC, DET, NYC, DEN, CHI, PHI),

and (DEN, NYC, PHI, DET, CHI, WDC).

Algorithm Iterative Focusing;
    Initialize focus-region to the entire search space;
   repeat
       Randomly generate and evaluate several candidate
         solutions from each focus-region;
       Obtain new focus-regions, centered around
         the better candidate solutions found so far;
       Reduce focus-region size;
   until the focus-region size is small enough, or
       computational bounds are exceeded.

Figure 7.5
A random iterative focusing search algorithm.

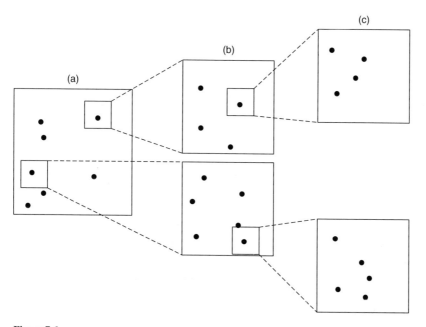

Figure 7.6
Modified random search. Boxed areas in (a) indicate most promising regions. Blown-up versions of these are shown in (b), where boxed regions show the most promising regions, further explored in (c).

286

Their respective costs are 4,962, 4,908, and 5,108. Of these, the second is the best, hence three more individuals are randomly generated in its vicinity, each of which is at Hamming distance of ≤ 4 from (WDC, DET, NYC, DEN, CHI, PHI), e.g., the following tours:

(WDC, DET, DEN, NYC, PHI, CHI) with cost 5,188,

(DET, WDC, CHI, DEN, NYC, PHI) with cost 4,750,

and (NYC, WDC, DET, DEN, CHI, PHI) with cost 3,943.

Of these, the third is the best, hence three more individuals are randomly generated in its vicinity. The following are three tours, at Hamming distance ≤ 2 from (NYC, WDC, DET, DEN, CHI, PHI):

(WDC, NYC, DET, DEN, CHI, PHI) with cost 4,118,

(PHI, WDC, DET, DEN, CHI, NYC) with cost 3,873,

and (NYC, WDC, DEN, DET, CHI, PHI) with cost 4,301.

Of these, (PHI, WDC, DET, DEN, CHI, NYC), with cost 3,873, is the best found so far, and we may choose to terminate the search or to continue with another search in the neighborhood of this solution. We have thus obtained a suboptimal tour similar to the optimum tour, (PHI, WDC, DEN, CHI, DET, NYC), whose cost is 3,809, and the quality of this suboptimal tour is better than the average tour found using the Hopfield network. The iterative focusing approach works in this case because it satisfies the property that similar tours tend to have similar costs.

7.5   Evolutionary Computation

We have examined various artificial neural network models motivated by the marvelous workings of animal brains. How did such a complex organ originate? How did human beings come into being, for that matter? How and why does the human brain differ from that of a macaque monkey, a parrot that can "speak," and a dog? The solutions to some of these riddles lie in the theories of evolution and genetics, discussed briefly here in order to motivate the algorithmic details of *evolutionary computing*.

All human beings are structurally similar, but not identical: there are obvious visible differences (e.g., hair color) as well as physiological differences (e.g., susceptibility to certain diseases) between different individuals. Some properties are inherited from parents, while others (in a small number of individuals) result from random perturbations of the genetic structures. Both parents contribute different parts of the chromosomal structure of an offspring. Imagine that each parent has some "good" genes that increase its "fitness" or ability to survive and reproduce, and some not-so-good genes (e.g., those that increase susceptibility to diseases) that lower the fitness of the individual. If an offspring picks up more of the not-so-good genes from both parents, it has reduced chances of survival and reduced chances of generating offspring. Its offspring that have similar chromosomal structure will also have reduced chances of survival and reproduction. On the other hand, if an offspring were to be generated by the coming together of fitness-enhancing genes from both parents, we would expect the result to survive longer, and reproduce more often; this property would also likely be shared by its offspring.[4]

A change in perspective is useful. We may focus attention on changes in the number of occurrences of specific combinations of genes in various generations. When an individual of high fitness survives and reproduces, its constituent gene combinations also survive and proliferate in the next generation. The fitness of an individual hence contributes to the survival of the gene combinations. In a population that has evolved for a long time, the presence of a gene combination in many individuals implies that individuals containing that gene combination are likely to have high fitness. Thus, genetic operators and selection propagate gene combinations that lead to high fitness; these gene combinations are the *building blocks* of the selected successful individuals. Section 7.5.7 presents theoretical results and hypotheses supporting these arguments in the context of evolutionary computation.

7.5.1 Evolutionary algorithms

Evolutionary algorithms are stochastic state-space search techniques modeled on natural evolutionary mechanisms. These methods have been successful in solving many difficult optimization problems. Unlike neural networks and most other traditional search techniques, they maintain a *population* of candidate solutions, and attempt to improve the overall quality of these populations as time progresses. In methods such as simulated annealing, a single candidate solution is perturbed in the hope of achieving a better solution. By contrast, evolutionary algorithms can obtain new candidate solutions (*offspring*) by combining elements from multiple existing members of the population (*parents*), so that each offspring has a chance of improving on its parents and the best candidate solution found so far. *Selection* mechanisms provide a driving force, weeding out candidate solutions of poorer quality from the existing population, in favor of solutions of better quality.

---

4. The playwright George Bernard Shaw was reportedly courted by an actress who argued that their children would be likely to inherit her beauty and his brains. Shaw replied that their children may instead turn out to be handicapped in appearance as well as intellect.

There are three broad classes of evolutionary algorithms, with many similarities.

1. *Evolutionary Programming (EP)*, developed by Fogel et al. (1966), emphasizes direct representations of candidate solutions, and "mutation" as the primary operator for generating new candidate solutions.

2. *Evolutionary Strategies (ES)*, developed by Rechenberg (1973), use real-valued vectors and self-adapting "strategy" variables (such as covariances) in the search process.

3. *Genetic Algorithms (GA)*, developed by Holland (1975), manipulate fixed-length binary string representations, using "crossover" operators that combine segments of parent candidate solutions to generate offspring.

All these methods can be used to find suboptimal solutions of optimization problems, using evolutionary operators to generate new candidate solutions, and a selection method that leads to gradual improvement in the average quality of the population. All three methods use a mutation operator, though with varying emphasis. ES also employ a *recombination* operator, and genetic algorithms employ similar *crossover* operators. The size of the population is small in EP and ES, while Goldberg (1989) recommends population sizes for GAs of the same order as the number of bits in a candidate solution's representation.

The quality of a candidate solution is gauged by a *fitness function* f, often required to be positive by evolutionary algorithms. For the TSP, for instance, a natural choice of fitness function is $(M - \text{tour length})$, where M is a large positive number. For instance, in the six-cities problem discussed in section 7.1.1, we can take $M = 8,000$.

EXAMPLE 7.4   Choosing $M = 8,000$ and $X = (\text{NYC, WDC, CHI, DET, DEN, PHI})$, we have

$$f(X) = 8,000 - d(\text{NYC, WDC}) - d(\text{WDC, CHI})$$

$$- d(\text{CHI, DET}) - d(\text{DET, DEN}) - d(\text{DEN, PHI}) - d(\text{PHI, NYC})$$

$$= 8,000 - 237 - 709 - 279 - 1,283 - 1,739 - 101 = 3,652.$$

A *parent* is a candidate solution to which an operator is applied, by biological analogy, and the resulting candidate solutions are called *offspring*. The *population* or *generation* $\mathcal{P}(t)$ refers to the collection of candidate solutions present at time t, where $t \in \{0, 1, 2, \ldots\}$. $\mathcal{P}(0)$ is the initial population. In most algorithms, the size of the population $| \mathcal{P}(t) |$ does not vary with time. Note that the population may contain multiple occurrences of the same candidate solution.

Figure 7.7 describes a generic evolutionary computation algorithm, in which operators are repeatedly applied to parents to generate offspring. A *selection* strategy is also used to ensure improvement in solution quality with time. Selection may be applied at either the "reproduction" stage (with candidate solutions with higher fitness having more offspring)

Algorithm Evolutionary Computation;
  Initialize the population $\mathcal{P}(0)$;
  while termination criterion is not satisfied, **do**
   • Determine potential parents from current population $\mathcal{P}(t)$;
   • Apply evolutionary operators, yielding offspring $\Omega(t)$;
   • Obtain $\mathcal{P}(t+1)$ from $\mathcal{P}(t) \cup \Omega(t)$;
  end-while;
  return best candidate solution from current population.

Figure 7.7
A generic evolutionary computation algorithm.

or in determining the composition of the new generation $\mathcal{P}(t+1)$ (choosing the better among members of the old generation $\mathcal{P}(t)$ and their offspring).

7.5.2   Initialization

The population is often randomly initialized. If a bit-string representation is used, for instance, each member of the initial population ($\mathcal{P}(0)$) contains 0 or 1 with equal probability at every position. For problems in which random initialization fills the population with candidate solutions of extremely poor quality, some members of $\mathcal{P}(0)$ may instead be obtained by using fast "greedy" heuristic algorithms, or by hill-climbing on randomly generated candidate solutions.

7.5.3   Termination criterion

In many problems where the fitness of the optimal solution is unknown, the only termination criterion is based on the number of generations. Unlike gradient descent approaches, lack of progress in improving fitness of the best individual in the population is not a very useful termination criterion, since evolution often proceeds in "punctuated equilibria," with sudden improvements interspersed between long periods in which fitness remains relatively unchanged; this is illustrated in figure 7.8.

An important termination criterion is based upon testing whether the evolutionary algorithm has "converged" to a state from which little progress is possible, i.e., whether many candidate solutions in the current population are so similar to one another that no further progress is likely to occur in the next few generations. The extent to which such convergence may have been achieved can be estimated by examining the variance of the population fitness, with computation being terminated when the variance of the fitness of candidate solutions in the population becomes very small.

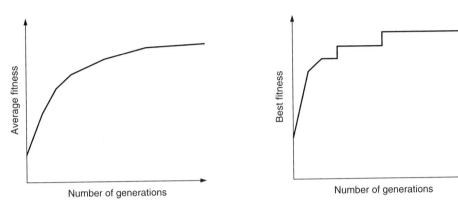

Figure 7.8
Graphs illustrating the improvement in average and best population fitness as the number of generations increases, in a typical genetic algorithm.

Eshelman (1991) and Maresky et al. (1995) report that performance improvements are sometimes obtained by "restarting" the algorithm when convergence occurs, replacing existing elements in the population by random or selectively generated candidate solutions.

7.5.4   Reproduction

How do we select elements in the current population to which the evolutionary operators are applied? The simplest reproduction strategies are to select all members of $\mathcal{P}(t)$ with equal probability, or to apply operators equally often to all members. These strategies are useful if *selection pressure* (to increase preponderance of solutions of better quality) is applied at the *replacement* stage, i.e., when determining which candidate solutions to retain for the next generation.

If selection pressure must instead be applied in the reproduction stage, fitness governs the number of times evolutionary operators are applied to a member of the current population. The canonical genetic algorithm proposed by Holland (1975) uses *fitness-proportionate* reproduction selection, in which the probability of choosing a candidate solution x is directly proportional to its relative fitness

$$\frac{f(x)}{\sum_{y \in \mathcal{P}(t)} f(y)},$$

where it is assumed that $f(y) \geq 0$ for every candidate solution y. For instance, if a population contains three elements (x, y, z) with fitnesses 10, 30, and 60, respectively, then the evolutionary operators are expected to be applied twice as often to z than to y, and six times more often to z than to x. If these were the only members of a population, then 10% of the offspring are expected to have x as a parent, and the corresponding fractions are 30% and 60% for y and z, respectively.

The quality of results obtained (using fitness-proportionate reproduction) is sensitive to the exact choice of the fitness function f. Different results are obtained using fitness functions whose values differ by a constant, since

$$\frac{f(x)}{\sum_{y \in \mathcal{P}(t)} f(y)} \neq \frac{(f(x) + a)}{\sum_{y \in \mathcal{P}(t)} (f(y) + a)},$$

for $a \neq 0$.

This problem does not arise with the *ranking* strategy, which examines how an individual ranks when compared to other members of the current population, instead of using the raw performance measure to determine the expected number of offspring for each individual. The population is first sorted by fitness to determine how many members of the population have higher fitness than a given member. The rank $r(x)$ is defined as the number of candidate solutions in $\mathcal{P}(t)$ whose fitness is $\geq f(x)$. Evolutionary operators are applied more often to those elements for which rank $r(x)$ is smaller. In a *linear* ranking strategy, the probability of selecting x as a parent is proportional to $1 - (c\, r(x))$, for some positive constant c. The expected number of offspring of each element is unchanged by many simple transformations on the fitness function, e.g., using f_2 instead of f_1, when $f_2(x) = a + bf_1(x)$ where $b > 0$.

EXAMPLE 7.5   Consider the instance of the traveling salesperson problem with six cities {CHI, DET, PHI, WDC, DEN, NYC}, illustrated earlier in figure 7.2. Assume fitness function described in example 7.4, with

$$f(x) = 8,000 - \sum_{i=0}^{5} d(x_i, x_{(i+1) \bmod 6}),$$

so that

$f(\text{NYC, WDC, CHI, DET, DEN, PHI}) = 3,652$

and

$f(\text{WDC, NYC, CHI, DET, DEN, PHI}) = 3,510.$

Using fitness-proportionate selection, these two tours (when present in a population) are chosen for operator application with relative probability 3,652:3,510, which scarcely differentiates between the two tours, so that the selection pressure is weak. Using a different fitness function defined by $f_1(x) = \max(0, f(x) - 3,500)$, however, we have

$f_1(\text{NYC, WDC, CHI, DET, DEN, PHI}) = 152$

and

$f_1(\text{WDC, NYC, CHI, DET, DEN, PHI}) = 10,$

so that the ratio of probabilities of using them (using fitness-proportionate reproduction selection) is 152:10, giving significantly greater emphasis to the former tour, and implying a greater selection pressure. For ranking selection, the same results are obtained whether we use f or f_1. If there are ten members in the current population, and if the two tours mentioned above are the best of the ten, and linear ranking is invoked, then the ratio of the probabilities of selection of the two tours is $1 - c : 1 - 2c = 0.9 : 0.8$ for $c = 0.1$, whether we use f or f_2.

7.5.5   Operators

Many evolutionary operators have been proposed in the literature, informally surveyed in this section. Each operator maps one or more parent candidate solutions to an offspring.

Mutation   Traditional mutation is a unary operator that performs a small perturbation of a candidate solution real-valued vector x, resulting in $x' = x + z$, where $z = (z_1, \ldots, z_n)$ is a vector randomly obtained from a multivariate normal distribution (see appendix A), whose mean vector is $\mathbf{0} = (0, \ldots, 0)$. For a GA that uses a bit-string representation, each component of the string is modified from 1 to 0 (or from 0 to 1) with a low probability of mutation (p_m). Choosing the value $p_m \approx 1/$(the number of bits in the bit-string) ensures that the expected number of bits mutated is one (in each candidate solution). When each gene can take on many values, traditional mutation is equally likely to result in any of these values. Variants of the mutation operator may violate this condition.

EXAMPLE 7.6   Consider the instance of the traveling salesperson problem with six cities {CHI, DET, PHI, WDC, DEN, NYC}, illustrated earlier in figure 7.2. Assume the representation and fitness function described in example 7.4, consider the solution $x = (\text{NYC, WDC, CHI, DET, DEN, PHI})$ whose fitness is

$$f(x) = 8{,}000 - \sum_{i=0}^{5} d(x_i, x_{(i+1)\bmod 6}) = 3{,}652.$$

A mutation operation may be defined as one which changes such a candidate solution at some location, e.g., replacing NYC by WDC to yield (WDC, WDC, CHI, DET, DEN, PHI). However this is not a valid tour since NYC is not visited. For TSP, a better definition of a mutation operation is: "Interchange the positions of two randomly selected cities." In the current example, such a mutation operation may exchange the positions of NYC and WDC, changing $x =$ (NYC, WDC, CHI, DET, DEN, PHI) to $x' =$ (WDC, NYC, CHI, DET, DEN, PHI). The result of performing this mutation is a slight decrease in fitness, since

$$f(x') = 8,000 - 237 - 809 - 279 - 1,283 - 1,739 - 143 = 3,510.$$

Crossover The operators emphasized by genetic algorithms are referred to as *crossover* operators. In a traditional GA, there are precisely two parents to which each crossover is applied, and every gene has a value inherited from either parent. The frequently used "1-point crossover" (1PTX) operator cleaves parents at the same randomly chosen position. 1PTX generates two offspring, each of which is obtained by concatenating the left fragment from one parent with the right fragment from the other parent. If i is a randomly chosen integer such that $1 \leq i < n$, 1PTX may be represented as follows (where the vertical bar indicates the position at which crossover occurs).

$$(x_1 \ldots x_i \mid x_{i+1} \ldots x_n) + (x_1' \ldots x_i' \mid x_{i+1}' \ldots x_n')$$

$$\rightarrow (x_1 \ldots x_i \mid x_{i+1}' \ldots x_n') + (x_1' \ldots x_i' \mid x_{i+1} \ldots x_n)$$

In some GAs, there is a chance that the parents are left unchanged and potential parents may be crossed over with a "crossover probability"< 1. Typical values for crossover probability are high, exceeding ≥ 0.7.

EXAMPLE 7.7   Consider the problem of discovering the explicit form of a polynomial in binary variables, where addition denotes the OR operation and multiplication denotes the AND operation. The fitness of a candidate solution (polynomial) is given by the number of binary vectors for which the candidate gives the same answer as that of the unknown polynomial.

For instance, consider a problem in three binary variables x_1, x_2, x_3, where the goal polynomial (to be discovered by the GA) is $x_1 x_2 + x_2 x_3$. Let the binary vector abc stand for the variables $x_1 = a, x_2 = b, x_3 = c$. The fitness of $x_1 + x_2 + x_3$ is 4, since it generates the same answers as the goal polynomial for four binary vectors (000, 011, 110, and 111) and different answers for other binary vectors.

Input string	Guessed polynomial $(x_1 + x_2 + x_3)$	Target polynomial $(x_1 x_2 + x_2 x_3)$
000	0	0
001	1	0
010	1	0

Input string	Guessed polynomial $(x_1 + x_2 + x_3)$	Target polynomial $(x_1 x_2 + x_2 x_3)$
011	1	1
100	1	0
101	1	0
110	1	1
111	1	1

How do we represent each polynomial, in order to apply genetic operators? One choice is to use a 7-bit representation, with each bit standing for the presence or absence of a term. For instance, the first bit stands for x_1, the second for x_2, the third for $x_1 x_2$, the fourth for x_3, the fifth for $x_1 x_3$, the sixth for $x_2 x_3$, and the seventh for $x_1 x_2 x_3$. The polynomial $x_1 + x_2 + x_3$ is hence represented as 1101000, while the polynomial $x_1 x_2 + x_1 x_3$ is represented as 0010100. Let these be the two parents for the 1-point crossover, with the crossover point chosen between the third and fourth bits. Crossover has the following result:

$$(110 \mid 1000) + (001 \mid 0100) \rightarrow (110 \mid 0100) + (001 \mid 1000)$$

(with the cut-points shown by vertical bars). The first fragment from the first parent is 110, while the second fragment from the second parent is 0100, and concatenating these yields the offspring 1100100, that represents the polynomial $x_1 + x_2 + x_1 x_3$. Similarly, the other offspring is 0011000, representing $x_3 + x_1 x_2$. Note that if the crossover point were chosen to be between the fifth and sixth bits, the resulting offspring would have been identical to the parents.

Many applications are incompatible with the restriction that each gene of an offspring come from either parent. Instead of direct genetic inheritance, problem-specific features of both parents may need to be inherited by offspring. For instance, it may be necessary for each offspring sequence to be a permutation of the elements in the parents, so that the ith gene of an offspring may be different from the ith genes of both parents. This is sometimes accomplished by patching up the results of applying a traditional crossover operator such as 1PTX.

EXAMPLE 7.8   For the six-city TSP described earlier, applying 1PTX to (DEN, CHI, PHI, NYC, DET, WDC) and (CHI, DET, PHI, WDC, DEN, NYC), with the crossover point chosen in the center of the vector, gives the offspring (DEN, CHI, PHI, WDC, DEN, NYC), and (CHI, DET, PHI, NYC, DET, WDC), respectively. Unfortunately, DEN occurs twice in the first offspring but DET does not occur at all. To obtain valid tours, one must perturb these tours, e.g., randomly selecting one of the occurrences of DEN in the first offspring and replacing it by DET (and conversely in the other offspring).

Recombination operators similar to crossover are used in Evolutionary Strategies. Since the operator may be applied to vectors of real numbers, recombination may involve arithmetic operations such as averaging. For instance, if the goal is to determine the best possible values for two dials x, y in a control system, and f is the fitness function, two parents (x_1, y_1) and (x_2, y_2) may be recombined to yield the following offspring.

$$\left(\frac{x_1 f(x_1, y_1) + x_2 f(x_2, y_2)}{f(x_1, y_1) + f(x_2, y_2)}, \quad \frac{y_1 f(x_1, y_1) + y_2 f(x_2, y_2)}{f(x_1, y_1) + f(x_2, y_2)} \right)$$

7.5.6   Replacement

Replacement refers to the method chosen to obtain the composition of the population in each succeeding generation. In the *wholesale replacement* strategy used frequently in GAs and ESs, for instance, all the members of the previous generation may be replaced by the offspring resulting from reproduction. This is the strategy adopted in the simple canonical genetic algorithm suggested by Holland (1970).

EXAMPLE 7.9   Figure 7.9 depicts a labeled graph in which each edge is associated with a cost. A genetic algorithm is applied to partition the graph into two groups of equal size, minimizing the total cost of cross-edges (edges that connect nodes in different groups). Each candidate solution is represented as a bit-string containing as many bits as the number of vertices in the graph to be partitioned. The jth bit in a bit-string identifies the group into which the jth vertex of the graph is placed by the corresponding partition.

A population size of 8 is used. The initial population is generated randomly. In each generation, new candidate solutions were generated using 1-point crossover with fitness-proportionate selection. Fitness is defined as 1/(total cost), where total cost is the sum of lengths of cross-edges that connect nodes placed in different groups by the partition. The minimum cost is 3, as indicated in the figure, hence the maximum fitness is $1/3$.

After crossover, each bit of each offspring is mutated with a probability of 0.1. The resulting offspring may not equally partition the graph, since the number of ones in the generated bit-string may not equal the number of zeroes. An adjustment is therefore performed, making the least possible change that will equalize the number of ones and zeroes in the bit-string. Wholesale replacement is used, and each new generation consists of all the resulting (adjusted) offspring.

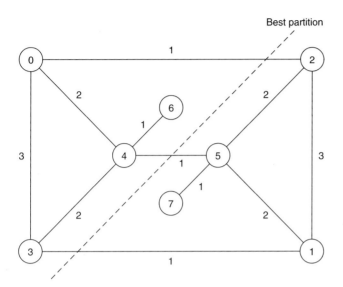

Figure 7.9
A graph with 8 vertices is to be bipartitioned; the broken line represents the lowest cost partition.

Candidate solution in randomly generated initial population	Cost
00110011	14
00011011	8
10000111	12
01010011	12
11000101	13
11100100	8
01110100	8
01000111	8

In the initial population, the average cost is 10.4, and the least cost is 8. The results of 1-point crossover, mutation, and adjustment are shown in the following table, whose last two columns indicate the composition of the next generation and the fitnesses of the new members of the population.

Parents (from initial population)	Results of crossover	Results of mutation	Results of adjustment	Costs of members (of generation 1)
11000101	11000101	01000101	11000101	13
01110100	01110100	01110100	01110100	8
11100100	00100011	10100011	10100011	12
00110011	11110100	11110100	11100100	8
00011011	01011011	00011011	00011011	8
11100100	10100100	10000100	10011100	8
00011011	00011011	00011011	00011011	8
01000111	01000111	01000111	01000111	8

In the new generation, the average cost is 9.1, and the best cost is 8. The following table depicts the average cost and best cost as the population evolves through various generations.

Generation no.	Average cost	Best cost	Number of occurrences of optimal solution
0	10.4	8	0
1	9.1	8	0
2	8.5	5	0
3	10.2	5	0
4	9.6	8	0
5	9.6	5	0
6	9.4	5	0
7	8.8	8	0
8	8.9	5	0
9	8.9	8	0
10	9.8	8	0
11	7.5	3	1
12	8.1	3	1
13	7.6	3	2
14	6.4	3	4

Generation no.	Average cost	Best cost	Number of occurrences of optimal solution
15	4.9	3	5
16	4.0	3	7
17	5.1	3	6
18	5.6	3	5
19	5.9	3	5
20	6.2	3	5

We observe that neither average fitness nor best fitness monotonically improves; many implementations address this difficulty by forcing the next generation to include the best solution found so far. The best possible solution has been reached by the eleventh generation, after which its frequency in the population rapidly increases until over half the population consists exclusively of this optimal solution. Mutation ensures that diversity in the population is not entirely lost, and new candidate solutions continue to be explored.

7.5.7 Schema Theorem*

The success of GAs is sometimes explained in terms of Holland's *Schema Theorem*, discussed below.

A *schema* is a set of states obtained by fixing some of the elements in a structure that can represent an individual in a population manipulated using a GA. Using "#" to represent the "don't-care" condition, for instance, when the GA is applied to bit-strings of length 9, the schema 1#0#10100 represents the following set containing four individuals.

{100010100, 110010100, 100110100, 110110100}

When 1-point crossover is applied to two individuals, bits that have the same value in both parents are inherited by both offspring. In other words, if both parents are members of a schema, then the offspring will also be members of that schema. In general, since offspring are not identical to the parents, offspring and parents will not belong to all the same schema. A schema to which only a parent (but neither offspring) belongs is said to be "disrupted" by the crossover operation, while a schema to which a parent and an offspring belong is said to be preserved by crossover.

The *order* of a schema refers to the number of fixed bits in the schema. Shorter schema (with smaller order) are less likely to be disrupted than longer schema. For instance, since crossover may separate the last bit from the others, 10## is less likely to be disrupted than 10#1.

The *defining length* of a schema refers to the distance between the farthest fixed bits of a schema. Among schema with the same number of fixed bits, 1-point crossover is less likely to disrupt schema with short defining lengths, in which the positions of fixed bits are near each other. For instance, 10## is less likely to be disrupted than 1##0, since the latter is vulnerable irrespective of which position in the string is chosen as the crossover site.

If instances of a schema have high fitness (relative to a population), we may say that the schema itself has high fitness. Selection pressure ensures that these instances produce relatively more offspring than instances of other schema with lower fitness. Since offspring have a good chance of preserving schema to which their parents belong, the next generation is likely to have relatively more instances of higher fitness schema present in the previous generation. The repeated reproduction-selection cycle thus results in a steady increase in the number of offspring of schema whose instances have higher fitness. This increase has been quantified in Holland's Schema Theorem, stated below for fixed-length bit-string representations.

THEOREM 7.2   Consider a genetic algorithm executed with large population size, fitness-proportionate reproduction, 1-point crossover performed with probability p_c, random mutation performed at each bit with probability p_m, and wholesale replacement of each generation by its offspring, In successive generations, the number of instances of any schema S (in the population) grows at a rate exceeding

$$\frac{\text{fitness (instances of } S \text{ in the population)}}{\text{average population fitness}} \left(1 - \frac{p_c.(\text{defining length of } S)}{\text{length of individual}} - p_m.\text{order}(S) \right).$$

The Schema Theorem has led to the formulation of Goldberg's (1989) *Building Block Hypothesis*, which states that GAs seek near-optimal performance through the juxtaposition of short, low-order, high-fitness schemata (called *building blocks*). There is no guarantee of the existence of such building blocks in every problem, but many practical problems do possess such internal structure that enables the successful application of GAs.

The capabilities of GAs are also attributed to a property called *implicit* (or *intrinsic*) parallelism, which refers to the exploration of a large number of schema using a small population. This property is a consequence of the fact that each individual bit-string of length L belongs to 2^L schema, each obtained by fixing some bits of the individual. Implicit parallelism is not to be confused with the ability of genetic algorithms to be scalably parallelized on appropriate hardware.

7.6   Conclusion

Several optimization methods have been discussed in this chapter, including neural and non-neural techniques. These optimization methods have been used successfully to solve many important problems, such as placement and global wiring of integrated circuits, computer-aided design of integrated circuits, folding, test pattern generation, logic minimization, compaction, graph theoretic problems (partitioning, coloring, Steiner tree), scheduling, designing error-correcting codes, and image restoration.

Among the optimization methods surveyed in this chapter, Hopfield networks are the fastest, but simulated annealing and evolutionary algorithms are much more likely to give good quality solutions for difficult problems characterized by a large number of local optima. Simulated annealing is guaranteed to yield global optima if extremely large amounts of computation are performed, but is not cost-effective for problems with few local minima. Faster variants of simulated annealing perform better than Hopfield networks, but do not guarantee that global optima will be reached. Genetic algorithms work well in problems where good solutions consist of good components or substructures ("building blocks"); suboptimal solutions that possess some such building blocks are recombined (or crossed over) to yield better solutions. Although more computationally expensive than Hopfield networks, evolutionary methods are easily parallelizable and can make effective use of various parallel computers.

This chapter has discussed genetic algorithms in more detail than other evolutionary computing methods such as evolutionary programming (EP) and evolutionary strategies (ES), which differ from genetic algorithms in operators and in reproduction and selection strategies. EP uses direct representations of individuals, with no bit-string encoding. Unlike genetic algorithms, mutation is the primary operator, and operators resembling crossover are absent or rarely used. The first successful application of EP was in evolving finite state machines capable of responding to environmental stimuli, using operators for effecting structural and behavioral change over time. ES have been used for building systems capable of solving difficult real-valued parameter optimization problems, using real-valued vector representations. ES emphasize the role of self-adapting strategy variables in the search process in addition to the input parameters specific to the problem. These strategy variables may include up to n different variances and $n(n-1)/2$ covariances, represented by a symmetric $n \times n$ matrix C, where $C[i, i] = \sigma^2$ represents the variance for the ith variable and $C[i, j]$ represents the covariance between i and j.

There have been many attempts to combine evolutionary algorithms with neural networks, surveyed by Schaffer, Whitley, and Eshelman (1992). These attempts broadly fall into the following categories.

1. using genetic algorithms to evolve optimal values for neural network parameters such as the number of nodes, connectivity, weights, learning rate, and momentum

2. using genetic algorithms to extract features, preprocessing inputs to be fed into neural networks

3. using neural networks to obtain good quality initial populations for genetic algorithms

4. using genetic algorithms and neural networks in parallel to solve the same problem, in order to increase the confidence in the correctness of the solutions obtained independently by each method

The phrase "Soft computing" is sometimes used to describe the set of methods comprising various neural networks, genetic algorithms, simulated annealing, and fuzzy computing techniques, several of which may be combined in a single application. We note that there is no panacea—none of these methods guarantees that an optimal solution will be found without resorting to exhaustive search of the entire state space. This is a property of the problem, not of the solution methods; no method can provide a best solution to all problems. Solving difficult problems requires using problem-specific heuristics as well as adaptive methods that learn problem characteristics and can determine the best applicable algorithm for a given problem.

7.7 Exercises

1. Solve the following problems using the methods discussed in this chapter. Compare the performance of various operators for the GA, and suggest suitable problem-dependent operators where appropriate.

   a. For example 7.7 on page 294 with ten variables $x_0, \ldots, x_9$, find the polynomial $x_0 x_1 + x_2 x_3 + x_2 x_4 + x_5 x_6 x_7 + x_9$.

   b. Solve the eleven-city TSP problem for data given in appendix B.6, using the methods discussed in this chapter.

   c. Solve the IC placement problem for 16 modules $\{A, \ldots, P\}$ in a 4×4 square configuration, with the following required connections.
   AC, BD, EF, AF, GH, GI, IK, GI, JL, JM,
   JO, NP, AP, BO, CN, DJ, HK, HL, HF, EO.
   Total wire length must be minimized. Assume that it is permissible for connections to "jump" over other connections, at an extra cost of 1 unit (equal to the cost of 1 unit distance of wire length).

2. For a five-city TSP, what is the number of distinct (non-equivalent) tours? What is the maximum number of local optima for the tour length, and how many trials of iterated gradient descent would be needed to obtain the global optimum with a probability ≥ 0.90?

3. Define an "energy" function to be minimized, for the clustering or vector quantization problems. Can this problem be solved using Hopfield networks?

4. Discuss how the Hopfield network, simulated annealing, and genetic algorithm may be applied to the following version of the classroom scheduling problem, in which a set of classrooms and times must be assigned to a set of courses, subject to the following constraints.

- No classes meet on Fridays; the same class must be held in the same time slot on Monday and Wednesday; the same class must be held in the same time slot on Tuesday and Thursday.
- Each time slot is of length 80 minutes, with a five-minute break between classes.
- Classes do not meet before 8 AM, and no class should extend beyond 10 PM.
- As many classes as possible should be scheduled after 5 PM.
- The number of students is given for each class, and cannot exceed the room size of a classroom in which it is scheduled.
- We are given the building location of the department that offers each course. We are given the physical distances between buildings, and must minimize the total distance between classroom buildings and corresponding department buildings.

5.   a. The *2-point crossover* (2PTX) operator randomly chooses two crossover points at which each parent is cleaved and produces offspring consisting of three segments of which the middle segment comes from a different parent than the other two segments. Using the vertical bars to indicate the positions at which crossovers occur, this can be described as follows.

$$(x_1 \dots x_i \mid x_{i+1} \dots x_j \mid x_{j+1} \dots x_n) + (x'_1 \dots x'_i \mid x'_{i+1} \dots x'_j \mid x'_{j+1} \dots x'_n)$$

$$\rightarrow (x_1 \dots x_i \mid x'_{i+1} \dots x'_j \mid x_{j+1} \dots x_n) + (x'_1 \dots x'_i \mid x_{i+1} \dots x_j \mid x'_{j+1} \dots x'_n)$$

b. The *uniform crossover* (UX) operator generates offspring whose bits are equally likely to come from either parent, not depending on any crossover point.

Apply GAs using each of 2PTX and UX to example 7.7 with ten variables $x_0, \dots, x_9$, to find the polynomial $x_0x_1 + x_2x_3 + x_2x_4 + x_5x_6x_7 + x_9$, and compare the results to those obtained using 1-point crossover.

6. Hill-climbing has been suggested as a means of improving the performance of evolutionary algorithms. For example 7.7, hill-climbing can be defined as the process of repeatedly adding a term or removing a term from a polynomial, if such addition or deletion improves fitness. On the problem with ten variables $x_0, \dots, x_9$, where the goal is to find the polynomial $x_0x_1 + x_2x_3 + x_2x_4 + x_5x_6x_7 + x_9$, compare the performance of a GA with hill-climbing and a GA without hill-climbing. Assume the same crossover operator for

both GAs, and use the same parameter values. Count the number of fitness evaluations required to achieve results of the same quality.

7. The probability of mutation in evolutionary algorithms is analogous to the temperature parameter in simulated annealing. An evolutionary algorithm can be used, applying mutation alone as the evolutionary operator, steadily decreasing the probability of mutation in each generation, using a rule such as $p_m(t+1) = 0.99 p_m(t)$, where initial mutation rate is high, e.g., $p_m(0) = 0.3$. For the polynomial discovery example discussed earlier, apply and compare the results of using such a hybrid algorithm with a GA, and with an evolutionary algorithm using no crossover but only mutation with fixed probability, say $p_m = 0.01$.

8. Given a set of points S in two-dimensional Euclidean space, it is easy to generate a *minimal spanning tree*, a graph whose nodes are points $\in S$, and the sum of whose edge lengths is as small as possible. Apply any of the methods discussed in this chapter to construct a *Steiner tree*, whose nodes are a superset of S, and the sum of whose edge lengths is as small as possible. Note that the Steiner tree can contain new points (not in S), to be discovered by the algorithm.

9. A practical optimization task is to arrange components on a circuit board such that the length of the wires is minimized, with additional constraints that require certain components to be connected to certain others. Consider the special case in which each component or module is a square of the same size, which must occupy slots in a rectangular array. The cost function estimates the amount of wiring, using the sums of the Manhattan distances between components that are to be directly connected. Use the simulated annealing algorithm to obtain a solution of the problem in figure 7.10.

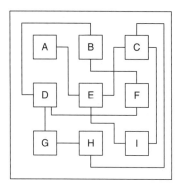

Figure 7.10
A layout of components on a circuit-board that can be improved by rearranging components.

10. Consider the solution of TSP by Hopfield network as described in section 7.1. Is it possible to use an energy function in which the constraints are represented by

$$\lambda_1 \sum_x \left(1 - \sum_j M_{x,j}\right)^4 + \lambda_2 \sum_j \left(1 - \sum_x M_{x,j}\right)^4$$

in the second component of equation 7.3?

A Appendix: A Little Math

The sections of this appendix are intended to reacquaint the reader with elementary mathematical notions invoked in parts of the text. Needless to say, these sections are no substitute for complete courses in college mathematics!

A.1 Calculus

This section recapitulates definitions of elementary calculus terminology used in the text.

Intuitively, a function is continuous if it has similar values for similar inputs. More precisely, a real-valued function f (whose domain of definition is the set $S \subseteq \Re$ of real numbers) is *continuous* at x if given $\epsilon > 0$, we can find a $\delta > 0$ such that $| f(x) - f(y) | < \epsilon$ for all y in S with $| x - y | < \delta$. A function is continuous on S if it is continuous for every $x \in S$. The extension to multiargument functions is straightforward; an n-argument function f is continuous over S if $| f(x) - f(y) | < \epsilon$ for all $y \in S$ with $| x - y | < \delta$. Here, $S \subseteq \Re^n$ is a subset of n-dimensional real space and $| \cdot |$ denotes the Euclidean distance.

If f is a real-valued continuous function, its *first derivative* (or *slope* or *gradient*) at x is defined to be

$$f'(x) = \frac{df(x)}{dx} = \lim_{\epsilon \to 0} \frac{(f(x + \epsilon) - f(x))}{\epsilon},$$

provided the limit exists. If the function has a first derivative at all $x \in S$ then we say that it is differentiable on S. Similarly, the *partial derivative* of an n-argument function f with respect to its ith argument variable is defined as

$$\frac{\partial f(x_1, \ldots, x_i, \ldots, x_n)}{\partial x_i} = \lim_{\epsilon \to 0} \frac{(f(x_1, \ldots, x_i + \epsilon, \ldots, x_n) - f(x_1, \ldots, x_i, \ldots, x_n))}{\epsilon},$$

if the limit exists. A function is *differentiable* over $S \subseteq \Re^n$ in all its arguments if its first partial derivatives exist everywhere in S, with respect to all its arguments.

The *second derivative* of a one-argument function is the first derivative of the first derivative of the function.

$$f''(x) = \frac{d}{dx} \left(\frac{df(x)}{dx} \right)$$

The *Hessian* of an n-argument function f is a matrix such that the element in its ith row, jth column is $\partial(\partial f(x_1, \ldots, x_n)/\partial x_j)/\partial x_i$.

Higher order partial derivatives are similarly defined. A function is *smooth* if all its ℓth partial derivatives exist everywhere in the region where the variables can take their values, for every positive integer ℓ. A smooth function $f(x)$ of one argument can be approximated in the neighborhood of any value x_0 using the (infinite) Taylor series expansion

$$f(x_0 + \epsilon) = f(x_0) + \epsilon f'(x_0) + \frac{\epsilon^2}{2!} f''(x_0) + \ldots + \frac{\epsilon^k}{k!} f^{(k)}(x_0) + \ldots$$

for small ϵ, where the $(k+1)$th term is proportional to $f^{(k)}(x_0)$, the kth derivative of $f(x)$ evaluated at x_0. Many applications use approximations that ignore all but the first few terms of the Taylor series expansion.

EXAMPLE A.1   The function $f : [0, 1]^2 \longrightarrow \Re$ defined by $f(x, y) = 3x^3 + 5x^2y + y^2$ is continuous in both arguments. To see that f is continuous at $(x_0, y_0) = (\frac{1}{3}, \frac{1}{3})$, we choose $\delta = 0.05$. Then, for any (x, y) whose coordinates are at a distance less than 0.05 from $(x_0, y_0) = (\frac{1}{3}, \frac{1}{3})$,

$$| f(x, y) - f(x_0, y_0) | = | 3x^3 + 5x^2y + y^2 - (3x_0^3 + 5x_0^2 y_0 + y_0^2) |$$
$$\leq 3 | x^3 - x_0^3 | + 5 | x^2 y - x_0^2 y_0 | + | y^2 - y_0^2 |$$
$$\leq 3 \times 0.05^3 + 5 \times 0.05^3 + 0.05^2$$
$$\leq 0.05.$$

This property can be verified for any choice of δ and at any point in $[0, 1]^2$.

This function has partial derivatives in both arguments. From the definition of the partial derivative, it follows that

$$\frac{\partial f(x, y)}{\partial x} = 9x^2 + 10xy$$

and

$$\frac{\partial f(x, y)}{\partial y} = 5x^2 + 2y.$$

The Hessian of this function is a 2×2 matrix whose elements are given by

$$\begin{bmatrix} \frac{\partial^2 f}{\partial x^2} & \frac{\partial^2 f}{\partial x \partial y} \\ \frac{\partial^2 f}{\partial y \partial x} & \frac{\partial^2 f}{\partial y^2} \end{bmatrix} = \begin{bmatrix} 18x + 10y & 10x \\ 10x & 2 \end{bmatrix}$$

When the derivative of a function is difficult or computationally expensive to obtain, it must be approximated. Gradient descent and other update rules require such approximations. Note that $\partial f(x)/\partial x$, evaluated at $x = 0.3$, $y = 0.6$, is equal to $9 \times (0.3)^2 + 10 \times 0.3 \times 0.6 = 2.61$. This quantity can be approximated by using the definition of the partial derivative by

$$\frac{\partial f(x, y)}{\partial x} \approx \frac{f(x + \epsilon, y) - f(x, y)}{\epsilon}$$

where ϵ is some small real number. The exact value of $\partial f(x, y)/\partial x$ at $(x, y) = (0.3, 0.6)$ is 2.61, whereas if we take $\epsilon = 0.05$, then its approximate value is given by

$$\frac{1}{0.05}\{[3 \times (0.35)^2 + 5 \times (0.35)^2 \times (0.6) + (0.6)^2]$$

$$- [3 \times (0.3)^2 + 5 \times (0.3)^2 \times (0.6) + (0.6)^2]\} \approx 2.9$$

When all first and second derivatives exist, local minima of a function occur at points where the first derivatives are zero and the second derivatives are positive. Gradient descent methods attempt to find such points, moving in the direction of the negative gradient to a point where the function value is smaller.

A.2   Linear Algebra

We assume readers are familiar with the "array" construct available in most programming languages. A *vector* is a one-dimensional array, denoted in this text using boldface lowercase letters. A *matrix* is a two-dimensional array, denoted in this text using uppercase letters. Following traditional practice, equations containing vectors have been typeset by showing each vector as a matrix containing a single column. For ease in reading, a vector that occurs in narrative text is represented as a sequence of vector components separated by commas, e.g., $(x_1, \ldots, x_n)$.

The *dot product (scalar product)* of two vectors $\boldsymbol{x}$ and $\boldsymbol{y}$ (of equal length) is defined as $\boldsymbol{x} \cdot \boldsymbol{y} = \sum_i x_i y_i$. This is distinct from the matrix product of two matrices $A = (a_{i,j})$ and $B = (b_{i,j})$, which is a matrix AB whose j, kth element is defined to be $\sum_\ell a_{j,\ell} b_{\ell,k}$, assuming that the number of columns of A equals the number of rows of B. If λ is a scalar (number), and A is a vector or matrix, λA represents the vector or matrix whose components are obtained by multiplying all components of A by λ.

Two vectors $\boldsymbol{x}, \boldsymbol{y}$ are *orthogonal* if their dot product $\boldsymbol{x} \cdot \boldsymbol{y} = 0$. They are said to be *orthonormal* if they are orthogonal and have unit length, i.e., $\sum_i x_i^2 = 1$ and $\sum_i y_i^2 = 1$.

Some square matrices have an *inverse* (denoted by attaching the superscript -1), defined such that $AA^{-1} = A^{-1}A = I$, the identity matrix. In general, the inverse of a matrix may not exist. This happens when one of the rows (columns) of the matrix can be expressed as a linear combination of the other rows (columns). By contrast, every matrix has a unique *pseudo-inverse*, defined to be a matrix A^* that satisfies the following conditions.

$$AA^*A = A$$
$$A^*AA^* = A^*$$
$$A^*A = (A^*A)^T$$
$$AA^* = (AA^*)^T$$

If A is a matrix, x is an *eigen-vector* of A if and only if x has a non-zero component, and there exists a constant λ (called an *eigen-value*) such that $Ax = \lambda x$.

Simple iterative methods are known for computation of inverses and eigen-vectors, and have been cast into the framework of some neural network models.

A.3   Statistics

Let x be a discrete random variable[1] which takes values $x_1, x_2, \ldots, x_n$ with probabilities $p_1, p_2, \ldots, p_n$. In other words, $p_i = \text{Prob}(x = x_i)$ where $i = 1, 2, \ldots, n$; $p_i \geq 0$; and $\sum_{i=1}^{n} p_i = 1$. Then the expected value of x, denoted by $\mathcal{E}(x)$, is

$$\mathcal{E}(x) = \sum_{i=1}^{n} p_i x_i$$

and the variance of x, denoted by $\text{var}(x)$, is

$$\text{var}(x) = \sum_{i=1}^{n} p_i (x_i - \mathcal{E}(x))^2.$$

This idea can be generalized as follows. If f is a function of x, then

$$\mathcal{E}(f(x)) = \sum_{i=1}^{n} p_i f(x_i)$$

and

$$\text{var}(f(x)) = \sum_{i=1}^{n} p_i (f(x_i) - \mathcal{E}(f(x)))^2.$$

For a continuous random variable, the probability is replaced by the density function, $p(x)$, whose interpretation is

$$\text{Prob}[x_0 \leq x \leq x_0 + \delta x_0] \approx p(x_0)\delta x_0,$$

where δx_0 is a small positive real number. The expected value and variance are now evaluated as

$$\mathcal{E}(f(x)) = \int_u p(u) f(u) du$$

---

1. Conventional notation is to use X to denote a random variable and x to denote its particular value. We do not use this convention in this brief introduction.

and

$$\text{var}(f(x)) = \int_u p(u)(f(u) - \mathcal{E}(f(x)))^2 du.$$

The integral is over all values in the domain of f.

One of the most used continuous random variables is the Gaussian, also known as the normal distribution. The density function of the Gaussian random variable, with expected value μ and variance σ^2, is

$$p(x) = \frac{1}{\sqrt{2\pi}\sigma} \exp\left(-\frac{1}{2}\left(\frac{x-\mu}{\sigma}\right)^2\right); \qquad -\infty < x < \infty. \tag{A.1}$$

Naturally,

$$\mu = \int_{-\infty}^{\infty} x p(x) dx, \quad \text{and} \quad \sigma^2 = \int_{-\infty}^{\infty} (x-\mu)^2 p(x) \, dx.$$

When $\mu = 0$ and $\sigma^2 = 1$, then

$$\Phi(x) = \int_{-\infty}^{x} p(u) \, du$$

is a standard notation for the distribution function of the "standard Gaussian" random variable.

In general, the Gaussian random vector x has a density function

$$p(x) = \frac{|\Sigma|^{-1/2}}{(2\pi)^{n/2}} \exp\left(-\frac{1}{2}(x-\mu)^T \Sigma^{-1}(x-\mu)\right), \tag{A.2}$$

where n is the dimensionality of x, μ represents the vector of expected values and Σ represents the matrix of covariances;

$$\mu = \mathcal{E}(x)$$

where ith element of the vector of expectation is $\mu_i = \mathcal{E}(x_i)$ and

$$\Sigma_{n \times n} = (\sigma_{ij}); \qquad \sigma_{ij} = \text{cov}(x_i, x_j) = \mathcal{E}\left((x_i - \mu_i)(x_j - \mu_j)\right).$$

Note that $\text{var}(x_i) = \text{cov}(x_i, x_i)$ for $i = 1, 2, \ldots, n$. The correlation between x_i and x_j is related to the covariance by

$$\text{corr}(x_i, x_j) = \frac{\text{cov}(x_i, x_j)}{\sqrt{\text{var}(x_i) \, \text{var}(x_j)}}.$$

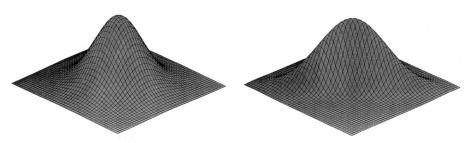

Figure A.1
Graphs of the bivariate Gaussian density functions: correlation coefficient = 0, and correlation coefficient = −0.8, respectively.

A positive covariance value of σ_{ij} implies that the random variables x_i and x_j are positively correlated, i.e., if x_i increases in value, then chances are that x_j will also increase in value and vice versa, because $\sigma_{ij} = \sigma_{ji}$. Plots of the density functions of two-dimensional Gaussian random vectors for three different values of correlations, presented in figure A.1, illustrate this property.

Information is quantified as the number of bits needed to represent an object or abstraction. *Information gain* refers to the amount of decrease in the number of bits needed for representation, when our knowledge relevant to a scenario improves. When various alternative states are not equally likely, then the information gain is expressed in terms of a measure called "entropy" that takes into account the probabilities of different states. *Entropy* is a measure of disorder or lack of knowledge, formally defined as $-\sum_x p(x) \log_2 p(x)$ when the variable x ranges over a discrete number of states, and as $-\int_x p(x) \log_2 p(x) dx$ when x ranges over continuous space with a probability density function $p(x)$.

EXAMPLE A.2   If our initial knowledge indicates that a cat is equally likely to be in any of sixteen rooms, the probability that a cat is in one room is $1/16$, and we need $\log_2 16 = 4$ bits to specify exactly which room the cat is located in. If our knowledge improves later so that the cat is now constrained to be in eight of those rooms, only $\log_2 8 = 3$ bits are now needed to identify the specific room containing the cat. Hence, the information gain is $4 - 3 = 1$ bit.

If our initial knowledge indicated that the cat could be in any of sixteen rooms, but is more likely to be in the eight rooms upstairs than in the eight rooms downstairs, with probability $1/12$ for each room upstairs and probability $1/24$ for each room downstairs, and if our final knowledge ruled out downstairs rooms completely (so that the new probabilities are $1/8$ for each upstairs room and 0 for each downstairs room), then the information gain is better described by the change in entropy. The old entropy is

$$-8\left(\frac{1}{12}\log_2(\frac{1}{12})\right) - 8\left(\frac{1}{24}\log_2(\frac{1}{24})\right) \approx 3.92.$$

We may express the probability for the downstairs rooms as $0 = \lim_{x\to\infty} 1/x$ so that $0\log_2 0 = \lim_{x\to\infty} \frac{1}{x}\log_2(\frac{1}{x}) = 0$. Hence the new entropy is

$$-8\left(\frac{1}{8}\log_2(\frac{1}{8})\right) - 8(0\log_2 0) = 3 + 0 = 3.$$

The information gain is hence $\approx 3.92 - 3 = 0.92$ bits, which is smaller than the corresponding information gain of 1 bit obtained earlier. In other words, the first initial state (in which all rooms were equally likely) contained less information than the second initial state (in which upstairs rooms were likelier), and the final states were the same in both cases, hence the information gain was more in the first case than the second.

Just as the "difference" between two vectors can be compared in terms of the Euclidean distance between them, different probability distributions can be compared using a measure called *relative entropy* or *cross-entropy*. The cross-entropy between two distributions P and P' is defined as follows:

$$H(p, p') = \sum_s p_s \ln(p_s/p_s')$$

in the discrete case, and

$$H(p, p') = \int_s p(s)\ln(p(s)/p'(s))ds$$

in the continuous case, where s is a variable that ranges over all possible network states. Note that $H(p, p') = 0$ when the difference between p and p' is least, i.e., when $p = p'$.

B Appendix: Data

In this appendix, we present several example data files to serve as fodder for the neural network algorithms and programs discussed in this text.

B.1 Iris Data

This classic data of Anderson and Fisher (1936) pertains to a four-input, three-class classification problem. The first four columns of the table indicate petal and sepal widths and lengths of various iris flowers, and the fifth column indicates the appropriate class (Setosa, Versicolor, and Virginia).

50	33	14	2	1	49	36	14	1	1	60	29	45	15	2
67	31	56	24	3	44	32	13	2	1	50	36	14	2	1
69	31	51	23	3	58	26	40	12	2	58	27	51	19	3
46	36	10	2	1	63	27	49	18	3	54	34	15	4	1
65	30	52	20	3	50	23	33	10	2	64	31	55	18	3
58	27	51	19	3	51	38	16	2	1	49	24	33	10	2
57	28	45	13	2	50	30	16	2	1	55	42	14	2	1
63	33	47	16	2	64	28	56	21	3	60	22	50	15	3
49	25	45	17	3	51	38	19	4	1	52	27	39	14	2
70	32	47	14	2	49	30	14	2	1	44	29	14	2	1
48	31	16	2	1	58	27	41	10	2	58	27	39	12	2
63	25	50	19	3	59	30	42	15	2	69	32	57	23	3
56	28	49	20	3	57	29	42	13	2	50	35	16	6	1
67	25	58	18	3	52	41	15	1	1	77	28	67	20	3
63	23	44	13	2	60	30	48	18	3	55	26	44	12	2
63	25	49	15	2	56	27	42	13	2	48	30	14	3	1
51	25	30	11	2	49	31	15	2	1	48	34	19	2	1
69	31	54	21	3	54	39	17	4	1	61	26	56	14	3
72	36	61	25	3	60	34	45	16	2	58	40	12	2	1
56	29	36	13	2	50	20	35	10	2	62	28	48	18	3
68	30	55	21	3	47	32	13	2	1	56	30	45	15	2
48	30	14	1	1	62	29	43	13	2	46	32	14	2	1
57	38	17	3	1	51	34	15	2	1	57	44	15	4	1
66	30	44	14	2	60	22	40	10	2	63	34	56	24	3
51	37	15	4	1	49	31	15	1	1	72	30	58	16	3
67	30	50	17	2	44	37	15	2	1	71	30	49	21	3

64	28	56	22	3	61	28	47	12	2	63	29	56	18	3
63	28	51	15	3	57	28	41	13	2	57	30	42	12	2
62	22	45	15	2	54	39	13	4	1	77	26	69	23	3
61	30	46	14	2	65	32	51	20	3	66	29	46	13	2
56	25	39	11	2	69	31	49	15	2	50	34	15	2	1
68	32	59	23	3	55	25	40	13	2	55	24	37	10	2
62	34	54	23	3	45	23	13	3	1	46	31	15	2	1
67	33	57	25	3	51	38	15	3	1	74	28	61	19	3
55	35	13	2	1	68	28	48	14	2	50	35	13	3	1
64	32	45	15	2	52	35	15	2	1	73	29	63	18	3
59	30	51	18	3	63	33	60	25	3	67	31	47	15	2
64	32	53	23	3	65	28	46	15	2	56	30	41	13	2
54	30	45	15	2	46	34	14	3	1	64	29	43	13	2
67	33	57	21	3	59	32	48	18	2	65	30	58	22	3
44	30	13	2	1	60	27	51	16	2	51	35	14	3	1
47	32	16	2	1	65	30	55	18	3	61	29	47	14	2
72	32	60	18	3	51	33	17	5	1	64	27	53	19	3
61	30	49	18	3	77	38	67	22	3	48	34	16	2	1
50	32	12	2	1	76	30	66	21	3	57	25	50	20	3
43	30	11	1	1	67	30	52	23	3	55	23	40	13	2
67	31	44	14	2	61	28	40	13	2	54	34	17	2	1
51	35	14	2	1	55	24	38	11	2	58	28	51	24	3
50	34	16	4	1	52	34	14	2	1	53	37	15	2	1
57	26	35	10	2	79	38	64	20	3	77	30	61	23	3

B.2   Classification of Myoelectric Signals

The following data are extracted from a problem in discriminating between electrical signals observed at the human skin surface. The first four columns correspond to input dimensions, and the last column indicates the class to which the signal belongs.

0.138	−0.168	−0.289	0.193	1	−0.030	0.003	−0.050	0.028	0
0.255	−0.029	0.134	−0.163	1	−0.001	0.019	0.016	0.023	0
0.044	0.003	0.048	−0.017	0	−0.009	0.008	−0.008	0.018	0

0.023	−0.004	−0.026	0.027	0	−0.031	0.002	−0.021	0.029	0
0.020	−0.034	0.030	−0.033	0	−0.018	0.056	−0.034	−0.012	0
0.003	0.006	0.006	0.032	0	0.023	−0.044	−0.045	0.020	0
−0.436	0.319	0.110	−0.215	1	−0.107	−0.031	−0.003	0.185	1
0.026	−0.012	0.029	−0.006	0	0.211	−0.060	−0.053	0.105	1
−0.009	0.008	−0.008	0.018	0	0.210	−0.274	−0.177	−0.086	1
0.026	−0.012	0.029	−0.006	0	−0.245	0.135	−0.135	−0.046	1
0.161	−0.091	0.296	−0.226	1	0.141	−0.174	−0.068	−0.038	1
−0.002	−0.009	0.001	0.019	0	0.034	0.173	0.480	−0.280	1
0.066	−0.076	0.078	0.138	1	0.157	−0.317	0.373	−0.373	1
−0.103	0.191	−0.161	0.084	1	−0.026	−0.113	−0.246	0.253	1
0.614	−0.634	−0.437	0.084	1	−0.058	0.114	0.040	0.017	1
0.502	−0.525	−0.098	0.274	1	−0.010	0.026	0.008	0.013	0
0.006	0.026	−0.013	0.052	0	0.033	−0.011	0.002	0.021	0
0.049	−0.169	−0.180	0.071	1	0.005	0.016	−0.007	0.000	0
0.133	0.097	0.293	−0.072	1	−0.004	0.071	−0.005	0.042	0
0.160	0.011	0.168	0.112	1	0.063	0.005	−0.021	−0.021	0
0.152	−0.089	−0.342	0.111	1	0.418	−0.178	−0.302	0.856	1
0.153	−0.250	0.051	−0.056	1	0.045	0.015	0.117	0.010	0
0.030	−0.038	0.026	−0.035	0	−0.076	−0.013	−0.148	0.070	1
0.003	0.006	0.006	0.032	0	0.011	0.054	−0.012	0.061	0
0.042	0.033	0.082	−0.031	0	0.302	0.029	0.588	−0.245	1
0.095	0.341	−0.102	0.111	1	0.013	0.051	0.035	−0.009	0
−0.001	0.019	0.016	0.023	0	0.020	−0.034	0.030	−0.033	0
0.009	0.020	−0.034	0.049	0	0.044	−0.002	0.069	−0.023	0
0.025	0.020	0.015	0.003	0	0.024	0.016	0.046	0.003	0
0.041	−0.000	−0.032	0.069	0	0.382	0.097	0.368	0.133	1
0.027	0.004	−0.007	−0.017	0	−0.044	−0.062	0.171	0.240	1
0.184	0.107	0.097	0.241	1	−0.015	0.018	−0.014	0.036	0
0.222	0.098	0.109	0.055	1	0.146	0.185	0.165	−0.009	1
0.166	0.127	−0.073	0.098	1	−0.018	0.056	−0.034	−0.012	0
−0.030	0.003	−0.050	0.028	0	0.040	0.026	−0.007	0.032	1
0.022	0.012	−0.003	−0.057	0	−0.253	0.042	−0.138	−0.010	1

B.3   Gold Prices

The following numbers indicate daily gold prices on international markets; the task is to
develop a neural network that can forecast these prices. Prices on successive days are given
on the same line, and the first entry in a line pertains to a date that follows the last entry on
the preceding line.

329.95	329.60	329.95	328.20	330.15	329.55	329.75	330.51
329.75	328.50	328.65	324.75	328.45	328.35	328.15	326.32
328.05	327.80	328.15	327.34	328.15	327.75	328.05	327.28
327.95	328.30	328.50	329.00	328.85	331.80	330.15	328.92
331.55	331.25	331.80	329.84	330.95	328.80	328.35	329.66
328.55	328.80	328.55	329.09	329.25	332.00	331.65	330.26
331.85	330.10	330.30	331.87	330.15	330.00	330.00	327.90
330.95	329.90	330.65	331.20	329.25	327.85	330.00	331.20
329.45	333.50	329.60	328.55	330.55	329.20	330.15	330.73
329.85	329.50	329.55	329.31	329.35	328.15	328.75	327.78
329.15	328.35	328.55	327.63	328.95	329.40	330.10	328.57
330.05	328.80	329.45	330.40	328.45	328.75	328.25	330.40
329.65	329.60	330.15	331.41	328.75	327.00	327.35	326.87
327.35	326.75	326.45	328.47	326.75	326.15	326.55	326.03
326.75	327.00	327.10	327.11	327.05	327.90	327.15	325.86
328.05	329.05	328.65	327.71	329.15	328.85	329.00	329.10
328.55	328.80	329.35	329.10	329.45	330.25	330.45	330.00
330.65	331.50	331.30	331.94	332.45	332.70	332.60	331.97
331.75	331.60	331.75	331.90	331.25	332.20	331.35	330.90
332.65	332.50	332.15	332.78	332.65	332.25	332.50	333.81
332.05	332.00	332.05	331.92	333.15	336.35	335.75	332.20
337.25	336.75	338.35	338.34	336.95	338.20	336.75	336.93
339.45	340.00	340.35	338.28	339.45	339.10	339.30	338.52
338.05	337.50	338.40	338.85	337.35	337.75	336.60	337.47
337.85	337.00	337.30	336.94	337.85	337.00	337.25	336.94
337.85	336.50	337.30	336.94	337.15	336.95	336.65	336.32
337.25	338.50	339.20	338.66	339.55	336.60	338.65	339.71
337.25	338.50	339.05	338.23	340.55	339.90	339.85	340.19
341.15	339.90	340.55	341.08	339.15	339.25	338.85	339.01

337.15	339.60	339.70	339.09	341.15	346.50	334.00	340.87
348.75	352.00	350.10	349.04	352.25	350.00	350.75	352.28
349.75	353.00	351.60	349.64	354.65	355.90	354.90	355.49
354.25	355.80	354.95	354.22				

B.4   Clustering Animal Features

In the following data, each line describes features such as teeth that characterize one animal. A clustering algorithm may be applied to determine which animals resemble each other the most, using eight-dimensional input vectors.

2	3	1	1	3	3	3	3	3	3	1	1	4	4	1	2
3	2	1	0	3	3	3	3	3	3	1	1	3	3	1	2
2	3	1	1	2	3	3	3	3	3	1	1	4	4	1	2
2	3	1	1	2	2	3	3	3	3	1	1	3	3	1	2
2	3	1	1	1	2	3	3	3	3	1	1	4	3	1	2
1	3	1	1	2	2	3	3	3	2	1	1	3	3	1	2
2	1	0	0	2	2	3	3	3	3	1	1	3	2	1	1
2	1	0	0	3	2	3	3	3	3	1	1	3	2	1	1
1	1	0	0	2	1	3	3	3	2	1	1	4	4	1	1
1	1	0	0	2	1	3	3	3	2	1	1	4	4	1	1
1	1	0	0	1	1	3	3	3	2	1	1	3	3	2	2
1	1	0	0	0	0	3	3	2	1	1	1	4	4	1	1
1	1	0	0	1	1	3	3	0	4	1	0	3	3	3	3
3	3	1	1	4	4	2	3	0	4	1	0	3	3	3	3
3	3	1	1	4	4	2	3	0	4	0	0	3	3	3	3
3	3	1	1	4	4	3	2	0	4	0	0	3	3	3	3

Reproduced with permission: SAS® Users Guide: Statistics, 1982 edition, Cary, NC: 1982. © SAS Institute, Inc.

B.5   3-D Corners, Grid and Approximation

The first three columns of each line in the following data correspond to input dimensions. The data may be used for clustering, using the first three columns alone. Some of the points fall in the vicinity of a corner of the unit cube, indicated by the fourth column, that may be used as desired output for a classification problem. The same three-dimensional input data may also be used for a three-dimensional chessboard or "grid" problem, in which

adjacent clusters belong to opposite classes; the fifth column in each line indicates the
desired class-identifier. The same three-dimensional input data can also be used to perform function approximation. The sixth and seventh columns in each line each give values
for two functions of the three inputs: the sixth column represents the polynomial function $x_3(x_1 + x_2 + x_3) - x_1^2$, and the seventh column represents the trigonometric function
$\tan(x_1) + \cos(x_2) + \sin(x_3)$.

0.99	0.95	0.08	1	1	1.984	1.496
0.95	0.99	0.96	1	1	1.847	2.789
0.97	0.06	0.55	0	0	1.238	2.437
0.53	0.96	0.55	0	1	0.771	1.680
0.05	0.09	0.56	0	0	−0.282	1.680
0.02	0.10	0.01	1	1	0.002	1.025
0.01	0.97	0.55	0	0	−0.282	1.191
0.95	0.05	0.08	1	1	1.005	1.886
0.09	0.03	0.60	0	0	−0.291	1.769
0.92	0.03	0.52	0	0	1.074	2.365
0.07	0.54	0.56	0	1	−0.238	1.555
0.56	0.54	0.98	0	1	0.200	2.861
0.01	0.58	0.59	0	1	−0.336	1.507
0.56	0.50	0.02	0	1	0.604	1.429
0.92	0.50	0.54	0	1	1.524	2.279
0.56	0.09	0.54	0	1	0.373	2.124
0.93	0.91	0.51	0	0	1.942	1.969
0.59	0.10	0.92	0	0	0.090	2.869
0.95	0.59	0.56	0	1	1.699	2.274
0.99	0.94	0.01	1	1	1.917	1.430
0.94	0.59	0.60	0	1	1.654	2.324
0.51	0.55	0.06	0	1	0.571	1.404
0.60	0.09	0.09	0	0	0.457	1.648
0.94	0.55	0.53	0	1	1.603	2.250
0.98	0.57	0.04	0	0	1.541	1.710
0.92	0.09	0.08	1	1	1.007	1.874
0.02	0.99	0.59	0	0	−0.323	1.234
0.00	0.52	0.52	0	1	−0.266	1.442
0.96	0.50	0.99	0	0	1.392	3.218

0.01	0.59	0.59	0	1	−0.341	1.515
0.59	0.51	0.02	0	1	0.656	1.448
0.94	0.03	0.57	0	0	1.134	2.448
0.97	0.57	0.96	0	0	1.508	3.096
0.04	0.51	0.10	0	0	0.015	1.010
0.96	0.06	0.95	1	1	0.999	3.221
0.91	0.96	0.95	1	1	1.672	2.769
0.09	0.52	0.02	0	0	0.055	0.973
0.91	0.91	0.54	0	0	1.865	2.009
0.95	0.95	0.95	1	1	1.811	2.802
0.02	0.52	0.91	0	0	−0.798	2.187
0.58	0.53	0.94	0	1	0.291	2.793
0.56	0.51	0.52	0	0	0.617	1.980
0.98	0.04	0.58	0	0	1.229	2.491
0.99	0.58	0.98	0	0	1.562	3.146
0.95	0.96	0.56	0	0	2.033	2.013
0.90	0.01	0.10	1	1	0.902	1.885
0.94	0.98	0.53	0	0	2.038	1.947
0.92	0.51	0.94	0	0	1.287	3.049
0.91	0.51	0.03	0	0	1.311	1.688
0.98	0.05	0.05	1	1	1.055	1.878
0.10	0.98	0.54	0	0	−0.127	1.249
0.56	0.05	0.90	0	0	0.033	2.801
0.00	0.55	0.56	0	1	−0.314	1.492
0.97	0.90	0.07	1	1	1.880	1.515
0.59	0.02	0.95	0	0	0.020	2.972
0.52	0.09	1.00	0	0	−0.155	3.045
0.55	0.59	0.96	0	1	0.240	2.800
0.59	0.01	0.05	0	0	0.376	1.605
0.02	0.96	0.97	1	1	−0.893	2.050
0.52	0.52	0.92	0	1	0.167	2.692
0.56	0.08	0.10	0	0	0.404	1.625
0.01	0.56	0.53	0	1	−0.270	1.444
0.09	0.05	0.91	1	1	−0.740	2.386
0.57	0.59	0.59	0	0	0.659	2.038
0.09	0.02	0.54	0	0	−0.230	1.684

0.93	0.93	0.52	0	0	1.929	1.968
0.55	0.02	0.53	0	1	0.316	2.112
0.01	0.91	0.08	1	1	0.007	0.707
0.92	0.07	0.02	1	1	0.930	1.810
0.54	0.00	0.98	0	0	−0.128	2.999
0.06	0.07	0.57	0	0	−0.282	1.687
0.55	0.02	0.94	0	0	−0.047	2.897
0.91	0.59	0.00	0	0	1.366	1.622
0.90	0.03	0.94	1	1	0.812	3.143
0.05	0.54	0.98	0	0	−0.880	2.395
0.60	0.05	0.97	0	0	0.016	3.035
0.53	0.51	0.92	0	1	0.182	2.687
0.58	0.52	0.09	0	1	0.693	1.511
0.06	0.03	0.55	0	0	−0.268	1.669
0.57	0.51	0.54	0	0	0.625	2.013
0.03	0.58	0.56	0	1	−0.271	1.491
0.07	0.91	0.53	0	0	−0.178	1.277
0.92	0.60	0.57	0	1	1.605	2.265
0.51	0.91	0.06	0	0	0.754	1.161
0.10	0.99	0.09	1	1	0.108	0.737
0.59	0.05	0.95	0	0	0.029	2.959
0.91	0.60	0.01	0	0	1.395	1.632
0.96	0.54	0.92	0	0	1.491	2.991
0.50	0.04	0.96	0	0	−0.164	2.902
0.96	0.60	0.99	0	0	1.477	3.176
0.52	0.50	0.99	0	1	0.057	2.894
0.97	0.05	0.98	1	1	0.982	3.307
0.94	0.51	0.56	0	1	1.582	2.302
0.05	0.97	0.98	1	1	−0.860	2.118
0.52	0.54	0.57	0	0	0.528	2.001
0.53	0.95	0.06	0	0	0.810	1.149
0.07	0.08	0.06	1	1	0.010	1.121
0.07	0.51	0.98	0	0	−0.858	2.431
0.08	0.50	0.04	0	0	0.051	0.996
0.58	0.55	0.52	0	0	0.687	1.973
0.08	0.00	0.99	1	1	−0.888	2.592

0.93	0.60	0.03	0	0	1.445	1.659
0.50	0.90	0.59	0	1	0.650	1.779
0.06	0.98	0.09	1	1	0.060	0.711
0.91	0.90	0.99	1	1	1.553	2.942
0.09	0.52	0.98	0	0	−0.813	2.438
0.97	0.95	0.97	1	1	1.865	2.870

B.6   Eleven-City Traveling Salesperson Problem (Distances)

	Anch	Calg	Chic	Daws	Edmo	Hali
Anchorage		2182	3690	1629	1999	5111
Calgary	2182		1608	553	183	3175
Chicago	3690	1608		2001	1691	1627
Dawson Cr.	1629	553	2001		370	3482
Edmonton	1999	183	1691	370		3112
Halifax	5111	3175	1627	3482	3112	
Montreal	4300	2332	847	2671	2301	828
New York	4499	2427	809	2870	2500	923
Ottawa	4172	2236	736	2543	2173	951
Prince Rupert	1666	949	2602	709	911	4023
Quebec	4448	2441	1010	2819	2449	668

	Mont	NYC	Otta	PrRu	Queb
Anchorage	4300	4499	4172	1666	4448
Calgary	2332	2427	2236	949	2441
Chicago	847	809	736	2602	1010
Dawson Cr.	2671	2870	2543	709	2819
Edmonton	2301	2500	2173	911	2449
Halifax	828	923	951	4023	688
Montreal		382	127	3212	160
New York	382		430	3411	566
Ottawa	127	430		3084	283
Prince Rupert	3212	3411	3084		3360
Quebec	160	566	283	3360	

B.7 Daily Stock Prices of Three Companies, over the Same Period

Company G:

Day	Open	High	Low	Close	Vol.	Day	Open	High	Low	Close	Vol.
0	19.50	19.75	18.25	18.75	4948	40	24.00	24.00	23.13	23.50	5205
1	18.63	18.63	18.00	18.25	5624	41	23.00	23.50	22.38	23.25	7410
2	18.25	18.25	18.00	18.00	6631	42	23.38	23.75	23.13	23.38	8874
3	18.13	19.00	18.00	19.00	16329	43	23.38	23.50	23.25	23.50	2666
4	19.00	19.00	18.25	18.88	7877	44	23.25	23.50	23.25	23.25	2895
5	19.25	19.75	19.00	19.50	9066	45	23.38	23.38	22.13	22.50	3254
6	19.63	19.75	19.25	19.50	4215	46	22.25	22.50	21.50	22.25	5502
7	19.50	20.00	19.50	20.00	5251	47	22.13	22.63	22.13	22.25	1417
8	19.88	19.88	19.50	19.75	3792	48	22.38	22.50	22.13	22.13	1178
9	19.88	19.88	19.50	19.75	4775	49	22.13	22.50	21.00	21.63	5040
10	19.75	19.88	19.25	19.88	4086	50	21.88	21.88	20.75	21.38	5371
11	19.63	20.75	19.63	20.75	8789	51	21.38	21.63	20.50	20.75	6259
12	20.50	21.13	20.38	20.75	8331	52	20.88	20.88	19.75	20.00	8160
13	20.75	21.88	20.75	21.63	14729	53	20.13	20.13	19.00	19.25	13108
14	21.75	22.50	21.75	22.13	12251	54	19.38	20.13	19.25	20.13	8950
15	22.38	22.63	21.00	21.00	11599	55	20.00	20.13	19.25	19.38	5340
16	21.00	21.75	21.00	21.50	8895	56	19.50	19.50	18.88	19.38	5418
17	21.63	21.75	21.00	21.63	3911	57	19.38	19.50	18.50	19.38	5317
18	21.63	22.75	21.50	22.50	12108	58	19.25	19.50	18.75	18.88	2794
19	22.63	23.50	22.38	23.13	6969	59	18.88	19.00	17.25	17.63	11542
20	23.25	24.38	23.13	24.13	9003	60	17.75	18.63	17.63	18.00	7856
21	24.50	24.75	22.5	23.13	16155	61	18.13	18.50	17.75	18.38	12074
22	23.25	23.75	22.63	23.38	9558	62	18.50	20.38	18.50	20.38	11396
23	23.38	23.75	23.25	23.75	7187	63	20.00	20.00	19.25	20.00	5014
24	23.75	24.00	21.63	21.88	10214	64	20.25	21.13	20.25	20.50	4354
25	21.00	22.38	20.50	22.13	16471	65	20.75	20.75	19.13	19.75	5213
26	22.38	22.88	21.75	22.50	5185	66	20.25	20.50	19.50	19.50	3421
27	22.75	23.25	22.50	22.75	3534	67	19.63	19.75	18.88	19.00	5114
28	23.00	23.00	21.75	22.00	4116	68	19.13	19.38	18.75	19.00	2015
29	21.00	22.00	20.50	21.25	8520	69	19.00	19.00	18.00	18.13	5063

30	21.50	22.63	21.25	22.25	6976	70	18.00	18.25	17.63	18.00	8043
31	22.50	23.00	22.25	22.63	2942	71	17.63	19.50	17.63	18.75	5450
32	22.50	23.00	22.50	23.00	4577	72	19.00	19.00	18.00	18.38	2737
33	22.88	23.25	22.38	22.50	5588	73	18.13	18.63	17.63	18.50	3273
34	22.63	22.63	22.13	22.50	3560	74	18.75	19.00	18.00	18.50	2210
35	22.50	23.13	22.25	23.00	3103	75	18.75	19.38	18.50	19.06	5424
36	23.13	23.50	23.00	23.25	4908	76	19.25	19.88	18.63	19.50	6214
37	23.25	23.63	23.00	23.13	6103	77	19.75	20.25	19.75	19.88	3604
38	23.25	23.88	23.13	23.63	4517	78	19.88	20.63	19.88	20.63	2534
39	23.88	24.13	23.75	24.00	6871	79	20.50	20.75	19.88	20.25	3026

Company I:

Day	Open	High	Low	Close	Vol.	Day	Open	High	Low	Close	Vol.
0	56.88	57.75	56.88	57.63	14308	40	52.88	53.88	52.50	53.63	20349
1	58.13	59.13	58.00	59.00	18468	41	52.75	53.50	52.13	53.00	27221
2	59.00	59.88	58.50	59.50	25700	42	52.88	53.38	52.63	52.63	16165
3	60.00	60.00	58.50	58.50	23798	43	53.25	53.25	52.38	52.63	17217
4	58.50	59.38	58.00	58.88	14586	44	53.00	53.00	52.13	52.25	17837
5	58.88	59.50	58.50	59.25	17350	45	52.13	54.88	51.38	54.75	46445
6	59.13	59.38	58.50	58.63	16906	46	55.00	55.75	54.75	55.38	37401
7	58.75	58.88	58.13	58.13	15031	47	55.50	56.25	55.13	56.00	30275
8	58.25	59.00	58.25	58.75	18042	48	56.13	56.25	55.25	55.88	16883
9	58.75	59.50	58.38	58.63	15860	49	56.13	57.88	55.88	57.50	29160
10	58.50	58.50	57.13	57.50	15281	50	57.75	58.38	57.38	57.38	24525
11	57.38	57.38	56.38	57.13	22559	51	57.63	58.25	57.13	58.25	18834
12	56.75	57.00	55.75	56.00	19595	52	58.25	58.25	57.50	57.88	18941
13	55.88	55.88	55.13	55.25	22785	53	57.88	58.25	56.75	57.13	32562
14	55.13	55.63	54.75	55.25	31766	54	56.88	58.88	56.75	58.63	27010
15	55.75	58.75	55.75	58.63	42193	55	58.00	58.63	57.75	58.25	18493
16	58.88	59.38	55.38	58.25	101549	56	57.00	57.38	56.63	57.25	26629
17	58.75	58.75	56.00	56.38	40896	57	56.88	57.13	56.00	56.38	20409
18	56.63	57.50	56.50	57.13	22152	58	56.50	56.50	53.63	54.00	29835
19	58.13	58.13	57.50	57.75	15439	59	54.38	54.63	52.50	53.63	33565
20	57.88	57.88	56.50	56.50	20924	60	53.63	54.38	52.50	52.63	31647

21	56.88	57.38	56.50	56.50	18584	61	52.50	55.00	52.50	53.50	41325
22	56.50	56.50	55.50	56.38	21532	62	54.00	54.63	52.00	54.63	34604
23	56.25	56.88	55.75	55.75	17638	63	53.00	53.50	52.25	53.00	27650
24	55.50	55.63	52.00	52.00	35599	64	53.50	54.13	53.00	53.38	23391
25	52.38	54.63	52.25	54.25	41188	65	53.50	53.55	52.75	53.13	19300
26	54.75	54.75	53.38	53.63	20088	66	53.25	53.25	52.25	53.13	17749
27	53.88	54.25	53.13	53.13	19791	67	52.88	53.13	52.38	52.50	13091
28	53.38	53.63	52.75	52.88	15656	68	52.63	53.38	52.25	53.00	13023
29	52.50	53.38	52.00	53.25	19855	69	53.75	53.88	52.50	52.88	18882
30	53.38	54.63	53.38	54.00	18737	70	52.88	53.38	51.88	52.38	34961
31	54.38	54.63	54.00	54.50	17274	71	52.50	53.88	52.50	53.88	26280
32	55.25	55.25	54.50	54.63	14957	72	53.88	54.50	52.63	53.00	26390
33	54.88	55.00	52.50	52.75	22902	73	52.88	54.13	52.75	53.38	31200
34	52.63	52.88	52.13	52.63	26787	74	53.50	53.75	51.38	53.38	20975
35	52.63	53.88	52.63	53.63	12769	75	53.25	53.50	51.75	52.25	22077
36	53.75	54.25	53.25	53.50	11952	76	56.13	58.63	54.00	58.38	87581
37	53.25	53.38	52.63	52.88	16529	77	58.38	59.50	58.00	58.75	56605
38	53.38	53.38	52.63	52.88	10617	78	58.50	59.25	58.25	59.25	30623
39	53.13	53.25	52.63	52.88	9607	79	58.88	59.25	58.50	58.50	22172

Company A:

Day	Open	High	Low	Close	Vol.	Day	Open	High	Low	Close	Vol.
0	29.50	30.00	29.00	29.88	16208	40	36.75	36.75	35.75	36.25	18917
1	30.25	31.50	30.00	31.50	25462	41	35.25	36.25	34.75	35.63	26263
2	31.75	33.88	31.75	33.75	54655	42	35.75	36.25	35.50	35.75	16828
3	33.75	34.00	32.50	32.75	32724	43	36.00	37.50	35.75	36.75	20254
4	32.00	33.25	31.25	33.13	26678	44	37.00	38.13	36.75	37.88	27714
5	33.00	33.88	32.75	33.63	17999	45	38.00	38.00	36.75	37.00	16612
6	33.50	33.75	31.75	31.88	31732	46	36.63	37.50	36.00	37.50	22191
7	32.00	32.25	30.50	30.50	39207	47	37.25	37.63	36.75	37.25	12836
8	30.00	30.75	29.75	30.63	47464	48	37.00	37.75	36.75	37.25	14450
9	30.75	31.75	30.50	31.00	19153	49	38.50	38.50	37.75	38.13	39438
10	31.00	31.50	30.00	30.38	13010	50	38.25	38.25	37.25	37.63	18263
11	30.25	30.25	29.00	29.38	32393	51	37.50	37.75	36.50	36.75	13140
12	29.25	29.75	28.75	29.25	25142	52	36.75	37.00	36.25	36.50	13949

13	29.50	30.75	29.50	29.88	23936	53	36.75	36.75	35.75	36.38	19971
14	33.25	33.50	32.25	33.38	87507	54	36.38	36.50	35.25	35.50	22010
15	33.25	35.25	33.25	35.00	61799	55	35.25	35.50	34.50	35.00	21681
16	34.75	35.00	33.25	33.88	39494	56	35.50	35.50	34.25	35.13	19347
17	33.75	34.00	33.25	33.50	14804	57	35.13	35.25	34.00	34.50	16794
18	33.50	34.25	33.00	34.13	11808	58	34.75	34.75	32.75	32.75	30682
19	34.25	34.75	33.75	34.00	12182	59	33.00	34.00	32.75	33.25	25230
20	33.50	33.75	32.75	32.75	21284	60	33.25	33.75	32.25	32.75	19064
21	33.00	33.50	32.25	33.25	13993	61	32.50	33.25	31.75	32.50	15163
22	33.25	33.25	32.50	33.00	13076	62	32.50	33.50	31.50	33.25	18666
23	33.00	33.63	32.50	33.50	12321	63	32.25	33.25	31.75	33.25	15027
24	33.50	35.00	33.25	33.50	31608	64	33.75	34.25	33.50	33.50	8741
25	33.50	37.13	33.50	36.50	64772	65	34.00	34.00	32.75	33.50	11526
26	36.00	36.50	35.25	35.75	25481	66	33.50	33.75	32.75	33.19	6908
27	35.75	36.50	35.25	36.25	16693	67	33.75	34.00	33.25	33.50	15790
28	36.25	37.50	36.00	36.50	26967	68	33.50	33.50	32.50	33.50	9538
29	36.25	37.50	36.25	37.00	14665	69	33.38	33.38	31.75	32.00	12217
30	37.00	38.00	36.75	37.00	21924	70	32.25	32.50	31.25	31.75	20816
31	36.75	37.50	36.25	37.13	11587	71	30.50	31.75	30.00	31.50	19821
32	37.50	37.50	36.75	36.75	10895	72	31.25	31.50	30.00	30.25	16817
33	37.25	37.88	36.25	37.00	12960	73	30.50	30.50	29.25	29.63	20562
34	36.50	37.00	36.25	36.25	13310	74	29.75	30.00	28.50	29.00	14854
35	36.25	37.50	35.75	37.25	19158	75	29.25	30.00	28.00	28.25	25166
36	37.25	38.25	37.00	37.25	23262	76	28.50	30.50	27.00	29.63	36655
37	37.00	37.25	36.25	36.63	17666	77	31.25	32.00	28.50	29.75	62306
38	37.00	37.25	35.50	36.00	21170	78	29.75	31.00	29.50	31.00	32075
39	36.25	37.00	36.00	36.50	11033	79	31.50	31.50	31.00	31.25	14663

Extracted from University of California—Irvine database.

B.8   Spiral Data

This classic data pertains to a two-input, two-class classification problem. The first two columns of the table indicate location of a point in a two-dimensional space, and the third column indicates the appropriate class membership. Each class contains data belonging to a separate spiral. The spirals are intertwined, thus presenting a non-linear classification problem.

0.000000	0.000000	0	0.164155	0.038695	1	0.274010	0.213270	0
0.000000	0.000000	0	−0.162325	−0.074425	0	−0.274010	−0.213270	1
0.009725	0.001955	0	0.162325	0.074425	1	0.233070	0.270615	0
−0.009725	−0.001955	1	−0.152495	−0.110795	0	−0.233070	−0.270615	1
0.018300	0.007670	0	0.152495	0.110795	1	0.180020	0.319895	0
−0.018300	−0.007670	1	−0.134385	−0.145980	0	−0.180020	−0.319895	1
0.024645	0.016690	0	0.134385	0.145980	1	0.116495	0.358540	0
−0.024645	−0.016690	1	−0.108120	−0.178085	0	−0.116495	−0.358540	1
0.027825	0.028290	0	0.108120	0.178085	1	0.044680	0.384325	0
−0.027825	−0.028290	1	−0.074270	−0.205230	0	−0.044680	−0.384325	1
0.027130	0.041525	0	0.074270	0.205230	1	−0.032770	0.395475	0
−0.027130	−0.041525	1	−0.033830	−0.225655	0	0.032770	−0.395475	1
0.022095	0.055270	0	0.033830	0.225655	1	−0.112835	0.390790	0
−0.022095	−0.055270	1	0.011805	−0.237805	0	0.112835	−0.390790	1
0.012560	0.068300	0	−0.011805	0.237805	1	−0.192230	0.369685	0
−0.012560	−0.068300	1	0.060885	−0.240430	0	0.192230	−0.369685	1
−0.001310	0.079355	0	−0.060885	0.240430	1	−0.267550	0.332265	0
0.001310	−0.079355	1	0.111365	−0.232660	0	0.267550	−0.332265	1
−0.019045	0.087235	0	−0.111365	0.232660	1	−0.335420	0.279355	0
0.019045	−0.087235	1	0.161005	−0.214070	0	0.335420	−0.279355	1
−0.039850	0.090850	0	−0.161005	0.214070	1	−0.392630	0.212480	0
0.039850	−0.090850	1	0.207455	−0.184730	0	0.392630	−0.212480	1
−0.062675	0.089335	0	−0.207455	0.184730	1	−0.436295	0.133825	0
0.062675	−0.089335	1	0.248360	−0.145225	0	0.436295	−0.133825	1
−0.086245	0.082065	0	−0.248360	0.145225	1	−0.463985	0.046185	0
0.086245	−0.082065	1	0.281500	−0.096640	0	0.463985	−0.046185	1
−0.109120	0.068745	0	−0.281500	0.096640	1	−0.473860	−0.047165	0
0.109120	−0.068745	1	0.304860	−0.040565	0	0.473860	0.047165	1
−0.129805	0.049415	0	−0.304860	0.040565	1	−0.464750	−0.142555	0
0.129805	−0.049415	1	0.316770	0.020980	0	0.464750	0.142555	1
−0.146785	0.024495	0	−0.316770	−0.020980	1	−0.436255	−0.236090	0
0.146785	−0.024495	1	0.315995	0.085605	0	0.436255	0.236090	1
−0.158645	−0.005250	0	−0.315995	−0.085605	1	−0.388780	−0.323800	0
0.158645	0.005250	1	0.301800	0.150645	0	0.388780	0.323800	1

−0.164155	−0.038695	0	−0.301800	−0.150645	1	−0.323550	−0.401810	0
0.323550	0.401810	1	0.496410	0.442040	0	0.751005	0.285910	1
−0.242575	−0.466505	0	−0.496410	−0.442040	1	−0.688305	−0.433625	0
0.242575	0.466505	1	0.405500	0.539145	0	0.688305	0.433625	1
−0.148610	−0.514700	0	−0.405500	−0.539145	1	−0.596510	−0.567635	0
0.148610	0.514700	1	0.295550	0.617445	0	0.596510	0.567635	1
−0.045060	−0.543780	0	−0.295550	−0.617445	1	−0.478615	−0.682200	0
0.045060	0.543780	1	0.170480	0.673205	0	0.478615	0.682200	1
0.064160	−0.551850	0	−0.170480	−0.673205	1	−0.338735	−0.772245	0
−0.064160	0.551850	1	0.034925	0.703510	0	0.338735	0.772245	1
0.174745	−0.537810	0	−0.034925	−0.703510	1	−0.181985	−0.833555	0
−0.174745	0.537810	1	−0.105905	0.706405	0	0.181985	0.833555	1
0.282195	−0.501460	0	0.105905	−0.706405	1	−0.014270	−0.862995	0
−0.282195	0.501460	1	−0.246445	0.681000	0	0.014270	0.862995	1
0.381975	−0.443510	0	0.246445	−0.681000	1	0.157915	−0.858630	0
−0.381975	0.443510	1	−0.380995	0.627540	0	−0.157915	0.858630	1
0.469735	−0.365610	0	0.380995	−0.627540	1	0.327750	−0.819870	0
−0.469735	0.365610	1	−0.503940	0.547425	0	−0.327750	0.819870	1
0.541465	−0.270275	0	0.503940	−0.547425	1	0.488355	−0.747485	0
−0.541465	0.270275	1	−0.609985	0.443180	0	−0.488355	0.747485	1
0.593690	−0.160835	0	0.609985	−0.443180	1	0.633075	−0.643630	0
−0.593690	0.160835	1	−0.694395	0.318380	0	−0.633075	0.643630	1
0.623645	−0.041305	0	0.694395	−0.318380	1	0.755735	−0.511775	0
−0.623645	0.041305	1	−0.753185	0.177535	0	−0.755735	0.511775	1
0.629385	0.083745	0	0.753185	−0.177535	1	0.850940	−0.356600	0
−0.629385	−0.083745	1	−0.783315	0.025915	0	−0.850940	0.356600	1
0.609915	0.209385	0	0.783315	−0.025915	1	0.914260	−0.183820	0
−0.609915	−0.209385	1	−0.782840	−0.130635	0	−0.914260	0.183820	1
0.565240	0.330505	0	0.782840	0.130635	1	0.942480	0.000000	0
−0.565240	−0.330505	1	−0.751005	−0.285910	0	−0.942480	0.000000	1

Bibliography

Abe, S. Theories on the Hopfield neural network. *Proc. IEEE International Joint Conf. Neural Networks*, I:557–564, 1989.

Ackley, D. H., G. E. Hinton, and T. J. Sejnowski. A learning algorithm for Boltzmann Machines. *Cognitive Science*, 9:147–169, 1985.

Aiyer, S. V. B., M. Niranjan, and F. Fallside. A theoretical investigation into the performance of the Hopfield model. *IEEE Trans. Neural Networks*, 1(2):204–215, 1990.

Al-Sehibani, A., K. G. Mehrotra, C. K. Mohan, and S. Ranka. Multiprocessor document allocation: A neural network approach. *IASTED International Conference on Applied Modelling, Simulation, and Optimization*, June, 1995.

Amari, S.-I. A theory of adaptive pattern classification. *IEEE Transactions on Electronic Computers*, EC-16:299–307, 1967.

Amari, S.-I. Dynamics of pattern formation in lateral–inhibition type neural fields. *Biological Cybernetics*, 27:77–87, 1977.

Amari, S.-I. Neural theory of association and concept–formation. *Biological Cybernetics*, 26:175–185, 1977.

Amari, S.-I. Topographic organization of nerve fields. *Bulletin of Mathematical Biology*, 42:339–364, 1980.

Amari, S.-I. Mathematical foundations of neurocomputing. *Proceedings of the IEEE*, 78(9):1443–1463, 1990.

Amari, S.-I., K. Yoshida, and K. Kanatani. A mathematical foundation for statistical neurodynamics. *SIAM Journal of Applied Mathematics*, 33(1):95–126, 1977.

Amit, D. J. *Modeling Brain Function: The World of Attractor Neural Networks*. Cambridge University Press, New York, 1989.

Anderson, J., and E. Rosenfeld, editors. *Neurocomputing—Foundations of research*. MIT Press, 1988.

Anderson, J. A. A simple neural network generating an associative memory. *Mathematical Bioscience*, 14:197–220, 1972.

Anderson, J. A., M. T. Gately, P. A. Penz, and D. R. Collins. Radar signal categorization using a neural network. *Proceedings of the IEEE*, 78:1646–1657, 1990.

Anderson, J. A., J. W. Silverstein, S. A. Ritz, and R. S. Jones. Distinctive features, categorical perception, and probability learning: Some applications of a neural model. *Psychological Review*, 84:413–451, 1977.

Andes, B., B. Widrow, M. Lehr, and E. Wan. MR III, a robust algorithm for training analog neural networks. *Proc. International Joint Conference on Neural Networks*, 1:553–536, 1990.

Anton, D. Block-start neural networks. Unpublished, personal communication, 1994.

Barron, A. R. Complexity regularization with application to artificial neural networks. *Nonparametric Function Estimation and Related Topics*, pages 561–576, 1991.

Barron, A. R. Universal approximation bounds for superpositions of a sigmoidal function. *IEEE Trans. Information Theory*, 39:930–945, 1993.

Baum, E. B. and D. Haussler. What size net gives valid generalization? *Neural Computation*, 1:151–160, 1989.

Beurle, R. L. Properties of a mass of cells capable of regenerating pulses. *Phil. Trans. Roy. Soc. London, B*, 240(669):55–94, 1956.

Beurle, R. L. Functional organization in random networks. *Principles of Self-Organization*, 1962.

Bryson, A. E. and Y. C. Ho. *Applied Optimal Control*. Blaisdell, New York, 1969.

Carpenter, G. and S. Grossberg. The art of adaptive pattern recognition by a self-organizing neural network. *Computer*, March:77–88, 1988.

Chakraborty, K., K. G. Mehrotra, C. K. Mohan, and S. Ranka. An optimization network for solving a set of simultaneous linear equations. *Proceedings of the International Conference of Neural Networks*, 1991.

Chakraborty, K., K. G. Mehrotra, C. K. Mohan, and S. Ranka. Forecasting the behavior of multivariate time series using neural networks. *Neural Networks*, 5:961–970, 1992.

Cohen, M. A. and S. Grossberg. Absolute stability of global pattern formation and parallel memory storage by competitive neural networks. *IEEE Transactions on Systems, Man, and Cybernetics*, SMC-13:815–826, 1983.

Courant, R. and D. Hilbert. *Methods of Mathematical Physics*, volume 1. Wiley Eastern Private Limited, New Delhi, 1975.

Cover, T. M. Geometrical and statistical properties of systems of linear inequalities with applications in pattern recognition. *IEEE Transactions on Electronic Computers*, EC-14:326–334, 1965.

Cowan, J. D. *A mathematical model of central nervous activity*. PhD thesis, University of London, 1967.

Cowan, J. D. Statistical mechanics of nervous nets. *Neural Networks*, pages 181–188, 1968.

Cowan, J. D. Neural networks: The early days. *NIPS*, 2:828–842, 1990.

Cragg, B. G. and H. N. V. Temperley. The organization of neurons: A cooperative analogy. *EEG and Clinical Neurophysiology*, 6:85–92, 1954.

Cybenko, G. *Approximation by Superpositions of Sigmoidal Function*. Center for Supercomputing Research and Development, University of Illinois, Urbana, 1988. (Also in *Mathematics of Control, Signals, and Systems*, 2:303–314, 1989.)

De Vries, B. and J. Principe. The gamma model—a new neural network for temporal processing. *Neural Networks*, 5(4):565–576, 1992.

DeSieno, D. Adding a conscience to competitive learning. *Proc. IEEE International Conference Neural Networks*, I:117–124, 1988.

Dreyfus, S. The numerical solution of variational problems. *Journal of Mathematical Analysis and Applications*, 5(1):30–45, 1962.

Dueck, G. and T. Scheuer. Threshold accepting: A general purpose optimization algorithm appearing superior to simulated annealing. *J. Computational Physics*, 90, No, 1:161–175, 1990.

Durbin, R. and D. E. Rumelhart. Product units: A computationally powerful and biologically plausible extension to backpropagation networks. *Complex Systems*, 1:133, 1989.

Erwin, E., K. Obermayer, and K. Schulten. Self-organizing maps: Ordering, convergence properties and energy functions. *Biological Cybernetics*, 67:47–55, 1992.

Eshelman, L. J. The CHC adaptive search algorithm: How to have safe search when engaging in nontraditional genetic recombination. In G. J. E. Rawlins, editor, *Foundations of Genetic Algorithms*, pages 265–283. Morgan Kaufmann, San Mateo, CA, 1991.

Fahlman, S. E. An empirical study of learning speed in backpropagation networks. Technical Report CMU-CS-88-162, Carnegie-Mellon University, Pittsburgh, PA, 1988.

Fahlman, S. E. and C. Lebiere. The cascade-correlation learning architecture. *Advances in Neural Information Processing Systems II (Denver, 1989)*, pages 524–532, 1990.

Feldman, J. A. and D. H. Ballard. Connectionist models and their properties. *Cognitive Science*, 6:205–254, 1982.

Feller, W. *An Introduction to Probability Theory and Its Applications*. John Wiley & Sons, Inc., New York, second edition, 1957.

Fletcher, R. and C. M. Reeves. Function minimization by conjugate gradients. *Computer Journal*, 7:149–154, 1964.

Fogel, L. J., A. J. Owens, and M. J. Walsh. *Artificial Intelligence Through Simulated Evolution*. Wiley Publishing, New York, 1966.

Frean, M. The upstart algorithm: A method for constructing and training feedforward neural networks. *Neural Computation 2*, pages 198–209, 1990.

Fritzke, B. Growing Cell Structures—a self-organizing network for unsupervised and supervised learning. *Neural Networks*, 7(9):1441–1460, 1994.

Fukushima, K. Neocognitron: A self-organizing neural network model for a mechanism of pattern recognition unaffected by shift in position. *Biological Cybernetics*, 36:193–202, 1980.

Fukushima, K. Neural network model for selective attention in visual pattern recognition and associative recall. *Applied Optics*, 26(23):193–202, 1987.

Fukushima, K., S. Miyake, and T. Ito. Neocognitron: A neural network model for a mechanism of visual pattern recognition. *IEEE Tran. on System, Man, and Cybernetics*, SMC-13:826–834, 1983.

Gabor, D. Theory of communication. *Journal of IEE*, 93:429–457, 1946.

Gabor, D. Communication theory and cybernetics. *IRE Transactions on Circuit Theory*, CT-1:19–31, 1954.

Gallant, S. I. Optimal linear discriminants. *Proceedings of the Eighth International Conference on Pattern Recognition (Paris, 1986)*, pages 849–852, 1986.

Gallant, S. I. and H. White. There exists a neural network that does not make avoidable mistakes. *Proceedings of the International Conference on Neural Networks*, I:657–664, 1988.

Gee, A. H., S. V. B. Aiyer, and R. Prager. An analytical framework for optimizing neural networks. *Neural Networks*, 6:79–97, 1993.

Geman, S. and D. Geman. Stochastic relaxation, Gibbs distributions, and the Bayesian restoration of images. *IEEE Transactions on Pattern Analysis and Machine Intelligence*. PAMI-6:721–741, 1984.

Ghosh, J. and K. Tumer. Structural adaptation and generalization in supervised feed-forward networks. *Journal of Artificial Neural Networks*, 1(4):431–458, 1994.

Giles, C. L. and T. Maxwell. Learning, invariance, and generalization in high–order neural networks. *Applied Optics*, 26(23):4972–4978, 1987.

Girosi, F. and T. Poggio. Representation properties of networks: Kolmogorov's theorem is irrelevant. *Neural Computation*, 1:465–469, 1989.

Goldberg, D. E. Sizing populations for serial and parallel genetic algorithms. *Proc. Third Int'l. Conf. Genetic Algorithms*, pages 70–79, 1989.

Gray, R. M., J. C. Kieffer, and Y. Linde. Locally optimal block quantizer design. *Information and Control*, 45:178–198, 1980.

Grossberg, S. Classical and instrumental learning by neural networks. *Progress in Theoretical Biology*, 3:51–141, 1977.

Grossberg, S. *Studies of Mind and Brain: Neural Principles of Learning Perception, Development, Cognition, and Motor Control*. Reidell Press, Boston, 1982.

Guez, A., J. Eilbert, and M. Kam. Neural network architecture for control. *IEEE Control Systems Magazine*, pages 22–25, 1988.

Hartman, E. A high storage capacity neural network content addressable memory. *Network*, 2:315–334, 1991.

Hassibi, B. and D. G. Stork. Second order derivatives for network pruning: Optimal brain surgeon. In Stephen José Hanson, Jack D. Cowan, and C. Lee Giles, editors, *Advances in Neural Information Processing Systems 5*, pages 164–171. Morgan-Kaufmann, San Mateo, CA, 1993.

Hassoun, M. and A. Spitzer. Neural network identification and extraction of repetitive superimposed pulses in noisy 1-d signals. *Neural Network Supplement: INNS Abstracts*, 1:143, 1988.

Haykin, S. *Neural Networks: A Comprehensive Foundation*. IEEE Press, Macmillan, New York, NY, 1994.

Hebb, D. *The Organization of Behavior*. John Wiley, New York, 1949.

Hecht-Nielsen, R. Applications of counterpropagation networks. *Neural Networks*, 1:131–139, 1987.

Hecht-Nielsen, R. Counterpropagation networks. *Applied Optics*, 26:4979–4984, 1987a.

Hecht-Nielsen, R. Counterpropagation networks. *IEEE International Conference on Neural Networks*, II:19–32, 1987b.

Hecht-Nielsen, R. Theory of the backpropagation neural network. *Proceedings of the International Joint Conference on Neural Networks*, 1:593–611, 1989.

Hertz, J., A. Krogh, and R. Palmer. *Introduction to the Theory of Neural Computation*. Addison Wesley, New York, 1991.

Hestness, M. R. and E. Stiefel. Methods of conjugate gradients for solving linear systems. *Journal of Research of the National Bureau of Standards*, 49:409–436, 1952.

Hinton, G. E. Connectionist learning procedures. Technical Report CMU-CS-87-115, Carnegie-Mellon University, Pittsburgh, PA, 1987.

Hodgkin, A. L. and A. F. Huxley. A quantitative description of membrane current and its application to conduction and excitation in nerves. *Journal of Physiology (London)*, 117:819–829, 1952.

Holland, J. *Adaptation in Neural and Artificial Systems*. University of Michigan Press, Ann Arbor, 1975.

Hopfield, J. and D. Tank. Neural computation of decisions in optimization problems. *Biological Cybernetics*, 52:141–152, 1985.

Hornik, K., M. Stinchcombe, and H. White. Multilayer feedforward networks are universal approximators. *Neural Networks*, 2(5):359–366, 1989.

Huang, W. Y. and R. P. Lippmann. Neural net and traditional classifiers. In D. Z. Anderson, editor, *Neural Information Processing Systems*, pages 387–396, New York, NY, 1988.

Hubel, D. H. and T. N. Wiesel. Receptive fields, binocular interaction and functional architecture in a cat's visual cortex. *Journal of Physiology (London)*, 160:106–154, 1962.

Hubel, D. H. and T. N. Wiesel. Functional architecture of macaque visual cortex. *Proceedings of the Royal Society of London, Series B*, 198:1–59, 1977.

Ingber, L. Simulated annealing: Practice versus theory. *Math. Comput. Modelling*, 18(11):29–57, 1993.

Josin, G., D. Charney, and D. White. Robot control using neural networks. *Proceedings of IEEE 1988 International Conference Neural Networks*, pages 625–631, 1988.

Karhunen, J. and J. Jontsensalo. Representation and separation of signals using nonlinear PCA type learning. Technical Report A-17, Helsinki University of Technology, Lab. of Computer and Information Science, 1993.

Kirkpatrick, S., C. D. Gelatt, and M. P. Vecchi. Optimization by simulated annealing. *Science*, 220:671–680, 1983.

Klopf, A. H. Drive-reinforcement learning: A real-time learning mechanism for unsupervised learning. *Proc. IEEE First International Conference Neural Networks*, pages II:441–445, 1987.

Kohonen, T. Self-organized formation of topologically correct feature maps. *Biological Cybernetics*, 43:59–69, 1982.

Kohonen, T. *Self-Organization and Associative Memory*. Springer-Verlag, New York, 1988.

Kolmogorov, A. N. On the representation of continuous functions of several variables by superposition of continuous functions of one variable and addition. *Doklady Akademii Nauk USSR*, 114:953–956, 1957.

Korst, J. H. M. and E. H. L. Aarts. Combinatorial optimization on a Boltzmann machine. *J. of Par. and Dist. Computing*, 6:331–357, 1989.

Kosko, B. Differential Hebbian learning. *Proceedings of the American Institute of Physics: Neural Networks for Computing*, pages 277–282, April 1986.

Kosko, B. Bidirectional associative memories. *IEEE Transactions on Systems, Man, and Cybernetics*, SMC-18:49–60, January 1988.

Kosko, B. *Neural Networks and Fuzzy Systems*. Prentice Hall, Englewood Cliffs, NJ, 1992.

Kung, S. and J. Hwang. An algebraic projection analysis for optimal hidden units size and learning rates in backpropagation learning. Technical report, Department of Electrical Engineering, Princeton University, 1987.

Kurkova, V. Kolmogorov's theorem and multilayer neural networks. *Neural Networks*, 5:501–506, 1992.

Lampinen, J. and E. Oja. Clustering properties of hierarchical self-organizing maps. *Journal of Mathematical Imaging and Vision*, 2:261–272, 1992.

Landahl, H. D., W. S. McCulloch, and W. Pitts. A statistical consequence of the logical calculus of nervous nets. *Bulletin of Mathematical Biophysics*, 5:135–137, 1943.

LeCun, Y., J. S. Denker, and S. A. Solla. Optimal brain damage. In David S. Touretzky, editor, *Advances in Neural Information Processing Systems 2*, pages 598–605. Morgan Kaufmann, San Mateo, CA, 1990.

LeCun, Y. A theoretical framework for back-propagation. *Proceedings of the 1988 Neural Network Model Summer School*, 1988.

Li, M., K. G. Mehrotra, C. K. Mohan, and S. Ranka. Sunspot numbers forecasting using neural networks. *Proceeding of the IEEE Symposium on Intelligent Control*, 1:524–529, 1990.

Lin, W., J. G. Delgado-Frias, G. G. Pechanek, and S. Vassiliadis. Impact of energy function on a neural network model for optimization problems. *Proc. IEEE International Conference Neural Networks*, VII:4518–4523, 1994.

Lippmann, R. A. An introduction to computing with neural nets. *IEEE ASSP Magazine*, pages 4–21, 1987.

Lloyd, S. P. Least squares quantization in PCM. *IEEE Transactions of Information Theory*, IT-28, 1982.

Lo, Z. P. and B. Bavarian. On the rate of convergence in topology preserving neural networks. *Biological Cybernetics*, 65:55–63, 1991.

Luttrell, S. P. Self-organization: A derivation from first principles of a class of learning algorithms. *Proceedings of the Third IEEE International Joint Conference on Neural Networks*, II:495–498, 1989.

Luttrell, S. P. Self-supervised adaptive networks. *IEE Proc. F [Radar and Signal Processing]*, 139(6):371–377, December 1992.

MacQueen, J. Some methods for classification and analysis of multivariate observations. *Proceedings of the Fifth Berkeley Symposium on Mathematics, Statistics, and Probability*, pages 281–297, 1967.

Mao, J. and A. K. Jain. Regularization techniques in artificial neural networks. *Proceedings of the World Congress on Neural Networks*, July 1993.

Marchand, M., M. Golea, and P. Rujan. A convergence theorem for sequential learning in two-layer perceptrons. *Europhysics Letters 11*, pages 487–492, 1990.

Maresky, J., Y. Davidor, D. Gitler, G. Aharoni, and A. Barak. Selectively destructive re-start. In L. J. Eshelman, editor, *Proceedings of the Sixth International Conference on Genetic Algorithms*, pages 144–150. Morgan Kaufmann, San Francisco, CA, 1995.

Martinetz, T. M., S. G. Berkovich, and K. J. Schulten. "Neural-gas" network for vector quantization and its application to time-series prediction. *IEEE Transactions on Neural Networks*, 4:558–569, July 1993.

Mattson, H. F., Jr. *Discrete Mathematics with Applications*. John Wiley & Sons, Inc., New York, 1993.

McClelland, J. and D. Rumelhart. *Explorations in Parallel Distributed Processing*. MIT Press, Cambridge, 1988.

McCulloch, W. S. and W. Pitts. A logical calculus of ideas immanent in nervous activity. *Bulletin of Mathematical Biophysics*, 5:115–133, 1943.

Mehrotra, K. G., C. K. Mohan, and S. Ranka. Bounds on the number of samples needed for neural learning. *IEEE Transactions on Neural Networks*, 6:548–558, 1991.

Mezard, M. and J.-P. Nadal. Learning in feedforward layered networks: The tiling algorithm. *Journal of Physics A 22*, pages 2191–2204, 1989.

Minsky, M. L. and S. A. Papert. *Perceptrons*. MIT Press, Cambridge, 1969.

Moody, J. The effective number of parameters: An analysis of generalization and regularization in nonlinear learning systems. *Advances in Neural Information Processing Systems*, 1992.

Mozer, M. C. Neural network architectures for temporal sequence processing. In A. S. Weigend and N. A. Gershenfeld, editors, *Time Series Prediction: Forecasting the Future and Understanding the Past*, pages 243–264. Addison-Wesley, Reading, MA, 1994.

Neter, J., W. Wasserman, and M. Kutner. *Applied Linear Statistical Models*, third edition. Irwin, Boston, MA, 1990.

Nguyen, D. and B. Widrow. Improving the learning speed of two-layer neural networks by choosing initial values of the adaptive weights. *Proceedings International Joint Conference on Neural Networks III*, pages 21–261, 1990.

Nguyen, D. H. and B. Widrow. Neural networks for self-learning control systems. *IEEE Control Systems Magazine*, pages 18–23, 1990.

Novikoff, A. On convergence proof of perceptron. *Symp. on Mathematical Theory of Automata*, 1963.

Oja, E. and J. Karhunen. On stochastic approximations of the eigenvectors and eigenvalues of a random matrix. *Journal of Mathematical Analysis and Applications*, 108:69–84, 1985.

Pao, Y. H. *Adaptive Pattern Recognition and Neural Networks*. Addison–Wesley, Reading, MA, 1989.

Parker, D. Learning logic. Invention Report S81-64, File 1, Stanford University, Office of Technology Licensing, 1982.

Peterson, C. and J. R. Anderson. A mean field theory learning algorithm for neural networks. *Complex Systems*, volume 1, pages 995–1019.

Platt, J. C. and F. Faggin. Networks for the separation of sources that are superimposed and delayed. In S. J. Hanson, J. E. Moody and R. P. Lippmann, editors, *Advances in Neural Information Processing Systems*, volume 4, pages 730–737. Morgan Kaufmann, San Mateo, CA, 1991.

Poggio, T. and F. Girosi. Networks for approximation and learning. *Proceedings of the IEEE*, 78, no. 9:1481–1497, 1990.

Poggio, T. and F. Girosi. Regularization algorithms for learning that are equivalent to multilayer networks. *Science*, 247:978–982, 1990.

Rashevsky, N. *Mathematical Biophysics*. University of Chicago Press, Chicago, 1938.

Rechenberg, I. *Evolutionsstrategie: Optimierung technischer Systeme nach Prinzipien der biologischen Evolution*. Frommann–Holzboog, Stuttgart, 1973.

Reed, R., S. Oh, and R. Marks III. Regularization using jittered training data. *Proc. IEEE International Joint Conference Neural Networks*, 3:147–152, 1992.

Ritter, H. and K. Schulten. Topology conserving mappings for learning motor tasks. *Proceedings of the AIP Conference, 151: Neural Networks for Computing*, pages 376–380, 1986.

Rose, K., E. Gurewitz, and G. C. Fox. Statistical mechanics and phase transitions in clustering. *Physical Review Letters*, 65(8):945–948, 1990.

Rosenblatt, F. The perceptron, a probabilistic model for information storage and organization in the brain. *Psych. Review*, 62:386–408, 1958.

Rosenblatt, F. *Principles of Neurodynamics: Perceptrons and the Theory of Brain Mechanisms*. Spartan, New York, 1961.

Rudin, W. *Principles of Mathematical Analysis*. McGraw-Hill, New York, 1964.

Rumelhart, D. E., G. E. Hinton, and J. L. McClelland. A general framework for parallel distributed processing. *Parallel Distributed Processing: Explorations in the Macrostructure of Cognition*, 1, 1986.

Rumelhart, D. E., G. E. Hinton, and R. J. Williams. Learning internal representations by error propagation. *Parallel Distributed Processing*, 1, 1986.

Salim, S. Z. and M. A. Ismail. k-means-type algorithms: A generalized convergence theorem and characterization of local optimality. *IEEE Trans. Pattern Analysis and Machine Intelligence*, 6:81–87, 1984.

Sanger, T. D. Optimal unsupervised learning in a single layer feedforward neural network. *Neural Networks*, 2:459–473, 1989.

Schaffer, J. D., D. Whitley, and L. J. Eshelman. Combinations of genetic algorithms and neural networks: A survey of the state of the art. *Proceedings of the International Workshop on Combinations of Genetic Algorithms and Neural Networks*, pages 1–37, 1992.

Shewchuk, J. R. An introduction to the conjugate gradient method without agonizing pain. *Technical Report* CMU-CS-94-125, Carnegie-Mellon University, 1994.

Shin, Y. and J. Ghosh. The pi-sigma network: An efficient higher order network for pattern classification and function approximation. *Proceedings of International Joint Conference on Neural Networks*, 11:205–210, 1992.

Shin, Y. and J. Ghosh. Ridge polynomial networks. *IEEE Transactions on Neural Networks*, 6(2):610–622, May 1995.

Sietsma, J. and R. Dow. Neural net pruning – why and how. *Proceedings IEEE International Conference on Neural Networks*, 1988.

Simpson, P. K. *Artificial Neural Systems: Foundations, Paradigms, Applications, and Implementations.* Pergamon Press, 1990.

Sirat, J.-A. and J.-P. Nadal. Neural trees: A new tool for classification. *Preprint, Laboratoires d'Electronique Philips*, 1990.

Taylor, W. K. Electrical simulation of some nervous system functional activities. *Information Science*, pages 314–328, 1956.

Taylor, W. K. Cortico-thalamic organization and memory. *Proceedings of the Royal Society of London, Series B*, 159:466–478, 1964.

Tiao, G. C. and R. S. Tsay. Model specification in multivariate time series. *Journal of Royal Statistical Society, B*, 51:157–213, 1989.

Tikhonov, A. N. On solving incorrectly posed problems and method of regularization. *Doklady Akademii Nauk USSR*, 151:501–504, 1963.

Tolat, V. V. and B. Widrow. An adaptive broom balancer with visual inputs. *Proceedings of IEEE 1988 International Conference on Neural Networks*, pages 625–631, 1988.

Uttley, A. M. Conditional probability machines and conditional reflexes. *Automata Studies*, pages 253–276, 1956.

Uttley, A. M. Temporal and spatial patterns in a conditional probability machine. *Automata Studies*, pages 277–285, 1956.

Uttley, A. M. A theory of the mechanism of learning based on the computation of conditional probabilities. *Proceedings of the First International Conference on Cybernetics*, 1956.

Uttley, A. M. The transmission of information and the effect of local feedback in theoretical and neural networks. *Brain Research*, 2:21–50, 1966.

Valiant, L. J. A theory of the learnable. *Communications of ACM*, pages 1134–1142, 1984.

Vitushkin, A. G. Some properties of linear superposition of smooth functions. *Doklady Akademii Nauk USSR*, 156:1003, 1964.

Vitushkin, A. G. On representation of functions by means of superpositions and related topics. *L'Enseignement mathématique*, 1977.

Von der Malsburg, C. Self-organizing of orientation sensitive cells in striate cortex. *Kybernetik*, 14:85–100, 1973.

Von Neumann, J. Probabilistic logics and the synthesis of reliable organisms from unreliable components. *Automata Studies*, pages 43–98, 1956.

Wee, W. G. Generalized inverse approach to adaptive multiclass pattern classification. *IEEE Transactions on Computers*, C-17, No. 12:1157–1164, 1968.

Weigend, A. S., B. A. Huberman, and D. E. Rumelhart. Predicting the future: A connectionist approach. *International Journal of Neural Systems*, 1:193–209, 1990.

Werbos, P. *Beyond regression: New tools for prediction and analysis in the behavioral sciences.* PhD thesis, Harvard University, 1974.

Widrow, B. Adaptive sample-data systems—A statistical theory of adaptation. *WESCON Convention Record: Part 4*, pages 74–85, 1959.

Widrow, B. An adaptive "Adaline" using chemical "memistors". Technical report, Stanford Electronics Laboratory, Stanford University, 1960.

Widrow, B. Generalization and information storage in networks of Adaline 'neurons'. *Self-Organizing Systems*, pages 435–461, 1962.

Widrow, B., J. Glover, J. Kaunitz, C. Williams, and R. Hearn. Adaptive noise cancelling: Principles and applications. *Proceedings of the IEEE*, 63:1692–1716, 1975.

Widrow, B. and M. Hoff. Adaptive switching circuits. In *Western Electronic Show and Convention, Convention Record*, volume 4, pages 96–104. Institute of Radio Engineers (now IEEE), 1960.

Widrow, B. and M. A. Lehr. 30 years of adaptive neural networks: Perceptron, Madaline, and backpropagation. *Proceedings of IEEE*, 28:1415–1442, 1990.

Widrow, B. and F. Smith. Pattern-recognizing control systems. *Computer and Information Science*, pages 288–317, 1964.

Wiener, N. *Cybernetics, or control and communication in the animal and the machine*. John Wiley & Sons, New York, 1948.

Williams, R. J. Feature discovery through error-correlation learning. Technical Report ICS Rep. 8501, University of California, San Diego, 1985.

Williams, R. J. and D. Zipser. A learning algorithm for continually running fully recurrent neural networks. *Neural Computation*, 1:270–280, 1989.

Willshaw, D. J. and C. von der Malsburg. How patterned neural connections can be set up by self-organization. *Proceedings of the Royal Society of London, Series B*, 194:431–445, 1976.

Wilson, G. V. and G. S. Pawley. On the stability of the travelling salesman problem algorithm of Hopfield and Tank. *Biological Cybernetics*, 58:63–70, 1988.

Index